Symbols of AUSTRALIA

MELISSA HARPER has escaped the university and is now an honorary senior research fellow in Australian Studies at the University of Queensland where she was lecturer from 2003 to 2021. Her research interests include everyday cultural practices, in particular on bushwalking and dining out, Australian popular culture and national identity.

RICHARD WHITE was born in Sydney and taught Australian history and the history of travel and tourism at the University of Sydney for 23 years. He has been known to pontificate, occasionally intelligibly on national identity, tourism and popular culture. His publications include *Inventing Australia*, *The Oxford Book of Australian Travel Writing*, *Cultural History in Australia* and *On Holidays: A History of Getting Away in Australia*.

In Memory of Sylvia Lawson, 1932–2017

Just when we most need it, a lively reassessment of the symbols that define us and their commercial and political exploitation. A mixture of scholarly ease and irreverent playfulness that also defines us.

David Malouf, award-winning Australian writer

If the nation is imagined, the business of creating its meaningful symbols gives us the very essence of its history. The star-studded cast of *Symbols of Australia* takes us on a fascinating tour among kangaroos and pavlovas, baggy green caps and rainbow serpents, Holden cars and vegemite jars – and much more besides. On this splendid journey across desert and beach, reef and harbour, city and bush, we see and hear the nation in its full dignity, diversity and dagginess.

Frank Bongiorno, Professor of History, Australian National University

Humorous, insightful and profound, this book is a thought-provoking survey of twenty-eight of Australia's best-known and most significant symbols. Entries range from Indigenous symbols that resonate with meaning, such as the Rainbow Serpent or Uluṟu, to animals and the natural world, official symbols, cultural practices, and commercial items of consumption. Most importantly, it showcases the agency of ordinary Australians and the role of popular culture in forging national identity.

Associate Professor Hsu-Ming Teo, Macquarie University

Symbols of Australia, in this new revised edition, is essential reading for a sure-footed trek into our constant act of becoming 'Australian', sifting through the raging cacophony of opinions to distil the most pertinent elements … all while keeping a sense of humour firmly intact.

Miriam Corowa, journalist, presenter, producer and director

This book is a fascinating look at the symbols that have been used to define and represent our nation. At a time when Australian identity is so contested, *Symbols of Australia* provides invaluable insight and context, overturning long-held assumptions and rattling revered icons. *Symbols of Australia* will make you re-think who we are, and where we came from. Even better, it's a bloody good read.

Monica Dux, writer, columnist and social commentator

Symbols of AUSTRALIA
Imagining a Nation

Edited by Melissa Harper and Richard White

NEWSOUTH

A NewSouth book

Published by
NewSouth Publishing
University of New South Wales Press Ltd
University of New South Wales
Sydney NSW 2052
AUSTRALIA
newsouthpublishing.com

© Melissa Harper and Richard White 2021
First edition published by University of New South Wales Press and
National Museum of Australia in 2010.
This edition published 2021.

10 9 8 7 6 5 4 3 2 1

This book is copyright. While copyright of the work as a whole is vested in Melissa Harper and Richard White, copyright of individual chapters is retained by the chapter authors. Apart from any fair dealing for the purpose of private study, research, criticism or review, as permitted under the *Copyright Act*, no part of this book may be reproduced by any process without written permission. Inquiries should be addressed to the publisher.

 A catalogue record for this book is available from the National Library of Australia

ISBN: 9781742237121 (paperback)
        9781742249995 (eBook)
        9781742239149 (ePDF)

Design Josephine Pajor-Markus
Cover design Debra Billson
Cover illustrations Main image by Kuhar Yuri, Shutterstock and Opera House by Pavel Smolyakov, Shutterstock
Printer Griffin Press, part of Ovato

All reasonable efforts were taken to obtain permission to use copyright material reproduced in this book, but in some cases copyright could not be traced. The editors welcome information in this regard.

This book is printed on paper using fibre supplied from plantation or sustainably managed forests.

Readers should be aware that this book includes images and names of deceased people that may cause sadness or distress to Aboriginal or Torres Strait Islander peoples.

CONTENTS

Preface, Melissa Harper and Richard White		vii
1	Land of symbols, Melissa Harper and Richard White	1
2	Southern Cross, Jane Taylor	26
3	Kangaroo, Beth Hatton and Linda Thompson	38
4	Crown, Mark McKenna	53
5	Map, Alan Atkinson	65
6	Cooee, Richard White	77
7	Stamps, Dennis Altman	91
8	Gum tree, Lucy Kaldor	102
9	Shark, Helen Tiffin	116
10	Boomerang, Felicity Errington	128
11	Billy, Melissa Harper	142
12	Miss Australia, Marilyn Lake and Penny Russell	156
13	Flag, Elizabeth Kwan	168
14	Wattle, Libby Robin	183
15	Coat of arms, Bruce Baskerville	195
16	Digger, Graham Seal and Carolyn Holbrook	206
17	Australia House, Olwen Pryke	221
18	Vegemite, Robert White	232
19	The Great Barrier Reef, Iain McCalman	246
20	Sydney Harbour Bridge, Peter Spearritt	259
21	Lifesaver, Caroline Ford	270
22	Pavlova, Michael Symons	282
23	Holden, Robert Crawford	296

24	Uluru, Roslynn Haynes	308
25	Sydney Opera House, Richard White and Sylvia Lawson	322
26	Akubra, Philippa Macaskill and Margaret Maynard	335
27	Rainbow Serpent, Shino Konishi	347
28	Baggy green, Gideon Haigh	358
29	The Democracy Sausage, Judith Brett	371

Notes	383
Contributors	426
Index	435

PREFACE

National symbols never stand still. When we published *Symbols of Australia* in 2010, we were keen to trace the ways a range of national symbols changed, adapted and fell in and out of favour over more than two centuries. Since 2010 the process has continued. All of the chapters from the first edition – some more than others – have needed tweaking to take into account a symbol's new accretions and depictions, their growing or fading popularity and the subtle or not-so-subtle shifts in their meaning. A new edition also offers an opportunity to take into account new research and to deal with some gremlins that crept into the first edition's text.

It is also a chance to think about our original selection of national symbols. While the 26 chapters of the first edition only ever presented a selection of symbols, all have continued to tell stories about how national symbolism works. In addition, we felt that two other symbols of Australia – the 'democracy sausage' and the Great Barrier Reef – could not be ignored in 2021 when in 2010 there was no pressing need to include them. It has only been in the last decade that a new symbol representing the particular character of Australian politics has emerged, in the distinctive shape of the 'democracy sausage'. And in 2010 we considered including the Great Barrier Reef as a great 'natural' symbol, but discarded it on the grounds that Uluru then told a somewhat similar story and was easier to visualise. However, as the climate emergency has become ever more acute, the possibility that human action might destroy something so loved and so symbolic of

Australia raised a further set of questions about how symbols resonate in a community. And beyond Australia, the world increasingly sees the reef as a symbol of Australia's recalcitrance on climate change.

The rapidity with which symbols change can be remarkable. When we began updating the first edition, there was no COVID-19 pandemic; even in the time we have been working on a new edition, the Holden reached the end of the road, the Akubra was dropped as an essential prime-ministerial accessory, Uluṟu is no longer climbed. But more significant is the way the very debate around national symbols never stops moving on: worrying about national symbols in the 2020s seems almost quaint. Yet their history is not only fascinating, quirky and unexpected; many would agree that that history reveals a great deal about where we have come from and how we have imagined ourselves, perhaps even how we can look to the future. And that raises the most fundamental point: who is this 'we'? Symbols attempt the impossibility of defining 'us', whoever we are.

In 2018 *Symbols of Australia* 'inspired' – their word, we modestly note – Mike Dawson, Catherine Gidney and Donald Wright to produce *Symbols of Canada*.[1] Taken together, our two volumes provide illuminating insights into the nature of national symbols. As settler societies in which European migrants dispossessed and often destroyed indigenous communities, Canada and Australia are very similar communities historically, not least in their propensity to find symbolism in the very cultures they displaced (consider the canoe, the totem pole and lacrosse alongside the boomerang, cooee and the rainbow serpent). Nevertheless, incidental features of their geography and history give them quite different symbolic histories. Australia has access to a much wider range of 'natural' symbols because – being, uniquely, 'a nation for a continent' – so much of its flora and fauna is found nowhere else. Canada's symbols of necessity are more likely to acknowledge cultural creation (from the Canadian Pacific Railway, the Mountie and Anne of Green Gables to poutine, 'Eh?' and Tim Hortons). Both books also show, however, just how porous the distinction between nature and culture is, ever more so in the Anthropocene. And whereas like Canada Australia's symbols were often developed in the context of a historical relationship with Britain, often in reaction, Canada's symbols also developed in relation to France (the fleur-de-lys and Dollard-des-Ormeaux) and in reaction to the United States (the peacekeeper and universal health care). While present as an inspiration or a cautionary tale throughout Australia's European history, the United States has never loomed as large in Australia's symbol-making as in Canada's.

The first edition of *Symbols of Australia* was published in association with the National Museum of Australia, and we thank them for their continued interest and assistance. Building on the book, the museum developed a 'Symbols of Australia' travelling exhibition. Over three years there were precisely 309,936 visits to the exhibition (apparently) which perhaps says something about the power of the symbolic object in comparison to the written word.[2]

This book was edited on Jagera, Turrbal, Gadigal and Dharug lands, and written on lands throughout Australia that were never ceded. We would also like to express our heartfelt thanks to all the original contributors who readily took on the job of updating their chapters; to Professors Judith Brett and Iain McCalman for writing the new 'democracy sausage' and Barrier Reef chapters; to all the many individuals who helped along the way with suggestions and critique; to all those who allowed us to use their images (the list is long); to all at NewSouth Publishing for their faith in the project – Joumana Awad, Elspeth Menzies, Harriet McInerney, Paul O'Beirne and Jo Pajor-Markus have been a delight to work with; especially to Phillipa McGuinness who liked the idea back in 2007 and commissioned both the first and second editions; and finally to Cath Bishop and Bill Casey and all who have had to endure our obsessive symbol-hunting.

Land of
SYMBOLS

Melissa Harper and Richard White

> Loyalty to something is an ingredient in our moral constitution; and the more vague the object, the more rabid will be our devotion to the symbol. Any badge is good enough to adore, provided the worshipper has in some way identified the fetish with himself.

Joseph Furphy, 1903[1]

In 2003, the heroes of the feature-length animation, *Scooby-Doo and the Legend of the Vampire*, a gang of American teenage detectives, visited Australia for a holiday. To establish the setting as Australia, the film drew on a number of conventional symbols. The gang immediately visited the Sydney Harbour Bridge and admired the 'groovy ceiling' of the Opera House. They told each other to 'say Vegemite' when being photographed. They went to Bondi where they were chased by a shark, enjoyed a barbecue and were harassed by lifesavers ('What a sheila!' 'I'll say mate'). Then, wearing slouch hats, they headed outback, 'the wild inland part', riding a kangaroo and being chased by emus along the way. Their destination was a rock music festival at Vampire Rock, a mysterious natural feature 'right in the middle of Australia' – more like Kata Tjuta than Uluru – and it was there that the formulaic plotline got underway, enlivened by encounters with a crocodile, a 'wild kookaburra', dingos and gum trees. To the extent that Australia existed in the story, it existed as that collection of symbols. Most of Scooby-Doo's young international audience would have recognised some of them as standing for Australia, and might have stored away the others for future reference. That even children could so easily recognise Australia in just a few symbolic animations suggests how powerful symbols can be in the creation of national identities (Fig. 2). Nations cannot be imagined without them.

Australia is a land of symbols. All nations use symbols to make themselves visible. Perhaps because they were relative latecomers to nation-making, Australians have been particularly enthusiastic and seem to have spawned more than their fair share. They have hunted far and wide for symbols they want to identify with, and have also sought to shape those the rest of the world uses to distinguish Australia. They even, as we will see, claim as exclusively their own symbols that are in fact shared with other countries: the southern cross, the wattle, the pavlova, even Anzac. At the same time, Australia's symbolic extravagance suggests more than the usual disagreement as to what the 'nation' is, an uneasy sense that Australia is nothing more than its symbols. That might help explain what seems to be increasing vehemence in the battles they provoke, as statues are graffitied, critics of Anzac are 'cancelled' and symbolic acts around anything from the flag to Uluru meet with outrage on social media. In the process we perhaps forget what national symbols actually do.

This book explores in some detail the emergence and spread of 28 of Australia's many national symbols. Like a dictionary, we seek not to attach definitive meanings to them, but rather to record how they have been used. On the other hand, unlike a dictionary, we make no claim to be comprehensive, choosing instead to represent a fair range of the symbols that have stood for Australia: the official and the popular, the spontaneous and the imposed, the natural and the contrived, the solemn and the trite, the domestic and the internationally recognised, the commercially inspired and the communally owned.

Nations don't make symbols: people do. When people draw maps, hoist flags, buy souvenirs, design trademarks and stamps, they make the imagined nation a tangible reality (Fig. 1). The nation is a product of its symbols, which perform a range of different functions. Australia's provide a shorthand way of representing Australia to the world. They seek to foster unity within Australian society. They are sometimes used to discriminate between who is Australian and who isn't. They provide visitors with mementos to take home. They are used by advertisers to sell their goods. They can be mere gewgaws, thrown away without a thought, but can also accompany moments of deep emotion, such as the burial on Gallipoli of CJ Dennis's popular larrikin hero, Ginger Mick:

> 'We buried 'im,' sez Trent, 'down by the beach.
> We put mimosa on the mound uv sand
> Above 'im. 'Twus the nearest thing in reach
> To golden wattle uv 'is native land.
> But never wus the fairest wattle wreath
> More golden than the 'eart uv 'im beneath.'[2]

Symbols can unobtrusively enter our daily lives in all sorts of ways. We eat Australia when we scoff pavlova, we smell Australia when we burn gum leaves, we drive Australia in a Holden, we hear Australia in the cooee. When we throw a boomerang, don an Akubra, skol a Foster's or plant a wattle we can – if we choose – make a statement about being Australian.

For a symbol to work as an effective embodiment of the nation, there are a number of elements that need to be present. First, it has to be clear and distinctive, readily recognised as a kangaroo or a Sydney Opera House in a range of different graphic representations. Second, it needs to be readily reproducible, and easily disseminated to a wide audience. Mostly this means it can be replicated as an image but some symbols – the pavlova and the cooee, for instance – are reproducible in other ways, in a thousand Kooka ovens and along a thousand bush tracks. A third requirement has to do with its meaning but not, as might be expected, with any agreed meaning. In fact ambiguity seems to be a positive advantage. While everyone needs to know what a symbol stands for – in this case Australia – any attempt to prescribe meaning in a more fixed or definitive way is doomed to failure. This is why we can agree on graphic images of the nation but when we try to sum up Australia in words, in a constitutional preamble or an anthem for example, division, derision and tinkering are often the result. This is not to say that there were not fights about symbols in the past – famously around the flag, the coat of arms and the national flower – or that those fights do not continue in the present, but more often an effective symbol papers over disagreements. The best symbols remain ambiguous: in Victor Turner's words, 'a *unification of disparate significata*'.[3] Those that have broad reach seem to be almost infinitely pliable, able to mean different things to different people. In particular while many (certainly not all) Australian symbols are recognisable both domestically and internationally, the meanings they convey to locals can be very different from how they are interpreted by the rest of the world.

This is a book about Australian symbols rather than icons, so there are no chapters on Kylie Minogue or Dame Edna. The power of an icon lies internally, in its ability – or its imagined ability – to physically embody an essential Australianness. In that sense the original icon has more power than any reproduction. In contrast the power of a symbol lies in the way it can stand for an 'Australia' that is external to the object. Its power lies in its reproducibility. In other words, there is an original Kylie and she is assumed to express something Australian (though it is less and less clear what that might be) but photographs of her carry little symbolic weight. On the other hand the coat of arms has no original – the first was merely a design – and all representations of the coat of arms stand equally for Australia. The distinction between a symbol and an icon is not quite so clear-cut, however, and a number of objects manage to straddle the two. A flag, while standing for Australia, is regarded by some as having an *intrinsic* spiritual quality over and above its capacity to 'stand for' the nation. When some people eat Vegemite, especially overseas, perhaps they think of themselves as eating 'essence of Australia'. Uluru and Sydney's Harbour Bridge and Opera House are original icons – the real thing is often seen as having special power – yet they also spread far and wide as very effective symbols, often being recognisable from just a few abstract lines on a page. Australia House also has a real, original existence, but while it was always conceived as a way of symbolising Australia in London, it is not particularly reproducible or even recognisable.

This book is only concerned with symbols of *nation*. It does not attempt to cover all the other symbols that Australians use. We live in a whirl of symbols, and to make sense of the world around us, even as children, we need to become experts in attaching appropriate meanings to an immense range of images, logos, numbers and signs, from a McDonald's M to a skull and crossbones. Our capacity to use symbols defines our humanity. Only a small proportion of all the symbols that Australians use on a daily basis actually stand for the nation itself.

In the older cultures of the first Australians, everything seemed to take on rich symbolic meaning and for many Aboriginal and Torres Strait Islander people that remains the case: the places they live in, the work they do, the ceremonies they perform, everyday life itself. But before Europeans arrived, while their symbolic universe was intimately bound up with their identity as peoples and their connection to Country, none of their symbols could be said to be 'national' symbols representing what we now call Australia. Much of their symbolism was local, referencing particular Country and kinship connections, even individual identity. But even those Dreaming stories, rich in symbolism, that are extensively shared beyond linguistic boundaries, cannot be said to constitute symbols of a nation, marking the inhabitants of this continent as distinct from other nations. The Australian nation is largely a Western invention, as is much of the symbolism used to represent it.

As Anglo-Celtic Australians began to develop a national consciousness, the nation they conceived was unrelentingly white, despite its Aboriginal and Torres Strait Islander population and small but significant numbers of settlers who were not. As they built up a symbolic repertoire to express their Australianness, they were also engaged in a cultural dispossession of First Peoples, as the newcomers claimed their own identification with kangaroos, wattle and gum trees. Yet that did not prevent them from looking to Indigenous culture as a quarry from which the new nation would mine new symbols, as settler colonialism did in other parts of the world.[4]

The use of Indigenous cultural references in the development of Australian national symbols has fluctuated over time. Some formal symbols from the nineteenth century idealistically depicted the meeting of the two cultures (the City of Sydney's official seal from 1857, the South Australian flag between 1876 and 1904). The boomerang and the cooee were also adopted in a positive spirit: many settlers genuinely admired the boomerang's ingenuity and the cooee's efficacy, though others, in acts that might represent the ultimate form of cultural dispossession, would try to claim alternative non-Aboriginal origins for both. On the other hand, when Aboriginal figures were used in trademarks before World War I for example, it was usually in a derogatory, supposedly humorous context. Then between the wars, artists and craftspeople showed increasing interest in Aboriginal motifs. By the 1950s Aboriginal figures and artefacts were providing popular ornaments and garden statuary, as well as national decoration for the Commonwealth jubilee in 1951, and souvenirs of the Queen's visit in 1954. The boomerang in particular was commonly accepted as a symbol of Australia, dominating the souvenir market but also, for example, providing the logo of the Buy Australian campaign launched in 1961. At the same time, throughout those first two centuries of European occupation, First Peoples themselves were reworking their own symbolism and absorbing European culture into their own symbolic worlds.

From the 1980s the appropriation of First Peoples' symbols as Australian national symbols increased, often without reference to their creators and with little understanding or even in violation of their underlying significance. A newly assertive Australian nationalism often called on them to fill a symbolic vacuum left by the withering of monarchical ties and the fading of a pioneering bush culture. Many thought they provided a spiritual centre and a historical depth to Australian national imagery that was otherwise lacking. The development of the tourist industry, a new international market for Aboriginal art and the symbolic handover of Uluru to its traditional owners in 1985 were some signs of the cultural shift. The adoption of the 'red centre' of Australia as the symbolic heart was also evident in the (intentionally) understated symbolism of the forecourts of both the new Parliament House and the National Museum of Australia, which opened in symbolic years, 1988 and 2001 respectively. The Aboriginal flag, designed by Harold Thomas in 1971, found a wide acceptance among both Aboriginal and non-Aboriginal people, many suggesting its symbolism would be appropriate in any new national flag. The increasing recognition of the vibrancy and sophistication of Aboriginal culture has opened up a whole new field of national symbolism: consider the popularity of the Rainbow Serpent as a symbol of Australia at the beginning of the new millennium. The motives behind non-Indigenous Australians' identification with Indigenous symbols are ambiguous and not easy to unpick, however: they range from reconciliation and sincere imitation to appropriation, absorption by the dominant culture and the desire for the approbation of – and commercial advantage in – the outside world. The First Peoples responses to this widespread, multi-faceted development are complicated, varied and shifting. One response has been a resurgent Indigenous cultural movement in which First People artists and activists not only reclaim their own symbols but re-appropriate and rework non-Indigenous symbols of nation as a form of resistance.[5]

Looking for symbols

Perhaps the high point of symbol-making came when Australia became a nation-state in 1901. The process was at its most self-conscious as those formal symbols of power – the flag, the coat of arms, stamps and coinage – were given legal sanction. Around this time, national symbols mushroomed as trademarks and they also gained legal standing. Their use could be controlled and manipulated for commercial gain. Developments in printing technology, poster art and the arrival of the picture postcard all meant that symbols as graphic images were being disseminated in new ways and more effectively than ever before. At the same time these newly minted Australians took an interest in all things Australian: they developed an appreciation for the gum and the wattle; they looked for a distinctive national type in the bushman; they applied Australia's distinctive flora and fauna to the decorative arts.

But the existence of a nation-state was not necessary for national symbols to emerge. Well before Federation the continent of Australia had been identified by a number of symbols – the map being among the most common, the Southern Cross the most inspirational. Most of the symbols that emerged in the nineteenth century were 'natural', though the divide between 'nature' and 'culture' is itself a cultural construct. The kangaroo has been the most enduring and widely recognised of all Australian national symbols, but the emu, the lyrebird, the koala, the platypus and the kookaburra have also had their moments. The symbolic languages of flowers, of animals and of the heavens were seen as relatively neutral, but these symbols were not value-free. Originally they reflected the Enlightenment's scientific interest in astronomy and natural history, a European view of what was distinctive about Australia. Their acceptance as national symbols by descendants of immigrants was part of a colonial habit of deference. Non-Indigenous Australians were happy to define themselves with an eye to how others saw them.[6] So the kangaroo was considered representative of Australia because it was a scientific oddity in European eyes. Symbols of other nations – the British lion, the Welsh dragon, the American eagle or the Danish elephant – were often chosen because they represented national strength. Non-Indigenous Australians' emphasis on nature also reflected their belief that Australia had little history or culture to draw on to provide its symbolic armoury. The one exception was a cluster of symbols that grew up around the sheep industry and the people associated with it (the bushman and his billy, swag and drover's dog, the merino) but again these were symbols that were seen as making Australia distinctive in the eyes of the world. A particularly telling example of Australians' willingness to represent Australia with a foreign perspective was Baz Luhrmann's comment that one of the characteristics of the continent that he wanted to show in his 2008 film *Australia* was that it was 'far away'.[7] From what?

In the twentieth century new symbols were added to the repertoire as new ways of disseminating them – film and then television and then the internet and (in the twenty-first century) social media – were developed. With World War I, the bushman was transformed into the Anzac and his more informal incarnation, the 'digger', around whom a whole lot of new symbolic meaning developed. New commercial products, from Vegemite to the Holden, strove to identify themselves with the nation. The desire for a distinctive national dress or national cuisine saw hats, coats, boots, lamingtons, pavlovas and Aeroplane Jelly given a national significance. As Australia suburbanised, rural motifs were challenged by more urban symbols such as the Hills hoist and the Victa lawnmower, although it has always been remarkable how tenaciously Australians have clung to images of the bush. By now there were some built structures that came to represent Australia: the artificial landscape of Bondi, the Sydney Harbour Bridge, later the Sydney Opera House. They signified new ideas about Australia: a country with a leisurely lifestyle, industrial strength and cultural sophistication.

It is perhaps controversial to observe that by the later twentieth century, most of these newer urban symbols were associated with Sydney. Even general histories of Australia by eminent Melbourne-

Houses in Haberfield, a Sydney suburb developed by Richard Stanton from 1901. The rising sun was a popular decorative motif on houses built around Federation.

Photographs by Richard White

based scholars have images of Sydney's Harbour Bridge on their front covers, while the *Cambridge History of Australia* sported the Sydney Opera House.[8] Equivalent symbols from other cities – Melbourne's Flinders Street Station or Cricket Ground, Brisbane's Story Bridge, Adelaide's Festival Hall – could often very effectively symbolise a city, but why did they not acquire *national* symbolic status? It's not just that Sydney became decisively the biggest city: in fact Melbourne is likely to overtake Sydney in coming decades, if it is not already bigger.[9] Partly it was that symbols of Sydney had international recognition, and this became more important as tourism grew. Indeed the striking visual quality of the Harbour Bridge and the Opera House against the backdrop of the harbour were themselves important elements in the increasing promotion of Sydney as an international city. But Sydney's symbolic dominance might also be linked to its standing as an exemplary postmodern city, expressed in a preference for style over substance. When Melbourne was the economic centre of the nation, it exuded a solidity that Sydney lacked. But Sydney's very superficiality lent itself more easily to symbolic representation. Sydney has also easily withstood the challenge from Canberra. As the national capital Canberra is a city of symbols – Parliament House, the War Memorial, the National Museum – but as a planned city its symbolism seems too contrived to inspire popular attachment.

The history of Australia's national symbols is not simply a matter of dating the appearance of new symbols. Symbols come and go; they fall in and out of fashion. In Raymond Williams' terms, at any one time some are dominant, some are residual, living off past glory, others are emergent, ready to be embraced more widely.[10] An instructive example is the rising sun, another 'natural' symbol which was particularly popular around the time of Federation. It had the advantage of identifying the newly emerging Australia with the future. This in itself distinguished Australia from many older nations whose symbolism seemed preoccupied with the past. In 1901, Australians saw themselves as being 'in advance' of the rest of the world, not just because from 1884 the de facto agreement on an international date line meant they were among the first peoples to greet a new day. They also believed their social policies and their reputation for democracy, egalitarianism and social justice placed them in the vanguard of human progress. The rising sun appeared on the New South Wales and South Australian coats of arms. It often decorated the main gable of houses built in the popular architectural style known (later) as 'Federation'.[11] It featured on the logo of the Australasian Pioneers Club established in 1910. On Australia House in London the sun motif was represented by Apollo in a dramatic sculpture – assertively facing east – unveiled in 1924. The badge designed for the Australian military forces in 1902, based on an arrangement of swords, became commonly known as 'the rising sun', allegedly because of its similarity to Hoadley's 'Rising Sun' jam brand.[12]

However, the rising sun's popularity as an Australian symbol did not survive World War II. In 1941, the *Australian Women's Weekly* bravely and rather awkwardly announced: 'The sun never sets on the slouch hat and the rising sun' – just as it did so.[13] Six months later Japan entered the war under its own distinctive 'rising sun' flag, and so the symbol came to be associated not with Australia but its principal enemy. Sixty years further on it was making a tentative come-back: an enthusiastic group of Australian flag-designers began a campaign to revive it.[14] In 2003 the newly constituted Cricket Australia included a rising sun in its logo. The slogan for an Australian Army recruitment campaign in 2007 was 'Rise'. The television advertisement featured several shots of the rising sun badge along with a dramatic voiceover: 'Throughout history we've risen to the challenges that have confronted us under a rising sun. If you want to make a difference, challenge yourself and rise.' Today, so aggressive has been the promotion of the defence forces in Australian identity, there is little sense that the rising sun might have any national meaning other than its military one.

The popularity of other symbols has fluctuated considerably over two centuries of use. One era's daggy embarrassment can turn into another era's fashionable accessory, and vice versa. Some were the height of modernity when they first appeared on the symbolic landscape – the lifesaver and the Holden for example – but then came to depend on a patina of nostalgia for their power. Harking back to a past Australia, they could appeal to traditionalists confronted by newer symbols which will in their turn, one day, come to represent a past sensibility. Differences over what symbols stood for could be matters of political allegiance or social class. Republicans were more likely to fly the Eureka flag than monarchists. Ordinary Australians began identifying with Australian symbols in the nineteenth century, but the elite, those Australians who wanted and could afford their own personal coats of arms, tended to avoid overtly Australian symbols until the twentieth.[15] Nationalism, sometimes understood as radical or progressive, at other times regarded as conservative or reactionary, seems particularly prone to these kinds of social and generational vicissitudes.

Use and abuse

National symbols have always been political. There have been debates over the flag, over the relevance of British symbols to Australia, even over whether the wattle or the waratah was the better national flower. Some prime ministers – some more ostentatiously than others – identified themselves with national symbols for political advantage: Billy Hughes and the slouch hat, Ben Chifley and the Holden, Robert Menzies and cricket. Gough Whitlam pointedly sought to renovate formal symbols, making moves to 'secure our own symbols of nation'. He organised a competition to find a national anthem to replace 'God Save the Queen'.[16] But at the end of the twentieth century, politicians seemed more conscious of symbols and symbolic gestures than ever before, wrapping themselves in the flag as it were: quite literally, in the case of Pauline Hanson. Perhaps it was connected to postmodern politicians' belief that their policies were less important for their own sake than for 'the message' they send. Paul Keating and John Howard proved to be especially adept at the manipulation of national symbols. As part of a conscious attempt to re-imagine Australia's place in the world, Keating sought to rework Australian symbolism: kissing the ground at Kokoda in 1992, commemorating the Unknown Soldier in 1993, granting the Aboriginal and Torres Strait Islander flags official status as flags of Australia in 1995. He was a symbols man, believing symbolic acts to be important.

John Howard proved an even more enthusiastic symbols man while at the same time publicly denying their importance, playing favourites with symbols while insisting Australia had moved beyond endless debates about national identity. He worked actively to promote some symbols and demote others. He told Aboriginal and Torres Strait Islander people that symbolic gestures around reconciliation were meaningless, claiming to favour more substantive 'practical' measures. But one of his very first acts as prime minister was the symbolic refusal to move his family to Canberra, 'Canberra' itself having come to symbolise, and act as shorthand for, 'big government'. He showed a deep reverence for Australia's older official symbols and continually asserted their value. He created the first prime ministerial website, which provided a link celebrating 'Australia's national symbols', with information about the flag, the anthem, the national colours and the wattle. He proved a particularly staunch defender of the flag, proclaiming 3 September as national flag day and passing legislation requiring any design changes gain the consent of the Australian people through a referendum. He was a vigorous supporter of the mythology of Anzac but refused to commemorate the Eureka Stockade. He also promoted a select group of more popular symbols: under the heading, 'Australian icons', his website featured Vegemite and the Akubra alongside the Opera House and Uluṟu, a remarkable prime ministerial endorsement of commercial products (an endorsement left unaltered by Kevin Rudd until mid-2009).[17] Howard literally clothed himself in symbols – the Akubra, green and gold tracksuits and sprigs of wattle – for various photo opportunities. And as the nation's self-proclaimed number one cricket tragic he played an important role in the elevation of the baggy green cap as a national symbol.

Perhaps Howard's symbolic excess dissuaded later prime ministers from being quite so obvious. There were still symbolic *acts*, Kevin Rudd's apology to the Stolen Generations, Tony Abbott's reinstatement of knighthoods and damehoods, but few paraded symbols as overtly as Howard, although Scott Morrison might yet succumb. Significantly one of his first acts as prime minister was to appear for a photo opportunity with drought-stricken farmers *without* the prime ministerial Akubra hat that could look so bogus. Instead he took to wearing the flag like a school badge, replaced Indigenous art in the prime ministerial office with a portrait of the queen and adopted a flag face-mask for photo opportunities when being vaccinated against the COVID-19 virus. Politicians could see value in packaging themselves, like any other product, in accepted Australian symbols although in Morrison's case it was, as Julia Banks put it, 'Out with the new and in with the old.'[18]

On the other hand, some sites become the focus of political protest precisely because of their symbolic significance. The Harbour Bridge at its opening in 1932 and again during the 2000 reconciliation walk, Parliament House in 1975 and the Opera House in 2003 all provided foci for political activism in the sure knowledge that the symbolic place would attract attention. Perhaps the most poignant such protest took place in 1928, when an Dharug toymaker, Anthony Fernando, staged a lone vigil outside that other powerfully symbolic site, Australia House in London. He wore over his coat an array of toy skeletons and a placard declaring: 'This is all Australia has left of my people'.[19] During the disastrous bushfires of the 2019–20 summer Australia House was the site for another protest deploring Australia's sorry record addressing climate change (Fig. 40).

The other group with a particular interest in manipulating national symbols for their own purpose are advertisers. The ability to identify a particular product with the emotional attachment of nationhood has direct commercial advantages. Once a fully-fledged consumer market arrived in the late nineteenth century, with products being increasingly packaged and branded, those brands being protected with trademark legislation, and illustrated advertising brandishing images as never before, national symbols were exploited mercilessly. Around the turn of the century manufacturers were selling Kangaroo bicycles, Boomerang explosives, Possum wines, Lyre Bird baking powder, Emu chocolate and Cooee tomato sauce.[20] They recognised Australians might be attracted to locally produced goods or could be persuaded to have an emotional attachment to a product that proclaimed its national ties. And the overt Australian symbolism of the brand, the packaging and the advertising was a way of identifying the product as patriotic. This commercial use of symbolism was also a means of mapping the Australian domestic economy, particularly against imports from overseas, at the very time Federation was effectively creating a single, protected national market. This symbolic definition of Australia as a market – the way in which business first and foremost imagines the nation – was arguably a far more potent force in the creation of national sentiment than is generally recognised. The 'banal nationalism' of the advertising and the very goods themselves penetrated further into homes and into everyday life than more formal symbols of state ever could.[21]

Many of those trademarks failed to survive: consumers did not buy simply on the basis of national sentiment. Quality and price apparently counted for more. Nevertheless, through the twentieth century and into the twenty-first, manufacturers continued using national symbolism: its use ebbed and flowed along with the changing tide of nationalism itself.

In the 1980s there was an upsurge of nationalist advertising, much of it associated with the Mojo advertising agency. Their nationalist, often 'Ocker' style was used for a number of products (beer, sport and media particularly) that were in the process of moving from state to national markets. The images promoted by advertisers – those that survive – provide some of the most powerful national symbols: Billy Tea, Rosella tomato sauce, the Qantas kangaroo. Paul Hogan's 'Ocker' style promoting Winfield cigarettes only waned with restrictions on tobacco advertising.

But what is curious is the way other products in themselves came to stand for the nation – Vegemite, Aeroplane Jelly, Weet-Bix, Victa lawnmowers, the Holden – even when their initial advertising and branding was not overtly nationalist. This suggests that it is possibly even more valuable for a product to establish *itself* as symbolic, to sit in its own niche in Australia's repertoire of symbols, than simply to flaunt an overt nationalism. The attachment of affectionate, often nostalgic national sentiment to a product can happen despite rather than because of conscious promotion. Advertising can then reinforce the symbiotic relationship, as with Holden's claim to be 'Australia's own car'. Another strategy is the mutually beneficial use of endorsements, paid and unpaid, from national celebrities, which we saw whenever Greg Norman, Lee Kernaghan, Tim Fischer, John Howard, Anna Bligh or Barnaby Joyce sported their Driza-Bones, Akubras or R.M. Williams boots. A 1990s Mojo advertising campaign for the Australian petrol company Ampol was perhaps the cleverest attempt to position a commercial product in the marketplace through the use of national symbols. Billboards featured a bush worker astride a motorbike, dressed in a Driza-Bone and holding a kelpie dog under the slogan 'I'm as Australian as Ampol'. The brand itself, the billboards proclaimed, was the only true test of national loyalty, a claim effectively subverted by Chinese-born Australian artist Hou Leong when he photoshopped his own face into the advertisement.[22]

The cynicism of the commercial manipulation of national symbology becomes clear when we consider marketing in an international

Australian symbols behave differently beyond Australia's borders.
Kanga Café, Toronto, Canada, 2017.

Photograph by Michael Dawson

context. First, many of the companies that cloak themselves in nationalism are no longer Australian. Many Australians bemoan the fact that products such as Aeroplane Jelly, Arnott's biscuits, Billy Tea, Cottee's cordial, Foster's, Minties and Vegemite fell into foreign hands. Yet other companies that have made much of national symbolism in their advertising, from Holden to McDonald's, have never been Australian-owned. Readymade symbols are useful when international corporations seek to insinuate themselves into a national market.

Second, nationality itself is a kind of international commodity. Two campaigns show how transferable marketing nations can be. In the 1970s, the George Patterson agency developed a campaign around 'football, meat pies, kangaroos and Holden cars' which simply translated the American jingle 'baseball, hot dogs, apple pie and Chevrolet'. (In South Africa it was 'braaivleis, rugby, sunny skies and Chevrolet'.)[23]

In 2000, coinciding with the Olympic Games in Sydney, the Foster's 'I am Australian' advertisement reworked an earlier 'I am Canadian' campaign for Molson beer. It too had other imitators. The national template can be used by all-comers.

A third consideration, however, is the way advertising can use national symbols to sell products outside the local market. Australians readily buy German technology or Swedish design, French chic or English tradition. Equally, some Australian farm products used national symbolism to sell, say, Australia's clean and green credentials in seeking out international markets, though given Australia's international reputation for environmental irresponsibility, that possibility may have fallen another victim of climate change, buried under smoke, ash and coal-dust. Foster's beer promotes its Australian origins largely to an international audience, though neither owned nor much produced – and very rarely drunk – in Australia.

The commodity that makes most use of Australian symbols in non-Australian markets is of course tourism, where the commodity being marketed is 'Australia' itself. Tourism turns national symbols into commodities quite literally in the form of souvenir boomerangs, fluffy koalas and Opera House snow globes (sometimes, not always, made in China). From 1995 the totality of tourist symbols was being marketed by government as Brand Australia, though when Australia's Nation Brand Advisory Council unveiled a new national logo for international promotion, featuring the wattle rather than the more recognisable kangaroo, it was widely derided.[24] Not only does tourist promotion insert conventional symbols into its advertising – kangaroos, Uluru, the Opera House – but it also symbiotically feeds off national celebrities such as Paul Hogan, Steve Irwin, Elle Macpherson, Lara Bingle and Chris Hemsworth who both made and were in part made by tourism promotion. Such campaigns are usually carefully researched, tailoring them to what different markets regard as symbolising Australia.

Who owns national symbols? The question becomes especially pertinent when national symbols have commercial value. Some symbols themselves become commercial entities protected by copyright. The symbolism around Anzac was once held to be so sacred that legislation was passed to ban (or now to regulate) its commercial exploitation. No other national symbol had the same status until words related to the Australian Bicentenary in 1988 and then the Sydney Olympics in 2000 received similar legislative protection. In those cases, however, it was to allow for their more effective commercial exploitation when rights to their use were sold to sponsors. Those fortunate companies whose trademarks have acquired the status of national symbol can be very sensitive to their iconography being used in other non-commercial contexts; Kraft, for example, was particularly protective when it owned Vegemite.[25] On the other hand, the commercial exploitation of non-commercial symbols also raises intriguing issues around who, if anyone, 'owns' national symbols. In particular, conflicts can arise around Indigenous symbols, such as the Aboriginal flag or the Rainbow Serpent, that some would think of as communally owned, when copyright law designates individuals or business entities as owning particular designs.

Contrived or spontaneous?

The manipulation of national symbols for commercial and political advantage suggests that they are artificially imposed on a community. Rather than being the natural expression by 'the people' of national sentiment, they can be quite contrived attempts to promote patriotism and unity. Most symbols work to impose a particular view of nation and they usually represent and reproduce the interests of the already powerful, who are also best positioned to disseminate them. Thus they will often effectively exclude the less powerful – women, children, ethnic minorities – from national imagery. On occasions when imagery related to First Peoples or bush workers, for example, has been used, it has been on terms defined by the powers that be.

The Unjolly Swagman, 2001, by Judy Horacek.
Australians have often been willing to laugh at their popular symbols.
National Library of Australia

But there are also cases where national symbols emerge more spontaneously. Who then can make symbols? It is not always the doing of powerful men. Even children can be active participants in the processes of symbology, as the multiple grey-cardboard-clad Ned Kellys at school parades attest. Australia's numerous ethnic minorities have a complicated relationship to Australia's national symbols. Immigrants were dominant in symbol-making in the nineteenth century, but became more marginal in the twentieth. Australia is a much more ethnically diverse society than it was when Anglo–Australians forged most of its more recognisable symbols. Apart from the fact Anglo–Australians have been dominant, both numerically and politically, diversity itself is a difficult concept to conceptualise symbolically. Symbols tend to impose a dubious unity within the nation rather than acknowledging diversity.

Nevertheless people of non-British migrant heritage engaged in various ways with national symbols, giving them their own meanings.

For older migrants arriving by ship, the Sydney Harbour Bridge or Station Pier in Melbourne marked a symbolic moment of arrival and an intensely emotional new beginning. Organisations representing particular groups occasionally created their own logos and badges incorporating familiar symbols: Marconi Soccer Club had a red, white and green boomerang with a radio transmitter, Dalmacija Sydney Croatian Football Club took on the Harbour Bridge, the ACT Chinese Australian Association combined a kangaroo and dragon, Indian and Vietnamese associations mixed their respective flags and maps. Creative artists produced playful (though also powerful) subversions of conventional Australian symbols, such as Anne Zahalka's staged photographs, Shen Jiawei's self-portrait and the *Kevin Pappas Tear Out Postcard Book*, conceived by the multicultural All-Australian Graffiti design studio. Monumental constructions built by largely migrant workforces – the Sydney Opera House and the Snowy Mountains Hydro-Electric Scheme – hold special resonance. For others, their use of conventional Australian symbols demonstrates their sense they don't belong. For some refugees Australia would be identified with symbolic images of freedom and opportunity; for others of incarceration. A razor wire fence can become a symbol of Australia. Anyone can participate in the national hobby of symbol-making.

In the twenty-first century more effort has gone into trying to find or adapt symbols that more accurately reflect the population, as the voices of those feeling left out of older national symbols become more clamorous. It is all part of the ongoing symbolic renovation that every nation engages in and is nothing new, as debates around the first Australian coat of arms showed. But changes can be slow, even glacial. It is striking how few national symbols capture anything of Australia's cultural diversity. The ill-timed Tourism Australia 'Matesong' campaign, launched in Britain during the Queen's 2019 Christmas message, included Kylie Minogue, Adam Hills, Shane Warne, Ash Barty and Ian Thorpe, as well as koalas, lifesavers, Akubras, the Harbour Bridge, the Great Barrier Reef, Uluṟu, beer and a 'sausage in bread'. The tourism minister praised its presentation of Australia as a 'welcoming destination' identified with 'our white sandy beaches to our native animals and our famous laidback outdoor lifestyle'. On social media however, there was widespread criticism that the campaign's symbolism misrepresented modern Australia, which was both more sophisticated and multicultural and less than welcoming to refugees. The criticism failed to recognise how the repertoire of symbols adopted within a nation are not necessarily those that resonate internationally. In this case Tourism Australia was deliberately targeting an imagined audience of Britons fed up with debates around Brexit, whose ideas of a more mono-cultural Australia were a product of repeats of *Neighbours*.[26] Unfortunately its launch in Britain for Christmas coincided with international television coverage of bushfires burning much of Australia and the campaign was temporarily halted, and then not revived as Australia closed its borders to international travel during the pandemic.

Women too have directed a good deal of criticism at the often unrelieved masculinity of many Australian symbols. Making nations has commonly been the preserve of men.[27] Men generally fought the wars, participated in the public debates, wrote the constitutions, voted in the elections and dominated the parliaments that gave form to the great wave of democratic nation-making in the nineteenth century. However some tasks of nation-making fell as much if not more to women, and the crucial though often trivialised role of national symbol-making is one. The design and dissemination of symbols, in popular forms of music, writing and the decorative arts, is central to the process of imagining the nation. Women were usually left out of the imagined nation – it was a man's country – but women actively participated in the forging of its symbols. In 1806 Honor and Mary Bowman not only sewed but presumably helped design the 'Bowman flag', depicting an emu and a kangaroo in the first version of what became the coat of arms. The Eureka flag was sewn together by three women, the stars made from petticoat fabric. Elizabeth Lauder made the wattle a symbol of national grief in her very personal tending of the grave of Adam Lindsay Gordon. From the 1870s, Aboriginal women at La Perouse created shellwork souvenirs, some later depicting such national symbols as maps, boomerangs and the Sydney Harbour Bridge.[28] Maude Wordsworth James had a passionate enthusiasm for the cooee and promoted it through the production of souvenirs, jewellery, songs and poetry. Women were also prominent in developing the rituals and monuments that commemorated Anzac, particularly fostering its emotionalism as an antidote to masculinist glorification of war.[29] As wattle and gum-leaf gatherers, and in their flower painting, crochet designs, poker work and even cake decorating, women often incorporated – and perpetuated – national symbols, thereby giving the publicly imagined nation a place in the private home.[30] But the symbols themselves rarely reflected the presence of women in the nation.

Only some symbols come to be accepted as standing for the Australian nation. Those that do have considerable significance for the community. While it might be that symbols can be interpreted as standing for almost anything, over time particular meanings accumulate and adhere, and the habit of reading symbols in particular ways and associating them with particular values can often persist. Such meanings, the accumulations of interpretations and emotional attachments of the past, can have political power. However, in Australia it would seem the power associated with national symbols is not taken as seriously as it might be in some other countries. The curator of an exhibition of Northern Irish symbols felt that, in mounting the display:

> one had to employ great care and caution. If the exhibition contained a hint of irony or disrespect, then one felt that some huge foot might come out of the sky and squash the organisers flat.[31]

Symbols have rarely been as dangerous in Australia. Indeed one of the striking aspects of national symbology has been the readiness of Australians to mock their symbols. Jocularity and irony are common when Australians think of their symbols – the rich cartoon tradition in

Australia would be endangered if artists felt unable to send up national symbols. Perhaps it is an attitude left over from the first jokes made about kangaroos, and the colonial cultural cringe that acquiesced in them. Or perhaps the prevalence of both British symbols and Irish–Australian humorists meant a tradition of mocking national symbols was established. Or perhaps it relates to a commercial cynicism that sees any natural resource – including symbols – as something to make money from, so a line in men's underpants featuring the Australian flag scarcely raises an eyebrow. It is no coincidence that Joseph Furphy's commentary on the vagaries of symbols that opens this Introduction occurs when his narrator, Tom Collins, is discoursing on the meaning of national flags and the symbolic implications of his having unhappily lost his trousers.

A willingness to mock national symbols might well be a healthy perspective, especially in a society as complex and diverse as Australia. Australia Day, itself increasingly contentious and a day of mourning for many, is marked by flag-raisings, smoking ceremonies and citizenship conferrals: the attempts to impose a dress code for citizenship ceremonies seem uptight and wowserish, even 'unAustralian'. Those more sombre events sit alongside cockroach races, thong-throwing competitions and gnome conventions, suggesting a reluctance to take national symbolism too seriously. But before we pat ourselves on the back over our tolerant and whimsical approach to symbols, we should recognise that the tolerance can be very selective. There is an emerging undercurrent of symbol bullying within the Australian community – when, for example, particular individuals were forced to kiss the flag at a Big Day Out music festival. The manufactured tabloid outrage against the teenager who burnt a flag after the Cronulla riots saw him publicly hectored and dragooned into walking the Kokoda Track as a symbolic act of penance. Following a complaint from Prime Minister Malcolm Turnbull, sports reporter Scott McIntyre was sacked by SBS in 2015 when he condemned Anzac atrocities in a private tweet; two years later, Yassmin Abdel-Magied was hounded from Australia for remembering the plight of imprisoned refugees on Anzac Day. More broadly there would seem to be an increasing sentimentality and emotional attachment to Australia's national symbols in the early twenty-first century, along with a 'pall of censorship' descending on anyone who would criticise them.[32]

So national symbols are complicated beasts. This book tells the story of the journeys some of Australia's most popular symbols have made. It is arranged chronologically, in the rough order in which each symbol first achieved popular recognition as symbolic of the Australian nation. It can be neither comprehensive nor definitive. But by taking a representative sample of the symbols that stand for Australia – the curious, the folkloric, the formal, the ancient, the inspiring – it offers a way into understanding the processes by which the nation is imagined.

SOUTHERN CROSS

Jane Taylor

There is no question that the Southern Cross is the oldest of all Australia's symbols: after all, it can date its origins closest to the Big Bang. It is not just its unimaginable physical age, however, that gives it its cachet: it is also the great survivor in that it was used to stand for Australia well before European settlement and certainly before its most famous invocation at the Eureka Stockade in 1854. Yet the Southern Cross is still considered modern enough to be a popular fashion in contemporary tattoo design and to be chosen as the name for Melbourne's swank new rail terminus in 2005. How has this constellation achieved such longevity, popularity and affection? The tale is built around myth and rumour, and weaved its way in and out of Europe and the Americas before it reached Australia. It begins with the perhaps startling detail that until around 2000 years ago, due to the precession of the equinox, the stars comprising the Southern Cross were visible from some parts of the Northern Hemisphere. Celebrated ancient astronomer Claudius Ptolemy catalogued them in approximately 150 AD, although he located them not as an individual constellation but as part of the larger Centaurus.[1] European knowledge of the stars, however, lingered long after they had disappeared to an exile beyond the horizon, and their very existence became the stuff of legend.

Over a millennium later, in 1313, Italy's greatest poet, Dante, referred to them in his *Purgatorio*:

> Four stars ne'er seen before save by the ken
> Of our first parents ...²

To each of the four main stars, he attributed a moral virtue: Justice, Prudence, Temperance and Fortitude. By mourning the loss of these stars to the Northern Hemisphere, Dante made them the subject of legend and longing:

> O thou northern site! bereft
> Indeed, and widowed, since of these deprived.

With the advent of frenzied navigation in the fifteenth and sixteenth centuries, Renaissance sailors were given the chance to rediscover these stars. Academic debates centre around which Renaissance navigator was the first to observe the stars, and who first named them the 'Southern Cross'. Regardless of who deserves these honours, it is clear that in the early sixteenth century the Italian navigator Amerigo Vespucci made the link between the stars in Dante's poem and the stars of the Southern Cross explicit. He quoted the poem in his journal, declaring 'I have no doubt that what he says is true; for I noted four stars in the figure of an almond'.³ Myth was proven to be a reality.

Following this realisation, Dante's stars were routinely hailed as the most exceptional of all constellations by those venturing under southern skies. Navigator Andrea Corsali proclaimed that 'this crosse is so fayre and bewtiful, that none other hevenly signe may be compared to it', and fellow navigator Antonio Pigafetta similarly expressed his wonderment, declaring that the Southern Cross was the 'most glorious of all the constellations in the heavens'. French astronomer Augustin Royer declared it the constellation of *Crux Australis* in 1679 and its name and image was then widely disseminated throughout Europe in travel journals, globes and maps produced for an enthusiastic public (Fig. 4).⁴ While navigators jockeyed to join the exclusive club of those who had seen the famed constellation, the stars were also a consolation.

In the perilous and uncharted waters of the new world, their brilliance was a reassuring link to pre-existing European knowledge and the realm of the familiar. They also provided more practical comfort – as the focal point for celestial navigation under these new skies.[5]

Perhaps the most consoling feature of all was the religious symbolism attached to the constellation's name and shape: the 'Cross'. Of course, it was only the Europeans who saw it that way. Constellations are named after objects from one's cultural repertoire and, accordingly, the Southern Cross was described as a 'sacred fishing net' by some Polynesians, and a 'quadrilateral' by Arabic sailors; Aboriginal people had a range of designations including a stingray, an eagle, or two brothers and their campfires.[6] For the Renaissance navigators, Christianity was at the forefront of their consciousness and they scattered names such as Santa Cruz, Sacramento, Los Angeles and Australia del Espiritu Santo in their wake. The naming of these exalted stars followed the same pattern, giving them the conviction that God was protecting them. It was even postulated that the cross-like figure of the Southern Cross was single-handedly responsible for keeping away 'demons responsible for stirring up the waters', thereby maintaining the relative calmness of the Pacific Ocean.[7] The Southern Cross, then, not only reflected religious beliefs, but was also an immensely powerful symbol able to actively influence the world.

The Christian symbolism associated with the Southern Cross also had a more sinister aspect. There was a certain symmetry about the constellation disappearing from northern skies, and the Renaissance navigators' intention to reclaim the 'lost' lands of the Southern Hemisphere for Christianity. The Catholic imperial powers – until the eighteenth century, the Portuguese and the Spanish, and then the French – carried out imperial conquests under the guise of asserting Christian influence. They planted wooden crosses to mark their presence in and control over new territories. We can speculate that the Southern

Cross may have been a convenient symbol which encouraged them in the belief that their territorial claims over the southern lands were somehow pre-ordained.

Symbol for a new nation

How did the Southern Cross, representative of the Southern Hemisphere and often used as a metonym for South America, become a specifically Australian symbol? For despite its popularity, of all Australian symbols it is the one that Australia has the least distinctive claim to, even less than the wattle and the pavlova.[8] Visible throughout the Southern Hemisphere, it features on the national flags of New Zealand, Samoa and Brazil, among others. It was *only* in the eyes of colonial Australians that it was seen as unique to Australia – *the* land of the Southern Cross – and they certainly did not hesitate in claiming the national characteristic of 'southness' as their own. If the Southern Cross was synonymous with the Southern Hemisphere, so their reasoning presumably went, then in the British imperial context it was only proper that it should stand for what they self-righteously believed was Britain's most important possession. Sailor and merchant Captain John Bingle, who, with Captain John Nicholson, claimed to have designed the unofficial National Colonial Flag used by Australian ships from the 1820s onwards, described its Southern Cross as 'the emblem of our Hemisphere'.[9] His use of the possessive 'our' indicates his willingness to appropriate symbols of the Southern Hemisphere for Australia's own exclusive use. Above all others, Australia was the southern land that offered redemption to Europe, as the Southern Cross promised.

This tendency became more marked in the 1850s, perhaps due to the gold rushes and the fulfilment of Marco Polo's prophecies of a Great South Land containing valuable minerals, spices and – most importantly – 'greate plentye of gold'. After being disparaged as a barren land fit only for use as a prison, Australia began to redeem herself. In Henry Lawson's bush ballad, 'The roaring days' (1896), Australia was:

> the Land of Promise
> That beaconed in the South
> ... Their shining Eldorado
> Beneath the southern skies.

If the Australian colonies were the fulfilment of the hopes invested in the Great South Land – or *Terra Australis* – then it was only fitting that they should adopt the *Crux Australis* as their symbol.

The gold rushes brought upheaval, culminating in a rebellion that would catapult the Southern Cross into even greater prominence. On 30 November 1854, tensions between gold miners and colonial authorities in Ballarat over taxation and arbitrary administration were pushed to breaking point. The revolutionary miners gathered on Bakery Hill and swore an oath 'by the Southern Cross to stand truly by each other and defend our rights and liberties' (Fig. 3). A group of women hastily stitched up a flag, apparently to a design by 'Captain' Henry Ross, a Canadian, from silky blue dress fabric and bits of Indian cotton twill for the cross and fine white 'petticoat' lawn for the stars. Raffaello Carboni, an enthusiastic Italian spectator, thought no flag matched it in beauty, 'all exceedingly chaste and natural'. So began the bloody Eureka Stockade, with the flag and its constellation invoked as a symbol of freedom from tyranny, and loyalty to the continent of Australia. Indeed, the Eureka flag was referred to as 'the Australian ensign' in the popular press from the time of its first appearance.[10]

This emphasis on loyalty not only positioned the Southern Cross as a symbol working to join people together, but also indicated its potential to exclude: it embraced a wide mix of nationalities, but excluded those who acknowledged British authority. It would become a focus for a radical, anti-British strand of Australian sentiment. Indeed, the Eureka flag was referred to during the Stockade as the 'refuge of all the oppressed from all countries on earth'. On the other side, Governor Hotham feared it was 'the Australian flag of independence'. Government officials referred to it as 'the revolutionary flag', 'the rebellious flag', or as 'the symbol of the revolutionary League'. It was interpreted as a sign of republicanism and revolution, for the miners' demands clearly drew on English Chartism, continental revolution and the American Declaration of Independence. It certainly caught everyone's attention. The *Ballarat Times* wrote that 'There is no flag in Europe, or in the civilized world half so beautiful'. The Melbourne *Age* went further, and predicted that 'the triumphant unfolding of the banner of the Southern Cross may not be so far distant as is generally imagined', equating the flag with the independence of the Australian colonies from Britain.[11] It is significant that in 2004, on the 150th anniversary of the Eureka Stockade, Prime Minister John Howard, who usually preferred to invest Australian history and its symbols with a conservative bias, refused to have anything to do with the celebrations.

The Southern Cross, however, did not provide a refuge for people of *all* nationalities. Six years after the Eureka Stockade, it featured on the so-called 'Flag of Stars' raised at Lambing Flat in violent riots against Chinese miners. There were limits to those who could join the ranks of colonial Australians, and the Southern Cross was used to mark them out. Conversely, the symbolism of the Southern Cross was not always anti-British. Prior to the Eureka Stockade, the Australasian Anti-Transportation League, which led the opposition to convict transportation, used the Southern Cross on their 1851 flag. While symbolising their disagreement with British policies, their flag nonetheless displayed a Union Jack in the canton to make it clear that they did *not* have any republican purposes. The Southern Cross was meant to symbolise their motto: 'The Australians are one'.[12]

On this flag, the stars of the Southern Cross expressly represented the various colonies. For this purpose, Captain Bingle's old 'National Colonial Flag', with its four-star cross, was inadequate: a fifth star was added to the cross in the 1850s. Bingle was outraged, claiming the idea of each colony having a star was 'moved by American Notions'. In this case, the stars stood for Tasmania, Victoria, New South Wales, South Australia and New Zealand, ignoring Western Australia (Queensland was still part of New South Wales). This idea that the stars of the Southern Cross represented the constituent elements of the whole (Australia) was a recurring theme in this and other mid-nineteenth century flags (for example the Murray River shipping flag), although no-one specified exactly which colonies were included.[13] By Federation it had dropped out of fashion, as the fact that Australia would henceforth consist of six states presented a rather insurmountable obstacle. Ironically, the fact that the 'fifth' star is actually two – and that both will ultimately disappear from view – was not known to nineteenth-century astronomy.

In the competition held for a flag once Federation was achieved, the six-pointed 'Commonwealth star' came to represent the six states, but the idea of the Southern Cross in association with the Union Jack remained. The campaigners for Federation hurriedly assured the British: 'we do not wish to sever the silken thread that binds the old land to the new. We only want to make a Greater Britain under the Southern Cross.'[14] For a nation seeking to create its symbols, there was a sense that the Southern Cross was the most inspirational. Australians returning from Europe would stand on deck anticipating their first sighting of the Southern Cross with mounting emotion, the sign that they were coming home. Whereas other potential symbols had their detractors and critics, no-one ever laughed at the Southern Cross. The competition judges insisted that the flag include 'the Southern Cross in the fly as indicative of the sentiment of the Australian nation'.[15] The nature of this 'sentiment' was not further clarified, its very ambiguity no doubt the key to its success. It was able to simultaneously embrace different – and often conflicting – groups and beliefs. The choice of stars as symbols was appropriate in a time when astronomy was seen as 'a valid and important science … which a civilised community should support as a mark of its cultural maturity',[16] an appropriate choice identifying the rationality of modern science with the new nation.

There was, however, one notable absence in these public debates. In contrast to the religious overtones frequently attributed to it during its early life, and despite debates about the place of religion in the new constitution, it appears that by the late nineteenth century the specifically Christian connotations of the cross had all but disappeared. The design competition for the Australian National Flag resulted in lengthy discussions in the press, but no religious significance was attributed to the Southern Cross whatsoever. Of course, some church organisations continued to find religious meaning in the stars. The Southern Cross featured on the first coat of arms granted to the new Anglican Diocese of Australia in 1836, and it is also the name of the newspaper of the Anglican church to this day. Mary, as 'Our Lady of the Southern Cross', was made patron of the Catholic Diocese of Toowoomba and, in 1959, Billy Graham brought his Southern Cross Crusade to Australia. Such religious uses seem little different from the adoption of the symbol by a great variety of organisations, businesses and events with no thought of religious sentiment. However, in the late twentieth century, some Christians sought to reassert the Southern Cross's potent religious message. Pilgrims to World Youth Day in Sydney in 2008 were encouraged to consecrate themselves to 'Our Lady of the Southern Cross', and Cardinal Pell commissioned a painting and a hymn in her honour for Pope Benedict XVI's visit (Fig. 5). In response to the republic debate, some conservative Christians made more proselytising designs on the flag. The Christian Democratic Party insisted:

> Our Australian flag has four Christian crosses. In the Southern Hemisphere God has placed the Southern Cross which is specially incorporated into our national flag, along with the crosses of St Andrew, St Patrick and St George.[17]

Reinventing the Southern Cross

Through the twentieth century the Southern Cross was invoked in all forms of literature. It named hotels, a university, a motorway (to Sydney's airport), a railway station and the plane in which Charles Kingsford Smith made the first trans-Pacific flight. When the Labor government was considering replacing knighthoods with an Australian decoration in 1949, they recommended it be called the 'Order of the Southern Cross'.[18] It was pervasive in Australian marketing, advertising and business names, helping to promote radio stations, newspapers, mobile phones, ceramics, construction companies, banks and even pump systems, to name only a few. Why has it been so popular a symbol? The diversity of uses highlights its relative neutrality, yet also shows that its identity as a peculiarly Australian symbol remains uncontested in the eyes of Australian consumers.

When adopted by organisations, the colourful history of the constellation has often played a more important role than the simple meaning of 'Australian' usually drawn upon in marketing. The Australian cricket team's irreverent – yet highly respected – victory song, for example, invokes the patriotism of the nineteenth century:

> Under the Southern Cross I stand
> A sprig of wattle in my hand,
> A native of my native land,
> Australia you little [or bloody] beauty.

Beginning with the Amalgamated Miners' Association founded in Ballarat in 1884 and followed shortly after by the Amalgamated Shearers' Union (ASU), trade unions have had a long history of invoking the Southern Cross as a symbol of the Eureka Stockade and a battle of workers against authority: it remained a core symbol when the ASU merged into the Australian Workers' Union.[19] Poet Francis Adams

The 'Southern Cross' and crew arrive in Sydney to a heroes' welcome after the first flight across the Pacific, 10 June 1928. Broughton Ward and Chaseling Photographers.

State Library of New South Wales

wrote 'Fling out the flag' to celebrate the formation of the Australian Federation of Labour in 1889, returning to the Flag of Stars:

> Fling out the Flag! And let friend and foe behold, for gain or loss,
> The sign of our faith and the fight we fight, the Stars of the Southern Cross!
> Oh! Blue's for the sky that is fair for all, whoever, wherever he be,
> And Silver's the light that shines on all for hope and for liberty,
> And that's the desire that burns in our hearts, for ever quenchless and bright,
> And that's the sign of our flawless faith and the glorious fight we fight!

The spectre of republicanism also continued to loom large in late nineteenth-century Australia. In the tradition of Eureka, the trade unionists often expressed the most overtly republican sentiments. The Wagga Wagga *Hummer*, the organ of the Riverina Workers' Association, invoked the Southern Cross in its rousing republican call to arms:

> Every Australian-born, and every man who has made this land his adopted home because Royalty, aristocracy and plutocracy have made the old world a tyrannical hell for the poor and friendless, means to work for a better order, a newer and purer life under the Southern Cross ... Let young Australia snap the chain that binds her fair young form to the dying leper of Imperialism, and, standing supreme in her bright and sunny youth under the star-spangled Banner of Blue, inaugurate a reign of peace and plenty and justice and common sense, liberty, equality and fraternity for the happiness of the Australian people and the honour of the Australian flag.[20]

For radicals, the Southern Cross stood for independence, republicanism and a young and free Australia. Its revolutionary overtones continued to be harnessed in a large number of demonstrations, most notably the great shearers' strikes in the 1890s, but also throughout the twentieth century in strikes by groups that ranged from university students to building workers, women to miners, and protests against things as diverse as United States military bases in Australia and Prime Minister Gough Whitlam's dismissal. It was employed as a symbol by the Communist Party of Australia as well as by neo-Nazis.[21] It could be positioned to represent racism as well as multiculturalism, loyalty to Empire as well as republicanism, and democracy, liberty, freedom, independence, human rights and mateship. In short, the Southern Cross came to stand for pretty much anything.

In the first decade of the twenty-first century, the popularity of the Southern Cross as an Australian symbol once again surged in unexpected locations – this time, as the latest trend for tattoos

(Fig. 6). Tattoo parlours throughout the country noted the rise, which was mirrored on car bumper stickers; according to one tattooist, the clientele was largely 'young, white, male suburban rednecks'. There is no simple explanation for this sudden surge in patriotism, or for the choice of the Southern Cross over other popular symbols such as the flag or the Boxing Kangaroo. To begin with, the constellation on its own was less complicated as a popular symbol, given the Union Jack's link to a heritage that many Australians saw as no longer relevant. Its popularity among youth also pointed to a tinge of rebellion, resistance to adult authority, even extremism: an attitude expressed in the very act of getting a tattoo. Some commentators believed it heralded a patriotic racism, expressed most dramatically in the Cronulla riots.[22] In the same way as the Flag of Stars was raised against the Chinese miners at Lambing Flat in 1860, so too could it be raised as an exclusionary device against people of Middle Eastern background in 2005. Yet others seeking such tattoos saw it as a more benign symbol of the country they love, and the lifestyle it embodied – particularly the beach – while strongly denying any racist overtones. Perhaps these meanings for younger Australians, alongside the associations with Charles Kingsford Smith, inspired Virgin Blue's cheeky marketing when it chose the Southern Cross to feature on the livery of its long-haul airline, V Australia, launched in 2007.

As Australian symbols continue to be scrutinised for their relevance, the chances are the Southern Cross will survive. But the contest over its use will also continue. Will it lose significance for many because of its associations with division and exclusion? Indeed, perhaps due to that stigma, by 2018 its popularity as a tattoo was on the wane, being one of the most commonly requested targets of tattoo removal.[23] Or will its more benign meanings win out, given its significance for Australians from the oldest to the newest. In a country with little shared cultural heritage it can be a symbol of unity. After all, like it or not, everyone living in Australia is – in the words of the national anthem – 'Beneath our radiant Southern Cross'.

KANGAROO

Beth Hatton and Linda Thompson

While American comedian Jerry Seinfeld might consider the kangaroo 'one of the Earth's most beloved creatures', along with puppies and dolphins, its life as a cuddly national symbol was always in danger. For the American *National Geographic* magazine, 'Australia means roos and roos mean Australia'. How did these creatures, that the world thought decidedly odd, become synonymous with Australia? For early European visitors, the bizarre kangaroos and wallabies they encountered were emblematic of a 'fantastic land of monstrosities'. For Indigenous Australians, of course, the kangaroo was as ordinary as the horse or cow were weird, an essential source of meat and fibre and an integral part of their rich and ongoing cultural history. With songlines and dreamings across the country, the kangaroo featured in paintings, ceremonies and dance. In contrast, for the earliest European arrivals, recognisable patterns of nature did not exist and their first accounts of kangaroos showed bemusement and confusion. Dutchman Francisco Pelsaert thought wallabies grew straight out of their mother's nipples, while in 1697, William Dampier thought them 'Sort of Racoons'. When the *Endeavour*'s men first glimpsed the kangaroo in 1770, its unique physiology, especially the singular property of 'hopping upon only its hinder legs', was noted with delighted interest. Cook commented that 'It bears no sort of resemblance to any European animal I ever saw', while Banks thought it 'different from any European and indeed any animal I have heard or read of'.[1]

Although unique (and vaguely unsettling), the kangaroo was not yet a 'symbol' of the continent. It was simply a curiosity, as one might expect from the bizarre Antipodean world. In an age of international exploration and discovery, the audience for such oddities was not those experiencing the kangaroo firsthand, but the scientific community and interested public back home in London. The first European painting of the kangaroo by George Stubbs in 1772 did not attempt to draw connections with Australia. Instead, it depicted a fascinating scientific specimen positioned uncomfortably upon large, pointed legs in an indistinct picture plane (Fig. 7).[2] The same image accompanied an exhibition in London in 1773, where, for one shilling, Londoners could marvel at 'The Wonderful Kanguroo from Botany Bay', whose:

> extraordinary Qualities would ... [impress] the Beholder with Wonder and Astonishment, at the Sight of this unparalleled Animal from the Southern Hemisphere, that almost surpasses Belief.[3]

Kangaroos became a popular attraction in England as 'kangaroo mania' took hold. They were bred in captivity in 1794 and by 1800 were in numerous parks and zoos, so anyone could delight in the curiosities of the Antipodes.[4]

In Australia, on the other hand, kangaroos were of interest for more pragmatic reasons. As Ken Gelder and Rachael Weaver point out, 'To shoot a native species and to name that species are both colonising acts.'[5] Even while marvelling at them, Cook and his party also hunted and ate them. Cook found it 'excellent food' but Banks complained of its 'total want of flavour'.[6] Similarly mixed responses were recorded by the first colonists, though with food shortages they were grateful for fresh meat. As introduced crops and livestock flourished, kangaroo was eaten less but remained a staple in hard times; kangaroo tail soup remained something of a delicacy. Colonists also continued to hunt kangaroos for sport and for their pelts, with royal visitors such as the Duke of Edinburgh (1867) and the princes Edward and George (1881) partaking of what came to be seen as a national pastime.[7] Aboriginal people had long made cloaks by stitching trimmed skins together, and settlers did likewise, producing bedcovers and rugs. By 1811 locally tanned kangaroo skins were advertised in the Sydney *Gazette*.[8] A major export trade began in 1849, when 12,000 skins were shipped from Western Australia, and developed largely to service European and American processors, who found it good leather 'for the best kind of boots'.[9]

But as settlement took root, kangaroos damaged fences and crops, and competed with sheep and cattle for resources. A belief arose that land clearing and provision of watering places had enabled kangaroo populations to increase, although more perceptive settlers identified dwindling numbers of dingo predators and Aboriginal hunters as the cause. When long-accumulated reserves of vegetation were eaten and drought came, livestock died and landholders blamed the kangaroo. In the 1860s they called for action against these 'plagues'.

By the 1880s all eastern states had passed legislation to eradicate the kangaroo. Government bounties were placed on the scalps of this 'noxious animal' and more than a million were returned annually during the latter part of the nineteenth century, not counting private arrangements by stock owners. Settlers organised 'battues', chasing animals into fenced enclosures or pits where they were shot or clubbed to death. Poison was also used.[10]

Nationalising the kangaroo

A symbol must be recognisably of a place before it can stand for that place. The kangaroo could not symbolise the nation until it was adopted, accepted and recognised as something distinctly Australian. While settlers endured kangaroos as pests throughout the nineteenth century, the fact that they were an exclusively Australian 'vermin' began to give them a certain level of acceptance.

The trend to identify them symbolically as uniquely Australian was given form in the distinct visual iconography of the kangaroo. Probably the earliest surviving example is a flag showing a kangaroo and an emu, raised by Richmond farmer John Bowman to celebrate the British victory at Trafalgar in 1805. Appealing to international interest in the kangaroo as a curiosity, Australia often represented itself at international exhibitions using kangaroos, both in the objects on display and in the general decorations around Australian exhibits. At Paris in 1866, for example, the Wool Trophy was surmounted by kangaroos, and in 1878 (also in Paris) the French authorities represented Australia as an Aboriginal woman with a kangaroo at her side. Two sculptors proposed a similar statue for Sydney's 1879 Garden Palace Exhibition, entitled 'Advance Australia' and showing a young woman flanked by an emu and a kangaroo. The kangaroo's Australianness was reiterated in presentations to English royalty such as the wedding gifts of silver to the Princess of Wales in 1864 which were decorated with the bouncing animals. Kangaroos also appeared in numerous advertisements for goods, from bicycles to footwear, tea, perfume and medicine, as well as on business coats of arms.[11]

The kangaroo's elevation to a national symbol was confirmed when it appeared along with an emu on the national coat of arms first gazetted by the new federal government in 1908. One view, reflecting a common belief that neither animal can easily move backwards, had the coat of arms signifying a country moving forward,[12] even as the agricultural sector believed kangaroos were holding it back. Many younger nations have featured indigenous fauna on their coats of arms, in deference to the interest they excited abroad. Australia may be unique in elevating a declared noxious animal to that position.

Celebrating the kangaroo's national distinctiveness involved an unconscious exclusion of those who were not Australian. In 1881 when princes Edward and George and a British Naval squadron joined a kangaroo hunt, 'the sport par excellence of the country', Sydney's *Punch* gleefully pictured the princes being outwitted by the kangaroos.[13] Australia was not their homeland, and the kangaroo was not an English fox. Although Australians remained fiercely loyal to their British roots, there was a burgeoning sense of difference between the colonials and their imperial masters. In this separation of loyalties, the kangaroo hopped clearly onto the Australian side.

The national claims of the kangaroo were unexpectedly challenged in 2013, when the National Gallery of Australia attempted to purchase George Stubbs' 1772 painting, which had been on its 'wish list' since the gallery's inception. Sir David Attenborough and others launched a campaign in Britain to 'Save our Stubbs' on the basis that the kangaroo,

Kangaroo teapot.
Terence Lane collection, National Museum of Australia

or at least Stubbs' painting, Banks's collecting and Cook's voyages, embodied *British* heritage. The British Government placed a ban on the painting's export and eventually funds were raised to buy the work for Britain's National Maritime Museum, whose director, ironically, was Kevin Fewster, an Australian. As Will Gompertz, the BBC's Arts editor noted with some satisfaction, Britain's coup took place '*much to the annoyance*' of the 'extremely disappointed' National Gallery of Australia.[14]

Adding meaning to the kangaroo

So over the nineteenth century the kangaroo developed from merely being 'an' interesting creature, to representing what was thought of as exclusively 'Australian'. Popular recognition of its Australianness alone, however, did not make it a national symbol. Another stage was required whereby kangaroos were identified with specific, 'uniquely Australian' character traits. This was not a deliberate process, but evolved organically through a series of disconnected literary uses, popular entertainments and commercial strategies to produce a range of available meanings which continued to ebb and flow in the Australian imagination.

In Steele Rudd's 1899 bestseller, *On Our Selection*, for example, kangaroos were the scourge of perennial 'Aussie' battlers Dad and Dave. While kangaroo has always been a popular choice of meat for Indigenous Australians and by the late twentieth century had entered non-Indigenous foodways, when times were tough for struggling farmers, eating kangaroo represented their state of poverty. Dad chastised Dave for not hiding a kangaroo leg: 'Do you want everyone to know we eat it?'[15] Their struggles against the animals, which frustratingly destroyed their crops, reflected the wider hardships of life in the arid outback. Rudd's comic heroes were, for better or worse, forged through their experience of Australia, of which the kangaroo was an integral part.

On the other hand, the kangaroo has been increasingly associated with unusual and humorous behaviour: by 1999 a *Simpsons* character could 'dare you not to laugh at a kangaroo'.[16] As early as 1819, the kangaroo was celebrated as an amusing oddity. Barron Field in his *First Fruits of Australian Poetry* thought the animal must have been a 'divine mistake' which could only have been produced 'On Creation's holiday'.[17] The jokes became increasingly elaborate. Mr M'Intyre of Camperdown, for example, when visiting Melbourne in 1888, proposed to arrive in a vehicle drawn by kangaroos and other native animals, 'in order that his appearance may be duly recognized by the citizens'.[18] Perhaps the most startling example of kangaroos gaining distinction for strange behaviour was the proliferation around the world of 'boxing kangaroo' acts, in which kangaroos fought human opponents for the entertainment of paying audiences (Fig. 9). Australia's best-known 'marsupial warrior' was Fighting Jack, who first appeared at Kreitmayer's Waxworks in Melbourne in April 1891, and toured the east coast as far north as Brisbane. According to the Adelaide *Advertiser*, Jack:

> took the blows calmly for a time, cooly [sic] ducking his head to avert punishment, but one or two stiff clouts on the chest brought him up to his metal, and he stood ... on the end of his tail and his hind legs, every now and then attempting to strike with his long claws ... The whole time the animal was on stage the audience was kept in roars of laughter at the amusing manner in which he illustrated the feints and tricks of a boxer.[19]

The rigours of celebrity life took a toll on Jack, his life cut short by illness six months later. His lengthy obituary stated no other creature could have been as heroic or as virtuous as this 'ambitious young kangaroo pugilist'. *Table Talk* declared that no other country would dare to 'upset the theories formulated by naturalists' by being the birthplace of such an animal.[20] In the public eye, kangaroos were no longer simply Australian creatures, but animals revealing the 'uniquely' humorous spirit of the nation that had accepted them as its own.

That combination of humour and pugnacity crystallised in the boxing kangaroo flag, which was first used in Alan Bond's 1983 America's Cup campaign (Fig. 8). Designed by Steve Castledine, the rights to the image were bought by the Australian Olympic Committee (AOC) in 1993, becoming a semi-official sporting emblem. This was particularly controversial at the 2010 Winter Olympics when the International Olympic Committee objected to it being flown in the athletes' village, with Prime Minister Julia Gillard even stepping in to defend the symbol. In a not-so-subtle allusion to Australian athletes abroad, the AOC continues to vehemently defend the emblem:

> His unrelenting 'have a go' Aussie spirit makes him hugely popular with all Australians. BK [The Boxing Kangaroo] is not a lout, nor is he aggressive or arrogant. He is, however, assertive when it comes to defending his country's glory ... These same qualities are what drive Australia's pursuit of success on the international stage.[21]

Associations of the ludicrous continued to dominate kangaroo interactions. Another scene in *On Our Selection* had Dad being outwitted by a boxing kangaroo, which caused Dad to lose his pants. The ongoing popularity of 'animal yarns' was still evident in December 2007 when the *Geelong Advertiser* broke the story of a swimming kangaroo being eaten by a shark off the coast of Fisherman's Beach in Victoria.[22] The bizarre story involving not one but two national symbols was syndicated across the globe: one Indian paper's headline read 'The shark that jumped out of the sea to kill a kangaroo'.[23]

Perhaps the most far-fetched tales were found in the television series, *Skippy the Bush Kangaroo*. First aired in February 1968, it was syndicated in almost 30 countries and created a generation of childhood fans, renewed with a remake in 1991, *The New Adventures of Skippy*. With the help of two human sidekicks, the friendly orphaned kangaroo solves crimes in Waratah National Park, due in part to an ability to 'drive cars, pick locks, send Morse code, fly helicopters or even hold a conversation'. Episode synopses reveal the extent of kangaroo heroics: 'Paralyzed by nerve gas, Clancy wills Skippy to [deliver] … tape recorded evidence that leads to the capture of the animal thief' or '[when] an armed robber holds Sonny as hostage, Skippy "jumps" him, saving the lives of everyone'.[24] Unlike folk stories and spectacles such as Fighting Jack, Skippy was a consciously constructed national product, designed to appeal to domestic audiences through its familiarity, and to international viewers through its engagement with pre-established cultural stereotypes.[25] Perhaps as testament to its international appeal, the series also led to Australians of non-British descent coining the term 'skip' to refer to Anglo–Celtic Australians, a (usually) gently derogatory retort to some of the language applied to them.

The kangaroo's absurdity, whether intentional, as in Dad and Dave, or unintentional, as in *Skippy*, was adopted as part of its national meaning among non-Indigenous Australians – nowhere more than in the incomprehensible international hit, 'Tie me kangaroo down, sport'. Perhaps it is merely an extension of the first European sense of the animal's 'oddity', but Australians seem comfortable treating their national icon in a less than respectful way, and seeing in it a reflection of their own supposedly irreverent character. But larrikinism is only one of a number of narratives of 'Australia' and 'Australianness' that the kangaroo has been required to serve.

'The Spirit of Australia'

Competing with its irreverence was a figure of the kangaroo standing for the noble spirit of Australia, one that implied a break from the first European representations. Ethel Pedley's enormously popular children's book, *Dot and the Kangaroo*, published in 1899, depicted a young girl being rescued in the bush by a kangaroo. More than simply a progenitor of Skippy, the kangaroo is a soothing, wise presence. She is described as 'endearing', 'a noble kangaroo' who transforms Dot's understanding of the value of the Australian bush and creatures.[26] On the elaborate cover of the second edition in 1900, the kangaroo echoed the pose of Stubbs' first sketch, but rather than being an uncomfortable 'specimen', she was rimmed with soft gilt and surrounded by a triumphal ring of green leaves as she looked back over her shoulder with quiet dignity at Dot's happy reunion with her father.[27]

When boxing kangaroos began to appear on the noses of various Royal Australian Air Force (RAAF) aircraft during World War II, the image of trustworthiness and nobility was interwoven with a cheeky larrikinism. The 'Desert Harassers' of the No. 450 (Kittyhawk) Squadron, for example, added a digger's hat to the boxing kangaroo,[28] while the No. 460 Squadron (combining RAAF and Scottish personnel) adorned the marsupial with bagpipes and flying boots.[29] These images of bravado often accompanied a tally of aircraft destroyed or the words 'It's in the bag!' The RAAF's formal insignia was initially the same as

The evolution of the flying kangaroo: Qantas livery through the years.

Courtesy Qantas Airways Limited

the Britain's Royal Air Force: a red, white and blue roundel. When the United States accidentally shot down an Australian Catalina, mistaking its red markings for a Japanese fighter, the RAAF removed the inner red circle, and after the war a hopping red kangaroo officially took its place at the centre of the blue circle.[30]

Qantas also capitalised on the associations of the flying kangaroo, painting its planes from 1944 with the kangaroo from the penny coin (first minted 1938) and forging an indelible link between flying, service to country and the kangaroo. From 1947 the company was regularly flying its premier 'Kangaroo Route', which hopped between Australia and London, and intentionally marketed itself as the flying kangaroo and 'the Spirit of Australia'. This 'spirit' was intangible and flexible, a vaguely noble sentiment that could appear both contemporary and timeless. Qantas, Australia and the kangaroo became interchangeable concepts, promoted by 2005 as a 'legacy', with 'ANZAC as its inspiring character' and with 'deep foundations in the Australian community'.[31] A corporate rebranding of Qantas in 2016 coincided with the introduction of the Dreamliner, developing something 'more modern and dynamic'. Qantas CEO Alan Joyce celebrated the 80-year history of the logo, which had 'come to represent the spirit of Australia. When passengers see the Qantas tail at airports around the world, it's a symbol of home.' But home needed to have 'a more premium feel'. Designer Marc Newson aimed 'to retain the fundamental essence of the flying kangaroo but also move the brand forward'.[32]

The floating significance of the kangaroo took the symbol to its final stage, where it could be imagined as standing for just about any positive value associated with the nation. In 2004, Tourism Australia adopted the jumping kangaroo as its logo for all international tourism promotion, as the animal was 'symbolic of … warmth, boundless energy and forward looking optimism'. In 2007, executive general manager John Borghetti claimed the Qantas kangaroo represented the airline's 'long association with the qualities of Australia – natural, free spirited and confident'. The Australian Made Campaign continued to use their kangaroo logo because both international and domestic market research shows the kangaroo conjuring up a series of attributes that could be linked to products made in Australia: 'pure and natural', 'unique', 'innovative' and 'clean environment'.[33] But at the same time, as climate change became more menacing, the kangaroo was becoming, even internationally, a symbol of a fragile environment.[34]

Symbolicide

The ease with which the kangaroo can hop between these various meanings without undermining its authenticity demonstrates its successful transformation from mere animal into a powerful and ubiquitous symbol of Australia. Anyone can write their own 'Australia' onto the palimpsest of the symbol. However, the kangaroo's pervasiveness as a symbol means that living kangaroos must always carry the burden of being a national institution. As a result any debate on the kangaroo industry or any dispute about the ethical treatment of kangaroos necessarily has higher emotional stakes, getting caught up in questions of national sentiment.

Concerns about the killing of kangaroos were voiced early by individuals such as naturalist Charles Darwin (1836) but it was not until 1871 that the Royal Society for Prevention of Cruelty to Animals was established in Australia, in response to 'the carefree colonial attitude towards animals'. Australia's first Wildlife Preservation Society appeared in 1909, opposing battues but accepting that graziers had a case for humane culling. In the 1950s kangaroo meat began to be used in pet food and export of kangaroo as game meat began. Alarm was increasing at the huge numbers of animals being shot and the general lack of control over the industry. In 1969 the Australian Wildlife Protection Council was formed, opposing culling.[35]

Responding to pressure from American and Australian conservationists, the United States Government banned imports of kangaroo in

1974. Australian governments responded with management programs for the kangaroo industry. Commercial harvesting was limited to those species considered resilient (mainly reds, and eastern and western greys) and the annual quota was to be set by the National Parks and Wildlife Service or equivalent body in each state. The kangaroo industry became highly regulated, with trained shooters adhering to a code of practice. The United States trade ban was lifted in 1981.[36]

Harvesting continued to be opposed by some conservation groups, joined by animal rights activists in Australia and overseas, and driven by ethical concerns. Some scientists feared that commercial culling damaged the kangaroo's ongoing ability to survive. They challenged prevailing beliefs about the resilience of the kangaroo's reproductive cycle and warned that killing the large alpha males eroded the gene pool, forcing females to take weaker, younger mates.[37] Although opposition to culling focused mainly on survival and cruelty, especially the plight of the orphaned joeys, these groups were conscious of the symbol's power, highlighting the kangaroo's national status in, for example, images of its being shot off the coat of arms.[38] Widespread international recognition of the kangaroo enabled groups opposing harvesting to gain media coverage and popular support for their campaigns. VIVA! (Vegetarians International Voice for Animals) compelled British supermarkets to stop stocking kangaroo meat and (in another extraordinary case of icons colliding) persuaded soccer star David Beckham to discard his kangaroo leather boots. VIVA!, PETA (People for the Ethical Treatment of Animals) and other groups convinced the Californian government to reinstate its ban on the use of kangaroo products in 2016. In February 2021, a Kangaroo Protection Act was introduced to US Congress, proposing to restore a national ban on the import of kangaroo products. Australia's kangaroo industry has acknowledged the symbolic power of the kangaroo as a major problem, which forced it 'to spend a large proportion of its promotional effort simply defending what it does'.[39]

Industry advocates also recognised the kangaroo's symbolic power by arguing that the industry harmonised with the Australian environment. They pointed out that kangaroos, unlike sheep, have soft paw pads which do not trample and compact the soil; kangaroos eat and drink relatively little, and breed in synchrony with Australia's drought-and-flood cycle. Expanding the market for kangaroo meat (highly nutritious with low fat content) would increase prices and encourage graziers in Australia's fragile arid rangelands to replace sheep with kangaroos. Desertification of these severely degraded areas would stop and native vegetation would regenerate.[40]

The kangaroo industry may be more accepted in Australia than overseas, but ambivalence remains. A 1997 study found respondents agreeing that kangaroos should be exploited as a valuable resource yet also protected because they are unique to Australia. A *Herald-Sun* poll in 2002 found 87 per cent accepted commercial use of kangaroos. A *Sydney Morning Herald* Australia Day feature in 2008 argued that it was a patriotic duty to eat kangaroo rather than introduced livestock, which damage the land. The next day a letter suggested it would be more patriotic to eat un-Australian feral pests instead.[41] The debate around eating kangaroo continues into the twenty-first century with the arrival of 'kangatarianism', a largely vegetarian diet with the exception of kangaroo meat.[42]

As Peter Ellyard observed, our values about killing wildlife are culturally based, changing and arbitrary.[43] Hence Japan could respond to Australian criticism of its whaling program by pointing to Australia's killing of kangaroos and dingos. The emotions invested in national symbols make it hard to have reasoned debates and distract attention from other issues such as the plight of less prominent species which continue to slip into extinction.

Both advocates and opponents to culling admire the resilience of the kangaroo, which has managed so far to survive climatic extremes, changed habitats, eradication programs and harvesting. They are also united in using the kangaroo's symbolic attributes in their opposing arguments. Rural landholders may be less willing to accept kangaroos as an inevitable consequence of living in Australia, and less likely to romanticise the marsupial's national meaning. Nevertheless, years of popular use and official and commercial promotion have made the kangaroo more than just a way of identifying a place, but a symbol capable of representing all the attributes and emotions of the nation.

CROWN

Mark McKenna

To be a King and wear a Crown is a thing more glorious to them that see it than it is pleasant to them that bear it.

Elizabeth I, speech to parliament, 30 November 1601

At about the age of six or seven, one of my daughters' favourite storybooks was Tohby Riddle's *The Royal Guest*, which tells the story of Mrs Jones of Padstow. As her name implies, Mrs Jones is a woman whose chief virtue is her ordinariness. We know little else about her save that she lives at home with her two children. Her modest bungalow in Padstow, an outer working-class suburb of Sydney, barely has room for visitors. Nonetheless, in a fit of generosity, she offers to billet the Queen during her visit to Australia. The Queen, of course, happily accepts Mrs Jones's offer. Her Majesty arrives at Sydney airport carrying her sleeping bag and takes the bus to Padstow. There, she plays cards and drinks tea 'till all hours' with Mrs Jones. But it is the night before she is to address federal parliament in Canberra so the Queen finally retires, sleeping on the living room floor on an air mattress, which she inflates herself.

The Queen shows her appreciation to Mrs Jones of Padstow with the gift of her crown, in *The Royal Guest*, written and illustrated by Tohby Riddle, first published in 1993.

Courtesy Penguin Random House and Curtis Brown

The following day, after a hectic round of royal engagements, the Queen returns to spend her last night at Padstow. Before she leaves the next morning, she hands Mrs Jones a thank-you gift. It is the most delicately crafted jewelled crown, one of the Queen's old favourites. Mrs Jones, who is busy packing the Queen's lunch, accepts the crown, joking that this must make her 'the Queen of Padstow'. Here the story ends. But I've often imagined Mrs Jones sitting at her kitchen table, carefully placing the crown on her head. How strange it must have felt, this crown that jarred with her clothes and refused to sit straight on her hair. If the neighbours caught sight of her, they'd probably have thought she'd gone mad. After all, what good is a crown in Padstow? We know nothing of how long Mrs Jones reigned in her realm of Padstow, or whether she managed to find any loyal subjects, although given the wry delivery of her final line it would seem unlikely she persisted with the fantasy of being the Queen of Padstow.[1]

While Australians have claimed the monarchy as their own, given the Queen the title Queen of Australia, and stamped their own particular qualities on the function of executive, legislative and judicial power exercised in the name of the crown, they have never managed to fully naturalise the object of the crown itself (Fig. 10). The aura of the crown has been borrowed but it has not proved transferable. The sight of an Australian wearing the crown of royalty – like the sight of the crowned Mrs Jones in Padstow – has always retained a strong sense of the absurd. To think of the crown as a 'symbol of Australia' (rather than a symbol 'in' Australia), certainly requires more mental agility than imagining the Opera House, the Harbour Bridge, Vegemite, or any hapless marsupial conscripted to serve the same purpose.

The crown is at once abstract and concrete, at once foreign and indigenous. And one of the most interesting aspects of the crown as a symbol in Australia is its fluidity. It seems impossible to pin this symbol down. First, there is the crown as the object itself – the talisman that sits atop the monarch's head. Neither the Imperial State Crown (worn by the Queen at the State Opening of British Parliament, though not in 2019) nor the St Edward's Crown (worn by the Queen at her coronation) have been used by Queen Elizabeth II in Australia. The crown is heterogeneous, both as object and symbol. Different crowns have been the basis for the symbolic crown incorporated into badges, emblems and insignia. Yet, sanctioned by God, it remains a symbol not only of divine authority and wealth, but of a certain magic, the sight of which, like fire in the hearth, holds an almost instinctive allure. In Australia it seems to have lost its ability to serve as a unifying symbol, not least because the object itself is absent.

Second, there is the crown as synonym for the state. The crown is both the ultimate and singular source of authority – moral, legal and political – and yet, like the Holy Trinity, it is divisible, morphing at the will of its subjects into the crown of Canada, Britain, New Zealand, Queensland or Tasmania, thus representing quite distinct executive governments in different jurisdictions. Each 'crown' comprises a separate political and legal entity, each capable of declaring war with or without the other, each capable of introducing parliamentary legislation found in no other Commonwealth country, and each capable of independent legal action – of both suing and being sued.

The 'chameleon Crown', as lawyer and historian Anne Twomey described it in 2006, is ingenious. It symbolises the state, yet it also embodies the idea of the state in the person of the monarch, thus giving the state a personalised dimension. When needed, this personalised dimension surfaces, when not it retreats behind the arras of political and judicial power, separating the person of the monarch (the crown) from the day-to-day function of state power performed in the name of the crown.[2]

Australian liberals and democrats in the mid-nineteenth century understood this subtlety perfectly well, distinguishing between the objectionable policies of Downing Street and the benign person of the monarch to whom they appealed. They saw the crown as a symbol of those British birthrights such as trial by jury, representative assemblies and freedom from arbitrary rule, and they did so across the political spectrum – conservative, liberal and democrat – for two centuries. No surprise then that the crown is often seen as a disguise or foil, dignifying the more unseemly business of government. Perhaps this is why Ben Chifley, Labor prime minister from 1945 to 1949, referred to the crown as 'a handy constitutional fiction'. The astonishing thing is that Chifley's fiction was not designed: it simply evolved over time according to Darwinian logic, adapting to its changing environment.[3] Take, for example, the analogy drawn from a 1997 legal text:

> The Crown is in many ways like a corporation. It is governed in Australia in each jurisdiction by a written constitution, it has perpetual succession, it must necessarily act through natural persons and it takes on a legal status independent from those natural persons.[4]

How different this definition is from the one provided by the *Sydney Morning Herald*, on 22 June 1911, on the coronation of George V. 'The Crown', said the *Herald*'s editorial, 'is the one enduring symbol of Empire'. While the modern crown may behave like a corporation in some ways, history suggests it has more security of tenure than many corporations. Part of the reason for its longevity resides in its ability to change over time, from a symbol of Empire and absolute authority to one associated with Australia and democratic government.

In the service of the crown

In 1901, the Australian Commonwealth was founded as 'one indissoluble Commonwealth under the Crown'. The crown, through the person of the monarch, has underwritten every statute and law and all those who have acted in the name or in the service of the crown. And yet, through the person of the monarch, it has also acted as the source of appeal against arbitrary exercise of state power. Aboriginal people, from the early nineteenth century on, appealed to the crown to protect them from the actions of governments acting in the name of the crown. Even as the Australian people were voting in the republic referendum in 1999, Aboriginal leaders were visiting the Queen in London, appealing to the crown for support at the very moment the crown's survival in Australia was in doubt. The crown, therefore, has often been perceived by Aboriginal and Torres Strait Islander people as a symbol of the protection of Indigenous rights (Fig. 11). At the same time, it has also been an undeniable symbol of their dispossession. From the late 1990s,

Indigenous artists such as Darren Siwes began to draw attention to the fact that the sovereignty of the crown obscured Indigenous sovereignty. Each sovereignty was the inverse of the other; each inextricably bound with the other. Siwes' series 'Oz Omnium Rex Et Regina' revealed what had already been implied in earlier forms of Australian banknotes and coinage: that the flipside of the crown's sovereignty was Indigenous sovereignty. Now, however, Indigenous sovereignty was restored as 'the head' rather than the tail.

When James Cook reached the northerly tip of Cape York on 22 August 1770, after sailing almost the entire east coast of Australia, he wrote in his journal that while he had already 'taken possession' of several places along the coast during his journey, he would do so once again. On what he called Possession Island:

> I now once more hoisted English Couleurs and in the name of His Majesty King George the Third took possession of the whole Eastern coast from the above latitude down to this place by the name of New South Wales, together with all of the Bays, Harbours Rivers and Islands situate upon the said coast, after which we fired three volleys of small arms.[5]

Along with Governor Arthur Phillip's proclamation at Sydney Cove 18 years later, Cook's declaration of possession asserted British sovereignty over Indigenous land, a sovereignty legitimised by the authority of the crown. It was nothing less than a form of sorcery – the hoisting of the colours, the reading of an incantation, the firing of a few volleys into the air – and thousands of square kilometres, in British eyes, instantly became the possession of the crown. The crown thus sanctioned occupation, possession, settlement, and the imposition of British rule and British law on the Australian continent. It was the word that hovered above the colonial project – strangely distant and yet powerfully present – the word through which the invasion and settlement was executed. The term crown land, in use ever since, is the

A crown tops the booklet issued by the Commonwealth Government for the proposed visit of Princess Elizabeth and Prince Philip to Australia in 1952. The visit was cancelled when the death of King George VI was announced and Elizabeth became Queen.

Professor Peter Spearritt collection no. 2, National Museum of Australia

very echo of this process of dispossession. Consequently, the crown has been the symbol of both possession and dispossession, depending on who is speaking.[6]

For most of Australia's settler history, particularly for Australians of British origin, the crown has been the most powerful symbol of Australia's belonging to the wider British Empire. In the nineteenth century, the Colonial Office was well aware of the crown's symbolic power, quickly seeing the unifying potential of creating a colonial order of knighthood. Civil servant and historian Herman Merivale went further, writing in 1870 that: 'every honour which the Crown can bestow should be Imperial ... and open to every subject of the Crown, in all its dominions peopled by Englishmen'.[7] From the 1860s, when members of the royal family began to visit the colonies more frequently, the crown became flesh and blood, with visiting royals reminding their distant subjects that the crown was a rallying point for the loyalties of people as disparate as a Calgary farmer, a Sydney shopkeeper and a rural dean in New Zealand. Through the symbolism of the crown, the imagined community of a global British people was made possible. When this sense of belonging came under threat in Australia, as it did during the abdication crisis in 1936, Australians made their preference for the maintenance of the relationship clear. At the height of the crisis, the Australian Government was fearful of the consequences for the dominions if Edward chose to abdicate. Australian prime minister Joseph Lyons wrote to his British counterpart Stanley Baldwin, reminding him that 'the Crown is now the great unifying element in the British Empire'. Without the stability of the crown, Lyons feared the whole edifice, of a British people and community spread across the globe, could crumble.[8]

Monarchists and patriots

To understand the significance of the crown's ability to symbolise allegiance to both Australia and Britain we need to take seriously the mystical language of loyalty that the crown inspired. This means trying to understand, rather than mock, the likes of Prime Minister Robert Menzies, who, in Westminster Abbey for the coronation in 1953, had something of an epiphany. 'I realised', he wrote, 'more than ever before ... [that] we were one people.' After returning home, he explained, 'I am a monarchist just because to me, and millions of others, the crown is non-utilitarian; it represents a spiritual and emotional conception more enduring and significant than any balance sheet cast up by an accountant.' As Queen Elizabeth II left Australia in 1954 she echoed

Menzies' rhetoric in her final address, insisting that 'the Crown is a human link between all the people who owe allegiance to me, an allegiance of mutual love and respect and never of compulsion'. In federal parliament, only weeks earlier, she spoke of the feeling of 'comradeship' engendered by the crown, 'that sense of duty shared which we must all have as we confront our common tasks'.[9]

At its most purple, this language, which attempted to give meaning to the symbolism of the crown, expressed a human longing for total unity, for one indissoluble and homogenous community. It constantly returned to the theme of a common purpose and shared bedrock of cultural reference, projecting a sense of belonging that extended far beyond Australia's shores. Implicit in the countless examples of public expressions of fealty to the crown is not only the concept of belonging to the 'British race', as Menzies described it, but the idea of belonging to a predominantly Christian society. So long as the crown remains, the sense that the state is informed and guided by Christian principles lingers, at least for those who are aware of the crown's history. Remember the words uttered at the coronation, 'Receive this Orb set under the Cross, and remember that the whole world is subject to the Power and Empire of Christ our Redeemer.' Fusing concepts of race, Empire, nation, morality and faith, the crown constituted 'an active conscience' at the heart of society.[10]

But it was also a symbol of national euphoria and exultation. When Samuel Pepys described the coronation of Charles II in 1661 he described the 'great shout' that echoed throughout Westminster Abbey as Charles was crowned. As Pepys walked with the procession from the abbey to Westminster Hall, he took much pleasure 'to look upon the ladies and to hear the Musique of all sorts; but above all the 24 violins'.[11] Almost 300 years later, when Queen Elizabeth II was crowned with the same crown in 1953, the same shouts of joy echoed in Westminster Abbey, outside on the streets of London, and in the many Commonwealth countries across the globe, shouts that seemed to express mass relief, because the people once again possessed a sovereign.

The sense of national communion achieved through the symbol of the crown, at least up until the royal tour in 1954, eclipsed that of Anzac Day today. Despite Menzies' intention that 'The Crown should not become too familiar or commonplace', members of the royal family visited Australia with increasing frequency.[12] Since 1868, when Prince Alfred became the first member of the British royal family to visit Australia, the spectacle of more than 50 royal tours has always relied heavily on the image of the crown. In 1920, 12,000 schoolchildren were brought to the Sydney Cricket Ground to form a living birthday greeting to the Prince of Wales. Above their heads, the children held masses of self-made yellow, blue and red feathers and dutifully following the scripted choreography, formed a human crown, visible only from the highest points in the stands above.[13] In 1954, near Woodside in South Australia, the front gates of the immigration centre were decorated with an electrically lit St Edward's crown placed atop the letters EIIR, all wired successfully by a Polish electrician.[14] On other occasions, floats, public buildings, welcome archways, official commemorative publications and countless souvenirs (many of which ended their lives as treasured objects exhibited in kitchens and family living rooms across Australia) reproduced the image of the crown. The crown was thus a symbol that was not only handed down from above, but one that also existed in private and domestic space. As Prince Edward realised after touring Australia in 1920, through the presence of the crown, the Empire had entered the people's dreams.[15]

The crown's more mundane entry into everyday lives came through its role as a symbol in Australian coinage, which goes back to the days of the First Fleet. When Australia started producing its own coinage from 1911, King Edward VII and then George V wore crowns even though they (and even sometimes Queen Victoria) appeared bare-headed on British coins. It was only in 1937, when Edward VIII expressed the desire to appear bare-headed, that Australia was prepared to tolerate a king without a crown. A king without a crown was not a king at all.[16] Deep in the cultural consciousness of many of the settlers who came to

Australia were echoes of a time when coins bearing the image of a king or queen were thought to possess magical powers.

Marc Bloch has shown how in the Shetland Islands, up to 1838, crowns and half-crowns bearing the effigy of Charles I were handed down from one generation to another in the belief they would remedy scrofula. And 'in the Scottish county of Ross even during the reign of Queen Victoria, ordinary gold coins were held to be universal panaceas, simply because they bore the image of the Queen'.[17] To date, I have no evidence of the effigy of the crown on Australian coinage being ascribed such magical powers. But I can still remember my father coming home after work early in 1966 and tearing open his yellow pay envelope as he sat at the kitchen table while the family gathered around. We were eager to catch our first sight of the new decimal currency. As he pulled out the brightly coloured notes and passed them round for us all to see, my grandmother exclaimed, 'It's not real money!' She was disappointed that many of the new notes no longer bore the effigy of the Queen, while those that did, with their gaudy colours and busy design, she found undignified.

Losing the crown

By the end of the twentieth century, it was easy to assume that the crown had retreated completely as an Australian symbol. While it no longer underwrites the postal service in Australia, the crown still surfaces as a symbol in countless aspects of Australian public life. It appears on the numberplates of the official vehicles transporting the governor-general and state governors and in the design of Commonwealth and state coats of arms. Badges worn by the Australian Army, with few exceptions, are very close copies of British badges, almost all surmounted by the crown. Royal hospitals, racetracks, sailing clubs, golf courses, hotels and agricultural societies all display the crown, as does the badge of the Returned and Services

League of Australia (RSL), and the insignia of the Order of Australia.

But it is in retreat. What are the ramifications of the crown's disappearance as a unifying symbol in Australia, a symbol which no longer possesses the civic personality it once did? It is not, as is so often assumed, simply a case of the crown slipping quietly off into the night, disappearing without consequence. It had its defenders: Professor David Flint, head of Australians for Constitutional Monarchy (ACM), asserted that the crown is 'as Australian as our beaches and our forests', and Tony Abbott, on the cusp of entering parliament in 1994, claimed that 'the Crown is no more alien to Australia than cricket and Shakespeare'. But we quickly recognise such statements as little more than spin.[18] As a meaningful symbol, the crown has lost the depth of its appeal, lost its lustre and magnetism.

In the early 1970s, Paul Hasluck wrote that 'the Crown, being outside politics, attracts the same loyalty from all subjects all the time and stands for those matters on which the nation is undivided'. In 2003, Vice Admiral David Leach told the ACM national conference that 'the Crown embodies the union of the monarch and the people. As such it is a symbol of [Australian] nationhood'. But the 1999 republic referendum showed a great many Australians, perhaps a majority, were ready to sever the last constitutional ties with the crown. Clearly, the belief of Hasluck and Leach that the crown was a unifying symbol of nationhood no longer held true.[19] In this sense, Australia is a captive republic, stumbling on into the twenty-first century with a symbol that has lost its relevance and unifying power. Placing the earlier language of devotion to the crown in a contemporary context it soon appears as nostalgia or special pleading. We need only to recite such terms as 'Minister of the Crown', 'On His Majesty's Service', 'His Majesty's Opposition' and 'His Majesty's Government' in order to hear the emptiness of the crown as symbol today.

In the twenty-first century, the Australian crown appears much like a Tinseltown film set after the last take; a town that, from a distance, still glows, still appears magnificent, but on closer inspection is deserted.

MAP

Alan Atkinson

In the Australian Museum in Sydney, among a glittering geological display, including dappled green malachite, azurite of peacock blue and brilliant yellow sulphur, there are several gold nuggets. They are replicas, but they look real. The originals are beyond the resources of a mere museum. Beside the 'Welcome Stranger' and other iconic pieces there sits a lesser-known nugget, discovered at Ruby Plains Station, Halls Creek, Western Australia, in 1900, which carries the name 'Map of Australia'. It is small compared with some of the other nuggets, just 23.3 ounces (660.5 grams) and no more than 10 centimetres across. It certainly looks like a map of Australia, although there is a large inlet where Port Hedland should be, and no Tasmania.

The Map of Australia nugget was unearthed within a year of Australian Federation. Its discovery and its naming are nicely symbolic of the way the continent itself – not just the people, not just its political systems but the continental landmass – figured in talk about constitutional change. When enthusiasts for Federation pronounced 'Australia for the Australians!' they were not only excluding Indigenous Australians but thinking of an object (the continent) whose shape they could roughly guess and whose value they knew to be immense. No doubt the men who found the Map of Australia nugget and who claimed it for themselves also learned to know its bumps and indents, as they gloated over it.

By this time, it was supposed to be the duty of all Australians to know by heart the main bumps and indents of the continent itself, the Mercator projection, that supremely European way of imagining the world, being treated as the orthodox version. Twelve years earlier, the explorer and later Western Australian premier John Forrest had announced that 'The map of Australia ... must be familiar to all persons who claim Australia as their home.'[1] The map was certainly becoming more familiar (Fig. 12), which explains the naming of the nugget. A later generation, living at a time when that distinctive outline was synonymous with the nation, might have simply called it 'Australia'. Even with Federation the map had nothing like the symbolic power it has today, but the symbolising process had begun. The events of those dozen years or so gave the map lasting value, and gave it symbolic power as good as gold.

The nugget has no Tasmania, but Tasmania was sometimes seen as a jewel in its own right, a miniature nation. Nineteenth-century Tasmanians, when they said 'Australia', had always meant the mainland, not themselves, and it was still quite common to speak of 'Australia and Tasmania'.[2] Historian Elizabeth McMahon has found a couple of late nineteenth-century authors, both of them travel writers, who compared Tasmania with Ireland and Ceylon – the Emerald Isle and the Pearl of India. Tasmania, said one of them, should be called 'the Ruby of Australia', in memory of convict (and perhaps Aboriginal) bloodshed.[3] Even today, pieces of land are often referred to as gems, glittering and seductive to the eye of the stranger because of the way they look on maps. The Seychelles, according to a tourism website, 'are scattered across the Indian Ocean like a string of diamonds'. The outcrops of the Great Barrier Reef, says another, 'stretch like a glistening string of pearls' along the Queensland coast.[4]

The glory of precious stones and metal had a spiritual power for that generation largely lost later on. Can the loveliness of the country be symbolised now with such objects? Like coal, they might even suggest desecration and yet in the right hands, some might say, the imagery still works. So, in 'My country' (1908), Dorothea Mackellar made the midday sun 'hot gold' and the mountains 'sapphire-misted'. Mackellar's treasure island, lying 'opal-hearted' in a 'jewel-sea', still makes vestigial sense.

Such imagery encapsulated something big in something small. Something reaching far beyond the horizon was distilled as something intricate. The simplicity of its shape meant that the map of Australia could be very small and still recognisable, at the same time summarising an object and an idea of dazzling dimensions (Fig. 13). All cartography, whether of invaders or indigenous peoples, was a way of holding and fixing the imagination on something beyond ready comprehension, which is how all good symbols operate. Such map-based imagery only started to work with the mass of readers in the late nineteenth century, when large numbers started to be cartographically literate, mainly through instruction in schools. This was also the first generation to advertise tourism. Tourists, being buyers, had to grasp and admire the object on sale. As a symbol, then, the map of Australia mixed up poetry and trade.

The idea of the nation as an abstract shape was being drummed into citizens elsewhere too. In France, 'the national hexagon', as one historian puts it, the nation within its sacred borders was suddenly ubiquitous in the late nineteenth century, making the French imagine eternal unity. In Thailand, where European map-drawing was an innovation, the change was especially sudden, but by the early 1900s the delineation of the kingdom was just as effective as symbol and as propaganda.[5]

Taking shape

The idea of Australia as a single jewel, as a sceptred isle bigger and richer than Britain itself, dates back to the mid-nineteenth century. Two generations before, in 1786, the British Government, in issuing its instructions to Arthur Phillip, first Governor of New South Wales, had claimed only the eastern part, with seas adjoining, and even this was far beyond any envisaged need. Later on, in the same way, gold miners were to set their boundaries as wide as possible before digging, in case something turned up. When the Swan River settlement was formed in 1829 there was no immediate effort to peg out the rest, and the colony of Western Australia reached to meet the New South Wales border only in 1832.

Matthew Flinders, with George Bass, proved Tasmania to be a single, detached landmass in 1798–99, and he did the same for the Australian continent in 1803. Still, for most people of that and the next generation, the continent was not so much a nugget or a jewel as a curate's egg, partly good and partly bad. It had to be comprehended in sections. For new settlers, some of it was polluted by convict transportation. This was the message implicit in the first map of the entire landmass to be placed before a popular audience, in England in 1835, among the literature designed to persuade working men and women to emigrate to the new colony of South Australia. 'Australia is a great big island', readers were told, 'situated in the South Sea, or Indian Ocean; they used to call it, *New Holland.*' The writer conducted aspiring emigrants around the coastline in several stages. New South Wales and Van Diemen's Land were penal settlements and Western Australia had been founded on 'erroneous principles', which made it just as bad. He then asked them to fix their minds on South Australia and to understand, if they could, its relationship with the world at large, including southern Asia, the Cape of Good Hope, and England.[6]

Internal exploration and mapping kept pace, though in a stumbling way, with the rapid expansion of settlement inland from Sydney in the 1820s and 1830s, and then from the newer centres of public and private enterprise, Perth, Adelaide, Melbourne and Brisbane. In order to make their task manageable the government surveyors in Sydney drew a rough half-circle at about 300 kilometres' distance, called the 'Limits of Location', within which roads and towns were laid out and freehold land was made available. During the 1830s the land inside the

Limits was held to be identical with the colony of New South Wales for most practical purposes, although there was grazing and exploration far afield. Here, the curate's egg was more finely mottled, with various assessments of soil, landscape and population, according to period and perspective. Some of it was wilderness, some was garden, some the abode of Aboriginal people, snakes and bushrangers, and some a place of roads, bridges, good women and religious communion.[7] These were vast spaces for a generation whose cartographic literacy was extremely limited. The readers of the South Australian propaganda, for instance, were mostly southern Englishmen, who rarely had to stretch their minds further than the distance between London and Bristol. The almost childish language in this literature – 'great big island', 'they used to' – was part of a deliberate effort to reach into the minds of people ignorant about maps.[8] Some transported convicts, in their efforts to escape, showed a fair sense of direction – an awareness, for instance, that China was in the north and Timor somewhere in the north-west – but an utterly hopeless underestimation of the size of the landmass, which they thought would take only a few days to cross, as with England and Ireland.[9]

In the 1850s, with the discovery of gold, the south coast became much more interesting, as a doorstep to riches in Victoria. So did the interior. As a result, maps were much more sought after. The absolute interior was the Centre, and large parts of it remained unmapped and mysterious for the rest of the century. Focusing on the Centre gave a kind of unity to the coastal boundary. It might itself be imagined as a jewel, hidden within a varied landscape many miles across. Ernest Giles set out for those parts in 1872, fantasising about secret riches:

> There was room for snowy mountains, an inland sea, ancient river, and palmy plain, for races of new kinds of men inhabiting a new and odorous land, for fields of gold and golcondas of gems, for a new flora and a new fauna, and, above all the rest combined, there was room for me![10]

Not long afterwards some of the more remote desert parts did turn out to be fields of gold. Halls Creek, where the Map of Australia nugget was dug up, was one of the earliest.

Knowing the map

For centuries, the great aim of education had been the instilling of knowledge. During the nineteenth century a new purpose was added, the stretching of imagination in order to comprehend large expanses of time (using continuous, long-term historical narrative) and of space (using maps). Memories were trained in a more connected and comprehensive way, and new intellectual techniques had to be mastered. This was the great turning point in the comprehension of continents. Australia, vast within itself and set alone in a remote part of the world, was a neat puzzle for the mind to conquer. 'A line', it has been said, 'is a child's first instrument of depiction, the boundary where one thing ends and the other begins.'[11] The map reduced the country to a single line, a sudden, magical configuration. Making sense of the map was like discovering gold.

Schools in the late nineteenth century used two methods of teaching cartography. In some colonies they started with the whole world and moved inward, ending up with the relevant colony and taking in the continent on the way. More up-to-date and probably more effective was the method used in South Australia. Children there started with 'local geography', which meant drawing diagrams of the classroom, school buildings and neighbourhood. When they had learned how to convert the real world into two dimensions and back again, they were shown pieces of cartography on a larger scale. As a school inspector put it, each child was first told 'something about his own neighbourhood, the hills that surround it, the creeks which flow through it, the seas which wash its shores', advancing all the time 'from the known to the unknown'.[12] The great challenge lay in leaping between these two dimensions. As

'A handful of Australia' postcard, c. 1909.
Mapping could be an act of possession – and dispossession.
State Library of Victoria

another put it, 'the advance from the geography of the neighbourhood ... to that of all South Australia in the second is a very great stride'. The next leap outward, to the world as a whole, was more difficult again.[13]

Many adults baulked even at the first leap. In 1883 a Frenchman living in Sydney, Edmond Marin la Meslée, author of *L'Australie Nouvelle* ('The New Australia'), established the Geographical Society of Australasia with the hope of coaching ordinary colonists through such efforts of comprehension. La Meslée thought of geography as a world of knowledge which ought to be accessible to every citizen. In trying to convey a sense of the whole landmass of Australia he seems to have taken his cue from his compatriot, the historian Jules Michelet. Michelet's magisterial *Histoire de France* (1833–69) had presented France as a coherent bundle of history and geography. In it, the author boasted, France was revealed for the first time 'in the *living unity* of natural and geographical events'. Michelet had much to say about the

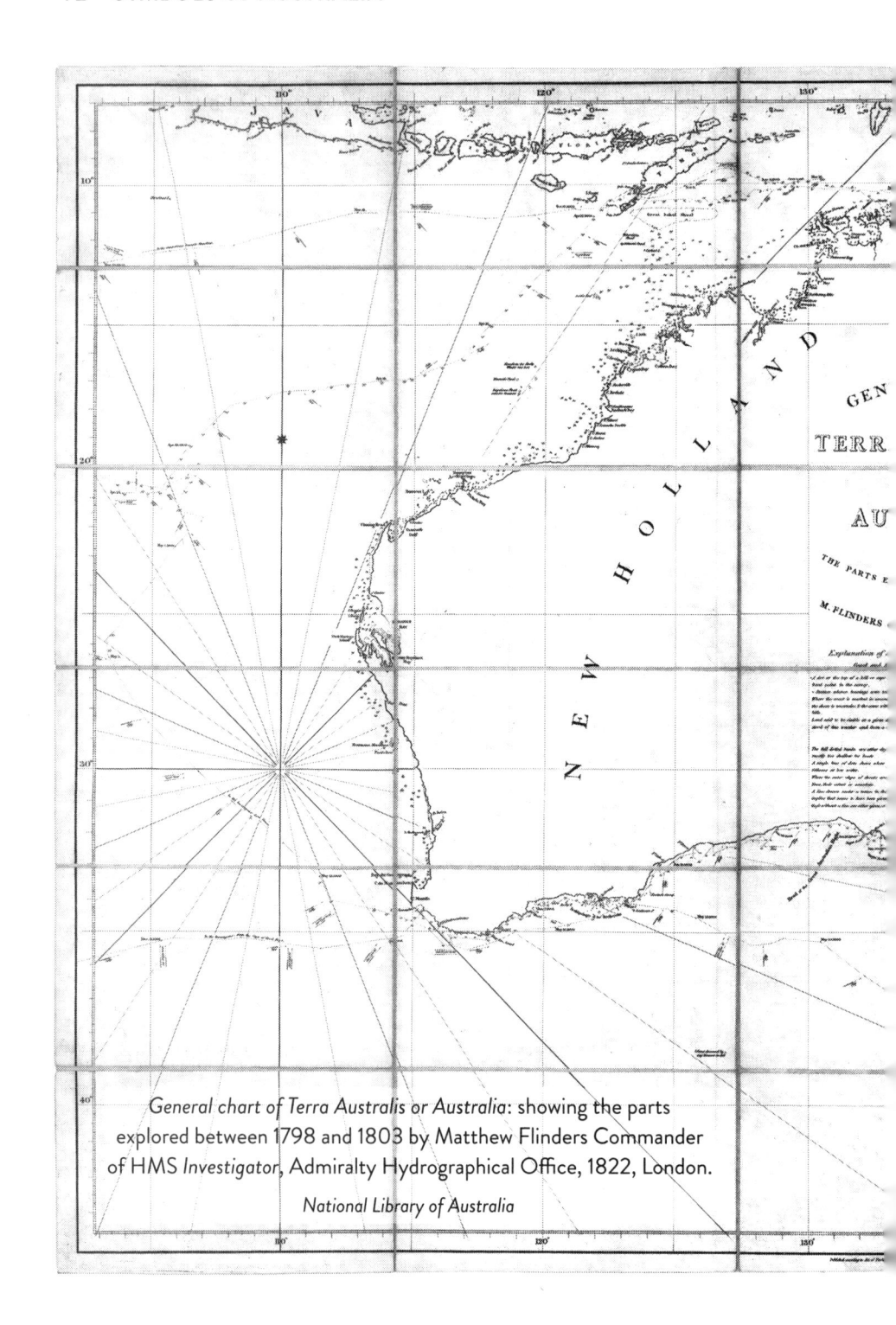

General chart of Terra Australis or Australia: showing the parts explored between 1798 and 1803 by Matthew Flinders Commander of HMS *Investigator*, Admiralty Hydrographical Office, 1822, London.
National Library of Australia

Map 73

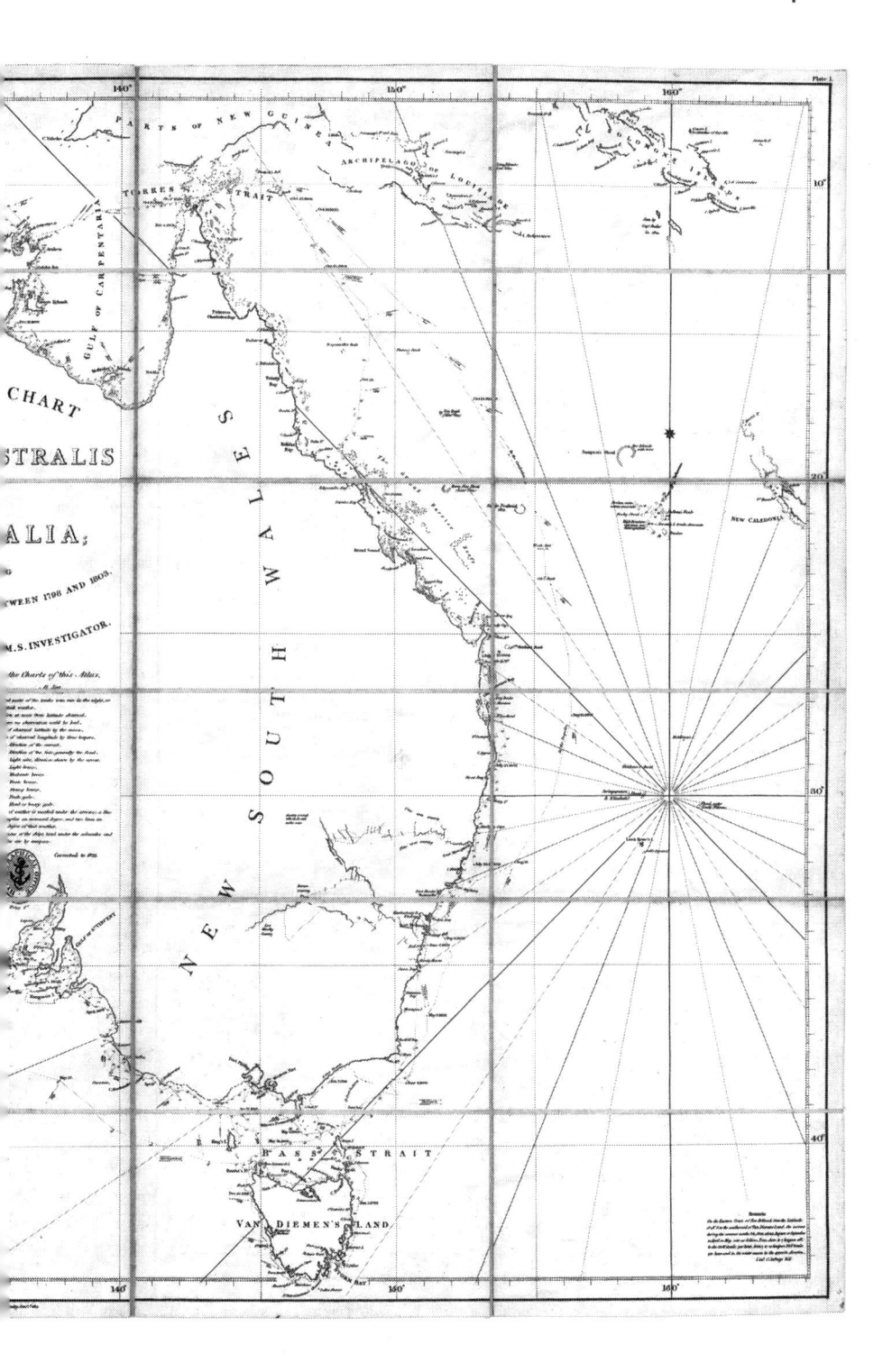

various provinces, but as provinces only, which history and geography made into a single nation.[14] La Meslée insisted on calling the Australian colonies 'provinces'. Their people 'do not hold the same ideas' but '[t]hey are the same men' and, as with Michelet's France, the provinces of Australia were fragments of a single whole. His Geographical Society was designed to create among their people 'a sense of national existence'.[15]

The society itself was theoretically a federation, orchestrated from Sydney and with self-determining branches in the other capitals. But, as it turned out, each branch worked in complete independence, succeeding and failing alone. The outcome of la Meslée's effort was the very opposite of his intentions. Obviously, in most minds colonial boundaries were still more heavily drawn than the coastline of the continent.

By this time, the 1870s and 1880s, the continent was being tied together by all kinds of traffic, by shipping, roads, railways, stock-routes and the telegraph. But traffic moves along lines, in this case mainly radiating from the capital cities. It made people familiar with distant places, but not necessarily with a single great expanse. A richer perspective altogether was offered by new work with weather patterns. Weather travelled en masse, as a series of 'fronts', and it took no notice of colonial boundaries. The telegraph made it possible for government meteorologists to explore changes in the weather across vast expanses, and for this the drawing of maps was crucial. In the mid-1870s HC Russell in Sydney, Robert Ellery in Melbourne and Charles Todd in Adelaide were all assembling large maps of weather movement.

In Spring 1879, Russell organised a conference in Sydney, where he, Ellery and Todd consulted with their New Zealand counterpart. It was already obvious that most atmospheric disturbances came sweeping across Australia from the west. Measurements made along the Overland Telegraph, which ran north–south through the middle of the continent, made it possible to predict weather along the east coast, and east-coast weather shaped weather in and across the Tasman. Russell wanted more stations in western New South Wales and Todd thought that if he had good information from points west of the Telegraph he could 'give the easterly colonies timely warning of approaching gales'. This meant bringing in Western Australia. The New Zealand meteorologist wanted more from Queensland. For Ellery, the key was Tasmania.[16]

They were ambitious – like la Meslée, too ambitious. In 1877 Russell had started publishing daily weather maps in the *Sydney Morning Herald*, the first such venture anywhere in the world. It was impossible to turn out completely new maps in time for each morning paper, and Russell invented a single printing block with small holes into which markers were inserted. It took only an hour a day to update. At first each map showed the entire eastern half of the continent, but Queensland being mostly a blank it was eventually cut back to the south-east, and in 1890 the whole effort was abandoned. The Melbourne *Argus* aimed higher, with maps of the continent, Tasmania and New Zealand, but they were small and thinly detailed, and lasted only three years, 1885–88. There were therefore no such maps during the most crucial years of the Federation movement. They reappeared afterwards, in the Adelaide *Advertiser* (1905), the *Sydney Morning Herald* (1907) and the Melbourne *Age* (1910).[17] These new efforts not only discarded New Zealand and featured the now familiar map of Australia, they also paid equal attention to every part. The curate's-egg view had given way to the single nugget, all the more valuable for being entire and perfect.

Sacred space

More than 100 years after Federation the map of Australia is not often seen as a jewel of any special value. There is no longer any need to drive the image home or to stress enchantment. The map, in broad outline, is so familiar that the vaguest approximation – the merest abstraction – is easily picked up. It is an image now made for scattering abroad, broadcasting through other countries, by depiction on backpacks for instance. Among Australians themselves its purpose has taken on new dimensions, more homely but also more profound. In travelling around the continent, Australians sketch out their own loyalties and their own sense of belonging on the sides of their panel vans, where the roads travelled are mapped within the single sacred space. As the founders of Federation intended, the shape is now completely synonymous with the people themselves. The longer the road the larger the boast of self-knowledge.

Salman Rushdie, in *The Enchantress of Florence*, tells the story of an artist who vanished while painting the portrait of a princess he had never seen. He had fallen in love with the image as it had taken shape, 'lambently beautiful', before him. He had wasted away, flattening himself into two dimensions. Then he disappeared, and he was located at last in the patterned border of the picture, 'crouching down like a little toad, with a great bundle of paper scrolls under his arm'.[18] Over several generations, the map of Australia, drawn and redrawn, read and re-read, has done something similar for Australians. It was taken up in the late nineteenth century as a symbol of themselves. Now it is much more than a symbol. It has become part of what they are.

And yet, at the same time GPS, Google Maps and the simple power of moving with a cursor around the globe has shrunk the magic of the map itself. So have the mighty, miscellaneous flood of refugees and global warming. Do borders still underpin freedom? The limiting line of surf, sacred in 1901, has been rendered almost banal by Indigenous notions of Country. That original jewel, to be held against the world, seems problematic, even imprisoning, in a new age.

COOEE

Richard White

Can a sound be a national symbol? The yodel immediately conjures up Swiss goatherds, lederhosen and Alpine scenery. The chimes of Big Ben resonate with British national imagery, of the home of constitutional monarchy, wartime grit and the mellifluous authority of the BBC. In Australia, the kookaburra's laugh was used on wireless and the 'talkies' as the aural equivalent of a national signature, conjuring up a cheerful vision of the bush. The cooee has historically had the same function, being used to stand for Australia both at home and overseas.

As a 'national call', the cooee came to function aurally in ways similar to visual symbols. It was generally recognised as being distinctive to Australia, it was connected to the bush, the traditional landscape of national sentiment, and, crucially, it was easy to reproduce. Indeed in the nineteenth century, teaching a 'new chum' the long drawn-out 'cooo' sound, followed by a sharp rising 'eee', was a kind of initiation into settler-colonial life. Samuel Butler, a temporary migrant to New Zealand before he established his literary reputation on his return to England, revelled in his sense of achievement:

> It requires some courage to give vent to a Coo-ey at first; the first attempts are generally abortive, not to say rather doleful and at the same time ludicrous; by and by however as one gains confidence one's Coo-eys are more successful; my own at present is quite

unimpeachable though in England nothing would have induced me to give utterance to such a noise on any consideration.[1]

Even if one's first cooee were self-conscious, it was nevertheless relatively simple – in this case with the voice rather than the pen – to produce something that was both recognisably a cooee and unlike any other sound in one's repertoire, and that was vital for a symbol to become accepted.

While the cooee worked aurally, national symbols almost irresistibly find a standardised visual shape. For the cooee this was a hand cupped around the lips, a forward thrust in the caller's stance (carrying the call just that 10 centimetres further) and, often, the written word itself issuing from the caller's mouth. Originally the spelling varied considerably, with over 20 attempts to capture the sound in letters. 'Co-wee' and 'Coe' were the first – the exact sound was hard to catch and the technology of writing was imprecise. In time this variety of spelling coalesced around 'cooee' or 'cooey', with or without a hyphen. A standard spelling was necessary for the written word to work as a visual symbol. The looping roundness of the letters in a cursive script gave 'cooee' a distinctively decorative look, and that would be a feature of its entry into national symbolism, particularly in its heyday in the period around Federation.

When Europeans invaded Australia they were intrigued and often discomfited by the sounds of the Australian 'bush'. One of those sounds was the cooee, which the new arrivals first heard being used by the Eora people through the disturbingly opaque woods around Sydney harbour. Disconcertingly, a cooee could summon crowds out of the trees where previously they had been invisible.

How widespread its use was among First Peoples and for how long is uncertain. Perhaps they had originally mimicked the call of the 'cooee bird', or koel (*Eudynamys scolopacea*), whose call can be heard down the east coast of the continent. The remarkable thing is that cooees or close approximations seem to have been used through much though not all of Aboriginal Australia, well beyond normal linguistic boundaries. It is perhaps less remarkable when we consider what a useful tool it was for people living in the bush, a communication and navigational technology that was a superbly effective forerunner of global positioning systems (GPS). It could carry through the bush as far as a gunshot. Aboriginal people used it in various practical ways – to call people together, to warn others of their presence – but also found symbolic uses for it in rituals associated with initiation, meeting and mourning.[2] However, it would only be in European Australia that the cooee would be appropriated to stand as a specifically 'national' symbol.

For some time it was a means of establishing cross-cultural contact (what Paul Carter has called 'the sound in-between'): as early as 1789 John Hunter (later governor of New South Wales) reported how an exploring party, on seeing some locals, 'called to them in their own manner, by frequently repeating the word *Co-wee*, which signifies, come here'.[3] In these cases it could have positive associations – of coming together, of friendship, of trust between cultures. But it also carried with it (or had imposed on it) an overtone of weirdness, potentially a visceral dread, a proof that the intruders did not really belong.

The newcomers began using it among themselves as they settled into the bush, which soon – it was said – rang with cooees. It became a conventional part of their developing bush culture, bush etiquette and bushcraft, with many uses: a work-call, a greeting, a call to come to lunch, a general eruption of high spirits, even, in the phrase 'within cooee', a unit of measurement. It acquired particularly solemn symbolic weight when it was a means of salvation: when a child or a 'new chum' got lost and cooees enabled search parties to find them. Nothing was sadder, in the stories of frontier life they told themselves, than the cooee of a lost child that no-one heard.[4] At this stage it was not seen as particularly Australian, and it readily spread to other settler societies – New Zealand and South Africa – where the frontier called for new techniques of communication.

Camping in subtropical forest around Cairns, 1907. The cooee had become convention by the time this staged photograph was taken.

*Photograph from Henry Hacker's photograph album,
John Oxley Library, State Library of Queensland*

Making it national

In the 1840s stories began circulating about another use of the cooee: as an ingenious means of re-uniting Australian colonists who had got themselves lost in the crowds or the fogs of London. Like other phenomena popular among Australians outside Australia – gum leaves, wattle and Vegemite for example – the cooee, in its self-conscious overseas application, got a particular fillip in its power to represent the nation. In 1864, an English Slang Dictionary gave Cooey as 'the Australian bush-call now not infrequently heard in the streets of London'.[5] The contrast between a cooee in the supposed emptiness of the bush and a cooee among the crowds of London could hardly be greater. It was in that context that it became specifically national, because it was a self-conscious performance of being Australian, and only Australians were expected to answer. The stories gleefully recounted the bewilderment of the English crowd hearing the call for the first time.[6]

The English accepted it as a mark of Australianness, an oddity which Australians were called on to perform as a demonstration of colonial difference. A most spectacular cooee was the climax of EW Hornung's first novel, *A Bride from the Bush* (1890), when the unhappy Australian heroine scandalised London society by impulsively letting out a cooee 'in the presence of Royalty'.[7] From then on it had its own trajectory within English literature, sometimes as an indicator of Australianness. Arthur Conan Doyle used it as a plot device for Sherlock Holmes a year later – if a villain cooeed, it was elementary that he must be Australian – and Agatha Christie would use it twice in the early 1930s. But it also entered ordinary English usage, where it lost its particular Australian association, to the extent the English imagined it was theirs.[8] DH Lawrence gave it to Lady Chatterley when, hearing the 'Papp! Papp!' of her crippled husband's extraordinary motorised wheelchair, crushing the bluebells as it made its inexorable way through the woods, 'She "Coo-eed!" in reply'.[9] Here the cooee stood not for

Australia but the vitality, freedom and naturalness of Lady Chatterley, against the mechanised paralysis of interwar Britain.

In Australia too the cooee entered literature as a self-conscious emblem of Australian identity. To begin a novel with 'COO-OĒ!', as Rosa Praed did in 1888, was to mark the setting as unambiguously Australian.[10] Henry Lawson also gave it national meaning as the 'battle cooey' of the republican movement in 1892, and as a contrast to Englishness when 'Jack Cornstalk' cooeed on London's Strand:

(and his voice was not low)
And – there's no room to coo-ee in London, you know.[11]

Cooees could be heard throughout the literary bush. Marcus Clarke, Joseph Furphy, Banjo Paterson, Henry Handel Richardson, Steele Rudd and Mary Grant Bruce were others who found them useful. From the 1880s a more nationalist literature was self-consciously competing with British imports and looking for means to brand their work as distinctively Australian.

The cooee also entered song. Isaac Nathan, Australia's first serious composer, used the cooee in the 1840s in loose adaptations of 'native aboriginal airs',[12] but from about 1860 there appeared a string of songs featuring the non-Indigenous cooee. Again it allowed composers to draw attention to the Australianness of their work (and help sales). It also became a distinctive contribution to musical language. One of the earliest of these songs told the story of a young man wandering in the bush and 'a pretty maid' who was lost. As suited the sentimental conventions of popular parlour music, they ended up husband and wife. Her cooee and his answer had brought them together. As with many of the songs that followed, the cooee was a strategic musical device. It marked the climax musically, when the 'ee' hit the song's highest note, and a *forte* cooee was often answered by a *pianissimo* reply.

In both literature and music, cooees were initially used light-heartedly, sometimes comically:

I'm riding on my pony with a view to matrimony
Cooee Mary My little gum tree queen. (Fig. 15)

Over time, in tandem with the elevated meanings being attached to Australian nationality with the approach of Federation, they carried increasingly weighty, generally sentimental significance. Lovers separated by oceans might doubt whether 'Love's message' – in the form of a cooee – could cross such distances. Fortunately, in the world of the imagination, it acquired a mysterious supernatural power.[13] In a poem called 'Bushed', Kenneth Mackay made the lost stockman's prayer a cooee to God, which God fortunately heard: 'Merciful God! Thanks unto Thee, Cooee! Cooee! Cooee-ee-ee!'[14] So the cooee had made a remarkable journey among European Australians during the nineteenth century, from being a bit of useful bushcraft borrowed from the original inhabitants to being something that carried a sufficient weight of meaning and elevated sentimentality that it could stand for the new nation itself.

By 1901 anything with national significance was sought out by local businesses for logos, trademarks, brand names or advertising slogans in order to identify their products with Australian consumers. Among the Billy Tea and Rosella tomato sauce, it was possible to buy 'Cooee' dairy foods, bacon, tobacco and cigarettes, galvanised iron, wine, spirits, motorcycles, cola, matches and ice-chests.[15] Many of these products of modern consumer society made an explicit feature of the cooee's Indigenous origin.

At the same time, ardent nationalists promoted the cooee as a consciously nationalist act. The South Australian president of the Australian Natives Association advocated the replacement of three cheers with three cooees.[16] Though that idea fell flat, ritualistic cooeeing at theatres, sporting events and parades became common, spontaneously erupting from the crowd. It was not always nationalistic – in theatres it could be just a disruptive cat-call – and there was often an element of disruptive jocularity in this chiacking, a raucous larrikinism that mocked formality.

But often it was an assertion of the crowd's Australianness: an older version of 'Aussie! Aussie! Aussie! Oi! Oi! Oi!'

It became a convention to welcome visiting celebrities with a cooee, a probably unconscious mimicking of Indigenous uses. Nellie Melba, having established her reputation in the opera houses of Europe, made her long awaited return visit to Australia in 1902, and was met in Melbourne by an orchestrated cooee from the well-behaved girls at her old school, Presbyterian Ladies' College. Boy scouts welcomed the visit of Lord Robert Baden-Powell with a cooee, and again, as the sailors of America's Great White Fleet paraded through Sydney in 1908:

> The crowd paused for breath, and then, with striking effect, the weird Aboriginal cry 'Coo-ee' rang through the ranks of the Australians. It had all the merits of a distinctive greeting: it was musical, and purely Australian.[17]

Despite the somewhat formal and elaborate national symbolism of the occasion, when King George V laid the foundation stone of Australia House in London in July 1913, the crowd cooeed spontaneously. One Australian reporter seemed both pleased and mortified that it was 'called all kinds of things by the English press – "strange, unfamiliar", "hooting", "yapping", "musical", "weird"'.[18]

Cooees, with their symbolic references to the new nation, were cropping up everywhere. Houses were often called 'Cooee', an echo of the call's domestic uses. Annette Kellermann, who developed an international career around her swimming prowess and daring figure-hugging swimsuits from the 1900s, would give a cooee before commencing her high-dive. The first troop of boy scouts formed in Australia christened themselves the Kangaroo Patrol and took cooee as their call sign.[19] Babies of both sexes were occasionally named Cooee, as was Annette Kellermann's pet cat. We can see then that the cooee came to work as a national symbol because it was distinctively Australian; it had an international exposure; it was easily learned and reproducible;

it had a ready use in literature and music; and it was associated with the bush, which was seen as containing all that was distinctive about Australia and the core values and sentiments of the nation.

Precisely because it was widely accepted as a national symbol, it generated controversy around its origin. In a nation whose whiteness mattered, it might be surprising how generally its Indigenous origin was recognised and celebrated. Those who played on the 'eerie mysticism of the bush and its ways' gave the Indigenous cooee an almost supernatural aura with a 'natural' origin in the distant past, sometimes drawing on that proto-fascist strand of nationalism which sought the origin of the nation in the 'volk' or the very soil itself.[20] In time, however, the Indigenous origin was worked loose. In 1914, it was merely '*said* to be an aboriginal mode of requesting assistance' as if there were doubt, and a *Bulletin* correspondent insisted the 'blacks' he recalled when growing up in the 1860s 'never used the coo-ee call ... Only one person as far as I know ever used the coo-ee around Armidale. That was my mother – and she was a Londoner, so perhaps it's only a cockney yell after all.' There were also indignant denials that it was widely used by country people; some saw it as merely an inauthentic souvenir produced for tourist consumption. According to *Truth* in 1915, cooees were 'used almost exclusively' by Australians watching Test matches in England 'and nowhere else in earnest; least of all in Australia'. In 1944 a *Bulletin* correspondent announced: 'I've been bushed myself and also in searches for bushed mates, and I'm blowed if I ever heard the bush "ring with cooees"'.[21]

Promoting the cooee

Despite the doubters, it is clear the cooee was a case of a symbol emerging organically, drawing on the experiences of ordinary people going about their ordinary business, rather than being imposed in any formal way. However, when a symbol takes on a distinctly national meaning, standing for Australia or some assumed Australian quality, it is often thanks to the enthusiasm of writers and composers and advertisers, along with a small minority of patriotic individuals who attach themselves to a particular symbol and become its enthusiastic advocates. They are what we might call practical symbologists, people who take on a social responsibility of embodying national sentiment by flying a flag in their front yard, organising celebrations around Wattle Day or tattooing themselves with a Southern Cross. Their motivations might be obscure but they are essential to the dissemination of national symbols. The cooee would have its share of devotees, and no-one was quite as devoted as Maude Wordsworth James.

While nation-making is frequently presumed to be the prerogative of men, women have played a considerable role – often undervalued – in the production and reproduction of national symbols.[22] James was one of those women, and, unusually, we know her motivation. She grew up in Bendigo in a prominent legal family. She was the great-granddaughter of George Crabbe, the English poet, and fancied her own literary pursuits, which she gave up after her marriage to Charles Wordsworth James, an engineer who took her and the growing family to the booming but barren goldfields of Kalgoorlie in 1897. There the marriage was under stress: her sense of martyrdom to her family, her husband's melancholy, the harsh climate, the lack of society and above all her sense of (relative) poverty. In 1907 she had a moment of inspiration. A keen Federationist, she saw national sentiment as a means to exercise her creative and organisational skills and, at the same time, make money. She described her epiphany in her journal:

> One night Charlie ... came home in a pessimistic mood, and talked as though money was the great thing in life ... when I went to bed that night I determined that I would not rest until I had thought of some plan ... for gaining wealth as quickly as possible ... just as the dawn was breaking, an idea came to me that immediately arrested

my attention ... Here is the idea which is entirely my own ... The Commonwealth of Australia has no <u>Souvenir</u> – Tasmania tempted Tourists with little golden maps – West Australia sold silver swans on spoons, and brooches, and jewellery intended for gifts – and the other states sent away Kangaroos and Emus and typical products of the country. But a present that embraced all the states and which could be used in any one of them was, I meditated, the one thing needful.

She hit upon the idea of 'making a fortune out of my favourite Australian word, Coo-ee', by using it as the inspiration for a line of souvenirs:

the more I thought of it the more I wanted to jump out of bed and start the thing right away ... from that day to this, I have tried to advance the idea, and to make out of it a satisfactory profit for the future.[23]

James registered the word as a trademark in Australia, Britain and New Zealand, patented various jewellery designs such as her cooee snake (Fig. 14), sold her designs for engagement rings, bangles and brooches to jewellers, attempted to claim copyright of the word 'cooee' itself and took every opportunity to promote her 'brilliant plan'. She moved on to cooee mementos, knick-knacks, china and pottery ware. She ran cooee competitions on the 'subject of the mystic word'; even laboured to concoct bad cooee jokes. She promoted the idea of Australian homes having a 'cooee corner' that could include a clock that bizarrely featured a mechanical 'Blackfellow with a Boomerang in his hand' who emerged to cooee the hour and half-hour. From 1908 she took to writing her own sentimental cooee songs, dedicating them to opera stars and inventing a strict ritual to go with them:

Before the singer commences, three 'Coo-ees', clearly rendered, and to carry well, must be given, with the hand or hands to the mouth, in true Australian fashion ... The compositions should never be sung until the Call is thus emphasised beforehand.[24]

James is an unusual case, but points to a significant feature of national symbols. They might appear as a spontaneous eruption of national sentiment, uniting all Australians, and that claim is an important part of their power. But often behind their dissemination there were patriots hard at work, creating, massaging, elaborating, popularising. Motives – often complex – were not always disinterested. James made over £118 from her various enterprises in the first six months, more than her husband earned.

Falling out of fashion

Once war broke out in 1914, and Australians answered the Empire's 'call', it was inevitable that the 'call' would be represented as a cooee. It provided a distinctively Australian motif for recruitment posters, in patriotic songs and most famously through the 'Cooee' recruitment march from Gilgandra to Sydney. Not surprisingly it supplied a title for soldiers' newspapers as it already had for school magazines. According to one soldier, 'one never hears the Cooee at home – but go abroad with Australians and one never hears anything else'.[25] Some even proposed it as a battle cry:

> Let it be – Coo'ee Australia – When
> You charge through the mud mixed with white men's blood.[26]

From the 1920s, perhaps because of the very excess of sentimentality brought to it by enthusiasts such as James, and then the over-the-top jingoism of the war, the cooee fell out of favour as a national symbol. It was still used in the bush and across backyard fences for everyday purposes. In London, Australian spectators could still be heard cooeeing at the rugby in 1957.[27] As hillbilly music evolved into country and western, it could still be used by singers such as Buddy Williams, 'The Yodelling Jackaroo', and the LeGarde Twins to evoke the simple values of the bush.[28] However, those bush values themselves were falling out of favour, coming to be seen as too 'daggy' to represent a nation that was in the process of industrialising and wanted to prove its modernity and sophistication to the world. As a national symbol, it became a joke: hence the facetious suggestions that Whitlam's new nationalism would mean Australian diplomats adopting the cooee as protocol to greet guests.[29] In ironic mode, cooee contests appeared from the 1970s associated with Australia Day entertainments and local celebrations, featured alongside other manufactured 'national' pastimes such as thong-throwing, cockroach-racing and billy-boiling competitions.

The fact that it could no longer be taken seriously might have suggested that, at the beginning of the twenty-first century, its survival as a national symbol was precarious. But symbols have a capacity for resurrection. Irony can segue into seriousness. It made a comeback as a popular business name: for cooee candles, Aboriginal art, backpacking hostels, children's clothing, plumbing, even a Swedish design company. During COVID-19 pandemic lockdowns in 2020 and 2021, the people of Tascott, on the NSW Central Coast, invented a ritual of cooeeing throughout the village at 5pm each day.[30] Vivienne Kelly's astute 2008 novel, *Cooee*, took the call seriously while in 2020 Tanya Heaslip began her account of Northern Territory life, *An Alice Girl*, with

'Cooeeeee!'
The call ripped through the hot, still air.

Libby Gleeson's 2006 children's picture book, *Amy & Louis*, revolved around a cooee that could be heard across oceans, echoing the mystic sentiments of nineteenth-century parlour songs. In the same year, at the commemorative service for Steve Irwin, the 'Crocodile

Hunter', whose marketing of Australian crikeyness straddled the border between irony and ingenuousness, a Gubbi Gubbi elder, Dr Eve Fesl, gave a solemn cooee, as if it could be heard beyond the grave. And in 2014, amid all the commemoration of the outbreak of World War I, Glasgow Cathedral played host to a particularly haunting rendition of the cooee. Actor Joanne Thomson read from Helen Thomas's account of her Welsh poet husband, Edward, leaving their Hampshire village for the war, only to be killed five weeks later:

> I stood at the gate watching him go; he turned back to wave until the mist and the hill hid him. I heard his old call coming up to me: 'Coo-ee!' he called. 'Coo-ee!' I answered keeping my voice strong to call again. Again through the muffled air came his 'Coo-ee'. And again went my answer like an echo ... 'Coo-ee!' So faint now, it might be only my own call flung back from the thick air and muffling snow. I put my hands up to my mouth to make a trumpet, but no sound came ... There was nothing but the mist and the snow and the silence of death.
>
> Then with leaden feet which stumbled in a sudden darkness that overwhelmed me I groped my way back to the empty house.[31]

But those cooees were not Australian at all.

STAMPS

Dennis Altman

Since their origin in the 1840s, stamps have been miniature conveyers of official ideology, and until recently they were a reliable guide to how governments wished to present the nation. Indeed stamps are a cheap form of asserting national identity and statehood. There are large numbers of stamps in existence from states that never came into actual being, such as the South Moluccas or 'free Latvia'. The literature on stamps as political icons is scarce, although as their production remains a government monopoly, and complete listings of all official issues are easily available, postage stamps are particularly amenable to analysis.[1] Because as symbols they carry the authority of government – but at the same time, unlike flags or coats of arms, have designs that are readily changed – they give a fascinating insight into changing whims in national symbolism. Stamps act to guarantee international postal delivery, as determined through agreements managed by the Universal Postal Union, the world's oldest international governmental agency. They therefore need to be sanctioned by recognised governments, and originally governments directly determined their subject and design. Over the past few decades, however, as postal services have been reorganised into semi-autonomous corporations such as Australia Post, the profit motive has become increasingly significant in determining what appears on Australian stamps. The search for hard currency from collectors, once seen as the preserve of small Caribbean and Eastern European countries, is now almost universal, and explains the profusion of stamp issues even as their use for postage decreases.

Colonial origins

This was not the case when stamps first appeared. The Australian colonies were among the first administrations in the world to issue stamps, with stamps appearing in New South Wales and Victoria in 1850, ten years after the first British issue that inaugurated the pre-paid mail service. Loyally, and predictably, most colonial stamps depicted the head of Queen Victoria, almost invariably facing left, though Western Australia was sufficiently radical to issue various sets showing a black swan, before an image of the Queen finally appeared on the final state issue of 1901.

But, for their time, the colonies displayed some imagination in stamp issues, an imagination no longer as apparent in the more market-driven issues of Australia Post. In 1888 New South Wales invented commemorative stamps, with an issue that marked the centenary of the colony: ten stamps depicting various animals and historical figures.

The colonies were also among the first in the world to introduce stamps that carried a surcharge for particular charities, an innovation that became very popular in Europe and is still used in Germany and Switzerland. In 1897 New South Wales issued two stamps to raise money for a home for consumptives, and Victoria produced two stamps to support hospitals. In a frenzy of patriotism Victoria followed these with two stamps to support the Empire Patriotic Fund, as did Queensland the following year.

In the nineteenth century stamps were considerably more meaningful. The Post Office was a major state instrumentality in that century, symbolising the importance of communications in developing the new colonies, and the role of government in representing the people. In the various state capitals the General Post Office (GPO) was built on the same sort of scale as were town halls and cathedrals, and the GPOs on Bourke Street (Melbourne), Martin Place (Sydney) and Queen Street (Brisbane) were central sites of civil culture. It is revealing that a century later many Australian post offices have been transformed into boutique hotels and shopping malls, marking a decline not only of the government's role in communications but also of the central role of the state.

Stamps for a Commonwealth

Although the new Commonwealth Government established a federal Postmaster-General's Department in 1901, it took 12 years for the new nation to issue its own stamps. The first stamps, with denominations ranging from a halfpenny to two pounds, showed a kangaroo astride a map of Australia. The map was white, to indicate, in the words of the then Postmaster-General, Charles Frazer (Kalgoorlie), 'the Commonwealth's policy in regard to its population'.[2] A change in government from Labor to the conservatives led by Joseph Cook saw these stamps supplemented by a series bearing the portrait of George V, framed by an emblematic kangaroo and emu. The same ambivalence between national and imperial themes has continued until today. The monarch's head had, by the 1970s, ceased to be the standard design for definitive stamps, that is, regular stamps issued across a range of postal rates. However, an annual issue for the Queen's birthday was inaugurated in 1980 and has continued ever since, almost always showing portraits of Queen Elizabeth II. No other Commonwealth country appears to follow this rather quaint habit, although it is commonplace to celebrate royal weddings and anniversaries.

For 50 years or so Australia Post produced commemorative stamps sparingly, and those early issues reflected a narrow view of what should be commemorated on stamps. Fairly standard images of explorers and settlement dominated, often in designs that balanced Australian themes with classical or British allusions. Examples included an allegorical female, a kind of 'Miss Australia', half-Ceres, half-Britannia, beside the image of the new Parliament House (1927), and London's Whitehall Cenotaph, which was used for the first stamps to commemorate Gallipoli (1935).[3] In 1947 the Postmaster-General's Department established a Stamp Advisory Committee, which sought to improve the standard of design so that stamps could 'play their part in advertising the Commonwealth as a land of progress, not to say culture'.[4]

During the Menzies government through the 1950s, Australian stamps expanded their subject matter, but still reflected a conservative view of the world, to the extent that I once drew on them as emblematic of the time:

> Largely in russet red and royal blue, these are the images of unquestioning respectability: cows and tractors exhorting us to PRODUCE FOOD; homage to the suburban volunteers of Red Cross, Rotary, the YMCA; nativity images of Christmas; and, most laden with symbolism of them all, the Queen's head set in an oval alongside our memorial to the American war effort: this was the Australia Menzies had created, and which we all in our different ways wished to escape.[5]

The 1950s were a bad time for stamp design everywhere, but Australia produced some of the very worst.

Stamps became brighter and the subject matter more varied in the 1970s, and began to depict a less restricted vision of Australia. Solemnity was lightened by stamps using cartoon characters, and the 1977 Christmas issue showed Santa Claus on a surfboard. This was a rarity as most Christmas stamps, issued annually since 1957, maintained a strong religious theme, unlike the United States, which preserved its nominally secular status by producing both religious and non-religious images. In 1988 a number of Australian cartoonists produced a new

Postage stamps brought national symbols into every home.
Postman delivering mail to 'Craigallen', Moonee Ponds, c. 1910.
By Commercial photographer Ruth Hollick (a neighbour).

Ruth Hollick collection, State Library of Victoria

(Top left) First stamp to feature an Aboriginal man,
issued for the Centenary of Victoria, 1934.

National Archives of Australia

(Top right) 'Aborigine' stamp, 1950. Warlpiri-Anmatyerre man Gwoya Tjungurrayi was the first living person to be depicted on an Australian stamp, despite a longstanding policy not to depict living people. Because he stood generically for 'the Aborigine' it was deemed not to matter.

Designed by Nicholas Freeman, Freeman Design Partners
Reproduced with permission of the Australian Postal Corporation

(Above left) Two-shilling stamp issued for the Melbourne Olympics, 1956.

National Philatelic Collection

(Above right) Surfing Santa stamp, 1977.

National Philatelic Collection

definitive set of stamps representing religion, trade unionism, primary industry and emergency services. Though controversial, this popular but short-lived series of stamps, celebrating the Bicentennial theme of 'Living Together', suggested a more informal and less pompous view of what 'Australia' might stand for.[6] As stamps proliferated, a particular image of Australia came to dominate, with a strong emphasis on themes of national development and achievements sporting and cultural, particularly painting. Flora and fauna, not surprisingly, remained key topics for Australian stamps. The introduction of a goods and services tax (GST) in 2000 led to new stamps being required for overseas postage, which is exempt from tax, and these have tended to feature tourist images of Australia.

Indigenous Australians were first recognised on stamps in 1934, when an Aboriginal man carrying a spear and gazing across the Yarra River commemorated the centenary of the modern city of Melbourne. Aboriginal art appeared on an issue in 1948, and has since been a popular way of giving recognition to Indigenous Australia. In the 1950 definitive series, the only non-royal image was that of Warlpiri-Anmatyerre man Gwoya Tjungurrayi, whose 1935 photograph in *Walkabout* by Roy Dunstan was intended to be a generic photograph of 'the' Indigenous Australian. It was so generic, presumably, that the Post Office broke their own rule of not depicting living persons.[7] The first Bicentennial issue in 1984 was devoted to 'the first Australians', and over the next four years leading up to 1988, the official story of settlement was told in 13 different series, 56 stamps in all. They culminated in a joint issue with the United Kingdom, which paid homage to the great men of Britain: Shakespeare, WG Grace and John Lennon. No named Australian appeared on the joint issue. Since then a number of joint issues have appeared, signalling Australia's cooperation with other countries and, incidentally, increasing the philatelic market for the stamps.

Stamp issues played their role in asserting Australia's presence in the region: there have been separate issues for Norfolk, Christmas and the Cocos islands, and since 1957 for the Australian Antarctic Territory. The latter are more related to a need to assert a dubious claim to sovereignty than they are for the postal needs of the several dozen scientists stationed there, and can be used for domestic postage in Australia. They tend to feature images of local flora, fauna and scientific endeavour, reassuring any doubters that the Australian presence is positive.

Until the 1990s one could read Australian stamps as echoing a particular perception of national identity: stamps told the nation what to celebrate and what it meant to be Australian. It was rare for anything not clearly national to be shown: the monarch was the major exception. Stamps conveyed the words of 'Waltzing Matilda', ushered in metric measurement, showed scenes from successful Australian movies and commemorated Australian history. If carefully non-partisan, there was a didactic and even hectoring note running through some of the issues, and a sense that Australians needed to be given a lesson in patriotism.

Popularising the post

That didactic function did not sit easily with a new economic rationalism that insisted that government instrumentalities be run like businesses. The profit motive came to dominate. The Whitlam government (1972–75) established a Postal Commission, and in 1989 the Hawke government created Australia Post, as a government-owned corporation. Gradually stamps began to reflect less an official picture of the nation and more what might appeal to a commercial market. In 1997 the annual issue for Australia Day was turned into an annual commemoration of 'Australian legends' and, while there is no evidence that John Howard, who became prime minister in 1996, influenced the decision, he was presumably pleased by the inaugural choice of cricketer Don Bradman, the first named living Australian to be depicted on a stamp. The selection of 'legends' was made internally by Australia Post, and was a closely guarded secret: Bradman was followed in 1998 by a number of Olympians, who also broke existing custom by being still living. They were succeeded in turn by painter Arthur Boyd, returned servicemen ('the last Anzacs'), country singer Slim Dusty, five medical scientists, two tennis players, Dame Joan Sutherland, six fashion designers, Barry Humphries, racing figures and notable philanthropists.

It is tempting to see here a perfect reflection of John Howard's Australia: even Barry Humphries, shown in drag as Edna Everage (another Dame) has a largely conservative view of Australia. But the emphasis on sport has become lopsided, ever since a decision to issue instantaneous stamps for every Australian gold medallist at the 2000 Olympics. The technology was impressive: you could go to any Post Office within a couple of days of the event to buy your own souvenir stamps of, say, Ian Thorpe or Cathy Freeman. Continuing this for the 2006 Melbourne Commonwealth Games meant more individual stamp designs were churned out in two weeks than in the first 40 years of Federation.

Increasingly stamps depicted a rather daggy and populist version of Australian life: signs of the zodiac, television shows, caravanning and 'big things' such as the Big Banana have all appeared on stamps in recent years. Nothing wrong with these, especially the inclusion of 'Kath and Kim', but there are some odd omissions, such as Patrick White, who does appear on a Swedish stamp commemorating Nobel laureates. No Australian university has appeared on a stamp, but neither have major business enterprises, except for Qantas, which at the time was government-owned. If every Olympian gold medallist deserves a stamp, why not an issue for Australian winners of the Booker Prize? Indeed, why should stamps only honour Australians? Most countries are willing to recognise international figures to an extent unknown in Australia.

As letters became less and less common, Australia Post produced a growing array of philatelic material, even though buying it at the local post office became more problematic. Increasingly Australia Post issued sheets and booklets that incorporated particular requests and personalised stamps. Australia was the first country in the world to offer customers their very own photograph inscribed on a stamp valid for postage. A stamp sheet featuring crocodile hunter Steve Irwin and his family was a result of a *New Idea* reader poll which voted the magazine cover featuring Steve and his children the most popular of the year. With stamps produced more and more to go into collections, rather than to be used in sending mail, what can we read into them, other than the assumptions of Australia Post about what might sell to collectors? Australia Post does its best to encourage collecting, although it is my hunch that this is a dying hobby, peopled mainly by men of a certain age (and collectors do seem to be overwhelmingly men).

In its eagerness to avoid controversy – guidelines for commemorative stamps preclude 'subjects likely to cause public divisiveness' – Australia Post produces stamps that are apparently apolitical, itself a political stance. Military service in the Vietnam War is recognised, the anti-war movement is ignored. There was an interesting exception in 2019 with two stamps marking the success of the marriage equality campaign, perhaps surprisingly without emphasising the role of Australia Post in managing the postal ballot (Fig. 16).

The current Stamp Advisory Committee is largely concerned with design standards, acting on advice from Australia Post's Board. Public input is encouraged, but this rarely means anything particularly imaginative or challenging. Stamps continue to represent a particular idea of the nation, but as they are increasingly seen as collectibles rather than central to everyday use, postal authorities compete for designs that are marketable. For Australia Post this appears to favour flora and fauna, military and sporting events and a fascination with the royal family. There is no evidence that Australia's committee is as prescriptive as its British counterpart, which insisted that a series depicting swans (British of course) include a couple 'to demonstrate that they form stable partnerships for life, like humans'.[8] Nor is there the same pressure to satisfy interest groups that is reflected in many American stamps, where the choice of famous Americans is a testament to the influence of particular ethnic and professional lobby groups. (More recently, in line with the apparently universal need to sell more stamps, the United States has featured increasing numbers of characters from contemporary animated films, a far cry from the more serious patriotic images of 50 years earlier.)

Of course, the search for popular subjects is not confined to Australian stamps. But while technically innovative, they appear increasingly anodyne and conservative beside those of countries such as Germany and Japan, or New Zealand, which has cashed in on several Hollywood blockbusters filmed in the country. This is not to advocate the sort of propaganda which is found on many issues from China and the United States. But many contemporary stamps from other countries show greater imagination and a willingness to recognise more than national achievements. Our stamps are clearly anchored in a mainstream and somewhat outdated vision of Australia.

GUM TREE

Lucy Kaldor

'There's nothing more Australian than a gum tree', declares the Australian Centre for Plant Biodiversity Research on a web page devoted to the eucalypt.[1] The claim capitalises on the gum tree's reputation as a cultural symbol of the nation to attract non-scientific viewers to the site's very scientific purpose: the promotion of a cutting-edge database to help 'ordinary' people identify different species of gum tree. This assertion of the gum tree's nationality is a cheeky nod to perpetual debates among non-Indigenous Australians about what is and what isn't 'Australian'. At the same time, however, it is a claim easily supported by scientific fact.

For the gum tree with its three constituent genera – *Eucalyptus*, *Corymbia* and *Angophora* – is more idiosyncratic in Australia than any other plant in any other nation-state, being highly unique biologically and, barring a handful of its 900-odd species, endemic to Australia alone.[2] The gum tree is also one of the most adaptable trees on earth and thrives right across Australia's diverse ecosystems, from desert to snow. The aim of the diagnostic database is to allow the easy identification of the different varieties of 'the one tree Australia is known for all over the world'.

It is an occupational requirement that any symbol of Australia be recognisably Australian, both within the nation-state and outside it. The gum tree, however, has an uncomplicated, scientifically irrefutable

Gum tree 103

'Big Ben', giant gum tree at Port Esperance, Tasmania, c. 1910.
Glass lantern slide by John Watt Beattie.

State Library of Victoria

claim to distinctiveness that many other national symbols cannot boast. According to the logic of botany and of national borders, the gum tree is more Australian than the national flower, the wattle (acacia is also native to Africa, Asia and the Americas), and its main competitor, the waratah (which is confined to Australia's east coast). However, the gum tree is no longer confined to Australia: large-scale export since the mid-nineteenth century has resulted in old and extensive stands of eucalypts overseas that far predate living memory.[3] Present-day citizens of the city of Les Eucalyptus in Algeria might as fairly profess fond childhood memories of the sweet scent of gum leaves after rain as Californians or Portuguese, who might reasonably assume that the eucalypts that have naturalised in their parks and street verges belong to their own corner of the globe.

Australians, however, like to remind the world that the gum tree is indeed *theirs*. From botanical reference books to the reveries of gum-loving patriots, seldom is the eucalypt mentioned in Australia without an accompanying remark, tinged with satisfaction or rosy with pride, on how wonderfully uniquely *Australian* it is, in its eccentric appearance and singular robustness. And somehow the qualities associated with the gum tree become characteristic of the Australian colonisers themselves.

Any history of national symbolism is also a history of strategic omissions of fact. As such, the gum tree's history as a symbol within Anglo–Australian nationalism does not incorporate the rich histories of Indigenous Australian societies that have always lived with gum trees, that hold enormous collective knowledge on gum tree ecology, and whose languages have given us names for many beloved specimens – karri, marri, coolibah, jarrah. The history of the gum tree as a national symbol is also distinct from (though not unrelated to) histories of white Australian appropriation of Indigenous land and destruction of eucalypt ecosystems. Here we are only concerned with national symbols – and the adeptness with which white Australians came to invest considerable national feeling in a tree.

Accidental hero

The gum tree was first seized as an object of a not-yet-national, Anglo–Australian pride at the end of the nineteenth century. As a symbol of beauty, the gum tree embodied an aesthetic of sun-bleached colours, otherworldly shapes and, unusually for Australia, a rare subtlety and sophistication. As a symbol of the physical environment, it represented the triumph of survival in a famously unforgiving climate. The gum tree was also invoked to represent a perceived national temperament and was throughout the twentieth century portrayed in terms otherwise reserved for the ideal Australian citizen: steadfast, long-suffering, dogged, loyal, humble, unpretentious and indomitable. Finally, the gum tree came to symbolise an Australian cultural victory, as the accidental hero of one of the founding myths of Australian nationalism about how the British failed, and the Australian-born succeeded, in learning to love and appreciate the curiosities of their new land.

Its economic, ecological, artistic and cultural value has been extolled by generations of Australia's scientists, writers, artists, photographers and nationalists – the latter sometimes calling themselves 'gumsuckers'.[4] Sweethearts and mothers have posted its dried leaves to soldiers at the front as a fragrant reminder of home, and these same diggers fighting overseas have photographed themselves grinning in front of expatriate gum trees, producing images indistinguishable from those taken in their own backyards, moments of escapism the length of a shutter-speed. It appears in the titles of books, such as *Tulips under the Gum Tree*, a history of Dutch immigration in Australia; *Outside the Gum Tree*, a study of multicultural art, where the gum tree represents a tired convention; or much earlier in *Gumsucker on the Tramp*, a bestselling travel memoir. Gum-tree green decorates the House of Representatives in Parliament House, Canberra, opened in 1988 and, in 2000, gum leaves were burnt at the opening ceremony for the Sydney Olympics, producing an olfactory sensation for those who were there that was never conveyed on television. The stylised limbs and leaves of a gum tree form the central motif of the Australian Overseas Humanitarian Service medal, representing Australians 'branching out' in aid of the world.

Of all the gum tree's features, the unmistakeable leaf is the most commonly replicated, particularly in tourist iconography, where it has played an important function in 'placing' Australia on the globe. A postcard printed in about 1907 featured a map of Australia with a dried gum leaf sewn onto it, and the verse:

A good old gum leaf! Doesn't it tell
Of a land 'neath the Southern skies.

This sentiment was echoed in another set of postcards, the 'Gum Leaf series', which depicted Australia's natural and architectural assets. Each print was a skilful *trompe l'oeil*, designed to look as if a real gum leaf had been painted with a tourist scene and affixed to the card (Fig.18). The gum leaf motif in the series clearly represented recently federated Australia, and provided, both literally and metaphorically, a common, national frame for the various state attractions. It harked back to a rather obscure tradition practised by a handful of Australian colonial artists who painted miniature landscapes on the dried, juvenile leaves of particular eucalypt varieties. Ostensibly born of necessity – a shortage of paper in the colonies – gum leaf painting had achieved minor fame by the time the postcard series was designed by the canny individual who recognised the symbolic potential of this quaintly colonial practice.[5]

The enthusiasm for the gum leaf declined in the mid-twentieth century but the image of the eucalypt still performs a similar function for the tourist market. In 2006, *Gum Tree: An Australian Icon*, by the prolific Australiana photographer Steve Parish, depicted a graceful Sydney red gum (*Angophora costata*), beneath whose silhouetted limbs is a view across the harbour to the Opera House and the Harbour Bridge.[6] The gum tree gave a national frame to these two über-iconic structures normally associated with Sydney.

'Uniquely Australian'

As with the silver fern of New Zealand or the maple leaf of Canada, the adoption of the gum tree as a national symbol revealed a cultural fascination with the unique biological character of the nation's natural landscape, coupled with 'a colonial habit of ... self-definition with an eye to how others see Australians'.[7] Symbols drawn from nature have the benefit of being ambiguous, politically neutral and malleable. They suited the symbol-making needs of settler societies still finding their footing as nations rather later than much of the Old World.

As a symbol of the natural landscape, the gum tree testified (if at times inadvertently) to a feeling, common in the British–Australian community around the time of Federation, that there was little but land and sea separating them, culturally, from their people 'back home'.[8] To others, it represented much more than mere geography. For the Australian-born – the gumsuckers – the assumption of the gum tree as a symbol of Australia mirrored a sentiment that the land and its eucalyptus-dominated character were wholly, and solely, responsible for the creation of a national 'type', a human character that was markedly and inherently different from that of 'his' colonial predecessors. 'We stand apart, like our own great tree', wrote Nathan Spielvogel in his 1913 poem 'Our Gum Trees'.[9]

The gum tree was a source of curiosity to European settlers long before there was any serious talk of nation. Initially, admiration for the gum tree was largely the province of the natural scientist; the species was named in the late eighteenth century. From the mid-nineteenth century onwards, the ever-pressing imperative of utility coupled with an enduring optimism about the continent's boundless wealth fuelled a new burst of scientific interest in the eucalypt. Suddenly, uses for the gum tree proliferated. Its various parts were examined, dissected, distilled and made into tinctures and floor tiles, roads and bridges, therapeutic oils and decorative furniture, and scientists and craftsmen preached its virtues to the world.

From the 1870s, science furnished the popular imagination with another reason to be proud of the gum's botanical endowments. The discovery of giant conifers in California and the less-than-coincidental unearthing of similarly enormous eucalypts in Australia sparked a cross-continental quest to find and name the 'World's Biggest Tree'. Australian colonists had reason to hope for the coveted title. Though the sequoias boasted unmatchable girth, some gum trees grew absurdly tall and one in particular – *Eucalyptus regnans*, the mountain ash of Tasmania and Victoria – was named optimistically by Australia's foremost authority on eucalypts as 'the loftiest tree in the British territory', having already bagged the honour of 'biggest flowering plant'.[10] Australian colonists, inspired by rumours of gargantuan gums and financial rewards, followed tantalising titbits of hearsay into the forest and sought supporting evidence with gusto, though disappointingly a winner was never announced.[11] Far from being a unifying national rallying point, however, at least until Federation the colonies competed against each other for the glory of Australia's – if not the world's – biggest tree.

The eye of the beholder

In the end, it was not botanical originality alone that elevated the gum tree to the status of a national symbol. For the most part, the genesis of a sense of national pride in gum trees was inversely related to the widespread perception that British colonists had found them to be ugly. To be sure, some did. Colonists clearing land to make room for livestock and crops typically resented the gum tree's brazen appearance, resistance to the axe and dictatorial command of the landscape they were attempting to conquer. So too did those habituated to an English or European aesthetic of landscape scenery, with its rich, comforting verdure and its generously canopied trees, find gum trees deficient. To their detractors, the most objectionable feature was the austere military green of their leaves and their lack of seasonal variation. Barron Field, who arrived in New South Wales in 1817 to head the Supreme Court and became one of the nineteenth century's most verbose critics of the gum tree's appearance, lamented: 'There is not a single scene of which a painter could make a landscape, without greatly disguising the character of the trees', and complained: 'What can a painter do with one cold olive green?'[12]

Equally, there were many colonists – artists, aestheticians and writers – who were enchanted with the gum tree's singular appearance and painted and wrote about it with admiration. By the 1830s, English-born-and-educated landscape painter John Glover had swapped emerald pigment for khaki green and turned both eye and hand to the eucalyptus-filled vistas of his adopted Van Diemen's Land. Glover, whose Australian pictures attracted especial attention in Britain for their originality and their naturalistic treatment of the native trees, admitted to being daunted by the appearance of the Australian land, but suggested it was he, rather than nature, who was at fault: 'there is a trilling and graceful play in the landscape of this country which is more difficult to do justice to than the landscapes of England' (Fig. 17).[13] Colonial attitudes to the peculiar look of the gum tree were far from unanimous and appear instead to have been closely related to one's gut feeling about the colonial project and the future possibilities of Australia.

By the time of Federation, however, feelings about the gum tree were no longer a matter of private opinion. An educated army of writers, artists and critics were making a concerted effort to discover a distinctive white Australian cultural identity. In the manner of national self-definition generally, where the 'self' is constructed positively against a conceptual 'other', 'England' emerged as the disparaged opposite of 'Australia': old-fashioned, overripe and out-of-step with an uncorrupted, young, free society on the brink of greatness. Nationalists grabbed wildly at anything they could call their own, anything noticeably not-English. The natural landscape, tangibly and unmistakeably Australian, proved the most powerful vehicle for national imaginings and, by the latter decades of the nineteenth century, the kernel of

Australian national identity was a romanticised vision of the bush, 'a sunlit landscape of faded blue hills, cloudless skies and noble gum trees, peopled by idealised shearers and drovers'.[14]

As the dominant botanical feature of the landscape and so undeniably, manifestly Australian, the gum tree became a central pillar of this ideal and its accompanying aesthetic. While the artists of the Heidelberg School painted bush vistas that venerated the brightness of the Australian sun and the special character of the Australian land, art critics, poets and journalists wrote reverently about the sunburnt palette and sophisticated, painterly shades of the Australian bush, and particularly of the ubiquitous gum tree.

The embrace of a new, all-Australian aesthetic was accompanied by a rejection of perceived 'English' aesthetics and a vociferous dismissal of the way that English colonists painted and wrote about the gum tree. The notion, however overstated, that British-born predecessors had singled out and publicly derided the gum tree for its peculiar appearance added vigour to the cause. Praise for contemporary artists' impressions of the gum tree and the landscape over which it lorded routinely included a dig at a perceived English inability to comprehend and convey the splendour of Australian scenery. Australia was considered too subtle for 'English eyes', which had been blinded by the facile prettiness of England. Australian beauty was thought visible only to those with their eyes 'opened' (namely, patriotic Australians). The cliché of the disgruntled, gum-hating British settler swiftly became a standard device by which twentieth-century Australian nationalists distinguished themselves as Australians. Loving the look of the gum tree was seen as a simple, reliable test of national feeling. Not loving it, on the other hand, was solid proof of unAustralian sentiment and a heretical, pitiable Anglophilia.

In an extension of this aesthetic morality, Australians indulged in derogatory comments on the showy colours of English scenery to contrast them with the inherent masculinity and subtlety of the eucalypt's khaki. When the artist Sir John Longstaff returned to

Australia in 1911 after a decade in England, he was reported to have said: 'When I first saw the brown, hot earth from the ship's deck at Fremantle I cannot tell you the emotion it gave me – after all that confounded sappy English green.'[15] In 1930, prominent eucalypt-loving poet and journalist Dorothea Mackellar scorned the fabled 'homesick English mothers' who, daunted by the omnipresent gum tree, pined for the gaudy greens of their homeland.[16] The real barb of her insult, however, lay in the implication of the effeminacy of her British male predecessors who also preferred English colours, and the superiority of their Australian descendants who were not daunted by gum-tree green.

In another passionate tribute entitled 'To the gums' (which began with the line 'You are Australia!'), Beryl Llywelyn Lucas in 1927 disdainfully likened the bright colours of the wattle and waratah to the kitsch of Old World scenery:

> Spin me no fair tales of wattle in its gold
> or the bright and burning waratah …
> Fragrant prettiness
> or scentless show
> are not Australia's soul.

Her deep admiration for the more utilitarian appearance of the gum tree, by contrast, stemmed from her belief that it was essential to the eucalypt's ability to withstand the vagaries of the Australian climate: 'Our lesser beauties' cannot cope with hardship or when 'desolations blow'.[17] The popular understanding that the appearance of the gum tree was a manifestation of its superior adaptation to the landscape led Anglo–Australians to associate the eucalypt's washed-out colours, tough leaves and untidy growth with the virtues of strength, fearlessness and forbearance that were now considered characteristically Australian.[18] Considering the often antagonistic historical relationship between settlers and the trees they settled among, it was hypocritical

'Washing day' postcard, 1934, by May Gibbs.
Gibbs gave gums a fairytale quality that normalised
them for generations of Australian children.

National Museum of Australia

for nationalists to see in the gum tree's struggle for survival a metaphor for the pioneer's struggle against the adversity of the climate. 'They hated trees' historian Keith Hancock (somewhat unfairly) commented in 1930.[19] Marjorie Barnard published a play in *The Home* magazine in 1938 portraying the British invasion and subsequent colonisation of the Australian continent as a duel between 'the Trees', an indomitable army composed mainly of eucalypts, and 'the White Man', a shrewd, alien force fated to succeed. The play concluded with the suggestion of a truce, and the formation of a coalition between the trees and the white-skinned invaders that would take the ancient land's 'strength [and] secret power and raise it to another plane'.[20]

This portrayal of the gum tree as an ally and supporter of white Australian domination of the land spectacularly misconstrues colonisation as being primarily about the subjugation of nature rather than people. With an ingenious sleight of hand, in this and many other fictive works, the gum tree's rugged, unadorned appearance veiled the brutal reality of colonisation and came to symbolise the Anglo–Australian overcoming of odds, inspiring in white Australians a new sense of pride in an otherwise rather unglamorous and discomfiting colonial past.

By the 1940s the gum tree was a distinctly empathetic character in the romantic narratives of Anglo–Australian nationalism. It was a wise and brave friend, a gallant comrade, a figure to be emulated and idolised – which is what celebrated photographer Harold Cazneaux did in 1941 when he published *Spirit of Endurance* (Fig. 19), an epic hero shot of a monumental, long-suffering river red gum in the desert that became one of his signature photographs and which he later described as 'My most Australian picture'.[21] The photograph represented the culmination of some decades of celebratory gum tree imagery from artists such as Hans Heysen and Henri van Raalte, as well as a host of amateur and professional photographers, led by Cazneaux. Reflecting on the Flinders Ranges expedition that led him to the now-famous gum tree of the photograph, Cazneaux recalled that 'some of the living element of this tree passed to me in understanding and friendliness, expressing the Spirit of Australia'.[22] The gum tree was, in a peculiar sense, the epitome of the perfect Australian. Testament to his title, the tree still stands, along with an interpretative panel for tourists (Fig. 20).

From the late 1930s to his death in 1959, an inadvertent populariser of the gum tree was Albert Namatjira, a prolific artist and one of the first Aboriginal people working in the Western tradition of landscape painting who became famous for his work.[23] In Namatjira's landscapes, gum trees – in particular, the ghost gum, *Corymbia aparrerinja* – frame spectacular landscapes of Central Australia. Namatjira did not paint in the service of white Australian nationalism, but borrowed a Western artistic form and compositional style to communicate the beauty of the trees and landscapes of which he, as an initiated Western Arrernte man, had special knowledge and connection. Through his attentiveness to the form and colours of the ghost gum, Namatjira's paintings made this tree iconic.

An evergreen symbol

Popular feeling for the eucalypt as a national symbol today lacks the imagination, the fervour and the sense of urgency of the first half of the twentieth century – unsurprisingly since, as a symbol firmly rooted, so to speak, in an older Anglo–Australian nationalism, it resonates for fewer and fewer Australians. By the 1960s, the gum tree's signature endurance and resilience was being referenced more ambivalently. In her elegiac poem 'Municipal Gum' (1965), Oodgeroo Noonuccal likens a gum tree in the city to herself and her people, displaced and oppressed but, notably, surviving:

> Municipal gum, it is dolorous
> To see you thus

Reclaiming the tree stolen both literally and symbolically by white Australians, Noonuccal portrays its resilience as bittersweet rather than heroic.

> Set in your black grass of bitumen –
> O fellow citizen,
> What have they done to us?[24]

In George Johnston's *My Brother Jack* of 1964, a sugar gum planted in the front yard performed a somewhat different role, a raffish protest against the stultifying neatness of Melbourne suburbia that led to a marriage breakdown.[25] This is doggedness, perhaps, but of a more militant sort.

Although it no longer inspires the excesses of Edwardian sentimentalism, the gum tree appears often in the lavish colour photography of Australiana for tourists, in Murray Bail's novel *Eucalyptus* (1998), and on the Australia Day website as an explanation for the nation's trademark khaki green. In the twenty-first century, however, gum tree symbolism is particularly fraught. Throughout Australia today, death and destruction of gum trees and the ecosystems they support proceeds apace, the result of climate change and extensive land-clearing. This paradox of white Australian national symbolism, where the image of a tree can be idolised even as *actual* trees are shown no mercy, contrasts with Indigenous relationships to trees, which are valued both individually and collectively. Still. In 2020, the Djab Wurrung people of Victoria protested against government felling of centuries-old sacred trees for the expansion of roadways. We should beware the hypocrisy that conceals reality and threatens all our natural symbols: it's not hard to imagine that the koala, now endangered due to the destruction of eucalypts, may remain a national symbol even after it has been rendered extinct. And, as the future threatens ever more ferocious bushfires, the futures of Australians and gum trees are inextricably linked, not just symbolically, but as a matter of survival.

SHARK

Helen Tiffin

When ecologists (and profiteers) suggested that kangaroos might be farmed for their meat on the grounds that they would prove less destructive of Australian ecosystems than sheep or cattle, there was an outcry both from within Australia and internationally. The most common response was outrage at Australians eating and exporting – especially on a commercial scale – their national symbol. After all, it was pointed out – somewhat irrelevantly – the British do not eat lions or unicorns, and Canadians do not eat the beaver. Such responses, received from both inside and outside the country, reveal the different levels at which national symbols operate: in Australians' self-perceptions, the images they wish to project, the reception of these symbols by other nations and their consequent images of Australia, all influenced by competing political agendas.

Originally regarded as the continent with the most bizarre flora and fauna on earth, Australia increasingly gained the reputation as the most dangerous in terms of its more cryptic biota. While it didn't have those land-dwelling animals that provided manly contests between man and beast – India's tigers, Africa's rampaging elephants or North America's grizzly bears – its deadly collection of spiders, snakes and sharks was seen as somehow more insidiously malevolent. That Australian settlement, from 1788 onwards, tended to cling to the shoreline ensured that the shark, though feared throughout the world, would be particularly associated with Australia. The emphasis on beach culture during the twentieth century necessarily reinforced this tendency. It is also particularly true of the settler colonies that their self-images and national symbols tend to emerge in contrast to those of the 'mother' country. The very different character of British beaches and the more formal 'seaside' attitudes of Britons to them, together with the less than central place of coastlines in their urban settlement patterns, have led Australians to emphasise both the superiority of their beaches, their attachment to them, and their easy familiarity with even their apparent dangers. More recently, Australians have cheerfully played 'the last frontier' to the United States' loss of it; here men are men and sharks are sharks and Australians still have the courage and know-how to take on the creatures of the wild.

Thus, while the kangaroo and the emu may be Australia's iconic animal symbols, more negative symbols of Australia carry particular potency outside the country. The favoured self-projection of 'the Australian' is almost always associated with apparently casual attitudes to 'dangerous' animals. It combines the bronzed surfer image with a *Crocodile Dundee* devil-may-care courage and is played most specifically to American and British audiences. In this particular projection, which foreigners accept as real and Australians are happy to encourage, sharks have played, and continue to play, a major role.[1] As historian Michael Sturma sees it, 'Sharks are part of Australia's international mystique.'[2] Long before 'the Chinese submarine theory', he writes, 'it was widely speculated by overseas journalists that Prime Minister Harold Holt was taken by a shark'. The Americans, he goes on to note, nicknamed champion golfer Greg Norman 'The Great White Shark'; while the mechanical great white in the blockbuster film *Jaws* was dubbed 'Bruce'.[3] Another, more recent, great white shark named Bruce was voiced in a broad Australian accent by Barry Humphries in the 2003 animated film, *Finding Nemo*. Nino Culotta, purportedly the Italian immigrant author of *They're a Weird Mob* (1957), was puzzled by the strange customs and attitudes of his adopted countrymen, who casually dismissed the threat of sharks: 'Yer'd be dead unlucky ter be taken by a shark.' Culotta took the statement literally, wondering (logically) 'Where is there a place where it would be lucky to be taken by a shark?'[4]

In 2001, well-known Anglo-American travel writer Bill Bryson wrote his account of 'Down Under', including the obligatory swim in potentially 'shark infested' waters. His focus was not sharks themselves but Aussie nonchalance about them:

'What about sharks?' I asked uneasily.

'Oh, there's hardly any sharks here. Glenn, how long has it been since someone was killed by a shark?'

'Oh, ages,' Glenn said, considering. 'Couple of months at least.'

'Couple of months?' I squeaked.

'At least. Sharks are way overrated as a danger,' Glenn added. 'Way overrated. It's the rips that'll most likely get you.' He returned to taking pictures.[5]

Admittedly sharks seem to be, in the minds of overseas visitors, only one of the contenders for top place in what Bryson refers to as 'a fat book titled *Things That Will Kill You Horridly in Australia: Volume 19*'.[6] The visitor's initiation into Aussie dismissal of dangerous animals is itself a part of the last frontier complex, since *Things That Will Kill You Horridly in Australia* are not cars, or other people (as in being murdered in the outback, shot in Melbourne, or left behind at the Barrier Reef) but *non-human* animals. And it is notable that it is this apparent fearlessness about sharks, rather than the presence or otherwise of sharks themselves, which engages the visitor, evoking his or her wonder and admiration (Fig. 21). Yet on the exclusively 'home front', when outsiders are not looking, Australian attitudes to sharks, while they may sometimes seem more casual, differ little from more general Western ones.

Ideas about sharks worldwide have always to some degree been ambivalent, generating mixed emotions of fear, awe and even hatred. Sharks in this context refer almost exclusively to the larger varieties. While there are over 340 known species – some adults small enough to fit in the palm of a human hand – popular understanding of the term 'shark' requires an animal of at least a metre in length. Australian attitudes to sharks shared this mixture of awe and fear, and, at least until the late twentieth century, generally participated in the promulgation of traditional Western shark stereotypes. Statistics clearly demonstrate that human fatalities due to shark attacks are very rare, and that more people die from dog bites, bee-stings or being kicked to death by donkeys each year; and road tolls so far exceed shark-caused injury or death as to be genuinely incomparable. Yet sharks generate greater fear in humans (even those of non-maritime cultures) than virtually any other animal species, and are often referred to as *the* primary human fear.

The calm surface of the ocean cut by the dark fin; the placid blue water under which can be seen lurking the dark torpedo mass, while human families swim and play unsuspectingly; the water surface savagely broken by the bloodied jaws and teeth of the shark:[7] why are these images so pervasive, so influential, and so frequently invoked by urban cultures whose quite unrealistic sense of individual or collective safety is profoundly disturbed by the images of sharks and shark attacks? An eyewitness to the Cottesloe (Western Australia) shark death in 2000 described her feelings in this way:

> I tried to swim and I kept wanting to move, but just nothing. It was just terror, pure unadulterated terror as you never experience. And I defy anybody to experience that because we're bred to be terrified of sharks. What brings most terror to your heart? It's a shark.[8]

Duncan Richards observes that sharks have 'teeth that cut, just by suggestion, especially in dreams'.[9] The shadow of the shark is the shadow of death, the image of an ultimate evil, or, like the whale in *Moby Dick*, of the inscrutability of a malign universe. This is one reason why shark fatalities attract the kinds of headlines they do, even though such incidents are rare (on average nine fatalities per year worldwide) and likely to be cases of mistaken identity. Great whites frequent the South Australian coast in the seal pupping season, and surfboard riders in flippers and wetsuits look very like seals. It did not help that, from 1997 to 1999, wetsuits filled with offal were towed behind tourist boats off South Africa and South Australia to attract great whites.[10] Though all these things are generally known outside the scientific community, single deaths by 'shark attack' still provoke disproportionately widespread fear and sensationalist media coverage.

It is clear that popular imagery is most strongly influenced by the shark's *symbolic* freight, based in human fears and human self-definition, and this is produced historically, psychologically, culturally, not scientifically. In this space of representation, these dominant animal images lend themselves to what art historian Steve Baker calls a 'vicious circularity' wherein 'only that which is already known will be readily recognised as having meaning'.[11] Peter Benchley's novel *Jaws* (and the even more influential film it inspired) deliberately exploited previously established shark stereotypes.[12] In the trailer for *Jaws*, the richly resonant voiceover, often mistakenly assumed to be that of Orson Welles,[13] encapsulated the shark mythos from which the film derived:

> There is a creature alive today that has survived millions of years of evolution without change, without passion, and without logic. It lives to kill; a mindless, eating machine. It will attack and devour anything. It is as if God created the Devil and gave him ... jaws.

DEVOURED BY A SHARK: SKETCH OF THE SHARK.

'Devoured by a shark': when a shark caught near Frankston on Port Phillip Bay was cut open, it was found to contain the remains of Hugh Browne, 20, who had drowned in a yachting accident in December, 1884. The shark was put on display in Melbourne. *Australasian Sketcher*, 14 January 1885.

State Library of Victoria

In its turn the film became notorious for (re)producing and perpetuating those stereotypes. Benchley himself was so horrified by the vengeful shark killing the film catalysed, that he subsequently donated money and time to the cause of shark preservation (Fig. 22).

There are a number of reasons why sharks conjure fear in humans. Such images of sharks as *Jaws* promulgated seem to help define what it means to be human, and parallel those once also applied to non-European peoples: savagery versus domesticity or 'civilisation'; 'cannibalism' as the extreme marker of barbarism and the not-human; inanimate, mechanistic behaviour as against an affective, 'human' way of being; and the extreme 'other'.[14] They also derive from our eagerness to separate ourselves, as top predators of the terrestrial food chain, from sharks, the top predators of the marine food chain. Humans distinguish between their own killing and feeding habits and those of sharks by applying different vocabularies to similar activities; while sharks kill, attack, maul and dismember 'prey', we raise, produce and 'process' our 'food'. The classic 'feeding frenzy' of sharks suggests a mechanistic, automatic set of 'savage' responses, bolstering the idea of sharks as biologically and emotionally alien, lacking any vestige of 'human' compassion. Kim Gamble, an eyewitness to the death of Ken Crow at Cottesloe in 2000, reported a description of the attack he had found particularly apposite. It was, he said, like 'sitting around watching a cricket match, enjoying your day when suddenly this alien comes over the top of the grandstand, chomps the slips fieldsman in half and goes away, leaving him bleeding on the pitch'.[15] Once again the shark is pictured as the inhuman, abrupt disturber of 'domestic' bliss and holiday relaxation; the 'devil' of the paradisiacal Australian summer of beaches and cricket.

Another reason for the exaggerated alarm is what has sometimes been described as the 'cannibal complex': our acute sensitivity to *what* and *whom* we eat, our taboos in relation to 'edibility' and our own fears of being eaten. Historically, humans have generally avoided eating those animals with reputations for eating us.[16] Thus we have generally not eaten lions, tigers and, in Australia, crocodile (at least until tourist promotions encouraged the sampling of wildlife as gourmet delicacies). The eating of shark flesh in Australia however has had a more ambivalent history. Originally providing the early settlers with sustenance and, in the early nineteenth century, trade with China in the form of shark fins, the eating of shark became unfashionable, requiring disguise. Since eating shark might seem to come too close to a kind of transmogrified cannibalism, shark has been consumed during the twentieth century as the unnamed generic in 'fish and chips', or sold as 'flake'.

Paradoxically, it is actually *because* shark deaths *are* so rare that the image of the shark as a malign, inscrutable force, like fate itself, persists.

Like death, the shark's unheralded attack can occur at any time and, like death itself, the shark seems cold and remote, erupting into life from 'nowhere' to carry the victim off. The 'shadow of sharks', as writer Peter Matthiessen notes, 'is the shadow of death' and it calls forth 'ultimate fears'. There is, he comments, 'something unholy in their silence'.[17] But as well as symbolising the forces of a malign universe and/or death, the shark is also figuratively represented as a savage disruption to domestic calm. Their presence at the heart of our holiday world, precisely where we feel most relaxed and 'safe', evokes the dangerous, unstable basis of life itself. It is also a reminder that the ocean depths represent one of the very few realms we have not yet totally 'conquered'.

Writing of growing up on the coast of Western Australia, novelist Tim Winton succinctly expressed the way in which 'the shark' came to symbolise much more than simply a large marine predator. 'While the sea was benign', Winton wrote:

> at the blurring perimeter of that boyhood, beyond the reach of conscious thought, there was an unacknowledged moving shadow. It was what the eye searched for when you weren't even looking. It was the reflex that made you swivel now and then as you trod water off the back of the boat, the thing that made your skin tingle as you snorkelled in a murky surge.[18]

Sharks do injure and kill humans, and exercising caution in the ocean is common sense. But although we practise a similar caution in relation to box jellyfish in our northern waters (box jellyfish, which, like the shark, can injure or kill us) and other species dangerous to humans, these are not feared in the ways in which sharks are. Though box jellyfish can kill unexpectedly, painfully and quickly, they are not imaged as evil or inscrutable, or even 'inhuman'; nor are they routinely used as negative images of humans and human behaviour in the ways in which the shark so pervasively is in our societies: 'loan sharks', lawyers, financiers.

Our oldest obsession

Settlers and whalers arriving in Australia after 1788 brought with them these European (and, with the whaling industry, American) attitudes to sharks. Historian Noel McLachlan called fear of sharks 'our oldest obsession', noting a '13-foot monster' being caught two months after the First Fleet arrived and, two months later, an attack on a fishing boat, where the shark took an oar and a rudder.[19] In 1804 the Sydney *Gazette* made the most of an incident on the harbour where three fishermen and a young girl were unnerved by a curious shark:

> Terror and trepidation were aroused when the voracious monster, whose bulk was probably magnified by fear, appeared close alongside the little boat, and ... threatened momentarily to dislodge the tremblers, who had no other expectation than to be hurled out to the mercy of the furious assailant ... The little girl clung to her father for protection and the poignant sensation that he endured must with difficulty come within the reach of conception.[20]

The authorities were aware that sharks were prevalent and relied on their presence as a deterrent to convict escape attempts from, for instance, Fort Denison (Pinchgut) and by water across Eaglehawk Neck in Tasmania. With all the Australian colonies being settled from the sea, sharks became an unexpectedly unifying symbol for the whole continent. While the first fears were associated with Sydney Harbour, in 1803 the first recorded shark attack in Australian waters took place in what became Western Australia, while a popular ballad later used 'teeth like a Moreton Bay shark' as a standard of ugliness.[21] Each colony would contribute its stories of shark horrors.

Nevertheless, some of the earliest written newspaper accounts of contact with sharks in Sydney Harbour are indicative less of 'attacks' on humans than of the killing of sharks for eating and trading in shark fins.[22] With the increasing dumping of offal and human waste into

Publicity shot for American wrestler, Vic Christy, posing with a shark at Double Bay, Sydney, before his appearance at Sydney Stadium, 1937.

Photograph by Sam Hood, State Library of New South Wales

the water, shark activity in the vicinity of Sydney no doubt increased, and during the nineteenth and twentieth centuries a caught shark was always a spectacle, whether in terms of size or, in an even more popular display, its stomach contents. Jaw trophies and shark tooth 'jewellery' also express a male triumphalism that has been a component of shark catching and characteristic of so many photographs where the proud fisherman stands beside a dead shark hung ignominiously by its tail, blood dripping from its mouth. Other favourite poses include children framed by shark jaw trophies and bikini-clad beauties tentatively touching the dead body.[23] While images such as those of humans in the jaws of a now very dead predator speak to that complex of eating and being eaten, many of them are also redolent of the savagery and vengefulness humans have inflicted on sharks since the Middle Ages.

(It is not only commercial convenience which still allows shark fins to be cut off and the sharks thrown overboard to die, sometimes slowly and painfully. Nor are the cruel practices of Renaissance sailors, such as cutting out the eyes of the shark and throwing it overboard alive, by any means unknown today.)

Stomach contents of sharks have been popular exhibits in Australia since the early 1800s. Their stomachs generally produced a wide array of inanimate as well as animate objects for display – a spectacle for which shark catchers often charged. A particularly bizarre incident occurred in 1935 at Coogee aquarium (Sydney), a favourite venue for the showing of live sharks. It was still the subject of popular magazine accounts 60 years later. On 25 April, a medium-sized shark was caught on a line off Coogee. Before it could be towed in, it was 'cannibalised' by a much larger shark which was then captured and exhibited in the Coogee pool. Not surprisingly this extremely large shark, watched by a crowd of eager onlookers, quickly began to exhibit signs of acute distress. Increasingly lethargic, it vomited up a human arm, distinguished by the presence of a 'boxing' tattoo. The arm had not been severed by either shark, but had been sawn off. The tattoo led the police to the Sydney underworld, a smuggling racket, the identity of the victim and his likely murderers.

The name by which this incident has been remembered, 'The Shark Arm Case', is indicative of the tale's enduring fascination.[24] While the shark initially appeared in its traditional role as dismemberer, harbinger of death redolent of unexpected and unjust fate, it was instead the (unwitting) instrument of justice, revealing a murder that would otherwise have remained undetected. Humans, not sharks, had dismembered the human body. The sobriquet 'shark arm' also confused both the obdurate difference between shark and human anatomy, while at the same time evoking the constant association of 'shark attack' with severed human limbs. Though obviously oxymoronic, the shark's persisting associations with human dismemberment and death made the phrase instantly and popularly intelligible, its ironic destabilisation by the facts of the case serving only, in the end, to reinforce the 'vicious circularity' of the shark's dangerous image.

An endangered symbol

In the twenty-first century, however, many sharks, particularly the large predatory and once prevalent species, are endangered, not only by overfishing, wanton destruction, marine pollution, longline by-catch and climate change, but by humans' increasing need for food. As the plague species of our planet, we – not sharks – are gradually eating ourselves and other species into oblivion. Most sinister of recent changes – in spite of efforts internationally to conserve species crucial to the marine food chain – has been China's repeal in 1987 of the ban on shark fin soup, which the Central Committee had previously categorised as a luxury 'throwback' to the imperial era.[25]

If attitudes to the destruction of sharks have changed, the image of the death-defying beach-loving Aussie has not. Over the last ten years, many, if not most people who have survived shark bites, have specifically requested that 'revenge attacks', still common in many parts of Australia, *not* be carried out in the wake of their injuries.[26] But just as, in Australia, *conservation* of endangered sharks, such as the grey nurse, is being increasingly accepted, so the overseas image of Australia as a continent surrounded by 'jaws' may itself be weakening. In Dean Crawford's 2008 cultural history of the shark and shark images, Australia barely rates mention. While, like the Tasmanian tiger, the image may outlive the species, the shark's peculiar association with Australia over the last two centuries may itself be endangered. From the time Mick Dundee caught the popular imagination, the crocodile began to dislodge the shark from its position as Australia's greatest symbolic terror.

BOOMERANG

Felicity Errington

The often surprising career of the boomerang has seen it travel from its obscure origins at least twenty thousand years ago to its position in the twenty-first century as one of Australia's most popular symbols. For Indigenous Australians its shape and purpose varied in different parts of the country: it had a role in games and music, was used for hunting and fighting, as a knife, a hammer and a digging tool. Its most famously striking characteristic is its aerodynamic properties that allow it to spin, and dependent on the design, to return to the thrower. Colonial Australia used it to market all manner of things from butter to brandy. Around the world, hundreds of enthusiasts compete in boomerang-throwing contests, admiring its unique aerodynamic properties; according to one manual, they 'practice [sic] regularly for the sheer enjoyment of throwing and for the beneficial exercise it affords'.[1] Boomerangs line souvenir shops in their thousands, inviting visitors to Australia to take this remarkable piece of the nation home with them as a symbol of both the country they visited and its First Peoples – whom they may or may not have met.

The boomerang is perhaps the best, or at least the most obvious, example of the way in which one object and image has functioned successfully as both a souvenir and a symbol of Australia. A popular souvenir will often be a well-known symbol of the country in question – a miniature pyramid in Egypt or Statue of Liberty key ring in the United

States.² These symbols and souvenirs belong to the same 'universal language of travel' that Roland Barthes invokes in his discussion of the Eiffel Tower.³ Just as the Tower symbolises Paris, the boomerang could be said to be a universal symbol of Australia. How do we explain this popularity? The boomerang's success as a souvenir is a result of its complex history. Just as the history of any given symbol will influence how it is interpreted, the exchanges and conversations the boomerang has been a part of over time have all contributed, layer upon layer, to the meanings that are associated with it. Souvenirs are interpreted within specific traditions.

What traditions of interpretation have grown up around the boomerang since those British interlopers, who often behaved like very early 'tourists', first encountered it?⁴ Among other objects, boomerangs have played a role on the 'front line' of cultural exchange since Europeans and Indigenous Australians first came into contact with one another.⁵ In 1770, on his first day in Botany Bay, Joseph Banks described two defiant Aboriginal warriors 'brandishing their crooked weapons', each 'about 2½ feet long, in shape much resembling a scymeter [sic]'.⁶ Long, sabre-like wooden 'swords' illustrated in the First Fleet journals of John White and Watkin Tench also appear to be boomerangs. Bungaree, a well-known Garigal man from Broken Bay who became an influential mediator and leader in Sydney, was probably the first to demonstrate the remarkable powers of the returning boomerang to Europeans in 1804.⁷

While intrigued, Europeans tended to see the boomerang as a sign of primitivism. Cook's great voyages of 'discovery' in the 1770s were motivated in part by scientific interest in flora, fauna and the origins of man. Here was a new, radical example of the 'primitive', providing a benchmark to measure how far their own civilisation had 'progressed'.⁸ Artefacts that seemed to crystallise that primitivism became favoured items for collection, and part of a thriving trade in curiosities in late eighteenth-century Britain.⁹ To European eyes, the boomerang's unusual shape and surprising aerodynamic properties epitomised primitive warfare – as well as having a fascinating strangeness.

The symbol as commodity

From these earliest encounters, both colonial appropriation and Indigenous agency played roles in the development of the boomerang as a national symbol. Remarkably soon after the European arrival in Australia, local people began manufacturing implements purely for the purpose of trading with the newcomers. In January 1822, Phillip Parker King and his crew anchored in Oyster Harbour, King George Sound, Western Australia, in order to replenish their supplies. King estimated 20 to 40 Minang/Menang Noongar men were soon busy manufacturing spears, 'throwing sticks' and other implements and weapons 'for the evening's barter'. By the time King's party left they had over 320 individually crafted items.[10]

Along with corroborees, displays of boomerang-throwing also became popular colonial spectacles (Fig. 23). In the 1880s, showman RA Cunningham took two troupes of Indigenous Australians from North Queensland (most belonging to a language group now known as Wulguru) around the world, billing them as 'Tattooed Cannibals, Black Trackers and Boomerang Throwers'. The troupes performed in the parklands, fairgrounds and baseball stadiums of America and Europe, and even at Moscow Zoo. The boomerang was an essential prop in their performance of 'cannibal savagery' for the entertainment of the masses, and the promotional rhetoric about 'The last of the Cannibals' was a typical example of the ways in which the marketing practices of mass tourism packaged otherness. If this was 'savagery', however, it was also admired; the crowds who viewed the troupes' performances professed considerable admiration for the boomerang's fascinating improbability and the skill required to control it. In 1884 the *London Standard* described their boomerang-throwing as 'accomplished', and it was noted that 'No other people have ever been able to master this extraordinary weapon.' Inevitably, the truth behind this light-hearted entertainment was much darker: the troupes' recruitment involved likely coercion, and all but three members of Cunningham's first troupe died from illness.[11]

By Federation, the Aboriginal people gathered at Botany Bay were making a regular living manufacturing boomerangs and displaying their capabilities. Boomerang-throwing became particularly popular, with such prestigious tourists as the British Admiral Lord Jellicoe and the Prince of Japan taking part.[12] In satisfying tourists' desires for the so-called 'primitive', the local people actively packaged and performed a certain image of Aboriginality. They controlled the production and sale of boomerangs, shell work and baskets, an Aboriginal-only industry, and ensured their essential value lay in their status as 'authentic' products of local Indigenous people. Manufacture, as well as consumption, shaped what the boomerang came to symbolise.

From the 1880s Aboriginal missions and reserves attracted tour groups, and tourist interest flourished in the 1920s and 1930s as popular interest in 'primitivism' swelled. Aboriginal initiative and ingenuity in producing boomerangs and baskets for sale challenged the then conventional idea that First Peoples would be unable to adapt and were doomed to die out. It was at sites such as La Perouse (New South Wales), Coranderrk and Lake Tyers (Victoria), Palm Island and Cherbourg (Queensland) and Tennant Creek (Northern Territory)[13] that local Indigenous people turned the boomerang into a souvenir, adding designs that catered for a tourist market (Fig. 24). The most common designs, burnt on with heated wire, were native fauna – in particular emus, kangaroos and koalas – and flora, such as wattle and waratahs. While identifying Australianness with the now conventional markers of the flora and fauna, and Botany Bay and other reserves as exotic tourist sites, these designs also reinforced the popular notion that First Peoples were 'close to nature'. But other popular markings at La Perouse were the phrase 'Greetings from Sydney' and images of the Harbour Bridge (which also appeared on at least one boomerang made in Lake Tyers). These designs placed the boomerang in a wider realm

Entrance to Bung Yarnda (Lake Tyers Aboriginal Reserve), 2004.
Lake Tyers, Victoria, was a principal site of boomerang tourism.
Photograph by Uncle Jim Berg, Gunditjmara Elder

of souvenirs functioning as mementoes that packaged an entire city for a tourist's later remembrance of a particular holiday. Significantly, both kinds of designs have endured in the boomerangs available from souvenir outlets today.[14]

But if the designs have endured, the national meanings attached to the boomerang have continued to evolve. Indigenous control over those meanings has had to contend with the constant colonial appropriation of Aboriginal culture, which has been recruited to play a variety of roles in the construction of a national heritage. Settler societies such as the United States, Canada, New Zealand and Australia have repeatedly looked to the cultural artefacts of their original inhabitants to give their nation-making a distinctive physical reality.[15] In a world that is getting smaller and more similar, what a nation can claim belongs to it alone is important.

If the boomerang was initially a sign of the 'primitive' to be contrasted with a self-conscious national modernity, it also bestowed on a new nation a sense of heritage and cultural depth it otherwise lacked.

As Jan Kociumbas put it, 'It is as if only Aboriginality can provide a meaningful, significant and unifying resonance in the otherwise diverse cacophony of local multiculturalism and global cosmopolitanism.'[16] It is a by now familiar story, perhaps most spectacularly evident in the opening ceremony of the 2000 Olympic Games, when a 20-minute sequence celebrated life before European arrival, and Yolngu songman and dancer Djakapurra Munyarryun and thirteen-year-old Nikki Webster enacted a sequence illustrating Australia's relationship with the sea.[17] Aboriginal culture is increasingly co-opted to fill the cultural – or spiritual – gap in the national psyche.

For a fledgling tourism industry, the boomerang turned this heritage into a commodity that could be packaged and sold. Increasing in professionalism and embracing new technologies, the tourist industry became a powerful image crafter and symbol producer. The first comprehensive study of the Australian tourist industry, completed by the American consultants Harris, Kerr, Forster and Company in 1965, saw 'The Aborigines of Australia' as an opportunity to promote 'a unique, primitive civilisation of great interest to the world'. So-called 'traditional' Aboriginal culture was the best cultural resource Australia could exploit, and its exhibition would 'be influential in convincing everyone of the dignity and achievements of the Aboriginal Australians before the days of white settlement'.[18]

The general assumption was that this 'traditional' culture only survived on remote reserves, where the policy of assimilation had not yet reached – far away in both time and place. Aboriginal 'protection' and tourism were closely linked. Toby Martin has shown how the Queensland Government Tourist Bureau promoted Indigenous Australians confined on the Palm Island Aboriginal Reserve, 65 kilometres off the coast from Townsville, as 'living examples of primitive peoples and their ancient cultures'.[19] Collectors had long sought to preserve what they saw as the last vestiges of an exotic otherness on the brink of extinction. As an Adelaide tourist inquired:

Mornington Island (Kunhanhaa) man carving a
returning boomerang at the local Presbyterian Mission, 1957.

National Archives of Australia

Where might one purchase Aboriginal weapons? My husband is most vitally interested in the Aboriginal question. He already has several boomerangs and spears from the Nullarbor Plain, and is particularly anxious to get a big collection before these unfortunate people are allowed to die out.[20]

But as the tourism industry developed, the primitive artefact desired by the collector turned into the tourist's souvenir. While the government pursued a policy of assimilation, designed to eventually eradicate the 'other', the industry had an interest in preserving this very 'otherness', which was where the tourism potential of the Indigenous population lay. The paradox was apparent when the Queen visited Australia in 1954. She was treated to a welcoming boomerang archway, and a dance performance by Palm Island residents, who had been released from incarceration specially to dance for royalty.[21]

Appropriating Aboriginality

From the late nineteenth century, the boomerang and other First Peoples images were available for use within popular culture, often with no reference to their Indigenous origin. Commerce particularly used the boomerang symbol simply to identify the essential 'Australianness' of the product being advertised. The 1890s saw products as varied as white ant exterminator, brandy and 'Boomerang Butter' seize hold of the image; 'Boomerang Tonic', glass and metal wares, cigarette papers and the Albert's Boomerang Harmonica followed early in the twentieth century. The widespread use suggests that advertisers were confident that their market not only recognised the symbol, but also viewed it positively and readily disconnected it from any associations with primitivism. Often, reinforcing a product's 'naturalness', the boomerang symbol was coupled with a native animal: a kookaburra in the 1917 trademark for Kimpton & Sons 'Finest Australian Rolled Flour', a kangaroo in advertising for Rosella Foods in 1934 and Boomerang Toys in 1945.[22] For obvious reasons, the boomerang featured in the advertising of the Australian travel industry, suggesting, for example, how easy it was to 'fly there and back' with Qantas.[23] Its capacity to 'return' also underpinned its use in the 'Buy Australian' campaign – 'Operation Boomerang' – launched in 1961.

The boomerang was appropriated in more explicitly nationalistic contexts, such as the Australia Day badge of 1918, where a kookaburra was depicted sitting atop a boomerang,[24] and in various Australian military emblems, from World War I on. The boomerang's associations with weaponry, the nation and the idea of return made it an appealing symbol for militaristic purposes, and even in the 1990s the Australian contingent of the United Nations peacekeeping forces in Cambodia incorporated the boomerang in their insignia.[25] In most of these popular uses, Aboriginality was eliminated from the range of meanings the symbol was supposed to contain. The embrace of Indigenous symbols as symbols of nation in the public arena took place alongside the ongoing marginalisation of First Peoples themselves: symbolic display co-existed with enforced invisibility. Philip Jones has pointed to the irony of the boomerang's proliferation in pubs in the 1950s – appearing on beers, bottle openers, glassware and drinking coasters – when actual Aboriginal people were barred from entry.[26]

Towards the end of the twentieth century, as respect for Indigenous culture increased, most domestic boomerang kitsch fell out of fashion, while other forms of Indigenous art regularly broke auction records. Many condemned the kitsch as crass, racist and offensive.[27] However, British–Australian sociologist Adrian Franklin has argued that the presence of objects of 'Aboriginalia' in people's homes from the 1940s to 1970s – pottery, wall-hangings, figurines, ash trays, tea towels – at a time when Aboriginal people were left out of official national symbols, recognised Indigenous culture's continuing and prior claim to what it meant to be Australian. Kerry Reed-Gilbert, Wiradjuri elder, activist, author and collector, undercut the debate by arguing 'we will decide what we see as being culturally right for us. I believe these objects represent who we are as people, from then to now. Each piece represents Aboriginal Australia and we will own them.'[28]

Beyond kitsch, the boomerang persisted as a cultural symbol in various forms. Its original hunting and throwing uses, functions forgotten in the plethora of boomerang images over the previous century, were picked up again in sporting uses. In the 1980s, the first Indigenous soccer club to tour internationally was named 'The

Boomerangs', and boomerang-throwing became an international sport.[29] Indeed, the Boomerang Association of Australia showed little interest in boomerang-throwing except as a sport.[30]

Authenticity and commercialisation

The boomerang has persisted – and flourished – as a popular souvenir into the twenty-first century. Once an Aboriginal-only industry, boomerang production had been transformed into a mass commercialised venture operating in a competitive souvenir market, often with no connection to Indigenous manufacture.

From the late twentieth century, Indigenous manufacturers have responded in creative ways to these tensions around authenticity. A re-appraisal of what could be considered an 'authentic' artefact, emphasising the link between the product and an individual, Indigenous manufacturer, meant the process of ensuring the authenticity of the product has become part of the tourist experience. When Maruku, Australia's largest regional craft centre, was opened at Uluṟu in 1995, the making, displaying and selling of souvenir crafts became a seamless chain. The Northern Territory Coomalie Art Centre included an artists-in-residence program, where tourists were able to watch artists and carvers at work.[31] In Sydney's souvenir shops, other means of identifying a souvenir with an individual producer were found: printing a portrait photograph on the back of the boomerang, or displaying a packaged version of the artist's life story, promising 'Her work portrays examples of her life experiences and appreciation of her cultural heritage'. Another shop displayed photographs of Aboriginal people holding up the same artworks that were on the shelves behind them, daring accusations of inauthenticity. While necessary, these attempts to reinvest some sense of individuality into what are still more or less mass-produced souvenirs inevitably turn the artist's life story into something of a commodity to be purchased by the tourist – a tourist who then 'possesses' as an individual the results of a cultural process rich with communal meaning and identity. The industry has also come up with creative ways to enable the savvy consumer to choose the 'real deal'. In 2019, Desart, the peak body for Australia's Central Desert Indigenous art centres, began trialling digital labelling technology to authenticate artworks by Aboriginal artists.[32]

However, given the market for Indigenous (and Indigenous 'style') souvenirs has grown into a multi-million dollar industry, the temptation to fake authenticity is strong and the rewards significant. A 2018 Parliamentary Inquiry explored the growing presence of inauthentic Aboriginal and Torres Strait Islander 'style' art and craft products for sale across Australia. It found that 80 per cent or more of these products sold in gift shops were inauthentic, including boomerangs and didjeridus displaying Indigenous imagery.[33] Given the centrality of art to the cultural identity, place and belonging of First Nations peoples, many artists and communities feel their culture is being stolen. In the words of Marjorie Williams from Tangentyere Artists:

> When I see fake art I get a really bad feeling. How can they steal our culture and our style, which we learned from our elders? After many years of practising, we paint our Dreaming of our country ... Fake art is destroying our identity and what we are. We are First Nations people and our arts and story must be protected for only us to share with our kids and the wider world.[34]

This imitation has a very real financial impact. Indigenous manufacturers, especially those operating from remote art centres, struggle to compete with cheaper imported products due to cost, scale, and lack of knowledge of or access to supply chains. In consequence, a large part of this multi-million dollar market is not accessible to those who have the right to benefit from it commercially, many of whom are operating from the most economically disadvantaged communities in Australia. In 2003 Australian Aboriginal Art Pty Ltd was accused by

'Tex Morton's Cowboy Roadshow: A cowboy with a boomerang', 1938.
Photograph by Sam Hood, State Library of New South Wales

the Australian Competition and Consumer Commission (ACCC) of misleading consumers, 'especially overseas tourists', when they falsely claimed that 'their hand-painted Aboriginal-style souvenirs were ... "authentic" Aboriginal art, produced by artists who were "Australian, Aboriginal by descent and Aboriginal"'.[35]

That case did not proceed to trial. However in 2019, an Australian-based company, Birubi Art, that sold Indonesian-made fake Aboriginal art was fined $2.3 million for 'false and misleading conduct' by the federal court. While existing consumer law penalises companies for misrepresentation, activists in the sector are calling for a new legal framework to protect artists' intellectual property against the misappropriation of Aboriginal and Torres Strait Islander culture. Such calls expose tensions between Indigenous and non-Indigenous understandings of art, cultural versus individual ownership, and the meanings attached to symbols themselves.[36]

What are the consequences when a cultural artefact is turned into a popular commodity and recruited to play a starring role in the nation's symbology? One version of the story, and a popular one, ends in despair: this postmodern, consumerist age has seen the death of the author – or in this case, the death of the local manufacturer. The individual identities of boomerang manufacturers are all but lost in the tourist transaction. Colonialist assumptions about Indigenous cultures endure, and cultural artefacts such as boomerangs are churned out like cheeseburgers to be devoured by mindless tourists, whose 'voracious demand' for authenticity is never satisfied, whose stomachs are never full.[37] The iconic status of the boomerang creates a stereotypical souvenir that the tourist desires, leading producers to conform to their expectations in a self-perpetuating cycle from which artists, and the boomerang, cannot escape. For Dean MacCannell this process represents 'a final freezing in ethnic imagery which is artificial and deterministic', the result of globalisation and consumerism.[38] The end point of this version of the story sees the boomerang swallowed by a commercialist popular culture, condemned to live out its days within the degrading genre of what anthropologist Nelson Graburn termed 'ethno-kitsch'.[39]

Sometimes, this story seems to ring profoundly true. In her critique of souvenir manufacturers in Canada, Valda Blundell asserted that mass-produced cultural expressions of First Nations and Inuit peoples perpetuated the idea that 'aboriginal peoples belong properly in the past along with the other heritage forms of the nation'.[40] Certainly, the version of Aboriginality often symbolised by the boomerang made for tourists has been 'primitive', natural, and spatially distant, bound to wide open spaces as opposed to urban environments, 'long ago and far away'.

And yet, the commercialisation of the manufacturer is not the same thing as the death of the manufacturer. Interpretations that assume so merely serve to perpetuate the myth that any cultural transmission from Aboriginal culture to a shared Australian culture is inherently inauthentic. Since the early nineteenth century, the development of the Indigenous artefacts market has brought many, many opportunities for income, agency, control, creativity and innovation to many different Indigenous groups in different times and places. Today, most non-Indigenous Australians, and indeed most tourists, encounter First Nations culture not through the people themselves, but through media, and various forms of cultural performance – as well as packaged and marketed symbols, often souvenirs. This means the messages embodied in popular national symbols such as the boomerang matter. How inclusive these messages are also matters. There is the danger that First Peoples can easily be constructed in their absence. But there is also the powerful opportunity for the boomerang as a symbol to represent not only its Indigenous origins, but also the complexities of Indigenous Australians' varied and creative lived realities today.

BILLY

Melissa Harper

Perhaps the most mundane Australian symbol is nothing more than a tin can – the unassuming billy. Used for cooking, carrying water and most especially for making tea, the billy, by the close of the nineteenth century, had become as natural, as widespread and as symbolic of bush life as the gum tree, the kangaroo and the wattle. It was cheap, light and versatile, ideally suited to the simplicity demanded by bush travel. But the elevation of the billy to the status of national symbol stemmed from more than its practicality. Australians attributed to it a far more potent range of meanings, investing it with human qualities such as reliability, hospitality and egalitarianism. And so the billy became a source of comfort and companionship; ultimately it became a mate.

In 1911 Edward S Sorenson gave romantic expression to the affection that the billy inspired:

> No utensil is so generally used in the bush as the billy-can; none
> is more widely distributed, none better known in Australia ...
> Shearers, miners, drovers, knockabouts, and even the poorest
> deadbeats on the track, carry it a-swing at their sides ... It is
> swung under wagons, bullock-drays, hawkers' vans ... The dainty
> housewife in town not infrequently sets it on her polished stove, and
> it often takes the place of the kettle in the cocky's home. Go into any

aboriginal camp in the bush, and you will see billy-cans there ...
All classes of people, whether city dwellers or backblockers, take it along with them when they go picnicking. There is scarcely a camp or hut in Australia without one, and some have a dozen.[1]

The billy became a necessity of life in the Australian bush – it was unimaginable without it – and that bush culture was increasingly coming to stand for an Australianness accepted throughout the continent. Sorenson attempted, perhaps too hard, to claim a universality for the billy in the bush and, unusually, sought to incorporate Aboriginal people into the nation it symbolised.

All nations have their origin myths which are often hotly contested. National symbols seem to have the same propensity for generating arguments about how they began and what they mean. The origins of the billy, both as an object and as a word, have attracted controversy

Family on a picnic, boiling a billy and toasting food over an open fire, c. 1910.
State Library Victoria

and these debates tell us a lot about the attachments people feel for their national symbols.

Historians, folklorists and others who are obsessed by such things agree that the billy established itself as an essential item of bush equipment during the 1850s gold rushes, but most find its origins a decade earlier and a few push it back even further.[2] Early bush travellers cooked in a frying pan or cast-iron pot, boiled water in a kettle or a quart pot, a lidless tin vessel with a side handle, and carried water in a canvas bag. By the 1840s, however, the billy had appeared. Tasmanian bushranger Martin Cash, incarcerated on Norfolk Island in 1846, later recalled that prisoners were each allowed 'a "billy" or tin kettle for the purpose of making tea'. Sarah Davenport, in a diary entry that recorded the departure of her husband and sons for Ballarat in about 1847, noted that they carried 'a tent ... and pick and spade and blankets billies and food'. In 1849, in what appears to be the first Australian use of the term in print, George B Wilkinson in *The Working Man's Handbook to South Australia* wrote of a shepherd in his hut preparing the evening meal and, 'singing near the wooden fire, is what is called the *billy*, or tea kettle'. However, as a forerunner of the great pavlova war, the *Dictionary of New Zealand English* gives a reference to J Heberley's unpublished autobiography of about 1839: 'boiled the Billy and made some tea out of Tawa bark'.[3] As with the cooee, the billy's convenience and versatility gave it early trans-Tasman appeal.

The billy did not immediately replace other cooking utensils but on the Victorian goldfields in the 1850s it certainly became more widely used. Miner John Rochfort felt it was such essential equipment that he 'needs must purchase 'a "billy"'' with the proceeds from the little gold he found on his first days on the diggings at Ballarat. He valued its versatility, describing the billy as a 'tin pot for boiling tea, coffee, meat, or anything you may have the luck to get'.[4] The billy was much lighter in weight than the alternatives, making it more practical for those who had to travel on foot. Its handle looped across the top, so it was far better suited than a quart pot for carrying, swinging and hanging over a fire. There was the further advantage in that while it was possible to buy one purpose-made, a makeshift billy could easily be fashioned from a used can and a piece of wire.

Origins

The most common suggestion as to its etymological origin, and one which adds weight to the billy's mid-century emergence, is that the word came from the French term *bouilli*, a beef soup popular on the goldfields and readily available with the recent development of canning technology. The empty tins or 'bouilli-cans' provided a suitable pot to boil water for tea. From the 1940s, with the upsurge of academic interest in Australian history and language, scholars enthusiastically joined the stoush. Philologist Sidney Baker dismissed the bouilli theory as 'academic nonsense' but his alternative explanation, that it derived from *billa*, a Wiradjuri word meaning creek or river and thus water, also had its detractors. Bill Ramson, editor of the *Australian National Dictionary*, argued that there was no evidence for such a derivation, preferring the explanation that the term came from the Scottish 'billypot' for cooking pot or 'bally' for milk pail which date back to the 1820s.[5]

The most intriguing possibility was Russel Ward's 1972 proposal that the term was a diminutive of William, named after King William IV who sat on the throne between 1830 and 1837. Ward cited a passage from an obscure account of life in 1820s Australia. In a bush house 'a royal George, *alias* a big kettle, for boiling' was slung over the fire to make tea. Once the damper was baked the pot was set on the floor and everyone scooped out a serve of the sweetened concoction with their pannikin. A royal George, suggested Ward, was named for King George (1820–30) and was quite possibly a large billy. With the accession of King William IV in 1830, he conjectured that 'what could be more natural than that a *royal* George should have become a *royal William*, hence a *William* and hence a *billy*'. It was an explanation that dated the use of the billy (if not the word) to a much earlier time than most others. Ward admitted his evidence was circumstantial; he did not provide any examples of royal William or even William being applied to a billy-like tin can.[6] His royal George may well have been an ordinary tea kettle or a large pot. Nevertheless, there is something rather appealing in the idea that British royalty, the centre of British power, pomp and prestige, might have provided the Australian name for a simple vessel for making tea.

Clearly, billy took its time to become entrenched in the vernacular. The use of italics or, just as often, inverted commas and the need to pair the term with a definition remained common practice into the 1870s, evidence that the billy was an aspect of Australian life that people needed to explain to the outside world. The billy was becoming more than just a utensil. The murky origins of the word – French, Aboriginal, English, Scottish or something else – only added to its mystique. Whatever its beginnings, by the late nineteenth century the billy became indelibly linked with Australia. Accounts of bush life almost invariably made mention of the billy. Every bushman, it seemed, carried one. Some carried more, nested one inside the other – a tea billy, a billy for cooking meat and perhaps a third for carrying water. It had been embraced as an Australian word, an Australian invention and an Australian symbol.

My mate billy

While the practical value of the billy to the bush traveller is obvious, it doesn't explain the fondness that Australians developed for their billies. Why should a tin can be put on a pedestal? Why should it grace the stove of the urban housewife and the wealthy squatter? The answers lie in its symbolism – in its evocation of a particular understanding of Australianness and a widespread desire to connect with it. The billy was democratic, used by men and women, rich and poor, black and white,

Advertisement for 'The Billy Tea', c. 1910.
Produced by James Inglis & Co. Tetley Group, TATA Consumer Products

workers and leisure-seekers, but it was its association with the bushman, and particularly with the swagman, that gave it national meaning.

In the upsurge of national sentiment that marked the last two decades of the nineteenth century, artists and writers identified the bush as the real Australia and the bushman as the real Australian. Colonial Australians from all walks of life imagined they could identify with the distinctive landscape and the life of independence and hardship it entailed. That life was said to have fostered a distinctive Australian character: practical, laconic, egalitarian. It was in this context that the billy could stand for the nation.

In the sketches of bush life that adorned the pages of illustrated newspapers such as the *Australasian Sketcher* and the *Bulletin*, in the stories and poems of Henry Lawson, Joseph Furphy, Barbara Baynton, Banjo Paterson and Edward Dyson, in the art of the Heidelberg School and in bush ballads and folk songs, somewhere there was nearly always a billy. Rarely did it take centrestage; more often it was simply there, an almost obligatory motif to establish the authenticity of the scene.

The swagman on the tramp was depicted carrying a billy in the hand or dangling it from the swag. When he stopped for a midday smoko or arrived for the evening camp, a fire was built, the billy filled with water and set to boil. Waiting for the billy to boil provided a moment for quiet reflection and rest. It was a precious moment. Frederick McCubbin captured its significance in 1888 when he painted a bushman resting on his side completely at ease in his surrounds and called it *While the Billy Boils*.

The sight of a boiling billy was also an invitation to the passing traveller – usually male – to throw down his swag, unpack his pannikin and share a mug of the hot brew. While some of the other accoutrements of the swagman, such as his swag and hat, also became objects of affection, only the billy symbolised the hospitality and sociability widely regarded as hallmarks of the Australian bush. The romance of the moment also drew on the hypnotic flames and companionable crackle of the campfire, which called up something deep in the human psyche. It was around the boiling billy that the great Australian yarn was spun. Henry Lawson wrote his short stories in the glow of that bush tradition and, when he published his first major collection in 1896, he too called it *While the Billy Boils*.

The ability to make a good brew was the sign of a good bushman (Fig. 26). Billy tea was strong and usually served black. Australians were con-vinced that billy tea was the best tea to drink but some brews were better than others. Connoisseurs debated when it was best to add the tea leaves, whether the tea benefited from a stir with a gum twig, how long it should sit and if it were necessary to swing the billy over the head to ensure the tea draw. There were also arguments over whether it was better to hang the billy over the fire on a pole held up by two forked sticks or to stand it on logs in the embers. The experienced bushman always filled his billy to the brim; he knew that if it were only half full the rim would soon burn off. Bushmen competed with one another as to who could boil the billy the fastest. The blacker a billy the more quickly it would boil.[7]

Though used by men and women, the billy, in myth, was masculine. Men (rather than women) took pride in the blackness of the billy not only because of its superior boiling qualities. They fetishised their billies. An old, blackened billy signalled the old hand as opposed to the new chum and that it was not spick and span spoke of the nonchalance that was supposed to define the Australian character. They also celebrated the improvised billy over the commercial product, taking it as a symbol of Australian ingenuity. With such qualities it is no surprise that it became the bushman's mate. Some of the more sentimental bush ballads of the twentieth century bordered on love poems to the billy. In 1912 James Lister Cuthbertson wrote 'To a billy' full of praise for a 'friend in all our tramping'. Edward Harrington also sang to his:

> Plain and sensible,
> Indispensable,
> Old black billy …
> I always find when the shadows fall
> My old black billy, the best mate of all.

Louis Esson's billy winked at him.[8]

While the boiling billy was usually a call to yarn and chat, in Henry Lawson's 1894 'Freedom on the wallaby', it was a call to arms:

> But Freedom's on the wallaby
> She'll knock the tyrants silly
> She's going to light another fire
> And boil another billy.
> We'll make the tyrants feel the sting
> Of those that they would throttle;
> They needn't say the fault is ours
> If blood should stain the wattle.

There was a precedent for the billy's rebellious spirit. The billies that Martin Cash remembered on Norfolk Island in 1846 had led to a mutiny. The prisoners had made their own cooking utensils and regarded them as their 'most cherished possessions'; when the authorities confiscated them, 500 men rebelled and four constables were killed.[9]

For Lawson the billy stood for the rebellion of workers against the bosses and so it symbolised the push for democracy and republicanism that marked late nineteenth-century Australian bush nationalism.[10] It was a theme he would return to in 1901 in 'The men who made Australia':

> Round the camp fire of the fencers by the furthest panel west,
> In the men's hut by the muddy billabong,
> On the Great North-Western Stock-routes where the drovers
>   never rest,
> They are sorting out the right things from the wrong.
> In the shearers' huts the slush lamp shows a haggard,
>   stern-faced man
> Preaching war against the Wool-King to his mates;
> And wherever go the billy, water-bag and frying-pan,
> They are drafting future histories of states!

Lawson was giving those conversations 'while the billy boiled' credit for the very creation of Australia as a nation.

The billy also symbolised the ambivalence that Australians felt towards the bush. As often as it provided comfort, it signalled the struggles that went hand-in-hand with bush life. It was hinted at in McCubbin's *The Pioneer* (1904), portraying a woman, downcast and chin in hand, while her husband tended the billy. McCubbin did a lot with the billy. In another major painting, *Down on his Luck* (1889), the hardship of the bush is writ large: the billy lies on its side, carelessly discarded. This evocative image of the overturned billy had been used before by Julian Ashton in *Lost! – A Sketch from Riverina* (1880). That even the billy could no longer provide the usual solace indicated the utter helplessness of an unfortunate bushman's predicament (Fig. 25). Edward Sorenson, who had a penchant for dying bushmen, saw in the billy 'the repository of the last words of many a perished swagman. Often it is found with the grim message scratched on the bottom, beside the dead owner.'[11]

Waltzing Matilda

The association between the billy and death found its clearest voice in Australia's quasi national anthem, 'Waltzing Matilda'. It is to the song that the billy owes much of its fame and conversely the song owes as much to the billy, or at least to billy tea. 'Waltzing Matilda', making the most of distinctively Australian words, tells of a swagman waiting for his billy to boil beside a billabong and singing to himself as he does so. A sheep strays into the scene and the swagman grabs it for his tucker. A squatter, presumably the sheep's owner, and three policemen descend on the hapless swagman, but rather than surrender he jumps into the billabong and drowns.

Here again origins, of both the lyrics and the music, have been the subject of heated debates, complicated by the fact that there are a number of versions of the song. The most commonly accepted account of its creation is that the lyrics were written in 1895 by Andrew 'Banjo' Paterson, by then well-known as a bush poet. On a visit to Queensland, he stayed at Dagworth Homestead, a sheep station north of Winton owned by the Macpherson family. One night, Christina Macpherson, the 30-year-old daughter of the station owner, played on the piano a tune that she had heard in Victoria. When Paterson asked if she knew the lyrics, she could not recall any and so he resolved to write some. Together they worked on the song, enabling Paterson to spend time with Macpherson, whom rumour has it he fancied. The lyrics were apparently inspired by a recent shearers' strike that had resulted in shearers burning down a number of woolsheds in the district, including one on the Macpherson's property. One of the suspected arsonists, Frenchy Hoffmeister, was later found dead at a nearby camp, though the swagman may have been based on a man who suicided by drowning in a waterhole near Dagworth.[12]

The song quickly became popular locally, and soldiers sang it in the Boer War, spreading it across state boundaries when they returned home. Paterson's version introduced the billy in the first verse – 'and he sang as he looked at his old billy boiling' – but this was the only mention. In the chorus he opted for the far less romantic waterbag. Curiously, given the song's popular appeal within his lifetime, Paterson was reluctant to end the debate about its origins and he did not publish 'Waltzing Matilda' in any of his collected verse until 1917.[13]

The version of 'Waltzing Matilda' that was to become the standard had its origins as an advertising ploy for Billy Tea. James Inglis and Co. imported Billy Tea from 1887, and by 1893 sold over 600,000 pounds (over 270 tonnes) of it each year.[14] From the 1890s the packet showed a swagman drinking his billy tea and conversing with a kangaroo carrying a swag and billy. Inglis had heard the song and in about 1902 he acquired the lyrics, though whether he was given them by Paterson or bought them from Paterson's publisher, Angus and Robertson, is not clear. Inglis planned to give away the sheet music with each packet of tea sold, but he wanted the lyrics to be rejigged. Given the story associated tea with death, it was not necessarily an obvious choice for a beverage marketed as a refreshing and uplifting brew. The task of commercialising the song fell to Marie Cowan, the wife of Inglis's manager. Cowan added the word jolly to the opening line and injected billy into the chorus, ensuring its repetition and its association with the product. She also capitalised the B and added inverted commas:

> And he sang as he watched and waited till his 'Billy' boiled,
> You'll come a-waltzing Matilda with me.

On the Wallaby Track, c. 1880–1901.
Tyrrell collection, National Library of Australia

The sheet music provided with the tea acknowledged Paterson as author and Cowan as the arranger of the music.[15] The song, the tea and the billy came together to firmly secure the popularity of all three.

The symbolic power of the billy then lies in the way it embodied the mythology of the bushman – like him the billy was dependable, resourceful, practical and egalitarian, even anti-authoritarian. The connection between these qualities and a widely accepted version of Australianness meant that it was commercially worthwhile for any business to associate itself with bush values.

Billy nostalgia

Drinking commercial Billy Tea provided a way for city-dwellers to imbibe a bush experience. But urban picnickers had long boiled the billy and perhaps were the most enthusiastic in engaging in its rituals, inhaling the gum smoke and swinging the billy dangerously. In the late nineteenth century it became as essential to the accoutrements of the bushwalker as it was for the swagman. Again it had its practical uses, but for early bushwalkers, many of them upper middle class gentlemen who got especially excited if mistaken for a genuine bushie, using the billy was a self-conscious attempt to give their own experience of the bush some authenticity. Australia's first bushwalking guidebook, published in 1906, was titled *With Swag and Billy*, and its author Henry Tompkins celebrated the billy as the embodiment of Australian egalitarianism, the 'shrine at which all colours and creeds pay homage'.[16]

Evenings spent around the campfire with a mug of billy tea continued to be a valued part of bushwalking and camping culture well into the twentieth century. However, by the 1980s the banal convenience of the teabag outweighed the romance of billy tea. More importantly the use of fire, particularly in national parks, was increasingly frowned upon and in many cases outlawed, resulting in a decline in the use of the billy. In 2000 one Sydney bushwalker complained that such legislation was a denial of an 'inalienable right to boil a billy and enjoy a campfire, a Cherished Birthright of all campers and picnickers across the land, for many generations'. Many national park managers do struggle to reconcile the damage and danger of fire with a recognition that attachment to the campfire (and billy) is an important cultural value for campers.[17]

The billy continues to be used in outback Australia. But as with many Australian symbols it also lives on through its commercial uses. Billy Tea, its packaging harking back to the original bushman and kangaroo, is still available in supermarkets. A small number of businesses, such as Billy Tea Safaris and Billys 'R' Us, seek to capitalise on the word's bush credentials by adopting it in their name. Tourist ventures in outback locations serve billy tea, and country shows hold billy-boiling competitions as a means of tapping into Australia's bush heritage. Its symbolic power has increasingly come to lie in its nostalgia for a bygone Australia. Contemporary bushwalkers are more likely to carry a portable espresso maker than a billy. For younger Australians in the twenty-first century, as much as for an international audience in the nineteenth, reference to the billy probably needs to be followed with a definition.

MISS AUSTRALIA

Marilyn Lake and Penny Russell

She made an early appearance in 1864, a timid young woman with soulful eyes gazing towards a prosperous future. Firmly identified by the rays of the rising sun and the stars of the Southern Cross at her back, she was flanked by images of a prosperous and civilised community. Australia, as the caption to the *Sydney Punch* cartoon made clear, was turning her back on her convict past, and seeking a new and gentler image.[1] It was a little surprising, in what was fast emerging as a 'man's country', that the new symbol should be a young woman.

In the twentieth century, the label 'Miss Australia' would become firmly associated with glamorous young women who represented the nation only in the limited context of beauty contests. But in the late nineteenth century, the tag applied to a cluster of graphic images of classically draped or fashionably dressed women who stood in as symbols of 'Australia' in allegorical paintings or political cartoons. We are concerned with this earlier allegorical symbol of nation here. It was not a symbol of local origin, like the boomerang or the kangaroo. Since the eighteenth century, similar young women embodying civic virtues such as justice, liberty or prosperity had become ubiquitous across Europe and the Americas. These figures were loosely derived from representations of Athena (Minerva to the Romans), daughter of Zeus and goddess of war and wisdom.[2] Some were armed and armoured, warlike and inviolable; others wore simple tunics or classical draperies, seemingly sufficiently protected by their virtue. The idea of Britannia, first used to represent the Roman conquest of Britain, was reinvented in the seventeenth century in patriotic mode and by the nineteenth century she was a popular way of depicting Britain's command of the seas. America had an equivalent emblem in Columbia. In France, Marianne performed more complex work, standing sometimes for Liberty, sometimes for the Republic, and only late in the century representing France itself.[3] Whatever her name, form or accoutrements, the warrior woman watched over the fields of battle and upheld the principles of civic righteousness for her chosen nation.[4]

In nineteenth-century Australian images, the female figure usually represented a colony rather than the nation. But she often embodied an explicitly 'Australian' spirit in a message intended for a British audience. When an unhappy Irishman put a bullet into Queen Victoria's son at a harbourside picnic in Sydney in 1868, the honour of the colony was at stake. Cartoonist Montagu Scott was swift to present New South Wales as 'Australia Vindex'. Her face distorted with anger and pain, she turned with vengeful fury upon the Fenian assassin, who had just stabbed her in the back. Dwarfing him with her magnificent, terrible height, she seized him around the throat with her left hand, while her right grasped the noose, ready to inflict summary justice.[5]

From the 1870s, images of the different colonies as young women proliferated, along with feminine figures representing more abstract qualities and virtues. As politicians began to make moves towards Federation, there was a growing need to represent the abstract idea of the prospective nation in visual form – not only in official and commemorative art and ephemera, but also in the rich satirical world of political cartoons. And, as Margaret Anderson has commented, 'the requisite iconography was already in place'.[6] The young woman was already recognised as a symbol of nation throughout the Western world, and she could better represent dignity and virtue than some of the alternatives, such as the kangaroo. She was also an appropriate object of desire for male nation-builders. By the 1890s Australia was, as John Hirst has noted, 'always imagined as female ... young, pure, virginal'.[7] He might have added, 'fair and white'.[8]

Miss Australia is born

Whiteness was central to the depiction of this conventional figure, and in specific contexts served to assert the superiority of Australia over other parts of Britain's Empire. In a coloured lithograph designed to accompany a commemorative medal at the *Colonial and Indian Exhibition* of 1898, a striking assemblage of symbolism shows Australia among those paying homage to Britannia.[9] India wears a sari; New Zealand is depicted as a bare-chested Māori man; Canada – of ambiguous gender – sports some unlikely robes and an 'Indian' feathered headdress. Australia alone bears none of the physical attributes of her Indigenous population, appearing instead in a simple cream-coloured tunic, the hem emblazoned with a kangaroo. Her long gold-brown hair is in striking contrast to the black locks of her three companions. Australia and Canada dominate the centre, and Australia alone seems directly comparable to the classical figure of Britannia. She holds a sword, point down, at her side; her stance, half turned away from Britannia, is not especially submissive. Here the representation of Australia as a woman – and, importantly, a white woman – seems to emphasise that she, of all the colonies, is most like the mother figure, Britannia: and, perhaps, most likely to become independent.

At the crucial moment of nation-making in 1901, images of a beautiful young woman – in flowing white gown, and usually unarmed, in direct contrast to the ever-present helmeted, armoured figure of Britannia – decorated the invitations and programs for the federal celebrations.[10] An official invitation to the opening of parliament placed the two women in a medieval rather than a classical setting. Showing Australia on a white charger, bowing her head before an imposing Britannia, the image drew explicitly on the commemorative poem, 'The Young Queen', which the Empire's poet Rudyard Kipling had written to celebrate the new Commonwealth. In a direct reference to Australia's contribution to the South African War, the 'Young Queen' arrived 'bright-eyed out of the battle' to be crowned.[11] The overtly militarist theme and the reference to Australia's emergence as a nation through bloodshed in war seemed to claim nation-making as a manly accomplishment, at odds with the womanly representation. But Kipling's poem added a further dimension. Although the 'Young Queen' was purely figurative, the 'Old Queen' evoked Britain's actual female ruler. A complex interplay of imagery and reference linked an allegorical figure of nation with the figure of Queen Victoria, the most powerful woman in the world. Kipling could thus celebrate 'feminine' qualities of love, humility and judgement at the same time as he sang the praises of Australia's military courage. The Old Queen, asked for her blessing, repeated the refrain 'we be women together': and as 'women together', Kipling asserted, both queens knew the vanity of 'lust' for dominion, and the value of the 'people's love'.[12] The embodiment of Australia in female form opened up a range of possibilities for gendered representation: possibilities that political cartoonists, in particular, would readily exploit. In their hands, a woman might be a symbol but she was also, always, a woman.

The personification of Australia as a woman did not of course have anything to do with women's status in the new Commonwealth of Australia. Although white women were given political rights at the federal level in 1902, the first female politicians were not elected to the Australian Parliament until 1943. In Australia, as elsewhere, the female figure worked as an abstract symbol in the public domain precisely because real women were excluded from politics and other formal power structures. Indeed, in 1901 Australia declared itself to the world as a white man's country; in 1908 the self-consciously nationalist *Bulletin* formally adopted the motto: 'Australia for the white man'. Real politicians were always men. Contemporary cartoons often depicted them in manly roles: for example, the tall, bearded, Alfred Deakin attempting to keep coloured immigrants at bay – although Prime Minister Edmund Barton was sometimes depicted as a fussy old woman.

In *The Sentimental Nation*, John Hirst wrote of the federal fathers as men who became 'passionate for the nation' and he quotes Federation poetry that depicts Australian nation-builders as seducers of a serenely inviolate Australia, set by God to sleep in 'summer seas':

He wrought her perfect, in a happy clime,
And held her worthiest, and bade her wait
Serene on her lone couch inviolate
The heightened manhood of a later time.[13]

As Hirst notes, the sexual theme is explicit. He thus gives us an important clue to one imperative of imagining Australia as a young woman; she was a fantasy of male political desire, an object to be possessed.

Staff at the *Bulletin* – more at home in the company of men – were less comfortable than the Federation poets with the idea of Australia as a woman. The *Bulletin*'s chief political cartoonist from 1883 until 1913, Livingston Hopkins, better known as 'Hop', explained in his autobiography that graphic artists generally found a 'mythical figure, usually of the gentler sex' a useful way to personify the 'national spirit', especially in cartoons of a 'prim allegorical character'. But when they wished to depict 'the more rugged phases of national life', they sought a masculine alternative that could 'stand more knocking about' – John Bull rather than Britannia, for example. Minerva was 'difficult to acclimatize' to the masculine environment of Australia. Casting about 'for a myth that was willing to make itself generally useful', Hop found one at last in the 'Little Boy at Manly', who represented, he thought, a 'more robust male impersonation'.[14] Although the Little Boy was popular at the *Bulletin* and variants were used elsewhere, he did not altogether displace Minerva as a national symbol. Cartoonists, Margaret

The Birth of the Commonwealth by George Dancey published in the *Melbourne Punch Annual*, 1901.

State Library Victoria

Anderson suggests, used the image they thought most appropriate to their purpose: an abstract feminine figure representing 'high ideals, an appeal to conscience or dignity'; or a little boy portraying 'cheekiness, or more boisterous behaviour'.[15]

High ideals were certainly apparent when George Dancey represented 'The Birth of the Commonwealth' in allegorical form, glorious against a backdrop of the rising sun, and product of a strange inversion: the 'child' of the 'six proud states' had become 'the mother of them all!'.[16] Such images linked a symbolically feminine Australia with dignity, beauty, fertility and maternalism. But a female figure might also be used in cartoons and sketches to represent more dubious feminine qualities. Australia was not always the goddess, robed, armoured and inviolate. She frequently appeared in modern attire, endowed with characteristics associated with contemporary women. As images of 'Miss Australia' and her precursors, the young female colonies, proliferated through multiple visual and satirical forms, she began to take on something of the reputation of the 'Australian Girl', plucky, healthy and independent. She was also placed in familiar relationships

– of sibling rivalry, filial deference or marital dispute, for example – which served as metaphors for the perceived relations between colonies, between colony and Empire, or between nations.

Portraying the colonies as 'girls of the period' blurred the ground between allegorical representation and social commentary, and created opportunities for satires on gender as well as on national and international relations. Thus New South Wales could appear as a sulky young woman who refused to join a game 'started by that minx, Victoria';[17] while the federated Commonwealth might be the object of rivalrous desire among lascivious politicians,[18] a beautiful debutante musing on the 'ugly little girl' she had once been,[19] or an extravagant spouse, wasting the country's wealth in a wild spending spree.[20] One aspect of these cartoons clear to us today is their apparent anxieties about female power, extravagance or vanity. They bore close resemblance to other images which derided women's incursions into the public sphere, mocked their transition to modernity or rebuked their campaigns for citizenship.[21] But it is also possible to see a sense of enthusiasm for the youth, style, modernity and fertile potential of the white Australian girl.[22]

Growing up

When Australia entered into international relations, however, the gendered symbolism took on further disturbing implications, for in this robust context nation-states were usually represented in masculine form. John Bull replaced Britannia; Uncle Sam stepped in for Columbia (the female representation of the United States of America); Germany, Russia, Japan and China most often appeared as male figures.[23] It must have been galling to 'Hop' that in the international scene of political cartooning, Australia repeatedly appeared as a young woman, and one in continuing need of chivalric protection. The portrayals of Australia in American and Australian cartoons during the visit of the Great White

Fleet in 1908 highlight the ways in which gender was used to encode power relations. The representation of Australia as a young woman pointed to Australia's continuing colonial condition and explains the political imperative that gripped leaders such as Prime Minister Alfred Deakin to assert Australia's manhood.

The United States fleet arrived in Sydney in August 1908, detoured south by President Theodore Roosevelt in response to a personal invitation from Deakin.[24] The welcome offered to the Americans was enthusiastic, even ecstatic. The people of Sydney and Melbourne went mad in anticipation, arranging all sorts of extravagant entertainments and invitations for the visiting officers and their crew. Deakin bade the sailors – all men, of course – thrice welcome: 'as guests … as the honoured representatives of a mighty nation [and as] blood relations'.[25] He hoped the future would see a 'perpetual concord of brotherhood' between the Commonwealth and the republic, imagining a transnational fraternity of white men as an alternative both to the hierarchical multiracial Empire and the cosmopolitan unity of mankind. In toasting the Great White Fleet's commander, the New South Wales premier described the visit 'as a further step towards the realisation of the common brotherhood of the English speaking races'. When Rear Admiral Sperry rose to reply – speaking, he said, 'as a white man to white men, and, I may add, to "very white men"' – he was met with loud cheers and a standing ovation.[26]

The occasion called forth many anxious affirmations of the mutual manhood of the Australian Commonwealth and the American republic. 'We are more than cousins', declared the Melbourne *Age*. 'We are brethren in thought, in speech, in aspiration'.[27] There was no room, insisted the paper just a few days later:

> for the weak craven spirit that might welcome the great white power merely as an Australian protection. One note seemed to be clear and strong and determined – it was the note of Australia's deep manly trust in herself; and was an augury perhaps that in the near future

> Australia herself will command her encircling seas even as America now controls the Western Pacific.[28]

The will to masculine power was clear, but the gender confusion registered by 'Australia's deep manly trust in herself' suggested a less certain, more ambiguous identity, indeed one befitting a nation-state that was self-governing, but not yet independent; federated, but still subject to the authority of the Mother Country. Australian politicians and publicists imagined dealing with the Americans 'man to man' and fondly invoked the 'ties of brotherhood'. Cartoonists were not so sure. The *Bulletin* could show a kangaroo – masculine-looking but with a convenient pouch to hold a bottle or two – roistering with the American eagle against a backdrop of the two flags, above the caption: 'What a time we are having'.[29] But to many, Australia was better understood as a young woman – the symbolic equivalent of the real young women who were courting American sailors in the streets of Melbourne and Sydney, flattered by the sudden attention of Uncle Sam. One American cartoon depicted 'Miss Australia' contemplating the impending visit, exclaiming: 'I never was so flustered in my life! I'll have to primp up for the occasion'. Another featured the avuncular gentleman in stars and stripes declaring to Miss Australia and Miss New Zealand: 'You are two of the nicest girls I have ever met'.[30] Miss Australia laid herself out to attract and please, hoping to capture the friendly interest and chivalric protection of the great republic. In newspaper cartoons, Uncle Sam dealt with Japan, Britain and Germany man to man, but saw the diminutive natives of Cuba, Hawaii and the Philippines, and those two attractive young women down under, as needing masculine protection.[31]

Another *Bulletin* cartoon used the Little Boy at Manly to register the power relations in generational terms. Uncle Sam farewells the lad, saying: 'Well, goodbye, sonny, you've done me proud: it's been one continual Fourth of July. I hope you'll return my visit before long, and bring your fleet with you.'[32] The connection between the Fourth of July and American naval power was clear. Australia still lacked manly independence; without a navy, Australians were powerless to defend themselves. But the little boy, unlike Miss Australia, had the potential to grow into manhood: with a fleet of great battleships such as those of the United States, Australia might at last dispense with its feminine need for protection and assert its national manhood. Without the power of self-defence, Australians would always be girls – or at best little boys – in the world of international affairs.

In the shifting landscape of international relations and political authority, gender mattered.[33] Powerful nations were male, weak ones were female. Men were preoccupied with asserting manhood, for the nation as for themselves. That Australia could be represented as a young woman among the world forces suggested she lacked the masculine accoutrements of international power, especially 'the arm of offensive power', a navy.[34] Deakin later said he wanted the United States navy to be an object lesson, precipitating 'a proclamation of Australian manhood, teaching our eyes to see and our feet to stand'. It was time for Australians to stand up like real men.

In this context, the depiction of Australia as a flustered young woman symbolised Australia's continuing colonial condition and spoke to Australians' anxieties about their place in the world. As 'daughters of empire', how could Australia and New Zealand be taken seriously as 'sons of Vikings'? In 1909, the Australian Government began building its own navy, that modern symbol of international power,[35] but the quest for the elusive condition of manhood persisted (Fig. 27). Just five years later, Australia followed Britain into World War I, Australia needing to prove 'her' virility still.

Coming of age?

The popularity of the young woman as a national symbol declined after the war. Examples survived into the 1930s, but the trend of representing the nation in the person of a young woman was on the wane across

Crowning of Maxine Morgan as Miss Australia with the other state finalists, *Herald & Weekly Times*, 1953.

State Library of Victoria

the Western world. Between the wars, and with increasing fanfare after World War II, Miss Australia transmuted from a symbolic to a corporeal figure, a beauty queen who in a different way also represented an ideal national 'type' – along with a shifting cluster of civic virtues.[36] As 'Miss Australia' became indelibly associated with a beauty contest, her earlier life as an allegorical and political symbol was largely forgotten (Fig. 28).

There were other reasons for her disappearance. It is tempting to attribute it to her displacement by the figure of the Anzac, a more comforting symbol of the virile nation in the war-ridden twentieth century. But paradoxically it may owe something, too, to women's increased participation in citizenship. As women became more visible, as voters, lobbyists and parliamentary candidates, indeed as they became more active cultural producers themselves, the use of a feminine figure to represent the nation became disconcerting, threatening even: too close to home.

Instead, gendered political imagery began to explicitly satirise actual women politicians. In the 1980s, Victorian premier Joan Kirner and Senator Cheryl Kernot were depicted in cartoons that reflect distinct unease about the presence of women in politics. Represented as either too feminine or not feminine enough, they were made to appear incongruous – symbolically out of place in the masculine domain of national politics.[37] The new millennium saw an early surge in the number and range of women representatives in the national parliament: in 2008 Australia was represented on the national and international stage by the first female governor-general, Quentin Bryce; in 2010 Julia Gillard became the first female prime minister. But the politics of gender took an ugly turn when some prominent men reacted with hostility and misogyny to real women wielding real power (Fig. 29). Our female prime minister was portrayed as not winsome but a 'witch'.[38]

As a national symbol, Miss Australia did not represent an intrinsic national quality. Formal graphic artists and cartoonists alike exploited the multiple possibilities of her female form, which proved a fertile site for the production of alternative meanings. Whether she appeared as inviolable Minerva, strong, pure, wise and warlike, or foolish girl, risking the future of the nation on an impulse, Miss Australia could be made to represent either the achievements or the failures of nation-making. As daughter, friend, mother, wife, lover, the allegorical female figure could play numerous roles. But in every guise, she represented feminine qualities and racialised virtues that have little place in modern Australia. Embodied representatives of nation – whether beauty queens or political figures – today more readily reflect the growing diversity of what it means to be Australian. While the women who now represent Australia in parliament or on the world stage still find themselves converted into contentious symbols of power and nation, the symbolic resonance of 'Miss Australia' has faded into obscurity.

FLAG

Elizabeth Kwan

In 2015, a number of far-right groups, including the anti-Muslim 'Party of Freedom', sought to hold a 'memorial' for the tenth anniversary of the Cronulla riots. Despite a court order, initiated by local councils, the police and Muslim community leaders, that any rallies not go ahead on the grounds they would stir up 'racial hatred', about 40 people gathered around a 'barbecue', with a (symbolic) spit-roasted pig, in the Cronulla sand dunes. National flags were prominent, as they had been during the original riots, the most obvious indication that this was a right-wing rally. It is ironic that, such are the shifting meanings attached to the symbol of the flag, had such a demonstration taken place in the 1920s, with those flags equally prominent, many would have considered the participants to be subversively left-wing.[1]

The flag is the chief national symbol for Australia and its people. Unlike the Australian coat of arms, the symbol of the Australian Government, which limits its use, the flag can be used by anyone. However, such availability widens the disputes about its symbolism. These disputes, especially about the changing attitude to Britain and its flag, are the focus of this chapter.

According to vexillologists – flag experts – the two Australian elements, the Commonwealth Star and the Southern Cross, are subordinate to the third element, the national flag of Britain, commonly

Battles around the flag and who and what it represents continue.
© Fiona Katauskas, *originally published in* The Chaser, 2006

known as the Union Jack, which has the place of honour in the Australian flag's canton. From 1967 a series of Morgan Polls found increasing numbers of Australians wanted a new flag; by 1998 the figure reached 52 per cent. Some believed that the British national flag in the canton indicated inferior colonial status; others that it represented the British core of the Australian nation. Since 1981 Ausflag, a non-profit company established by marketing consultant, Harold Scruby and others, has promoted design competitions to find an Australian alternative, while from 1983 the Australian National Flag Association (ANFA), led by its national spokesman, John Vaughan, flag designer and businessman, and supported by the RSL (NSW), has opposed change.

The misinformation and mythmaking surrounding the flag intensified with politicisation of the debate from the early 1980s. By 2001, when Australians celebrated the centenary of Federation, ANFA was quick to claim not just the flag's centenary, which was true, but also the flag's centenary as the national flag, which was not true.[2] In 1901 the Union Jack, not an Australian flag, had the place of honour in the celebrations, as it did at the Australian Commonwealth Jubilee in 1951. Although Australian blue and red ensigns were also flown, the Union Jack was still the national flag, taking precedence on the viewer's left, as protocol demanded.

The Australian blue ensign did not replace the Union Jack as the national flag until Queen Elizabeth II gave her assent to the Flags Bill in Canberra on 14 February 1954. Introducing the Bill to parliament on 20 November 1953, prime minister Robert Menzies concealed the change in national flags it heralded, assuring parliament it would make 'no change', when, in effect, the Bill reversed the order of precedence, from Union Jack to 'the Australian national flag'.[3]

Like prime ministers before and after him, Menzies struggled with a problem that has bothered Australian governments since Federation: how to manage a national symbol that is meant to unify the nation but in reality exposes divisions within it. From the early 1980s governments experienced a further problem: how to balance the growing demand for a new national flag against increasingly vociferous support for the old one. These problems remind us that the flag has always invited controversy, raising fundamental questions about the relationship between Australian and British nationalities.

Running up the flag

At its inauguration in January 1901, the Australian Commonwealth did not have an Australian national flag, though many Australians assumed it would be the Federation flag, a British white ensign with a blue cross throughout bearing five white stars. This popular unofficial shipping flag, originating in the 1820s, became the flag of the Federation campaign in the 1890s, with the motto 'One people, one destiny, one flag'. In 1901 it featured on invitation cards for the celebrations and in the streets. A few of the flags even appeared in schools, though they were overwhelmingly outnumbered by Union Jacks donated by Sir Frederick Sargood, or bought by schools at his suggestion. The prominent English-born Victorian MP arranged for public schools to participate in a telegraphically coordinated raising of their Union Jacks on 14 May 1901, five days after the opening of the new Commonwealth parliament's first session in the Melbourne Exhibition Building. He hoped that Australians, now federated, would still love 'the old mother country', the British Empire and its flag. His generosity could also be seen as an astute marketing exercise for his wholesale soft-goods business. Once in schools, the Union Jack became the focus of citizenship education.[4]

The British Government required the new Commonwealth Government to suggest a distinctive badge in a design for two shipping ensigns, blue for official and naval ships, and red for merchant ships. By the opening of the first parliament in May 1901, Edmund Barton's Protectionist government, unable to agree on a badge, had launched a public competition to settle the issue. Out of some 30,000 entries (Fig. 30), marine and naval judges chose a similar design entered by five separate entrants who shared the £200 prize. It featured the Southern Cross constellation – used in Victoria's ensigns and that of the Australasian Anti-Transportation League of 1851 – and also the Commonwealth Star, whose points represented the six federating states. Though not prescribed in the competition brief, the judges, familiar with British flag conventions, required the Union Jack in the canton of the ensigns. These were British flags.[5]

With minor modification to the stars, the ensigns were gazetted in February 1903. Five years later their Commonwealth Star gained a seventh point to represent Australian territories, matching the star in the coat of arms crest. In flag terms, the ensigns indicated British sovereignty. The Union Jack remained Australia's national flag – the symbol of Australians' British sentiment as well as nationality. The secretary of the Department of Defence, the source of flag expertise, determined that 'the Union Jack is not superseded in any way by the Commonwealth ensign'.[6]

Early governments were unhappy about the chosen design and uncertain about the blue ensign's use, especially in relation to the Union Jack. Barton was clearly disappointed in the choice, having persuaded the Australasian Federation League in the 1890s to adopt and promote the Federation flag as the flag for the new Commonwealth. Chris Watson's Labor government in 1904 was also dissatisfied, wanting a design 'more distinctive', more 'indicative of Australian unity'.[7]

The blue ensign began to gain greater acceptance after its strongest advocate, Richard Crouch from Victoria, the youngest member in the House of Representatives, persuaded the House in 1904 to accept his motion 'that … the Australian flag … should be flown upon all forts, vessels, saluting places, and public buildings of the Commonwealth upon all occasions when flags are used'. But cost and uncertainty delayed its implementation. In 1903 Barton had agreed to local naval forces using the blue ensign; in 1908 Alfred Deakin extended its use to forts coinciding with the visit of America's Great White Fleet, signalling Australia's determination to take greater responsibility for its defence.[8]

Three years later, Andrew Fisher's Labor government, urged on by the patriotic Australian Natives Association (ANA), made the blue ensign the saluting flag for all military parades and reviews.[9] But it found that the presence of vice-regal representatives still required the Union Jack – a sharp reminder that the Union Jack remained the national flag. Empire Day in Australian schools from 1905 reinforced that flag's standing. Much delayed legislation requiring merchant ships to fly the red ensign had a similar message. The *Navigation Act 1920*, which took effect in 1922, provided a system for registering Australian ships as British ships along the lines of imperial legislation.

Arguing about precedence

Clarifying the relationship between the two Australian ensigns and the Union Jack on land became more pressing as World War I intensified public interest in flags and debates about loyalty. All three flags featured in recruiting campaigns. Pride in the achievements of Australians at Gallipoli and the growing popularity of Australian ensigns prompted questions about the blue ensign: no longer simply a shipping flag, should it be for Commonwealth Government use alone? Should it have precedence when displayed with the Union Jack? Governments were reluctant to answer these questions because of the divisive impact of controversies during and immediately after the war. Some groups used the Union Jack to accuse others of disloyalty to the Empire, but advocates of the 'Australian' ensign ranged from Irish–Australians to middle-class patriotic associations such as the ANA.

In 1920 Irish-born Dr Daniel Mannix, Catholic Archbishop of Melbourne, chose Australian ensigns instead of the Union Jack to head Melbourne's St Patrick's Day. With a guard of honour of Australian Victoria Cross winners on white chargers, Mannix led an extraordinary procession of several thousand returned servicemen, most in uniform and a few hundred on horses, as well as the traditional Catholic schools and societies. It was coded support for Irish independence against Britain in the midst of the bitter Anglo–Irish war. Undaunted by Protestant loyalists' professed outrage, Mannix continued to use flags to push the Australian–British divide. Why, he asked, must Australian children on Anzac Day salute 'some other flag' than 'the flag of the Australian nation?' During the wartime conscription campaigns, when loyalty to Britain became a key issue, Mannix had been the most outspoken advocate of the slogan 'Australia first and the Empire second' in arguing against conscription. Mindful of this background, Victoria's director of education stressed that teachers were free to use either the Union Jack or an Australian flag, concerned that proscribing the latter 'might prove a welcome reinforcement to propaganda of disloyalists'.[10]

In Sydney the Australian Labor Party's preference for the red ensign encouraged the Nationalist Party to champion the Union Jack when appealing to voters, especially returned soldiers. In emphasising Labor's links to Irish republicanism and international communism, the Nationalists and their allies, the RSL and other conservative groups, saw an Australian ensign as a disloyal symbol, unless accompanied by the national flag, the Union Jack.

While politicians played politics with flags, public servants in the Prime Minister's Department responsible for flag protocol struggled to answer the public's questions. Grudging Commonwealth approval came in 1924 for state governments, but not state schools, to use its blue ensign for patriotic purposes. Private businesses and individuals wanting to use an Australian flag had to use the red ensign. For universal use there was the Union Jack, which the Commonwealth made clear was the national flag: 'It should never be flown in a position inferior to any other flag.'[11] When the Duke of York opened Australia's Parliament House in Canberra in May 1927, Union Jacks, not surprisingly, took precedence over Australian ensigns.

Victoria took the lead in the push for a national flag. The Country Party government, supported by Labor and influenced by the ANA, was keen to see the blue ensign used in state schools as the national flag. Early in 1939, the premier, Albert Dunstan, pressed the Menzies federal government to end restrictions on the blue ensign's use. Seeking advice from the Canadians, the Commonwealth learned that the Union Jack continued to fly from government buildings in Canada, but that from 1924 the red ensign, Canada's de facto national flag, was permitted to fly from Canadian government buildings abroad. Menzies, cautious in the midst of World War II but forced to act by Victorian legislation, removed restrictions on people's use of the blue ensign in 1941, rather than having an Australian national flag proclaimed. Still unresolved was the question of precedence: which flag was the national flag? The ANA's question to John Curtin, Labor prime minister, in 1943 underlined the problem: why did the Union Jack, not the Australian flag, drape the coffins of members of the Australian forces, both in Australia and overseas? The considered response came: the use of the Union Jack was 'a time-honoured custom', but next-of-kin requests for an Australian flag alone or with the Union Jack should be met 'without question'. Wary of Labor being branded anti-British, Curtin was mindful of Australians' British identity in his use of the Australian flag.[12]

After the war, both Canadian and Australian governments considered the matter of a national flag. The Canadian Government, as an interim measure in 1945, permitted its red ensign to fly from its buildings. In Australia the Labor government's committee established in 1949 to consider a range of flag matters wondered whether an ensign could be a national flag, since it carried another country's flag in its canton. A briefing paper was adamant: the ensign's design was 'typically colonial'; the Union Jack was 'an anachronism' in 'a truly Australian flag'.[13] But the committee recommended the blue ensign as the national flag on the basis of the earlier decisions of 1911 and 1941. Menzies' new government approved this recommendation in December 1950, following its acceptance of another Labor proposal: the presentation of an Australian flag to every school to mark the jubilee of Federation – and to familiarise Australians with their blue ensign. Fifty years after the Boer War, when Sir Frederick Sargood had placed Union Jacks in Australian schools to remind children that they were British, the federal government, in the midst of the Korean War, provided an Australian alternative to teach children to be Australian. With a large post-war immigration program and the negotiation of a defence treaty with the United States, Australia's place in the world was changing.

Menzies was well aware of the sensitivity required in handling the transition in national flags wrapped up so secretly in his Flags Bill of 1953. For generations of Australians, giving precedence to the Union Jack had seemed obligatory, especially for many from an English Protestant background who invested much emotion in the symbol. By designating the blue ensign as the *Australian* national flag, Menzies

Queen Elizabeth II and Prince Philip on the steps of Federal Parliament House, Canberra, 1954. For the first time the Australian national flag took precedence over the Union Jack.

National Library of Australia

allowed Australians to continue to think of the Union Jack as the national flag, in the same way that they accepted 'God Save the Queen' as the national anthem. Further, he made the point that the 'common practice in Australia' of displaying the Union Jack and the Australian national flag together would continue. There was not a word about the major change the Bill introduced: that the Australian blue ensign, now designated the Australian National Flag, must take precedence over all other national flags, including the Union Jack, when flown together in Australia.[14] Menzies then set aside the Bill for the Queen's assent when she visited Australia early in 1954. By the time she arrived at Parliament House to open the session, the day after she had signed the Bill, the flags had changed positions.

So subtle was the change in precedence from Union Jack to Australian national flag in 1954 that Australians took some 30 years to complete that transition. Only from 1964 did the Australian flag, once flown with the Union Jack only on special days, fly alone each day above the entrance to Parliament House, as well as from government buildings. That many Australians still treated the Union Jack as their national flag exasperated Arthur Smout, a stalwart campaigner for the Australian flag from 1968 to 1982 through several editions of his *Flag Book: Australia*. His claim in 1968, that the flag of the United Kingdom had 'no more significance in Australia than … any other national flag' denied the power of the Union Jack to unite and divide sentiment in Australian politics.[15] But by 1982 most Australians had come to regard the blue ensign as their national flag, with both major political parties using it as part of their logos.

Significantly, neither Menzies' government nor those of his successors described or explained the change of national flag that had taken place. The booklets they produced for schools and the general public encouraged readers to think that the blue ensign had been the national flag since 1901. That the Union Jack was the national flag until 1954 was ignored, as was the role of the red ensign as the people's flag. By 1977 the booklets' writers assumed that Australians knew they had the right to fly the Australian national flag and to give it precedence in displays with the Union Jack.

Changing the flag

In 1964, the Canadian parliament voted for a new national flag, its maple leaf a unifying symbol of hope for Canadians divided by their French and English backgrounds.[16] Some Australians too began a push for flag change, but they were a minority. In 1982, the Australian Labor Party policy began encouraging change in the flag and anthem, but according to a Morgan Poll, only 32 per cent supported them. Ausflag hoped Australia would have a new flag by its bicentenary in 1988. Bob Hawke's Labor government had 'Advance Australia Fair' proclaimed the national anthem in 1984, the same year Australians ceased being British subjects, but they were not prepared to tackle the more difficult issue of flag change. Opposing forces were significant. Within a week of Hawke's election in 1983, the RSL (NSW) with John Vaughan had begun organising a protest group, ANFA.[17] The strongest branch was in Sydney, home also to Ausflag. Conservative political parties also opposed change and, alarmed by Hawke's apparent ease in changing the anthem, sought to amend the Flags Act to make change more difficult.

By early 1992, after Paul Keating had succeeded Hawke as prime minister, popular support for flag change had increased to 42 per cent, although change was no longer Labor policy. Keating was keen to take up the issue – 'We can fly two symbols of our nationhood no longer', he declared in 1992 – but preferred the more popular cause of the republic.[18] His government's decision to have the Aboriginal and Torres Strait Islander flags proclaimed official flags in 1995 (following Cathy Freeman's use of the Aboriginal flag with the Australian flag at the 1994 Commonwealth Games) revealed enthusiasm for not only elements of the Aboriginal flag, but also the flag itself becoming the new Australian flag.[19] Freeman again carried both flags in her victory lap after winning the 400 metre race at the Sydney Olympics in 2000, carrying 'the hopes and dreams not only of Australia's Indigenous community, but of those in the country as a whole who were throwing their weight behind the reconciliation cause'.[20]

The growing popularity of the Aboriginal flag, particularly on clothing, would later prompt concern about the licensees controlling its use. In 2018, the flag's designer, Luritja artist Harold Thomas, granted commercial rights to the non-Indigenous profit-making company WAM Clothing, which served cease and desist notices on numerous groups using the flag. An Aboriginal-owned company, Spark Health Australia, which produced clothing under the 'Clothing The

Gaps' brand, campaigned to 'Free the Flag' (Fig. 31). A Senate Select Committee considered the possibility of the Commonwealth acquiring the rights in 2020. It recommended the copyright remain with Thomas, but wanted to negotiate for an independent Aboriginal body to take responsibility for ensuring the flag's integrity, dignity and appropriate use, similar to the governance of the Torres Strait Islander flag.[21]

Defence of the Australian flag and its British symbolism became a cornerstone of John Howard's coalition government from 1996. His use of the flag for wedge politics was reminiscent of the 1920s. Urged on by ANFA, Howard (who was a member) proclaimed 3 September Australian National Flag Day in 1996, and amended the Flags Act in 1998 to make flag change more difficult – the first year polls showed a majority of Australians wanted flag change. In 2002, the education minister, Brendan Nelson, approved ANFA's request to replicate and distribute their promotional video, *Our National Flag ... since 1901*, to all primary schools, funding it as 'an associated activity' of his department's Discovering Democracy program. Nelson introduced the video to school principals, with teachers' notes heavily influenced by ANFA, which insisted that its rival, Ausflag, and its views should not be mentioned. Rather than correcting misinformation about the flag's history, the video and notes added to it.[22]

To his credit, Howard resisted pressure from ANFA and the RSL to have schoolchildren pledge 'allegiance to our National flag of "Stars and Crosses"'. But, with war in Afghanistan and Iraq, he continued to push the flag onto schools.[23] Each promotion – flag ceremonies in 2002, subsidies for flagpoles in 2003, and the requirement in 2004 that schools accepting federal money must have a functioning flagpole and fly the flag – reopened the debate about the flag's design for those objecting to the Union Jack.

Australia's social composition had changed dramatically since the 1940s with the acceptance of non-British, and then from the 1970s, non-European immigrants. Although the percentage of Australia's immigrants from the British Isles dropped from 42.5 to 8.4 per cent between 1959 and 2000, Britons remain the largest immigrant group.[24] Promoting the flag in that context appeared to privilege those with a British background and alienate those without it – an interpretation confirmed by violent riots in Cronulla in mid-December 2005 between self-proclaimed 'Aussies' (Anglo–Australians) and 'Lebs' (Lebanese–Australians). Soon afterwards, at the Big Day Out concert on Australia Day, some flag-wavers tried to force people not of Anglo appearance to kiss their flags or risk a bashing, prompting organisers of the event in 2007 to ban Australian flags. The predictable outcry from politicians, shock-jocks and self-proclaimed defenders of the flag caused an immediate back-down.

Researchers interviewing youths from Cronulla and Lakemba involved in the 2005 riots found that their battles, centred on the Australian flag, reflected both local and global complexities about ethnic differences and security concerns in the new century. According to Amelia Johns, the interviews offered 'new insights into the experiences of racism, violence and belonging in young people's lives'. They revealed how the flag 'became a potently charged symbol of hegemonic white belonging and domination in the post-September 11 environment'.[25] A century after its design, the flag again became the focus of controversy precisely because of its popular use, with incidents of flag-burning and flag-wearing for patriotic and racist purposes highlighting the flag's ambiguous roles as a national symbol. Promoted by governments and people, the flag as a symbol – especially its Union Jack – signifies both unity and division. Flag skirmishes continued to mar Australia Day: patriotism had become provocation, though by 2010 multicultural clashes in Sydney seemed to have subsided.[26]

Perhaps prompted by repercussions from the Cronulla riot, a special telephone Morgan Poll was conducted immediately after Anzac Day on the nights of 28 and 29 April 2010. The timing, perhaps intentional, very likely inflated the pro-flag response. A greater majority than in February 1998 wanted to keep the Australian flag with its Union Jack: 69 as against 53 per cent. The percentage of those seeking a new flag design dropped from 52 to 29 per cent.[27] The Howard coalition government from 1996 had sought to end debate about the flag (its 1998 legislation) and the republic (the failed 1999 referendum). It seemed successful. The flag had become increasingly visible after 2001 with Australia's involvement in war in Afghanistan and the Middle East, and the fearmongering surrounding the arrival of asylum seekers by boat. Despite, or perhaps because of, the way the Australian flag had been misused in Sydney in 2005–09, those polled in 2010 overwhelmingly supported the current design. However, by 2016 polls showed significant signs of change with 64 per cent in one survey and 41 per cent in another calling for a new design.[28]

Even so, while debates around the flag became less prominent in the continuing discussions around national identity, the focus shifted to other symbolic formalities. Indigenous groups in particular objected to the date chosen for Australia Day, marking the anniversary of Britain's invasion and 'the beginning of tragedy for Indigenous people'.[29] As early as 1994, the Council for Aboriginal Reconciliation (Australia) (CAR) (now Reconciliation Australia) established by the Commonwealth Government in 1991 rejected Australia Day on 26 January as a national day. Sol Bellear, a respected Aboriginal spokesman who had served on the Council, declared that 'Aboriginal Reconciliation can never be achieved unless there is a new Australian flag without the Union Jack'.[30] When several local councils objected to citizenship ceremonies on 26 January, the Morrison coalition government in 2019 revised the code for the day and required councils to hold the ceremonies on Australia Day.[31] On the other hand, increasing calls to change the wording of the national anthem – its 'for we are young and free' a direct denial of Aboriginal occupation of the land and participation in nationhood – saw Scott Morrison authorise the change of 'young' to 'one' from 1 January 2021.[32] Australia's rugby union Wallabies went further in December 2020, singing the anthem in the Eora language for the first time before their game against Argentina's Pumas.[33]

Flags continued to be useful markers for Indigenous people in their struggle for rights. As thousands of protesters rallied outside Brisbane's Parliament House on Invasion Day in 2018, parliament staff agreed to the elders' request, via police, that they lower Aboriginal and Torres Strait Islander flags to half-mast until sunset as a sign of respect. While the circumstances did not conform to parliamentary protocol, Queensland's Speaker supported his staff's decision.[34] In racially divided Alice Springs, Aboriginal people struggled for years in the town council to have their flag flown with the Australian and Northern Territory flags on Anzac Hill, the site of the town's war memorial as well as a sacred site for Arrernte people. In 2018, the council narrowly agreed to fly the Aboriginal flag, but only for ceremonial occasions, such as National Sorry Day, National Reconciliation Week and NAIDOC Week. Further pressure by Arrernte/Mirning woman, councillor Catherine Satour led the council in August 2019 to agree unanimously to fly that flag throughout the year, the longed-for 'gesture of respect'. The only exception was Anzac Day, when Australian, Northern Territory and New Zealand flags were flown.[35]

The National Australia Day Council became much more direct in 2020 in explaining the point of Australia Day:

> Our First Peoples are the traditional custodians of our beautiful lands and waterways and have a fundamental role in the great Australian story. We aspire to an Australia Day that can increasingly include a recognition and celebration by all Australians of the importance of Aboriginal and Torres Strait Islanders to our nation.[36]

The growing use of the Australian and Aboriginal and Torres Strait Islander flags on Australia Day poses the challenge recognised by Ken Wyatt, Minister for Indigenous Australians in 2020. He hoped 'all Australians celebrate our indigenous heritage, promote and support truth-telling to recognise and acknowledge our shared history, and work together to heal these past wounds', for the sake of a 'reconciled future'.[37]

1 *Australian Binge*, plastic necklace by Peter Tully, 1977, features a range of Australian symbols.

Terence Lane collection, National Museum of Australia

2 When he turned seven, Australian-born Heath Parkin, living in England and alert to national symbols, wanted an Australian-themed birthday cake with a kangaroo sign and the Wallabies rugby union colours. Carole's Customised Cakes came to the party with a symbol-laden birthday cake, including a map, a boomerang, a koala, a crocodile and a rugby game all on a cork hat.

Photograph by Helaina Storey

3 Charles A Doudiet (Switzerland, c. 1832–1913) *Swearing Allegiance to the 'Southern Cross'*, 1854. Watercolour and ink on paper. 16.7 x 23.2cm.

Purchased by the Ballarat Fine Art Gallery with the assistance of many donors, 1996. Collection of the Art Gallery of Ballarat

4 *Haemisphaerium scenographicum Australe coeli stellati et terrae* (Drawing in perspective of the Southern Hemisphere, of the starry heavens and of the land), 1661, by Henricus Hondius. Note the Southern Cross making an entrance, bottom, centre.

Rex Nan Kivell collection, National Library of Australia

5 *Our Lady of the Southern Cross, Help of Christians*, 2008. This painting, commissioned for World Youth Day 2008, referred to national symbolism in the wattle headband, the Broome pearl, the iconic Streeton landscape (*The Purple Noon's Transparent Might*) and even, in Mary herself, the image of Australia represented by a young Australian woman.

© Paul Newman

6 Press image for the film *Bra Boys*, showing Koby Abberton's Southern Cross tattoo, 2007.

Photograph by Trudi van de Wint

7 *The Kongorou* 1771, by George Stubbs, now in the National Maritime Museum, Greenwich, United Kingdom. Stubbs painted his kangaroo from an inflated skin supplied by Joseph Banks, becoming the first non-Indigenous artist to exhibit a painting of the animal. The kangaroo rapidly acquired status as a symbol of Australian oddity.

Photo courtesy Parham House, West Sussex, United Kingdom

8 The boxing kangaroo flag goes up on Alan Bond's boat in his unsuccessful attempt to represent Australia in defending the America's Cup off Fremantle in 1987.

Photograph by Roger Garwood

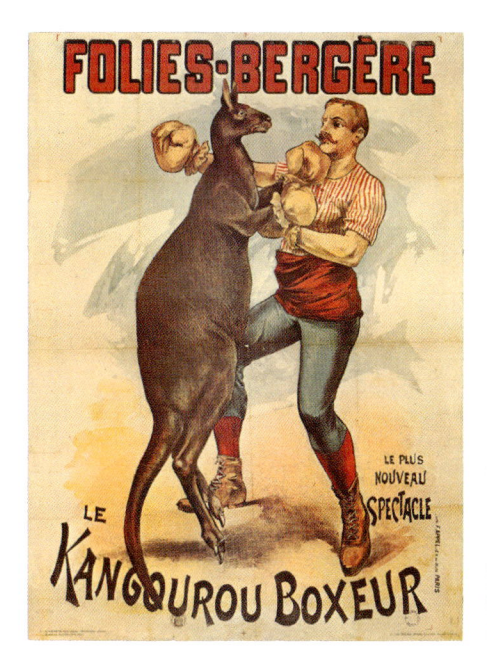

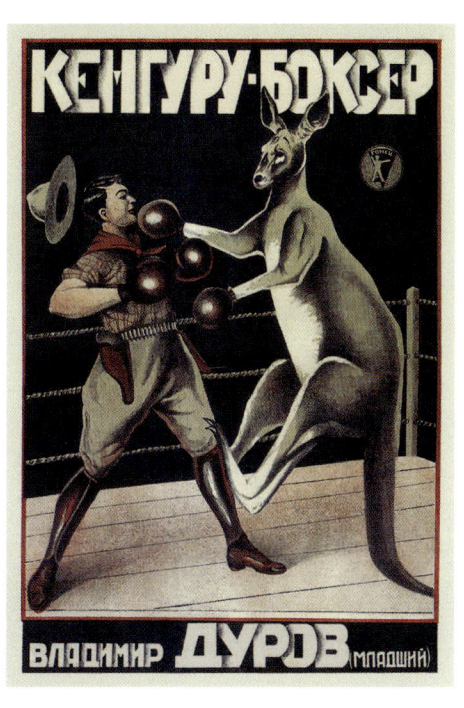

9 Boxing kangaroos became popular entertainments throughout the world from the late nineteenth century. (*Top left*) *Folies-Bergere, Le Plus Nouveau Spectacle, Le Kangourou Boxeur*, c. 1875; (*top right*) *Das Boxende Känguruh*, printed by Adolph Friedländer, Hamburg, c. 1895. Print is possibly related to the short German film of that name that appeared that year; (*below left*) *Time! The Boxing Kangaroo*, Litho Creber, Plymouth, c. 1910; (*below right*) Soviet circus poster, *Kangaroo Boxer* by Vladimir Durov Junior, c. 1933. This poster acquired a cult following when it appeared on the wall of Joey and Chandler's apartment in the sitcom, *Friends*.

National Museum of Australia; Wikimedia Commons; Courtesy Antipodean Books, Maps & Prints, Garrison, New York, United States of America; Courtesy JustPosters.com.au

10 *Her Majesty Queen Elizabeth the Second*, 1954, by William Dargie. The Australian state portrait of Queen Elizabeth II, wearing a Norman Hartnell dress embroidered with wattle, and the Girls of Great Britain and Ireland tiara, Queen Mary's wedding present. Often known as the 'wattle painting' it is one of the most familiar images of the Queen in Australia. Dargie painted several versions of his iconic portrait: Tony Abbott, and later Scott Morrison, retrieved this version for the prime ministerial office.

National Museum of Australia

11 Indigenous relationships to the crown are many and varied. Titus Nganjmirra holding his painting, *Queen Elizabeth*, acquired by the Commonwealth Government's Artbank in 2019.

Courtesy Injalak Arts, Gunbalanya, Northern Territory

12 Child's board game, 'Around the Commonwealth by aeroplane', c. 1910. Making the map familiar to children was not just the preserve of school.

National Library of Australia

13 'White Australia' badge, 1906. Drawing a map could be an act of possession, of belonging, of inclusion or exclusion, possession or dispossession.

National Museum of Australia

14 Pearls and turquoise gold snake brooch in the shape of the word cooee, c. 1910, designed by Maude Wordsworth James and made by Johnson & Simonsen, jewellers, Melbourne.

Photograph by George Serras, Trevor Kennedy collection, National Museum of Australia

15 Sheet music for 'Coo-ee Mary, (My Little Gum Tree Queen)', 1908. Words and music by Frank G King. The cooee, as a distinctively Australian sound, was readily adapted to popular music.

National Library of Australia

16 Stamps commemorating the postal vote on marriage equality, 2019.

Courtesy Dennis Altman

17 *Australian Landscape with Cattle: the Artist's Property, Patterdale* by John Glover, c. 1835. Though Glover would be criticised for seeing gums 'through English eyes', he captures their sinuosity very effectively.

National Library of Australia

18 'A bush home', one of the Gum Leaf Series postcards, c. 1907.

State Library of Victoria

19 *Spirit of Endurance*, 1937. Harold Cazneaux's iconic image of a Flinders Ranges river red gum has led to the tree itself becoming a tourist attraction.

Photograph by Harold Cazneaux, National Library of Australia

20 'Maddy at the Cazneaux tree', 2019.

Photograph by Stephen Norman

21 *Surfer insouciance. Surfers at Manly, Sydney,* after the shark siren had sounded, 2019.

© Photograph by Mike Gee

22 Large mature male bull shark, caught in Sydney Harbour, 2019. Originally tagged there in 2017, it had been detected travelling to the Great Barrier Reef in winter, returning to Sydney Harbour in summer.

Photograph by Dr Amy Smoothey, NSW Department of Primary Industries

23 (Above) Boomerang throwing at Coranderrk station, Vic., near Melbourne, a popular tourist attraction, c. 1909.

State Library of Victoria

24 (Left) Indigenous boomerang-makers tapped into a market for boomerang souvenirs, often by including other national symbols into their designs such as the coat of arms, the map, the Harbour Bridge and the rising sun.

(From top to bottom) Attributed to Lawrey Moffitt, Lake Tyers, Victoria, c. 1930s.

National Museum of Australia

Made by Albert Perrett, La Perouse, Sydney, 1934.

National Museum of Australia

Made by Jim Mullet Senior, Lake Tyers, Victoria, 1950.

National Museum of Australia

Incised and painted boomerang, Cherbourg style, Cherbourg, Queensland.

National Museum of Australia

25 The symbolism of the overturned billy. *Lost! A Sketch from Riverina* by Julian R Ashton published in the *Illustrated Australian News*, 3 July 1880.

State Library of Victoria

26 Boiling the billy, c. 1900.

Photograph by George Henry Hutson, State Library of Victoria

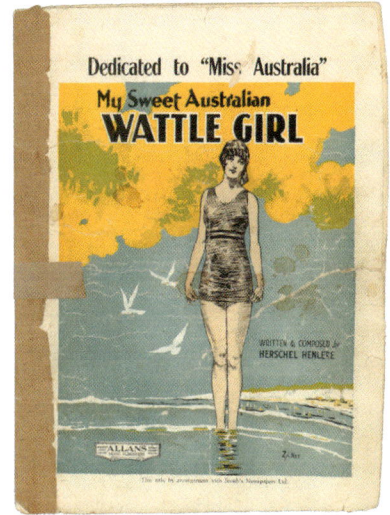

27 (*Top left*) A Royal Australian Navy pamphlet commemorating the arrival of the new Australian naval fleet in Sydney Harbour, 1913.

National Museum of Australia

28 (*Above*) Sheet music for 'My Sweet Australian Wattle Girl', 1925, by Herschel Henlere. It was sometimes a struggle to reconcile a modern beach-going Miss Australia with more traditional images of a feminised Australia.

National Library of Australia

29 (*Left*) Unlike the idealised depiction of Australia as a woman, Julia Gillard, as Australia's first female prime minister wielding actual power, attracted considerable hostility, which was directed towards her sex. Opposition leader Tony Abbott speaks at an anti-'carbon tax' rally outside Parliament House, 2011.

Photograph Andrew Meares, Fairfax

30 Flags we might have had: some of the unsuccessful entries in the 1901 flag competition, reconstructed by vexillologist Ralph Kelly.

31 Staff at Clothing The Gaps modelling some of the company's 'illegal flag products'. (*Left to right*) Laura Thompson, Sianna Catullo and Jesse Popple.

Photograph by Lena Charles

WATTLE

Libby Robin

Wattle has long been a symbolic flower for the Australian nation. Of course, various acacias were known as useful plants for the many Aboriginal nations long before 1901 and many are using the plants again in ways that reinvigorate Culture.[1] 'Wattle' became the Australian word – as opposed to mimosa and acacia, which are used in the rest of the world where the plants grow naturally or have been introduced – because of the verb, 'to wattle' which means to weave. The earliest colonists wove the flexible twigs and split branches of acacias between uprights, plastering them with clay to make insulated walls, particularly when bricks and stone were scarce. This 'wattle and daub' building technique, adapted from the practice of using hazel branches in the same way in Britain and northern Europe, gave the trees a distinctive *colonial* name.

When the colonies federated in 1901, they chose the wattle as a symbol because there are acacias in every part of the continent, and while their flowers and leaves vary, there is a local wattle for everyone. Wattles have appeared on postage stamps, banners and coats of arms, and most prominently in the national sporting colours of green and gold. Yet it was not until 1 December 1988 that the wattle was officially proclaimed the floral emblem of Australia, and 23 June 1992 that 1 September was declared 'National Wattle Day': 'an opportunity for all Australians to celebrate our floral heritage, particularly through the planting of a species of *Acacia* suitable for the area in which they live'.[2]

Choosing 1 September as a 'significant day' (though not a holiday) was a matter of administrative convenience. The decision to 'nationalise' the first day of spring moved away from earlier, more ecological traditions of celebrating wattles at different times in each state according to flowering seasons. The notional 'first day of spring' gave an affirmation to wattle as a 'harbinger', an earlier tradition. As poet Margery Ruth Betts put it:

Oh! The spring is here again, and all the ways are fair;
The wattle-blossom's out again, and do you know it there?[3]

On this day, new Australian citizens are often presented with a wattle to plant in their home garden, in an echo of earlier Arbor Days, where tree-planting was linked with civic virtue.

The decision provides food for thought about the mix of pragmatism and idealism in the wattle's use as a national symbol. It has always been a valuable resource, not just an attractive decoration, and its utility was significant to its claims to being a national symbol. The seeds of mulga (*Acacia aneura*), widespread in the desert country in Australia, not only provide a patriotic flavour for Anzac biscuits but are an important food for Aboriginal people.[4] As well as the seeds, mulga produces 'bush lollies', a sweet exudation, produced by the plant after attack by a sap-sucking insect, which can be sucked straight from the plant or dissolved in water to make a refreshing sweet drink, something that people in desert country enjoy.[5]

Wattle bark was also valuable in the leather tanning industry, wattle having been identified as a 'promising colonial export' in Tasmania.[6] January was the height of the 'barking' season, not the time when most wattles flowered, though some species do flower in summer. The useful 'nation building' virtues of holding 'Wattle Day' in spring came into their own in the Federation years.[7]

Choosing a floral symbol

The Australian Natives Association (ANA) was established in Victoria by middle-class Australian-born patriots who bridled at the dominance of British immigrants in public life. By the 1880s, it was a leading advocate of Federation, and one of its pet projects was to establish 'a national flower or emblem' for Australia, like 'the rose for the Englishman, the thistle for the Scotlander and the shamrock for Old Ireland'.[8] The ANA was impressed by Canada's successful campaign for the maple leaf, with its 1867 confederation song, 'The maple leaf forever', and its depiction on all Canadian coins. Wattle, like the maple leaf, was a natural not cultural symbol, and so could be used to symbolise an egalitarian, classless Australia:

> The wearing of the blossom at the same time alike by people of all classes and creeds and political parties ... is meant to impress upon the mind and the imagination of Young Australia in particular that on the day of its exhibition *everybody* stands forth as an Australian.[9]

Wattle blooms profusely all over the Australian continent. Its biogeographical ubiquity made it a popular choice as a national symbol, and the 'generosity' of its flowering was associated with an egalitarian ethos (Fig. 33).

Other flowers also represented the nation at this time. The waratah (*Telopea speciosissima*) and the flannel flower (*Actinotus helianthi*) were both popular in formal designs for decorative arts. Waratah was preferable to the wattle for floristry. Waratahs could travel successfully all the way to England, packed in ice, while wattle blossom fell quickly when cut. Richard Thomas Baker from the Technological Museum in Sydney was the leading champion of the waratah as a national flower. He and Lucien Henri also campaigned vigorously for the use of Australian trees and plants in arts and crafts, in everything from cabinet-making to jewellery.[10] Lucie Shorter, a student of Richard Baker's, whose

Golden Wattle – Our Australian Floral Emblem, 1921, by Archibald James Campbell.

Australian National Botanic Gardens

father, John, was the local agent for Doulton china, designed the 'Lu Lu Pattern' tea service, featuring a border of stylised waratah. Baker's argument for waratah as quintessentially Australian was that it was unique to Australia, while wattle also grew 'in other Countries in the world'. Wattle was also less suitable for fine arts and craftsmanship because it harboured 'wood borers and gall insects'.

Long after the campaign for wattle had won the day, in 1933, Baker was still promoting the waratah. Another reason to choose it, he claimed, came from a different fine art and a deeper history:

The *first* Australian flower printed in colour was the 'Waratah' in 1793
… Aboriginal people brought waratahs to the streets of Sydney, and
carved it in stone. Who can say it was not their National Flower? And
so I hold that had Australia adopted the 'Waratah' for its National
Flower, She would have one dating back to the Stone Age.[11]

These musings came all too late. By this time, wattle had gathered wartime patriotic symbolism and was entwined with the Anzac legend. The collective force of the rest of Australia had outnumbered the Sydney push.

Wattle had a passionate supporter in Melbourne every bit the equal of Baker in Sydney. Archibald James Campbell was a prominent field naturalist, ornithologist, pioneering photographer and newspaper columnist. He founded a private Wattle Club in Victoria in 1899 that held activities each September to celebrate the wattle season. The club invented a whole new pastime, 'wattling' (in this case, 'appreciating wattle') to enable city-dwellers to celebrate spring in the bush through days out visiting the 'wattle wilds' by railway and bicycle, to gather wattle blossoms (Fig. 32). This was an early manifestation of the hobby of bushwalking with a seasonal flourish. A hundred years later, this practice is echoed in the south of France where festivals and a 'Mimosa tourist trail' are still actively promoted, although acacia has nothing to do with national symbolism there.[12]

Wattle enthusiasm increased over the first decade of federated Australia. By 1912, Victoria's Wattle Club had been superseded by a Wattle Day League, a charity group that raised money by selling wattle sprigs to city workers for their lapels. The first Wattle Day League was established in Sydney in 1909, and the tradition of a 'Wattle Day' began there on 1 August 1910 with support from Joseph Maiden, the government botanist.[13]

On 31 August 1912 in Perth, the Western Australian Wattle Day League sold buttonholes of wattle and boronia (then the state emblem). Meanwhile, in Hobart, 'under the auspices of the ANA', the date was

10 September, when wattle blossom was 'everywhere in the city'. In 1913, Wattle Day went international: Selfridges filled its Oxford Street, London store with 'mimosa' to honour Australia's 125th birthday on 26 January 1913.[14]

Wearing wattle was a start, but planting wattle trees was even better, as Tullie Wollaston argued in his book, *Our Wattles*, published in 1916. In his celebratory rhetoric, the wattle became the nation and the generous blossom the spirit of the people:

> Is there anything quite so wonderful anywhere else? More gorgeous flowering trees there may be ... but where on all the habitable globe will you find a 30-feet tree seven years from seed which will yield you sprays ... packing 28 feet of it ... And then in another five years your tree is 50 feet and finally 70 to 100, if you treat it fairly. Well our bright Australia is like that ... Our chosen emblem is not only a true symbol of outward prosperity, but suggests a note of generosity in the people.[15]

Even so, Australia hesitated to declare wattle the official national emblem, perhaps because of persistent debate in New South Wales about the waratah. While Mary Grant Bruce described the scent of wattle as 'a breath of Australia', Baker sourly commented that wattle 'flowers when cut and placed in the house produce catarrh'.[16]

While men were the public face of wattle patriotism, women were often its most fervent devotees. The association of flowers with femininity gave women authority to promote wattle as a national symbol. It was Jane, Lady Franklin, the governor's wife, whose enthusiasm for Australian natural history inspired the first Wattle Day in Hobart in 1838, to mark 50 years of British settlement in the Australian colonies. The Wattle Blossom League inaugurated on 13 March 1890 in Adelaide was sponsored by the ladies' committee of the ANA No. 1 Branch. Journalist William J Sowden, founder of the ANA in South Australia and president of the Wattle Day League, argued that because South Australia was the first colony to have women's suffrage, *Acacia pycnantha* should also stand for women's rights. On Foundation Day, 26 January 1891, a banner embroidered with golden wattle represented the Adelaide ANA.[17] And perhaps there was no more devoted advocate of the wattle than Elizabeth Lauder. She had been romantically attached to Adam Lindsay Gordon, whose well-known poem, 'The sick stockrider', has the dying bushman asking his mates: 'Let me slumber in the hollow where the wattle blossoms wave!' When Gordon shot himself in 1870, Lauder planted a wattle on his grave, tended it for the next 30 years and each year sent its seeds to Victorian schools for planting in Gordon's memory. Victoria's Wattle Day League marked Wattle Day in 1912 with a visit to Gordon's grave at the Brighton Cemetery.[18] Through this association with the death of Gordon, the wattle acquired a commemorative role.

In the end, the wattle became the national flower because it was omnipresent. It gained military significance during the wartime years, when pressed wattles were sent to soldiers at Gallipoli and the Western Front, along with hand-knitted socks and homemade fruit cake, and wattle sprigs were sold on Wattle Day in aid of soldiers and their families. When the soldiers returned, they were honoured in 'Wattle Park' in Melbourne, where a seed of the Lone Pine of Gallipoli was planted alongside many wattles.[19]

Claiming the wattle

While the wattle (*Acacia* spp.) grows everywhere in Australia, *Acacia* grows in other countries, too, and that has led to a different kind of contestation, both popular and scientific. When the Union of South Africa chose *Acacia* to symbolise their nation on the king's coronation Stole in 1911, some Australians were affronted. William Ey wrote to the Adelaide *Register*:

Wattle Day, Martin Place, Sydney, 1935.

Photograph by Sam Hood, State Library of New South Wales

We have lost a great lot of the commercial value of our beloved wattle tree by selling them seed, justly or otherwise; but we shall certainly not permit South Africa, without protest, to plume and decorate themselves with our feathers.[20]

The 'mimosa' embroidered on the king's stole was almost certainly an African one, probably doringboom, *Acacia karroo*, not a wattle imported from Australia. While the majority of *Acacia* species are indigenous to Australia, South Africa is the source of species with the sharp thorns that gave the *Acacia* genus its name, which means 'thorn tree'. In 1910 the new Union of South Africa chose the doringboom, complete with thorns, for the garland encircling the arms on the governor-general's flag, in the vice-regal tradition of the maple leaf in Canada and the fern in New Zealand. But Australians remained adamant that wattle was uniquely Australian. NRL McLeod of Petersburg, South Australia, was forthright, even racist:

> The wattle is Australian; and just as Australians are like no other people, the wattle resembles no other flower. We as a race are clean and wholesome, which is a strong point of resemblance between us and the wattle ... So with Australians, God made wattles first, and then created Australians with the same characteristics. Therefore it is worse than neglect to allow our God-given birthrights to be filched from us by the grasping, yet aesthetic hands of our relatives across the sea. The South Africans cannot yet have realized the enormity of their offence ... Till we have our national glory restored let our clarion cry be – nay, let it always be – The wattle for white Australia.[21]

By the time the coronation dress was designed and embroidered for Queen Elizabeth II in 1953, wattle represented Australia (Fig. 10). Protea (the 'first cousin' of waratah!) represented South Africa. Neither country had an 'official' floral emblem at the time, though wattle and protea were often used in each place.[22]

Australian pride in wattle has a long history. Less celebrated is the plant's scientific name, *Acacia*. But there was a major outcry when international taxonomists proposed that the genus be split, and the Australian varieties renamed *Racosperma*. Southern Africans also frequently regard *Acacia* as a 'symbol of Africa', if not a national flower. Australia, with some 1000 endemic species of *Acacia*, took on the rest of the world to argue that the name should remain with the branch of the family that is predominantly Australian.[23] This decision outraged South Africans who did not think that *Acacia* should apply to spineless Australian varieties and resented the proposal to rename most African acacias *Senegalia*. Eugene Moll, chair of the Council of the Botanical Society of South Africa, argued that: 'Acacias and Africa are synonymous; our thorny savannas are historical and contemporary icons. We surely cannot allow the Australians to steal the name that is as much a part of Africa as cheetah and the Big Five?'[24] But the International Committee on Botanical Nomenclature in 2005 ruled that the scientific term *Acacia* should be associated with the sub-group that dominates the Australian flora, not the one associated with the historic type-specimen.

How much Australian pride is actually vested in the name '*Acacia*'? Australians took pride in 'wattle' certainly, but were they equally passionate about *Acacia*? An *Acacia* Study Group was established within the then-new Society for Growing Australian Plants in about 1959, and there was knowledge of the scientific name in horticultural circles, but little evidence of the sort of 'popular' symbolism that the *Acacia* carries in Africa. A few little girls were named 'Acacia', including Acacia Dorothea Maiden, daughter of Sydney Wattle Day enthusiast, Joseph Maiden, but this was rare. The botanists advocating the Australian case claimed that the status of *Acacia* as a symbol of Australia was pertinent to their claim. But perhaps it was simply that the horticulturally literate community did not like the alternative *Racosperma*. There may have been a commercial incentive in their reactions as there were valuable patents attached to some horticulturally improved *Acacia* varieties. Indeed the strong campaign against the alternative name for Australia's wattles has possibly led to 'acacia' gaining in popularity within Australia as a vernacular alternative to 'wattle', particularly in Western Australia, home of many endemic acacias.

When Maria Hitchcock edited a special issue of *Australian Plants* to 'celebrate the special relationship that Australians have with their beloved acacias', she urged Australians to rewrite the alphabet beginning with 'A is for Acacia, symbol of Australia'. In an echo of Tullie Wollaston's entreaty of 1916, she encouraged her readers 'to grow at least one Acacia'.[25] Wattle and acacia are increasingly interchangeable. The scientific Acacia website, maintained by Australian taxonomists, is called 'World Wide Wattle', apparently without irony. Meanwhile, an Acacia Appreciation Club has been established in Japan because an Australian acacia is believed to have been the first plant to rise from the ashes of Hiroshima after the atomic bomb was dropped there in 1945. Every year on Wattle Day the Japanese club sends hundreds of yellow ribbons to the Australian National Botanic Gardens in Canberra. The ribbons are made by the children of the Hiroshima Shudoin Orphanage, who have been sending and receiving messages from Canberra schoolchildren since 1999.[26]

Ritualising a symbol

The flower's increasingly official symbolism has seen a revival of the ritual of wearing wattle, not simply for Wattle Day but in state ceremonies relating to the deaths of Australians overseas. A new Wattle Day Association was established in the national capital, Canberra, in 1998. On 4 August 1999, another Wattle Day tradition was born. The governor-general, Sir William Deane, and his wife cast 14 sprigs of wattle into the Saxeten Gorge in Switzerland, one for each of the 14 young

Australians killed in a canyoning disaster eight days earlier. The flowers came from Government House in Canberra.[27] In 2002 Prime Minister John Howard continued the use of wattle as a symbol of mourning, this time to honour the Australians killed in the Bali bombings: 'As a simple unifying tribute could I encourage the wearing of a piece of wattle during the day and also where possible the planting of wattle seeds as a quiet personal gesture of remembrance and reflection.'[28] At the first anniversary of the bombings on 12 October 2003, Howard and his wife, Janette, wore sprigs of wattle from Australia in Bali. Janette dried her wattle sprig and saved it with other Bali memorabilia, offering it as a significant object for display in a 2006 exhibition at Old Parliament House, Canberra, entitled *Mrs Prime Minister*.

There is a tension between wattle as a symbol for mourning and wattle as a symbol for celebration. Wattle's historical symbolism was forged in the complex rhetoric of World War I and its aftermath and this was both about death and forging nationhood. By contrast, wattle's ecological symbolism is about spring and new life. Wattle is now central to ceremonies welcoming new citizens. Nature and nation are woven together in their complex associations with the golden wattle blossom.

COAT OF ARMS

Bruce Baskerville

It is a very curious thing that one of the best studies for understanding the symbolism of the Australian coat of arms, which were finally granted in 1912, was written in Britain about Canadian coats of arms by a Polish-Lithuanian-Canadian.[1] It suggests that heraldists (heraldry experts), like vexillologists (flag experts), are a particular breed. But it also points to a relative lack of interest in Australia in a national symbol that appears everywhere, on government buildings, documents, letterheads and publications.

At its simplest, a country's coat of arms symbolises the intangible supreme authority in a polity, not its geographical extent. The arms identifies the person or institution in which that authority is vested, and as such is known as Arms of Dominion and Sovereignty. They are not personal arms, and do not pass through personal inheritance, but by succession, election or conquest.

The coat of arms is not itself the abstract public authority, and representations of the arms, whether they be printed, painted, sculpted or otherwise manufactured, can only symbolise that authority. However, because they are physical objects, they can each be read and interpreted like any other historical record.

The principal element in any coat of arms is the shield. The design on the shield of Australia's, the Commonwealth Arms, is divided into six quarters (heraldic quarters do not have to be of four equal parts), each illustrating a state badge, surrounded by a border of ermine. The state badges are not formal coats of arms but simply identifying emblems originally intended for use on marine flags to distinguish the vessels of one colony from another.

There are several distinct elements surrounding the shield. The ermine border is used so that the whole shield design forms one 'device', rather than being a collection of separate emblems.[2] Ermine has been used in the mantling of the English and British Royal Arms since the fourteenth century,[3] and the ermine patterning of the border evokes the encompassing authority of the Australian crown. The naturally coloured kangaroo and emu supporters holding the shield suggest a native buttressing of the symbolised authority, which is reinforced by the golden seven-pointed Commonwealth Star as a crest above the shield, and the ornamental sprays of wattle blossom emblematic of the continental sweep of Commonwealth authority.

The constitutional division of powers in Australia vests all general powers in the states (or state crowns) except for particular powers reserved to the Commonwealth (or Australian crown). The Commonwealth Arms symbolise this federal structure, rather than federal authority over the states. Thus the Australian Arms do not try to marshal the state arms, but reflect the Commonwealth's limited federal authority.

The shield is, in a sense, a graphic representation of the preamble to the constitution: 'Whereas the people of [each state] ... have agreed to unite in one indissoluble Federal Commonwealth under the Crown ... and under the Constitution'. The people of each state are signified by their state badges, the federation established under the constitution by the equal distribution of the quarters, and the crown by the ermine border. The public authority represented by the arms symbolises the intangible, but limited, public authority of the Commonwealth and its vesting in a sort of mystical fusion of people, crown and constitution.

People and power

That at least is how a heraldist reads the coat of arms, but what of its popular meaning? In 1806 settlers in the Hawkesbury District near Sydney designed a coat of arms, now known as the Bowman Flag. The arms included a kangaroo and emu as supporters, and are credited with being the inspiration for the supporters of the present Commonwealth Arms.

By the 1820s a coat of arms with a motto of 'Advance Australia' was being used in Sydney. The shield was divided into four quarters, each depicting a symbol of commerce: a golden fleece, a ship, a crossed harpoon and anchor, and a wheat sheaf. It also displayed a Southern Cross and emu and kangaroo supporters. These nativist symbols worked to localise the arms. The 'Advance Australia Arms' were widely used across eastern Australia throughout the nineteenth century with many variations in its colours, and the devices in the quarters often changing position, or being replaced by others.

The Advance Australia Arms were used on building facades and in stained glass windows (where many examples survive); they adorned furniture, bookplates, embroideries, crockery and many other household goods; they appeared on newspaper mastheads, within commercial labels and advertisements, on trade tokens, and so on.[4] Later they formed the basis for the coats of arms granted to New South Wales (1906), Adelaide (1929) and Melbourne (1939 and 1970),[5] but were never formally granted or otherwise officially recognised. Their popularity as a symbol of colonial patriotism is reflected in their long-lasting and broad-ranging uses, and in their commercial uses to attract customers to purchase 'Australian' goods and services. Despite the lack of an authorised or official version, the many representations are remarkably consistent. They reflect a certain level of heraldic literacy among the colonial populations. Heraldic forms allowed colonial, national and imperial aspirations to be symbolically expressed in a manner that others could read and understand. They also suggest that,

William Gullick's designs for a Commonwealth coat of arms.
National Archives of Australia

though formal coats of arms were expressions of authority, there was a sense of the popular imagination using familiar heraldic forms to explore evolving new identities.

The ability of ordinary people to read the language of heraldry can be seen in the 'kingplates' or breastplates awarded to Aboriginal people from the 1810s to the 1930s.[6] Usually made of brass, and invariably crescent-shaped with a neck chain, the plates were often decorated in a quasi-heraldic manner. Kangaroos and emus were the most common motifs, often in heraldic poses such as a 'regardant' (looking over their shoulder). Other motifs included platypus, lyrebirds, snakes, lizards, grass trees, weapons, Aboriginal figures and crowns. The use of such heraldic-like motifs relied upon the viewer being able to 'read' the symbolic values depicted on the plate, at least enough to attribute to its presentation some element of public authority.

Popular heraldic literacy was also reflected in extensive debates about the Commonwealth Arms which were to be the formal symbol of the nation as authority. Two aspects of these debates can illustrate the point: the argument about a motto for the 1908 arms, and proposals to replace the 1837 arms with the Commonwealth Arms in 1915.

King George V granted the present Australian coat of arms (formally the Arms of Her Majesty in right of Australia) on 19 September 1912, replacing arms granted in 1908. Until then, the official arms used federally and in the states were the successive British Royal Arms, most prolifically the version adopted on Queen Victoria's accession in 1837.[7]

When Prime Minister Alfred Deakin was reported in 1908 to be considering mottos for the arms then being designed, he received a number of suggestions from the public. 'Semper respublica primus' was suggested because it was patriotic, classical in form, and unique. Another suggestion was the more complicated 'Commonwealth of Australia' or 'Australasia', and 'Commerce, Industry and Humanity'. One writer submitted a list of 18 Latin mottos such as 'Est concordia fratrum' (Harmony makes brothers) and 'Vis unita fortior' (Strength united is stronger). Wilson Dobbs, the arms' designer, suggested 'Semper Australiensis' (Always Australian). Finally Deakin settled on the old motto of the popular colonial arms, 'Advance Australia', and this appeared on the scroll of the ill-starred arms of 1908 (Fig. 34).[8]

Within four years the 1908 coat of arms had been replaced with the enduring 1912 version. Why did it last such a short time? Trouble began even before the 1908 arms had been granted when a story appeared in the British press describing their design. The St Andrew Society in Edinburgh protested that the inclusion within the design of a cross that resembled in any way a St George's Cross, without also including the saltire crosses of Scotland and Ireland, failed to recognise the four nationalities (including the Welsh) of Britain, concluding that, for the non-English part of the Australian population, 'a very grave and serious blunder has been committed ... unnecessarily and improperly casting a slight on the national sentiment'. The English heralds in London, who were ultimately responsible for the granting of arms, were also aggrieved. They privately reminded the government that the authority to design arms did not belong to Australians, and that as a draft the design should not be in the public domain. They would also prefer a design that would avoid any British or English emblems 'and bring in only the Southern Cross'.

The Scottish Patriotic Association (SPA) in Glasgow, a vocal campaigner for Scottish home rule and Scottish interests abroad, then became involved. The SPA wrote to Deakin in 1908, protesting that the proposed design would be 'not only heraldically incorrect, but highly distasteful and offensive', pointed out that the English heralds were not the only heraldic authorities in the Empire and urged Deakin to also consult the Scottish and Irish heralds. They concluded that if the three British kingdoms could not all be acknowledged in the Commonwealth Arms, 'it would be better to adopt an entirely non-controversial emblem, possibly symbolic of Australia, which would give offence to no one'.[9]

The first problem was that the SPA's protest was made too late, coming on the day that the king signed the royal warrant granting the arms. The second was that, the more Dobbs tried to vary the design to take account of such protests, the more it looked like a shield bearing a Union Jack. It became less 'Australian'.

The SPA began to gather allies. The Victorian Scottish Union in Melbourne wanted the arms to be referred to the Scottish and Irish heraldic authorities as well as the English, and stated its support for the views of the SPA. The story received coverage in the British and Australian press. The St Andrew Society claimed the Commonwealth was anti-Celtic, and pointed out that the English part of the Australian population was only 5 per cent larger than the combined non-English part. A circuit breaker was needed and, at this moment, William Gullick, the New South Wales Government Printer who had designed the New South Wales Coat of Arms in 1906, came to the rescue.

Gullick had just 'discovered', he said, 'what is absolutely the origin of the so-called Australian Coat of Arms, dating back to ... 1805'. This is the coat of arms now referred to as the Bowman Flag. It must have seemed a godsend to the Commonwealth, especially as Gullick also told them of his long interest and researches into the heraldry of colonial Australia. Wilson Dobbs was swiftly dropped when Scottish-born Labor Prime Minister Fisher asked Gullick to prepare some designs for a revised Commonwealth coat of arms, perhaps derived from the 'old Australian Emu and Kangaroo Flag'. Gullick prepared four options. After further design work, including adding the kangaroo and emu supporters and ermine border, and rearranging the order of the state badges in the quarters, the arms were finally granted by the king in 1912 (Fig. 35).

The 1908 arms were tainted with ethnic division and called into question the nature of the Australian identity they portrayed. Dobbs had suggested that one way out of the mess was to patriate heraldic authority (giving Australians power to design arms) and avoid 'old world' national tensions, but ironically it was the English heralds who stated a preference for Australian symbols such as the Southern Cross. They did not want their heraldic eminence questioned and Dobbs's arguments were sidelined. His design for the Commonwealth Arms was a failure. Gullick offered a solution by invoking a sort of cryptic genealogy in the venerable kangaroo and emu arms, from which he derived a design that recognised the states, was obviously Australian, avoided the controversies whipped up by the SPA, subtly played to the Scots critics by including the eminently Scottish heraldic device of a border,[10] and sidestepped the issue of the location of heraldic authority.

During World War I popular opinion emerged as a factor as the old 1837 arms came to be replaced by the new Commonwealth Arms. In May 1915, C Marshall, a deputy foreman in the Postmaster-General's

Department in Hobart, suggested that the Commonwealth Arms should replace the 1837 arms in departmental advertisements and on public telephone cabinets. The chief clerk in Hobart, however, felt that as the 1837 arms 'is the insignia of the Empire of which the Commonwealth forms a part, and its use ... is in no way subservient of the interests of the Commonwealth' no further action should be taken.[11]

Further action, however, was taken. As the matter would affect other departments, it was referred to the Prime Minister's Department. The Postmaster-General's departmental secretary wrote, 'I presume the coat of Arms was intended to be used wherever Arms were required to denote Commonwealth property or authority' and sought a ruling on the correct arms to use.[12] Within a fortnight Prime Minister Fisher gave his ruling: all departments were to use the Commonwealth Arms 'over advertisements and on stationery, cabinets, and other government property'.[13] There were some setbacks: joint advertisements with states would continue to use the 1837 arms unless the premiers agreed to change; and the Government Printer had to be told as late as 1918 to use the Commonwealth Arms on the *Commonwealth Gazette*.[14] Nevertheless, Marshall's suggestion had been acted upon, and acted upon quickly, by the highest authorities in the land. It seems that, as in the conscription referenda in 1916 and 1917 and the flag debates in the 1920s, there was conflict between nationalists and Empire loyalists, but in the case of the coat of arms at least, the use of Australianist symbols was on the ascendant.

Marshall's foremanship in the department's workshops points to another area of popular interest in the nation's arms. The Sydney firm of Wunderlich operated a large foundry and workshops producing a huge array of stamped metal products, notably metal ceilings and wall linings. Catalogues of their products were distributed across the country, and included embossed metal coats of arms. The 1919 catalogue included arms 'suitable for peace celebrations'. The company produced Commonwealth Arms for use by the federal authorities. The moulds and stamps were all made in the factory, and there was a steady demand for the mass-produced arms for government, commercial and domestic use.[15]

Like the colonial-era Advance Australia arms, kingplate motifs, the quest for a motto and the programmed replacement of the 1837 arms, Wunderlich's mass-produced coats of arms illustrate the use of official heraldry as a popular medium for symbolically expressing some sense of Australian identities. People took part in arguments about their design and motto, they argued about replacing the 1837 arms, they bought representations for their houses and shops. Their interest in the 1908 and 1912 coats of arms revealed a heraldic literacy, even a poetic sensibility in the way they imagined their Australianness.

Arms as art

After the settlement of 1912, conflict over the arms has focused on the qualities of artwork and craftsmanship, architecture and graphic design. Sydney sculptor William MacIntosh fashioned the 1837 and Commonwealth Arms in white Portland cement for the facade of the (now) Old Parliament House in Canberra in 1926. The art deco architectural style of that Parliament House called for a sleek response, and MacIntosh agreed to show the left-hand supporter as a kangaroo 'regardant' to allow both supporters to be facing the 1837 arms (to the left of the Commonwealth Arms). Following some criticism of this adaptation, the chief architect argued for the need to allow some degree of artistic licence: 'Exact reproduction of every detail ... when applied to certain building works in certain materials and positions is difficult, and often not practicable, consistent with satisfactory appearance.'[16]

Following the accession of Queen Elizabeth II in February 1952 the British authorities produced optimistically modern representations of their 1837 arms and other royal emblems. This was also a period when many new post-war regimes were adopting new national emblems, often with a conscious rejection of heraldic rules and an adoption of a more modernist aesthetic. In 1954 National Gallery of Victoria director Darryl Lindsay persuaded the Commonwealth Art Advisory Board that the Commonwealth Arms were 'artistically bad' and needed to be redesigned.[17] The board approached a number of prominent artists, including Margaret Preston, Cedric Emanuel and Douglas Annand, but they were either unavailable or their designs considered unsuitable. Other artists were approached, but after nearly 18 months of work on the redesign, Eileen Mayo and others were questioning Lindsay's departure from heraldic practice. By this stage, the board had spent considerable funds on its project, with very little to show for it. Questions of whether the new arms would be the 'Royal' arms of Australia were being raised,[18] and earlier hopes that the project should involve 'as little publicity as possible' looked increasingly untenable. The Prime Minister's Office then stepped in, and after reviewing the situation, concluded that 'we should pay more attention to heraldic aspects'.

Contact was made with the College of Arms in London, which drew attention to the symbolic issues involved, especially a proposal to somehow combine the Commonwealth Star and a crown as the new crest of the arms. The College suggested (perhaps sardonically) that 'the Crown in heraldry is a conventional representation of an actual object, so if you want to show an Australian Crown with a seven pointed star on top, logic seems to me to require that you should start with an actual Crown of this form made and brought into use!'[19] The board however suggested to the artists that a case could be made for placing the star above the crown, regardless of any heraldic design rules. By this time funding for the project was almost exhausted, issues of heraldic authority were again being raised, and the 1955 federal election was looming. The committee accepted a preferred design – one of Mayo's which added both a crown and a stylised Aboriginal shield in a more 'modern' arrangement – and then the project was quietly shelved.[20]

The artists who have created the representations of the arms have

Design for a coat of arms, c. 1954, by Eileen Mayo.

Gift of Margaret MacKean-Taylor, 1993, National Gallery of Australia

often known or cared little about their formal heraldic symbolism (Fig. 36). It seems at odds with the controversy surrounding the design of the 1908 and 1912 arms, when every detail was subjected to much effort and consideration to ensure that it was just right. Symbolism has often been subverted by artistry, paradoxically allowing the Commonwealth Arms to avoid the controversies and debates surrounding the crown, the flag and other emblems of sovereignty and identity. This has made the arms the least appreciated of Australia's official symbols, despite their popular appeal.

Any attempts to revise or vary the coat of arms have inevitably raised uncomfortable questions about sovereignty for federal governments. Ironically the Commonwealth's apparent constitutional inability to assert authority over issues of heraldry has meant the depiction of the coat of arms has often been more artistic than accurate. Given many people have lost the ability to read arms, the symbolism of the Commonwealth Arms can seem somewhat ambiguous, but it is a cultivated ambiguity which intentionally glosses over problems of meaning. The visual poetry of a heraldic design can be lost in trying to explain it. It's not surprising that the symbolism of the Australian Arms has to be inferred from a study of the Canadian Arms.

DIGGER

*Graham Seal and
Carolyn Holbrook*

Large-scale wars involve significant numbers of a nation's military personnel in confrontation with an enemy or enemies. Less directly but no less profoundly involved are families, friends and the broader population. Soldiers therefore carry the hopes and fears of the national community they represent and, assisted by usually extensive official propaganda, are seen as both actual and symbolic representatives of their nation. The Australian experience of global war has been further charged by the complexities of a colonial relationship with Britain, or 'the mother country', as it was often called. As in sporting rivalries, Australian soldiers were impelled to project a distinctive 'Australian' image, not only in contrast to the enemy they fought, but even more perhaps, against their wartime allies. The combination of a cultural warrior role and traditional rivalry with ancestral friends invested the 'digger' with doubly potent national symbolism (Fig. 37).

The term 'digger', meaning the rank and file Australian foot soldier, is closely linked with the significance of Anzac, the more formal focus of military nationalism in Australian culture. 'Anzac' has come to represent the 'spirit of the nation' and the digger has become its physical embodiment, and so a powerful symbol of the ideals of national identity. Together, these two words, and the complex of historical, mythic and emotional meanings that they invoke, have been at the centre of popular ideas about national identity since World War I.

'Anzac' is derived from the telegraphic abbreviation of Australian and New Zealand Army Corps. It seems to have been used among members of the First AIF (Australian Imperial Force) during training in Egypt, perhaps even earlier, and was immediately applied to the beach where the Australian and New Zealand troops first landed, at Gallipoli on 25 April 1915. The term 'digger' did not become an accepted denomination until 1917 on the Western Front. Nevertheless, the term is commonly employed retroactively to refer to Australian (and New Zealand) soldiers who fought from the beginning of World War I.

The symbolic importance of the digger can perhaps be gauged by the large number of apocryphal stories about the origin of the word. One claim was that the military term was derived from the mid-nineteenth-century eastern colonies gold rushes in which those who hastened to the goldfields to seek their fortunes came to be known as 'diggers'. It is also often claimed, although without documentary evidence, that the word originated at Gallipoli when the Anzacs who landed there were quickly compelled by the Turkish resistance to 'dig in'. New Zealand variations of the story include the suggestion that it came from the local term 'gum diggers' and there are numerous other folkloric accounts that claim to pinpoint the origins of the word. The only certainty is that Australian troops did not begin to call themselves 'diggers' – or to be called so by others – until at least two years after the Anzac landings at Gallipoli.[1] Regardless of the lack of historical evidence for the wide use of the term digger before 1917, the subject is often still debated passionately in letters to the editors of newspapers and in ex-service associations around the country. In 2001, Athletics Australia was forced to withdraw the use of the word as a name for the Australian athletics team, mainly in response to a negative reaction from the Returned and Services League of Australia (RSL). The digger is celebrated in the Australian War Memorial and by millions of Australians on each Anzac Day. Why is the digger such a significant symbol within the larger legend of Anzac?

At the Landing and Here Ever Since, 1915,
by David Barker for *The Anzac Book*, 1916.

Australian War Memorial

This question can be answered by analysing the idealised figure of the Australian foot soldier. In his popular representations the digger is depicted as tough, resourceful, anti-authoritarian and a bit of a larrikin who likes to drink, smoke, swear, brawl and gamble. He is an ordinary, everyday bloke who is not much interested in military niceties such as saluting officers and approaches war as a bad job that must be done. The digger is a fierce but honourable soldier.

In many of these respects, the digger is very similar to an earlier Australian ideal, the bushman. This figure evolved from the mainly nineteenth-century Australian experience of pioneering and the related development of extensive pastoral industries. The bushman was to a large extent invented by writers and painters during the last few decades of the nineteenth century at a time when the economic and social realities that had given rise to the distinctive bush lifestyle were beginning to fade. AB 'Banjo' Paterson, Tom Roberts and many other writers and artists portrayed the experiences of shearers, drovers and bushrangers through a rose-tinted rear-vision mirror. In the process they romanticised into myth such enduring figures as Paterson's 'Man From Snowy River' and 'Clancy of the Overflow', as well as the more collective stereotypes of the rural landscape celebrated in folksong and verse, such as the tough cocky farmer, the carousing overlander and the taciturn swaggie.

The bushman was seen as the ideal Australian type at a moment when the country was having its first significant bout of questioning and discussion of its identity. In the lead-up to Federation, politicians, writers, artists and members of the public debated what it meant to be 'Australian'. What was distinctive, different, perhaps even unique about being Australian? The answer was provided in the figure of the mostly itinerant, anti-authoritarian, independent bushman.[2]

The bushman goes to war

When Australian troops went to war for the first time in the name of a relatively new country called Australia, those who now sometimes called themselves 'Australians' waited anxiously to discover if they would acquit themselves well as fighting men. At the time it was widely believed that nations needed a history of military glory to be self-respecting members of the British Empire and the world in general. Even though Australia had formally become a nation in 1901, there was little emotional investment in the idea of a single national community and the states had little in common, other than the colonising experiences of pioneering. The performance of the troops at Gallipoli, the first instance in which troops fought as Australians rather than as representatives of particular colonies, was therefore going to be a highly charged emotional experience for Australians, whatever the outcome.

In the event, the Australian troops were seen to have covered themselves in military glory, as were the New Zealanders beside them.

In Australia, the news of the heroic landings was greeted with relief, joy and patriotic fervour. The Australian foot soldier was now cast as the bushman in uniform and vested with all the characteristics of the bush hero, previously the only significant national stereotype available. The fact that the campaign was in the end a military disaster did not matter. Instead, it provided a magnificent backdrop against which the final withdrawal could be presented as a triumphant victory, a display of extraordinary courage, resourcefulness and resilience in appalling conditions. And they endured. Their valour in defeat was a vindication of the quintessentially 'Australian' qualities that originated in the nineteenth-century bush and were carried into the twentieth-century battlefields by the men who would become the 'diggers', the bearers of the national ideal and symbol of the nation itself.

The processes through which this symbolism arose were both public and private. They included the personal and family experiences of citizens hearing from their sons, husbands, brothers, uncles and sometimes from women at or near the front. They also included the need for the diggers themselves to assert a distinctive national identity amid the French, New Zealand, British, Canadian and, later, Americans they confronted in significant numbers for the first time. Much World War I digger folklore revolved around the need to define and project a distinctively Australian identity against the national identities of others, as in this yarn about a sentry on duty:

> 'Halt! Who goes there?'
> 'Ceylon Planters' Rifle Club.'
> Sentry–'Pass, friend.'
> A little later–'Halt, who goes there?'
> Answer–'Auckland Mounted Rifles.'
> ['Pass, friend.']
> As the next person arrives–'Halt, Who goes there?'
> Answer–'What the – has that got to do with you?'
> Sentry–'Pass, Australian.'[3]

Anecdotes of this kind are a staple element of digger lore, insisting on distinctiveness in the form of notably colourful speech and suggesting that the digger's 'Australianness' marks him out as not only different, but implicitly superior.

When the diggers returned, their presence and their desire for recognition were ongoing reminders of their great deeds. These were celebrated in reams of prose and rhetoric extolling the links between Anzac, the digger and the nation, even if at this time these ideas were closely tied to the role of Australia within the British Empire. The following is a typical example of the more formal jingoism inspired by war, also reminding us that at that time most Australians thought of themselves as British first:

> Red with their blood is our new charter of national life and of liberty, the expression of sacrifice which alone can make us a nation worthy of the noblest Commonwealth of Nations. British to the core, they lived and fought and died.[4]

Mythologising the digger

While many diggers were notoriously reticent about their experiences and often felt uncomfortable recalling them, there were others willing to speak on their behalf. Principal among these was CEW Bean, whose multiple roles as official war correspondent and historian, editor of trench newspapers and progenitor of the Australian War Memorial, allowed him to express and embed his view of the Australian fighting man. Before the war Bean had written extensively about the ideal bushman. When he joined the troops as correspondent and chronicler of the digger he interpreted their actions and attitudes through eyes already fixed upon the bush hero.

In his many dispatches home and other writings throughout the war Bean rarely failed to extol the Anzac virtues and the magnificence of the digger. He edited *The Anzac Book* (1916), a bestselling compilation of verse, prose and art by Gallipoli troops that sat on the sparsely populated bookshelves of many Australian homes. It selectively portrayed the Anzac troops largely in their own words and images, further entrenching the stereotype that had been established from the original landings of April 1915.[5] 'Parables of Anzac', for example, provided a glimpse of the sardonically nonchalant humour that would come to typify the digger:

> From a Correspondent in Australian Field Artillery, 'Sea View,' Boltons Knoll, near Shell Green.
>
> I was looking out front the entrance of my dug-out, thinking how peaceful everything was, when Johnny Turk opened on our trenches. Shells were bursting, and fragments scattered all about Shell Green. Just at this time some new reinforcements were eagerly collecting – spent fuses and shells as mementoes.
>
> While this fusillade was on, men were walking about the Green just as usual, when one was hit by a falling fuse. Out rushed one of the reinforcement chaps, and when he saw that the man was not hurt he asked: 'Want the fuse, mate?'
>
> The other looked at him calmly. 'What do you think I stopped it for?' he asked.[6]

After the war, Bean took the role of editor and part-author of the *Official History of Australia in the War of 1914–1918* and wrote related popular books of his own, always presenting the diggers as the ideal exemplars of the Australian spirit. By then, of course, he had almost single-handedly cast the mould and the works of many other writers, speechmakers, journalists and artists would continue the mythologisation of the digger and Anzac.[7]

In addition to his historical and popular writings, Bean was largely responsible for creating the Australian War Memorial and, crucially, shaping its character as a national shrine. He operated at the highest official levels but also had an impact on the broader population through his books and his championing of the Memorial. The Memorial, opened in 1941, simultaneously achieved the official endorsement of Anzac at the national level with the fulfilment of the grassroots need for memorialisation. There, the national mythology of Anzac was fused with the image of the larrikin digger as warrior culture hero, a profoundly symbolic conflation that was the basis of the enduring and, apparently, strengthening appeal of this tradition for many Australians.

As with all mythologies and the symbols they generate, the reality often turns out to be other than glittering. The abstract principles of duty, bravery and sacrifice, enshrined in such institutionalised legends as that of Simpson and the Donkey, reflected in the Hall of Memory at the Australian War Memorial, and celebrated each 25 April, are ideals. While there were many heroic diggers, there were also diggers who deserted, murdered prisoners of war, rioted and stole from their fellows, as there were in all other armies. But these are not realities that Australians choose to recall when celebrating Anzac and the digger, whether on Anzac Day itself, in the press, in books, films, art or television mini-series. The concept of being Australian includes such popular values as 'the fair go' and lovable larrikinism, represented by the 'digger', as well as more formal Anzac qualities. Australians like to reinforce both in public displays of nation. The purpose of such spectacles as Anzac Day is to present the positive facets of the digger as exemplars of what Australians like to see as the real, typical or characteristic Australian male.

The bush hero had been a totally masculine construction. He lived his life mostly away from women, engaged in tough and unpleasant physical work with other men. His legends, songs and verse had little place for women and certainly not for Indigenous peoples. They were the expressions of white males whose main activity was hard work and hard drinking and that carried over into the symbolism around the digger. The First AIF constituted the largest assemblage of Australian men that had ever taken place. They rendezvoused on troopships at Albany and jostled together in Egypt. While some women performed outstanding service, mainly as nurses, fighting at that time was an all-male activity, much like the itinerant lifestyle of the idealised swagman, overlander, shearer and other rural workers.

Through the experiences of the AIF the bushman effortlessly morphed into the digger. Instead of driving cattle overland, shearing sheep or riding herds of brumbies, the bushman now wore a uniform – more or less – and employed his bush skills and nous on Gallipoli in excavating 'dugouts' and 'possies', making jam tin bombs, sniping and generally trying to outfox wily enemies resisting an invasion of their homeland. Even though many members of the First AIF did not come from the bush and only a minority fought the Turks, contrary to a popular and persistent myth,[8] as a body they demonstrated the bushman's ingrained disdain for authority and independence, together with such masculine pastimes as drinking, fighting and gambling. It is no coincidence that two-up became canonised at Gallipoli as the unofficial national gambling game. The digger's symbolic status, rooted in the available traditions of the bush, was immediate and enduring.

Leaving behind more than 60,000 dead comrades, the surviving diggers returned to Australia. Many joined ex-service associations, the most lasting and influential of these being the organisation now known as the Returned and Services League, the RSL. 'The League' almost immediately took upon itself the role of defender and preserver of the national flame of Anzac and the digger. It agitated successfully for Anzac Day to be celebrated across the nation and for it to be a 'close' holiday, on which no commerce was allowed and few, if any, sports played. While not everyone shared this view, by 1929 the League and its allies had secured 25 April as 'the fifty-third Sunday', and standardised the various Anzac Day activities. From 1941, the Australian War Memorial stood as a monument to Anzac and a shrine to the digger.

Within this imposing national shrine and at many smaller but connected memorials, the image of the digger continued to express the essentials of national identity, as conceived in the late nineteenth century and transformed into the volunteer private soldier of World War I. The annual Anzac Day rites pivoting around memorials large and small served as the moment of combined celebration and commemoration of Anzac and of its essential figure. The birth of the digger hero was observed in the Dawn Service, mirroring and recreating the moment in which the Anzacs left the transport ships and made their fateful way towards the dark Turkish coast. Later in the morning the diggers paraded in an approximation of military formation, displaying the medals and ribbons they had won. They wore their by-now well-recognised accessories of the slouch hat and the rising sun hat badge, themselves tangible symbols adding lustre to the concept of 'diggerness'. After lunch the larrikin factor took over, with drinking, reminiscing, reuniting with old comrades and the symbolic replaying of two-up, generally illegal on any other day of the year.

Defender of the homeland

Word War II provided another pivotal historical moment for the nation and for the digger. Drawing on the now established traditions of Anzac, a younger generation of Australians again went to war in support of Britain. Events during that conflict, notably those at Tobruk, Kokoda and in the prisoner-of-war context of Changi and the Burma Railway, provided a new opportunity for the display and further elaboration of the fabled digger attributes. The digger image gained additional power, as Australia believed itself to be under direct threat from the Japanese advance after 1941. Now the digger could be seen not only as a warrior who went to fight wars on behalf of other nations but, for the first time, also as a defender of the homeland, a further dimension to the role of culture hero. Once again, after this war there was an upsurge of membership of the RSL and other ex-service organisations that provided another generation of marchers at each Anzac Day parade. There were further smaller scale opportunities for the digger to go to war again, in Malaya and Korea during the 1950s, though these did not resonate so powerfully through the already established Anzac mythology.

Anzac Day became especially contentious during the 1960s and 1970s as a younger generation questioned its values and purpose, antagonisms exacerbated by the conflicts over Australia's role in the war in Vietnam, the issue of conscription and feminist activism around rape in war. During this period, attendance at Anzac Day events reached perhaps the lowest point ever, and it was widely expected that the commemoration would die out along with the last of the old diggers.[9]

Since the 1980s, however, the Anzac mythology has undergone an extraordinary revival. The seeds of this resurgence can be found in the depths of its malaise, with the burgeoning interest of family historians in the experiences of their soldier fathers, uncles and grandfathers. The deaths of the last Anzacs attracted extensive media coverage: now high-blown rhetoric around Anzac heroes was no longer inconveniently contradicted by actual World War I veterans.[10] Backpackers were increasingly finding their way to Gallipoli as 'pilgrims', with cheaper air travel and Turkey opening to tourism.[11] Books such as Bill Gammage's *The Broken Years* (1974) and Patsy Adam-Smith's *The Anzacs* (1978) reiterated and popularised this new emphasis on the experience of ordinary, front-line soldiers. The success of Peter Weir's film *Gallipoli* (1981) gave massive impetus to Anzac 2.0. The film's naïve young hero Archy, crucified at the Nek as he charged, unarmed, towards the Turkish trenches, was far from the lionised warriors of the original Anzac mythology. This softer, gentler version of the digger was more amenable to the experiences of the 30,000 soldiers who had been prisoners of the Japanese during World War II. With the publication of his memoirs in 1986, 'Weary' Dunlop, officer and doctor, became the symbolic representative of those prisoners of war. Dunlop was canonised into a digger mythology that increasingly favoured tales of suffering and trauma over stories of military prowess and national pride.[12] By the late 1980s, politicians discerned the stirrings of this renewed sympathy towards the Anzac legend and inserted themselves at the centre of an emerging commemorative industry, which included educational resources, expanded museums and an extensive promotional effort by the Australian Defence Force to identify with the Anzac tradition, which originally defined itself in opposition to a regular army. Paul Keating oversaw the entombment of the Unknown Soldier at the Australian War Memorial in 1993 but it was John Howard who was most adept at promoting a more assertive, flag-waving form of Australian nationalism with the Anzac legend as its centrepiece. In the process the digger's legendary larrikinism was tempered by the ADF's preference for emphasising the professionalism of the Australian army.

The centenary of the Great War revealed the enormous appetite for the Anzac among the political class, particularly those with conservative leanings. With its outlay of more than $630 million, Australia far outspent all other nations, including the major combatants, in commemorating the war. In addition to ongoing efforts to include women within the Anzac fold, there was a new government emphasis during the centenary on incorporating Indigenous and non-Anglo–Celtic diggers into the legend in order to, somewhat cynically, 'up-date' and extend the appeal of Anzac.[13] Commercial interests too sought to profit from the centenary of the Gallipoli landing, though the more ham-fisted ones, such as Woolworths' 'Fresh in Our Memories' campaign, attracted condemnation and spawned the hashtag #Brandzac. Audiences largely spurned representations of World War I in television drama and documentary, prompting commentators to report that the public was suffering from 'Anzac fatigue'.[14] On the other hand, record crowds turned out for the ritualistic Dawn Service on 25 April 2015.[15] There is evidence that attendance at Anzac Day events is settling back into its pre-centenary levels.[16] Yet, the Commonwealth Government continues to bankroll the Anzac industry; following the opening of the

$100 million Sir John Monash Centre at Villers-Bretonneux in France in 2018, the government allocated $500 million in 2019 for a major renovation and expansion of the Australian War Memorial at a time when other museums and libraries were having funds cut.

A magnificent fiction

Not all Australians feel attached to the digger. There are strong and deep critiques from an intelligentsia concerned about jingoistic excess, though the cost of maligning the secular religion of Anzac and its digger idol is high.[17] Sports journalist Scott McIntyre was sacked by SBS for a series of tweets critical of Anzac Day in 2015; young Muslim commentator Yassmin Abdel-Magied left Australia after death threats and trolling following her tweet 'LEST WE FORGET. (Manus, Nauru, Syria, Palestine …)' on Anzac Day, 2017; artist Abdul Abdullah saw his tapestries of diggers taken down from a gallery in Mackay, Queensland, after complaints from the RSL and local politicians in 2019 (Fig. 38). Nor can it be expected that those who have migrated here from countries uninvolved in the conflicts that created Anzac and the digger will need or wish to acquiesce in his symbolism, though one extraordinary development is the way Australia's Turkish community has found a place for the Gallipoli story.

But for a majority the digger remains a powerful figure. His larrikin character, his slouch hat, its rising sun emblem, itself associated powerfully with the Federation of Australia and the notion of the 'birth of a nation', continue to project an idealised representation of Australian values and identity. The digger symbol is invariably invoked by politicians and the media whenever the need arises to send Australians to make war or to keep peace, as in East Timor, Iraq and Afghanistan. While these troops are professional soldiers rather than volunteers or conscripts, they are widely seen as bearers of the Anzac tradition. The risk for politicians of conflating modern-day professionals with

Spirit of the Digger, cast of the Braidwood
War Memorial, New South Wales.

National Museum of Australia

the volunteer diggers of World War I is evident in the revelations of the 2020 Brereton Report into alleged Australian war atrocities in Afghanistan. Following a four-year investigation, the report detailed credible evidence to support allegations that 25 Australian soldiers were involved in the unlawful killing of 39 Afghan civilians. These are the latest in a history of documented soldier atrocities, which began with the frontier wars and the Boer War at the turn of the twentieth century. Yet so powerful is the digger trope and so great the popular desire to believe in it, that the digger may well emerge from this latest scandal with his reputation somewhat tarnished, but largely intact.

The digger stands for the Australian nation, complete with his racist, masculinist bushman baggage, his naïve xenophobia and his rowdy larrikinism. He also stands for a young, barely conscious country of 'mettlesome gaucho-people'[18] aspiring to glorious feats of arms, of unprecedented heroism and suffering within a brutal Japanese captivity. He stands for every son, father and brother who has gone to war, or who will go in the future. The digger remains an essentially Australian symbol because he is at once the producer and the product of the national mythology and its profound connections with wars fought mostly in other places as an ally of Australia's most important strategic and cultural partners. In the aftermath of the 2019–20 bushfires, those who had died fighting the blazes were referred to as 'the fallen', resonating with the rituals and language of Anzac. The belated deployment of the army and navy to bushfire areas also contributed to militarising the understanding of tragedy and disaster. As with the Bali bombings, the symbolism and rhetoric of Anzac and the digger are providing new modes of commemoration and mourning for the national dead.[19] The idealised Australian soldier is a magnificent fiction, and a profoundly ambivalent one. But he is a convenient fiction in which are combined the worst and the best. The digger, like that other ambivalent national icon, Ned Kelly, is likely to stand with Australians and for Australia long into the foreseeable future.

AUSTRALIA HOUSE

Olwen Pryke

The first building designed to act as a symbol of Australia was located in London. Long before Parliament House stood in Canberra, Australia House was rising proudly in the Strand for all the world to see. For over two decades from its opening in 1918, it was the Commonwealth's only diplomatic mission overseas.

'I suggest that it might be called "Australia House"', wrote Sir George Reid, Australia's first high commissioner in Great Britain. He preferred 'House' to 'Chambers', 'Offices' and 'Buildings', which he thought hackneyed: 'It seems to me that the word "House" carries with it the idea of a "home" for Australia in London, and would mark out this particular part of London as Australian.'[1] The dignity of 'Chambers', the modern efficiency of 'Offices', the utility of 'Buildings', would each have represented a particular image of Australia in Great Britain. Reid wanted more: not only to represent Australia in London, which Australians imagined to be the centre of the world, but to mark out a part of London as Australian and make a particular part of the city, 'home'.

The uncertainty over the appropriate name for the Offices of the Commonwealth in London reflected a broader debate about the role Australia House was meant to play. Following the federation of the six Australian colonies in 1901, Australia remained dependent on the British Empire. Economically, politically, constitutionally, culturally,

Victory march through London, 3 May 1919. Members of the 1st AIF march around the impressive new symbol of Australia in the heart of Empire.

National Library of Australia

Australia's connection with Great Britain was its paramount focus, although increasingly constrained by a growing sense of Australia's separate interests and independent national aspirations. Australians wished to expand their markets, increase their white population through the immigration of appropriate settlers, convince London City of their financial stability and encourage investment. For all these reasons it was agreed that Australia should be represented in London by a high commissioner, in a high commission.

Expectations of Australia House were always complicated by the structure's symbolic tasks. Unlike many symbols, Australia House was to be a tangible manifestation of Australia. The very building was meant to be a physical representation of Australia: to take Australia itself to London, so all the world would see 'Australia' in architectural form. It was to be the symbolic means by which the new nation would physically exist in stone and timber, gold and marble.

Moreover, like the coat of arms and the national flag, Australia House was officially sanctioned as a national symbol. And in contrast to other structures that came to symbolise the nation over time – the Opera House or the Sydney Harbour Bridge – Australia House was erected with this function foremost in mind.

Yet questions over its meaning, its role, and who was supposed to benefit were never conclusively resolved. These tensions were evident in the ways in which Australia House attempted to accommodate the very different needs of its British visitors and Australian guests. Australia House acted as the public entrance for the nation: 'our national "foyer"', as one Australian journalist declared.[2] It was intended to be an imposing space as well as a welcoming space, providing the first official glimpse of Australia. For British visitors – intending investors, uncertain immigrants, inquiring schoolchildren, excited tourists – it formed an entry point to Australian life. But it was to serve Australians as well. At the outset it was to provide a stable and secure base for Australians, a 'home' from which to explore and return: somewhere to collect their mail, do their banking, read the newspapers and meet other Australians (Fig. 39). And it was expected to meet all these aims by portraying a single unitary idea of Australia at a time when there was little agreement on what Australia was or was to become.

Locating Australia House

To build Australia in London required an appropriate site. Extended parliamentary and press debate over the best location exposed tensions between the symbolic and practical functions of the high commission. Debates about the location of the nation's capital played out simultaneously. It would be easy to assume that the selection of the site for the capital in Australia would take precedence. But few questioned the assumption that securing a site in London was more pressing. Labor Senator James Charles Stewart pointed out that the amount proposed for the purchase of a mere block of land in London would be enough to build the Houses of Parliament in Australia.³ But these parallels were seldom drawn.

Indeed, when in 1911 Alfred Deakin (leader of the opposition and former prime minister) reflected on Australia's need for diplomatic representation, he argued that, from the Commonwealth's beginning, 'it was always recognised as one of the essentials that we should be represented in London, and on a fitting scale'.⁴ What exactly constituted a fitting scale proved a real point of contention.

A fitting scale demanded a fitting location. As Senator John Neild noted, there were tens of thousands of properties available in London, 'but they would not answer our purpose. We do not want a building in a back street.' Senator Edward Pulsford agreed: Australia 'does not desire merely to obtain so many square feet of land, but a site in the very centre of the heart of the Empire'.⁵ The Australian Government only seriously considered two sites: one in Trafalgar Square, the other in the Strand.

While there was a distinct 'push' from Australia for representation in Britain, there was a corresponding 'pull' from interested parties in London. The government was deluged with offers from across London. Commercial imperatives influenced which sites were suggested for consideration. The London County Council had radically rebuilt the Strand, Aldwych and Kingsway in the early years of the twentieth century, but was disappointed that it had failed to attract prestigious tenants and financial returns. One 'waggish' Australian visitor even suggested the neighbourhood was particularly suitable for the Commonwealth Offices, because it recalled the less populous parts of Australia.⁶ Keen to recoup on their investment, the London County Council offered the Australian Government options on three sites in the vicinity and was not averse to playing on intercolonial rivalries by making it known that Canada too was negotiating for a site nearby.⁷

Similarly, the consideration of Trafalgar Square – widely thought to be the heart of London – was influenced by the fact that Canada had an existing Immigration Bureau there. Canada was seen as an exemplar of the best representation and advertising in Great Britain and recourse to the Canadian example was often a clinching point in any discussion. Deakin took up this position, confessing, 'We have been rather tardy both in our choice and in this action, especially when we take into account the extraordinary success of the efforts which have been put forward by the great Dominion of Canada during all the years that we have been idle'.[8]

Astonished that more than a decade had slipped by debating the question, a *Sydney Morning Herald* contributor argued that: 'Plainly what is wanted is one great and imposing pile of Australian buildings in a central situation … It should be a prominent landmark, even in London, and set forth the pride and power of Australia in a way that would come home to the most unthinking.'[9] The sites were again considered and Sir George Reid, the newly appointed high commissioner, ultimately recommended the purchase of land on the Aldwych curve of the Strand. On 12 December 1911, Senate debated the resolution and the decision was made to acquire the entire corner site.[10] Australia had secured a location considered a particularly appropriate setting for a modern, progressive nation at the start of the twentieth century.

Designing Australia House

The Australian Government acted quickly to commence the design. The building was shaped by a mix of metropolitan, national and imperial agendas, as well as tensions between pragmatism and symbolism. Metropolitan pressure came from the London County Council, which required certain standards of design and the use of a specific building material, Portland stone, in its construction.[11]

In February 1912 the well-respected Scottish architect Alexander Marshall Mackenzie and his son Alexander George Robertson Mackenzie were appointed, causing consternation among Australian members of the profession. The architects produced a design influenced by beaux arts classicism, a style particularly fashionable in Britain late in the first decade of the twentieth century. It incorporated eclectic historical styles, revelled in a profusion of detail and gave prominence to grand public spaces. However, the question remained as to what, exactly, was an appropriate scale. The Melbourne *Age* was concerned by Australian pretensions to too much sophistication, alarmed by a scheme 'beside which the appearance of any European power at the Court of St James will be dwarfed into insignificance'. 'Of course', Labor's William Archibald argued in 1911, 'we do not want a building equal to Buckingham Palace, or to the Mansion House, but we should have, as near as possible to the city of London, a building which, without being gaudy or vulgar in style, will be creditable to Australia.'[12] This proved a delicate balance to achieve.

An advisory committee of Australian artists in London consisting of Bertram Mackennal (chair), George Lambert, Fred Leist, John Longstaff and Arthur Streeton had been convened to assist the architects. Upon examination of the architectural plans, they were satisfied that a workable balance had been reached between beauty and practicality of design.[13] The more utilitarian Arthur Atlee Hunt, permanent head of the Department for External Affairs, was less taken with the result. 'I cannot tell you how disappointed I am with the plans for the London Offices', he grumbled:

> The architects don't seem to have risen to the occasion at all. Everything internal seems to me to have been sacrificed to an attempt at grandeur which in my judgment might have been equally well achieved without the sacrifice of utility which is obvious in the present designs.[14]

To Hunt's chagrin, the pragmatic demands of an efficiently functioning office had been sacrificed to the less tangible goals of pleasing aesthetics and an impressive symbolic statement. It was a criticism that would continue to haunt Australia House.

Bertram Mackennal's bronze scultpure of Apollo driving the horses of the sun, facing east – and the future – above the main entrance of Australia House, London.

Photograph by Richard White

Constructing Australia House

The Australian Government was so eager to start construction that the excavations were completed even before the plans were officially approved by the London County Council. In July 1913 the foundation stone was laid, an event which was understood quite literally to cement Australia's relations with the Empire. But World War I brought delays, even though the British Government waived restrictions on non-essential construction due to the morale-boosting value of 'building the Empire' while at war. Transport difficulties hindered the supply of materials, particularly marble and timber shipped from Australia, and labour was scarce.[15] But eventually, in December 1917, the high commissioner and his staff were finally transferred to their still-incomplete premises in Australia House.

On stepping into the echoing entrance hall, visitors were struck by the cool marble features and fine gilt work. The architects' gesture towards creating a distinctively Australian space was their extensive use of Australian materials in the imposing interior, the *Argus* speculating that it was probably the first time they had been used in England. The builders estimated 1100 tonnes of Australian marble was used, including the dove-coloured Buchan from Victoria, light and dark Caloola marble from New South Wales, and white Angaston from South Australia. The ornate panelling in the high commissioner's offices and the main offices on the first floor featured Australian black bean timber. The Australian joinery and flooring timbers were selected to include varieties from the different states, and the furniture for the principal rooms, designed by the architects, was made in Australia. In addition, various symbols were employed to depict Australian industries and interests: rams' heads (sheep-raising), pickaxes (mining) and wattle were common motifs.[16]

The expenditure of up to £25,000 had been approved for the provision of painting and sculpture for the building, though a competition to secure mural art was suspended during the war. While Bertram Mackennal was chair of the advisory committee, he was acknowledged as Australia's greatest sculptor, and both he and Harold Parker entered into contracts to prepare works to grace the entrance. Parker's sculptures, which flank the main doorway – symbolic groups denoting the Awakening and Prosperity of Australia – were raised in 1918. Mackennal's dramatic double-life-sized bronze of Apollo driving the horses of the sun, which sits above the main eastern entrance, was finally positioned some five years later.[17]

On its completion in 1918, Australia House stood apart on its island site. Striking colonnades lined the Aldwych and Strand. Of modern steel-frame construction, with a distinctive copper roof, the building rose above the surrounding avenues to a height of seven storeys. As required by London County Council regulations, the exterior was fashioned predominantly of Portland stone, but secured on a base of

Australian trachyte.[18] This combination of stone – one characteristic of London, the other Australia – symbolised the relationship between Britain and Australia, brought together in the exterior of Australia House. Eileen Chanin's recent history further details the complications facing the Scottish architects and the Australian artists and sculptors who attempted to unite materials and symbolism in the building's composition.[19] While the result of compromise, as symbols often are, the outcome was a confident and impressive assertion of Australia's distinctive place in London.

Reconsidering Australia House

Once Australia House was set in stone, a version of the nation was authorised and given physical form, fixed in the architectural structure of the building and in its institutional practices. While many were pleased with the outcome, it was at this moment that the building's version of the nation made explicit the contestation symbols frequently attract. Arguments arose around both the elusive conception of the nation and the contradictions between the high commission's practical functions and its less tangible symbolic tasks.

Contemporary reviews applauded the monumental spirit of Australia House. The *Builder* could 'call to mind few modern buildings of importance which have occupied their sites with such good results'.[20] The British architectural community and construction industry praised the 'frankly modern' building, but opinion among the Australian population was mixed. Australian parliamentarians and officials in London pronounced the building a success, representative of the budding Australian nation. But even the *British-Australasian*, generally a keen supporter of the venture, bitingly referred to Australia House as 'the great Commonwealth palace in the Strand'.[21]

Its modernity was increasingly challenged as architectural design moved from the classicism espoused by the beaux arts tradition to embrace the minimalist styling of art deco in the 1920s. Certainly by the 1950s Australia House was widely considered passé. Though Australia House survived the London blitz of World War II with minor damage, little was being done to renovate the building. The very fact of its solid intransigence told against it as a symbol of 'modern' Australia. Newspapers disparagingly referred to its 'ugly, grey bulk'. For John Haskell, the architectural correspondent for the *Sydney Morning Herald* in the early 1980s, it was 'yet another overblown pile of Edwardian bombast', a 'hodge-podge' of out-dated styles, jarring to the modern eye, as if 'the jolly swagman had been dressed up in a doublet and hose'.[22] Its grandiloquence remained outmoded for many years.

Australia House continued to represent Australian interests in Great Britain, but in a world transformed. Originally Australia relied on channels of communication provided by the British Foreign and Commonwealth Offices for its international diplomacy. From 1939, the Australian Government established more independent representation abroad, seeking to take a more autonomous position in foreign affairs. Around the world, new Australian embassies, legations, high commissions, consulates and permanent missions were taking on the role of symbolising Australia. By the 1970s, Australia House had become just another of Australia's many missions abroad.

By 1992, Australia House's architecture had been sufficiently reconsidered to warrant English heritage listing as an important exemplar of imperial design.[23] A magnificent restoration and a subsequent role in the phenomenally popular Harry Potter films brought the building to public attention again. Celebrating its centenary in 2018, Australia House is the longest continuously occupied foreign mission in London.

Debates about the high commission's location, its design and the very fabric of the building demonstrate how porous and negotiable Australian national identity was, and how difficult it proved to symbolise. Australia House has always been more than marble and stone: an architectural affirmation of federation, trade emporium, recruiting office, library, polling booth (Australia's largest), diplomatic mission, meeting place, film set, and refuge for the homesick (Fig. 40). More than one hundred years on, high commissioner George Brandis echoed the first high commissioner's hopes for the building, stating that for Australians in Britain, it is 'their building' still.[24]

VEGEMITE

Robert White

In 2006, Mark Scott, the managing director of the Australian Broadcasting Corporation (ABC), trumpeted research that showed the only brand name more popular in Australia than the ABC was Vegemite.[1] How a by-product of the brewing industry came to acquire such affection – to be even named one of Australia's national icons on a prime minister's website – was as much a matter of clever marketing as the unlikely appeal of its distinctive flavour. The combination meant that by 2008 Vegemite, with its characteristic marketing opportunism, could claim to have sold its billionth jar. By 2020 the brand's latest owner, Bega Cheese, has been emboldened to widen its ambit, copyrighting as its exclusive trademark the ambitious phrase 'Tastes like Australia'.[2]

Vegemite's improbable origins date back to the invention of Marmite in 1902. Marmite was distributed in Britain and New Zealand by the Sanitarium Health Food Company, an arm of the Seventh Day Adventist Church whose promotion of healthy eating had considerable success in Australia. The fact that it was made with a waste product from beer, yeast extract, was always a source of embarrassment to the teetotal church. It soon made inroads into the Australian market, promoted to a health-conscious society excited about the recent discovery of vitamins. Rich in the vitamin B complex, Marmite was described as 'pure vegetable extract' and linked with the call to 'eat plenty of greens'. Advertising celebrated its versatility. It could be used to fill sandwiches and spread biscuits, to enrich all manners of soups, stews and savoury dishes, to provide 'a refreshing and invigorating "cup"' and, more surprisingly, to make a 'piquant' tasting custard, a change from sweet desserts. In the patriarchal society of Australia in the 1920s, Marmite was also advertised as 'a man's drink', with the advice, 'It is very economical in use – Ask your wife to buy the Large Jars'.

Fred Walker and Company was an Australian firm selling cheese and preserved meats to country areas in the eastern states of Australia. In 1922, flushed with the success of Bonox, a copy of Britain's Bovril, Fred Walker passed a jar of Marmite to his brilliant chemist, Cyril P Callister, asking, 'Could you produce a product like that?' Callister had never seen it before, but he researched the chemical makeup of Marmite and discovered it was made from brewer's yeast from the Burton-on-Trent Breweries. Callister wrote up his research in a thesis which was awarded a DSc from the University of Melbourne. Fred Walker used supplies from Carlton Breweries in Melbourne to simulate Marmite, and thus in 1923 was born a product sold in small amber jars. The name, Vegemite, was the winning entry in a competition.

Disappointed by poor sales, Fred Walker renamed the product Parwill – 'If Ma might, then Pa will' – although it was marketed under this name only in Queensland. Sales fell still further, and the name Vegemite returned for good in a new opal glass jar. Other suppliers of raw materials came on board: Tooheys' Brewery and Tooth and Company in New South Wales and later Foster's in Victoria. The fact that such well-known breweries were behind Vegemite gave it an added richness of Australian reference, bringing together Australia's favourite (allegedly) wholesome foodstuff with its favourite alcoholic beverage.[3] The link was made explicit in 2007 when the Victorian Ministry of Justice banned Vegemite from gaols, because prisoners – perhaps equally deserving of a DSc – had found a way of extracting the yeast to make alcohol.[4] Surely Ned Kelly's ambiguous status as rebel and rogue hovers somewhere in this story.

In the Depression years Vegemite was still losing the battle with Marmite for markets in Australia and New Zealand. In 1926 Walker amalgamated with the United States company Kraft Cheese to form Kraft Walker Cheese Company. More vigorous, American-style advertising strategies in the mid-1930s, such as offering with every Kraft Walker product a coupon that could be redeemed for a jar of Vegemite, really launched the product as a mass commodity. By 1946 it was being advertised with images of Walt Disney cartoon figures. Vegemite's success in the Australian market owed much to the genius of the American adman contracted by Kraft, J Walter Thompson, who has been described as 'the father of modern magazine advertising'.[5]

During World War II, both Marmite and Vegemite were considered essential to the war effort. The export of Marmite from England was curtailed and, in Australia, restrictions were imposed on civilian sales of Vegemite. Advertising turned the restrictions to Vegemite's advantage (Fig. 41), making much of both its use in the armed forces and its value in building up the nation: 'If you are one of those who don't need Vegemite medicinally, the thousands of invalids and babies are asking you to deny yourself of it for the time being.'[6] Before returning to those curious medicinal uses, it is worth noting that the out-moded word 'invalids' refers not primarily to convalescents from illness but to the war-wounded. As well as being identified with health and vitality, through the Depression and war years the company endorsed thrift as a social value by presenting two pieces of bread with Vegemite as a wholesome and rounded meal – breakfast or lunch. The increased wartime demand proved an opportunity for the manufacturers, who, faced with limited supplies of brewer's yeast, set up a factory producing baker's yeast. Vegemite would continue to be made from a blend of brewer's and baker's yeast, augmented by vegetable extract to soften the taste. In 1947 a huge supply of yeast waste, produced by the extraction of pure alcohol from sugar, was sourced from northern Queensland.

This enabled Vegemite production to expand and diversify throughout Australia and New Zealand.

After the war, Vegemite redefined its significance for the civilian population by shifting from its wartime associations with virile manhood to advertising its health benefits to the child-centred society of the 1950s. In 1954 one of Australia's most popular radio jingles went to air:

> We're happy little Vegemites as bright as bright can be.
> We all enjoy our Vegemite for breakfast, lunch and tea.
> Our mummy says we're growing stronger every single week.
> Because we love our Vegemite, we all adore our Vegemite,
> It puts a rose in every cheek.

In 1956 the song appeared on the new medium of television, sung by children in top hats, choreographed by their dance teacher Helen de Paul. In 2006 the original eight singers were reunited as a publicity event after a national search on the 50th 'birthday'. This revival led to another advertising strategy which interwove the original black and white commercial with children singing along to their grandparents' tune.[7] The symbolic intention was to associate Vegemite with nostalgia for school lunches in the 1950s, linking baby boomers and their grandchildren in an Australia that looked back to an imagined, secure past.

Health food of a nation

The main claim made for Vegemite was always its health benefits, as the jingle suggested. Scientists supported these claims, most notably Dr Keith Farrer, later a foundation fellow of the Australian Academy of Technological Sciences and Engineering. Cyril Callister hired him in 1938 to conduct chemical measurements of the amount of vitamin B1 (thiamine) in Vegemite. Developing his own equipment and

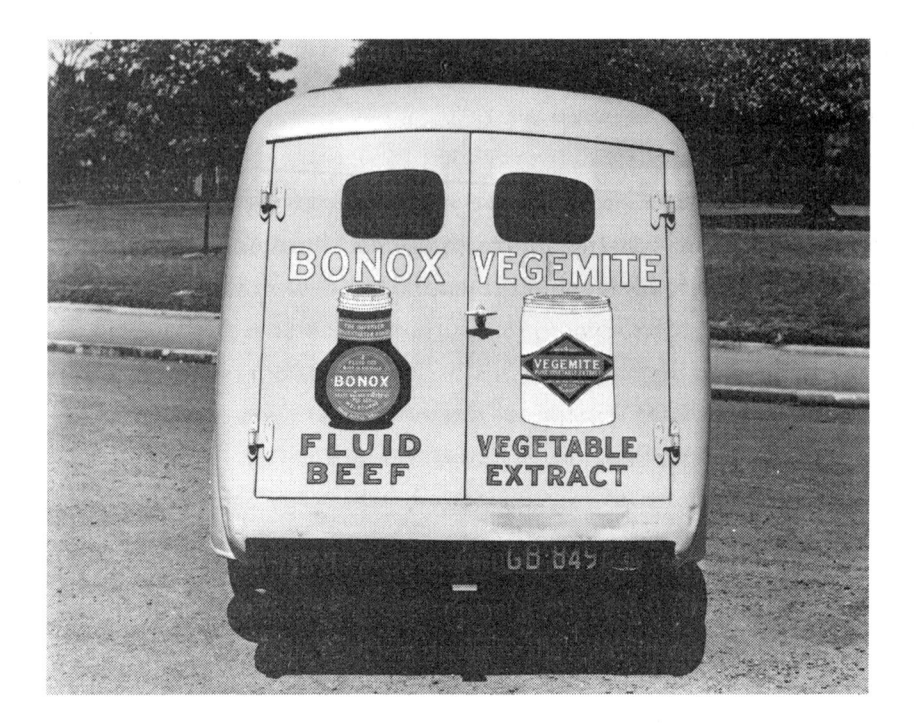

Delivery van, 1947.

Photograph by Lyle Fowler, Harold Paynting collection, State Library of Victoria

methodology, Farrer wrote a series of papers in scientific journals on the properties of vitamin B1 in foods. These led Professor Sir Cedric Stanton Hicks, director of the Australian Army Catering Corps, to include Vegemite in servicemen's rations, especially in the tropics as protection against beri-beri. Farrer wrote that, after the war:

> we extended this work to other B group vitamins, riboflavin, niacin (nicotinic acid) and folic acid and we were able to tell paediatricians how much there was of these factors in the product, so they were able to write Vegemite into the diets of young children which was then taken up by the baby health centres.[8]

Farrer built up the Kraft Research and Development team to about 65 people in their golden age of the 1960s. Gardeners would later agree on Vegemite's remarkable capacity to stimulate growth: apparently even plants thrive on its vitamin B as it helps the root development of cuttings.[9]

The health claims made for Vegemite were largely responsible for turning it into a national symbol by the 1950s. They connected it to the same longstanding ideas about the natural healthiness of the Australian and aspirations for the evolutionary fitness of the nation that produced the lifesaver. Products with claims to promote health and vitality had an advantage in the Australian market. One of the ironies was that thiamine, the component of the vitamin B complex that maintains the nervous system, is notoriously depleted by heavy drinking: in circular fashion it would be argued that it should be added to beer. Armed with their scientifically based health claims, the producers of Vegemite predictably stressed its health benefits. It has no fat whatsoever, very few kilojoules, no added sugar, no animal content and no gluten. The cult of the young, healthy and beautiful body was served by advertising for children assuring them that thriving brain cells, fully toned nerves, healthy skin, efficient digestion and sparkling eyes inevitably followed a diet of Vegemite. Its health reputation produced its own folk remedies: claims that Vegemite could cure mouth ulcers, that it was a useful antidote for insect bites in the bush, that it reduced swelling. Suggestions have been made that its folic acid content protects against spina bifida and that it can cure muscular dystrophy; it even alleviates dyslexia by increasing learning and memory capacities. Witnesses from World War II told remarkable stories of Vegemite's curative and reviving properties, with seriously debilitated prisoners of war from Changi treated with Vegemite for vitamin deficiency. In 2007, Sir Paul Nurse, Nobel Prize winner in physiology and medicine, suggested that research into Vegemite, or at least cell division in yeast, could eventually unlock a cure for cancer.[10]

In the late twentieth century, however, there was some resistance from the fringes of science to the curative claims and scepticism about the health benefits. The first attack was from the anti-salters. Dr Mark

Leggett and Susan Leggett, in *The Australian Food Report* in 1989, found both Marmite and Vegemite massively above the guideline levels for sodium. In a rather tart and frankly unAustralian throwaway line, they added '[Vegemite's] savouriness is, we felt, somewhat harsh, and unmellowed by the sugar content that helps make Marmite palatable'.[11] With such unashamedly personal taste, they had no compunction about opening up an area of nationalistic contention between Australians and Britons. Vegemite responded by drastically reducing the salt content. However, other researchers pursued the line that pure, concentrated yeast is not good for anybody, let alone children, particularly when coinciding with the huge post-war expansion in sugar consumption. They alleged that feeding yeast with sugar caused a kind of explosion which, enacted in the human body, could weaken the immune system and lead to allergies, thrush and asthma, all of which seem to have steadily increased in post-war Australia. The argument is that Vegemite's benefits before World War II were turned into drawbacks, because of the social context which introduced more sugar, pasteurised milk and preservatives in food. The ferociousness of the debate suggests the scientists moved beyond a scientific question to a national one:

> We are killing our children with food, says nutritionist Peter Dingle ... Everyone talks about Vegemite being so good for kids and rich in B vitamins ... But you are also getting a massive dose of sodium ... Does that make a nutritious meal? No.[12]

Dingle called for Australians to stop feeding their children 'toxic' food such as white bread and Vegemite sandwiches, and to resist the blandishments of advertising campaigns based on health claims. But were they heard? Scientists were no longer the unquestioned darlings of national progress, as they had been in the era of Callister and Farrer, and were now under suspicion from a cynical Australian public.

Vegemite in the world

In Australia Vegemite is so ubiquitous that it is taken for granted, but it has different meanings elsewhere. In Britain it quietly entered major supermarkets, corner shops and exclusive delicatessens in the 1990s, but seems to be bought by expatriate Australians out of homesickness or by sceptical English out of curiosity. Other countries proved less receptive. An attempt to market Vegemite in Japan, on the theory that it resembled soy sauce, failed when the sample consumers found it inedible. However, tastes change in surprising ways. In 2008 it was reported that the Vegemite headquarters at Fishermans Bend had become a regular tourist stop for Japanese who ask where they can buy supplies: 'Vegemite has been declared by Japanese gourmets to be *umami,* one of the few foods with an almost mythical fifth taste of deliciousness.'[13] United States citizens, unaware that they owned the product, recorded a dislike for Vegemite when in Fremantle for the America's Cup in 1987. The *Toledo Blade*'s outdoor editor reported back from Perth that Vegemite had the consistency of 'axle grease':

> It smells like a can of rusty nails, and tastes salty and yeasty
> – at best – or maybe like a bloody lip or an inadvertently
> bitten tongue. It definitely is an acquired taste, yet 15 million
> Australians consume something like 4,500 tons of it a year ...
> Now the stuff supposedly can be found in 9 out of 10 Australian
> households.[14]

He concluded that 'maybe the motto Down Under should be, "Vegemite – don't leave home without it"', stumbling onto a truism, for many Australians do just that. In 2006, despite a new free trade agreement, there were reports of American customs and border guards confiscating jars of Vegemite from visitors entering the United States, because of its high levels of folate, which under food and drug legislation was restricted to bread.[15] The controversy led to questions being raised at ambassadorial level – and an indignant open letter to President George W Bush from a reader of the *Geelong Advertiser*.[16] More recently, President Obama declared Vegemite to be 'horrible', and the product has been included in Sweden's Disgusting Foods Museum, much to Australian indignation.[17] But any suggestions of apparent parochial regionalism are implicitly refuted on the most recent website, which offers over 60 recipes adapting international cuisine by adding Vegemite, such as Beef Shawarma Skewers, Vegemite Pho, Beef and Black Bean Stir Fry, Vegemite and Cheese Spaghetti and a host of others.[18] International denigration served to embellish rather than diminish its symbolic role in the national imagination.

In their attachment to Vegemite, Australians travelling abroad supply a set of unconsciously symbolic readings which revolve around concepts of 'home', childhood, nationalism, and perhaps a fondness for Australian kitsch. It is remarkable how many people attest to having a relative abroad who regularly requests supplies of Vegemite, and many witnesses have told of Australian travellers in unlikely places producing their familiar yellow, red and black pot at mealtimes. While detained at Guantánamo Bay Interrogation Centre, David Hicks received Vegemite from his father, passed on by his lawyer, Michael Mori.[19] One of the accused 'Australian Nine' drug mules in Denpasar Prison in Bali was delivered a jar of Vegemite from his parents.[20] There are outposts for the desperate expat in the United States: according to Jessica Hart, the new face of fashion label Guess, Vegemite on toast is served in Rosie's, an Australian-owned café in New York, where Heath Ledger is said to have had his final breakfast.

Expatriate Australians in Britain may be the one group that genuinely attaches symbolic status to Vegemite, taking a cue from Barry Humphries' cult creations in the satirical *Adventures of Barry McKenzie*:

> Aunt Edna: Boys, boys. Your mother sent us some scrumptious things all the way from sun-drenched Australia. Close your eyes, close your eyes. A tin of lamingtons and three jars of Vegemite.

Barry: You beauty, fantastic ... best cook this side of the black stump mum, no risk.²¹

Various associations that would never occur to non-London Australians play around this exchange: recollection of a 'sun-drenched' childhood in the 1950s contrasting with the pitiable Pommies' dark, deprived environment, where abundant dog droppings litter the footpaths; mother's 'scrumptious' but simple cooking; naïve, simple culinary tastes at a time before multiculturalism; and an overall ambiguity, mingling affection and embarrassment for 'home' felt by those who left Australia for good in the 1960s. Many expatriates came to regard their birthplace as both stultifyingly conformist and yet a secure and reliable memory in times of homesickness – and Vegemite could stand for both sentiments. In the play *The Vegemite Tales* (the title echoing the pilgrimage motif of *The Canterbury Tales*), the characters, living in cheap, shared accommodation in West London, left Australia in their early adulthood to spend time between education and real life in the metropolis. Written by, and apparently for, a new generation of Australian expatriates, it achieved cult status in London, combining nostalgia and self-recognition for a largely Australian audience.

In 1950, the company became Kraft Foods Limited and was wholly American owned. Periodically there were rumours, the latest in 2007, that Vegemite production would move offshore. Kraft's biscuit-making operations shifted to China, but popular outrage fuelled by the media kept Vegemite production in Australia. The fear was partly industrial, that jobs would disappear in Australia, and partly sentimental, that a national symbol would lose its potency, but also gastronomic, that the taste would change if Australian beers were not used, as the Irish have worried that Guinness would taste different without the malodorous Liffey water. But in a global economy such nationalism may be too precious. Few of the comparable products that promote their Australianness are locally owned and produced: those that are include Victa lawnmowers, Akubra hats, Rosella tomato sauce and

Bonds singlets. Many are (or were) foreign-owned but produced here: Holden Commodore, Aeroplane Jelly, Hills hoist, Billabong fashion wear. Still others are owned and made overseas: Bushells tea, Speedo, Arnott's biscuits and Vicks VapoRub. Foreign ownership – even foreign manufacture – seems to make no difference to their status as iconic Australian products.[22] It suggests when it comes to commercial symbols, nationality is merely a matter of marketing. However, there has been something of a boomerang effect. In 2017 Vegemite was bought back from Kraft (or rather its then subsidiary, food giant Mondelez) by another iconic Australian company, Bega Cheese, for $530 million. Bega's shares soared and the patriotic public was gratified.[23]

The beauties of Vegemite

Nevertheless, its role as a national symbol has produced an aesthetics of Vegemite. The Powerhouse Museum in Sydney has a collection of Vegemite jars from the 1920s: they appear as a distinctive and evolving art form. The shape of the jar has undergone changes from time to time: copies of the Marmite jar were shaped and named after the French cooking pot; the current straight-sided jam jar of the 1990s was a throwback to an early prototype, as was its 'black gold' colour scheme. Perhaps it is a coincidence that the black, red and gold of the Vegemite jar were repeated in the Aboriginal flag. The colours on advertising seem to have darkened and intensified over recent years, adding a visual message which draws subliminally on indigeneity. Vegemite has also produced its own pictorial genre, at least in Western Australia. Diluted or undiluted, and applied with fingers or spatula on butcher's paper or card, Vegemite can produce an effect of sepia and charcoal. Vegemite painting, one of Australia's uniquely regional art forms, emerged among thrifty country people who lacked access to ready supplies of paints.

For something so familiar to every Australian, it has produced surprisingly few literary references. Julian Croft's poem, 'Strangeness and charm', speaks of 'north coast beaches' as epitomised by golden banksia:

> brought back in sprigs to dry
> into the faded blue of sailors' dungarees,
> stuck in vegemite jars in frosty
> tableland kitchens, their water rusty
> with age and neglect, like myself.[24]

The image seems to call up the banality of the everyday in Australia, and the quiet desperation of jars recycled as vases. More parodically glamorous associations appear in 'The spider', a short story by Georgia Savage, in the line 'To find her waiting for me with what looked like an entire jar of Vegemite on her eyelashes'.[25] The Australian rock band, Men at Work, was responsible for Vegemite's best-known literary reference in 1982, in the song 'Down under'.[26] The singer, finding himself in Brussels, asks a muscular man of 6'4":

> 'Do you speak-a my language?'
> He just smiled and gave me a Vegemite sandwich.

For an Australian overseas, nothing more needed to be said. Other cultural references occurred in children's books such as *Possum Magic* by Mem Fox (1983) and the alphabet book, John Brennan's *A is for Australia* (1984), reinforcing Vegemite's indispensable connection to an Australian childhood.

Just occasionally Vegemite has had deeper social resonance in its relation to Australian ethnic diversity. In school playgrounds of the 1950s, Vegemite sandwiches were the measure of an assimilationist Australia, positioned against the salami and pungent cheeses of the lunches of migrant children. Fifty years later Vegemite's positioning was more complex. The ultimate in 'fusion food' might be Vegemite-flavoured ice cream made by Italian-trained Gherardo De Florian in his Brisbane Gelateria Cremona in 2007.[27] It was described as a 'multicultural flavour'. In the 1980s, the Office of Multicultural Affairs produced a poster with the caption:

MULTICULTURALISM
OUR NATION WAS BUILT ON IT
SPREAD IT AROUND

Designed by a TAFE student, Michael Sarah, the poster called on a jar of Vegemite to stand for 'Multicultural Australia', an interesting example of Vegemite's symbolic capacity to cross social divides.[28] When John Howard was elected prime minister in 1996, multiculturalism, as a word and a policy, fell out of favour. The dominant symbolic references of Vegemite returned nostalgically to the 1950s and the White Australia Policy. In the 2007 election campaign, Labor leader Kevin Rudd was careful to assert his humble roots when he insisted that he was 'a very simple Vegemite-on-toast man … muesli, glass of orange juice and a cup of tea and that's about it'.[29] Vegemite suggested the common touch, a connection to the everyday in Australian cultural life. It has also acquired or retained a resonance evoking the 'outback'. When passengers alight from the Indian–Pacific train in some country town, they are often greeted by khaki-clad locals wearing Akubra hats and serving 'Vegemite scrolls' or 'swirls'.

Sceptics argue that the success of Vegemite is purely commercial and is based not on its innate virtues or deep national attachments but adroit marketing. They point to the apparently unnecessary 2009 ploy of mixing the product with cream cheese (patented by Kraft, of course). The company claimed this offered the convenience of not even having to butter the toast, and publicised the new blend with a competition to name it. So widespread was ridicule of the winning name, iSnack 2.0, that Kraft executives had agreed to abandon it within 72 hours of its announcement, later changing it to Cheesybite. Public opinion owned the brand.[30] The new owners, Bega Cheese, seem to have had more success promoting 'Squeezymite', now sold in tubes like toothpaste, and 'Bartymite', referencing the popular tennis star, Ashleigh Barty, to enhance the product's association with the alleged health and fitness benefits.[31] Nevertheless, in 2021, Vegemite, inevitably again paired with Marmite, came to symbolise what was at stake in post-Brexit trade negotiations with the UK.[32]

Playful humour has always accompanied Vegemite's cultural presence, and it continues to do so. In early 2016 a press release announced that a museum, appearing as a strangely aerial post-modern building called 'the Big Jar', would open in Port Melbourne. It was lovingly to chronicle the history of the 'Mitey Bite' and to offer 'a plethora of memorabilia, merchandise and VEGEMITE culinary creations'. The joke lay in the date of the press release – 1 April. Dreamed up by an ad man, the prank fooled even some of the media (Fig. 42).[33]

Having acquired the priceless cachet of being itself an Australian symbol, Vegemite has proved versatile in adapting to advertising fashions, political factions, and cultural shifts for almost a century, a trend which shows no signs of abating.

THE GREAT BARRIER REEF

Iain McCalman

The Great Barrier Reef, one of Australia's best-known and best-loved destinations, has always been difficult to symbolise because of its size and complexity. As the largest organism on our planet, only astronauts in outer space have seen it as a whole; the rest of us must be content with scale maps. The Reef matches or exceeds the size of many mid-sized countries: it's as big as Japan and the United Kingdom and larger than Italy and New Mexico.[1] And its geographies and ecologies are correspondingly diverse. Three thousand coral reefs and the same number of islands stretch along the north-east coast of Australia for 2350 kilometres to cover an area of 344,400 square kilometres.[2] Sovereign countries or states usually overcome this size problem by prescribing official symbols in the form of flags, coats of arms, or images of charismatic plants and animals. But the Reef is not a sovereign country: it was snatched from its original Indigenous custodians and then squabbled over by the federal and Queensland governments, who, since the establishment of the Great Barrier Reef Marine Park in 1975, have shared its management.

Terror or nurture?

Even so, since Captain James Cook's partial navigation of the Reef in 1770, it has been imagined symbolically and generated its own informal symbols in accordance with the changing opinions of Australians and others. Cook himself had no clue about the Reef's existence even after he'd sailed along its lagoon for 800 kilometres before crashing the HMS *Endeavour* onto an inner reef during the night of 10 June 1770. He had been cruising along comfortably unaware that the calm seas were caused by a vast coral barrier over the horizon, but which was now snaking in towards the coast. After jerking their wounded ship off the coral, the sailors spent the next five weeks repairing the hull at the site of today's Cooktown on Cape York Peninsula. But the marooning confronted Cook and his crew with extreme and unexpected challenges. A 'barren' countryside and elusive animals provided little fresh food at a time when scurvy was afflicting the sailors, a problem compounded by the refusal of local Indigenous peoples to trade fresh food for useless Western trinkets. Cook's surveys of the surrounding seascape from local hilltops also revealed a morass of reefs, shoals and sandbanks, which threatened to block their northward journey, while the prevailing trade wind prevented them from returning south.

Rescue from the dearth of food came through the chance capture on local reefs of thirteen giant green turtles (*Chelonia mydas*), each weighing between 90 and 135 kilograms. The relieved botanist, Joseph Banks, gloated that 'we may now be said to swim in plenty', but an armed party of Guugu Yimithirr warriors begged to differ. They were angry that these foreigners had barged uninvited into their country and then stolen a large number of their turtles. The green turtle was both a food staple and a cherished spirit figure within their cosmology. When ten warriors requested a modest payment of one turtle, they were roughly rebutted. The resulting skirmish culminated in Cook wounding one of the warriors with his musket. Having been instructed by the Admiralty not to antagonise any 'native' peoples, he and Banks were greatly relieved when a brave elder initiated a reconciliation. Even so, the European voyagers never understood that the turtles belonged to local clans who practised a sophisticated collective system of sustainable 'wild' farming .[3]

This encounter proved prophetic of the way the Reef would be interpreted and contested in future years – seen sometimes as a beneficent nature to be shared, sometimes as a resource to be exploited for money or pleasure, sometimes as an icon of health and beauty. The green turtle, as the Reef's earliest symbol, would reflect a range of these different meanings. During the 1920s, canneries were established on several Reef islands in an effort to meet Europe's longstanding taste for turtle soup.[4] And at this time when entrepreneurs were evading the ban on reef resorts by establishing them under the guise of 'naturalist expeditions', they lured tourists with a range of recreational attractions, including the sport of 'turtle riding'. This entailed tying a noose around the neck of a live green turtle and clinging to its back as the animal frantically tried to escape, culminating often in the strangulation of the turtle and the submergence of the rider.[5] Surviving photographs show that some tourists first killed the turtle then pretended to ride it while still on dry land. By the 1960s this behaviour was frowned on, as Reef turtles came gradually to be seen as beautiful, ecologically wondrous and vulnerable marine creatures. Today, the green turtle remains a widely used symbol to evoke the Reef's natural wonders, as may be seen in the lovely underwater paintings of Indigenous artist Melanie Hava (Fig. 45) and in a series of commemorative 'Barrier Reef Coins' issued by the Perth Mint in 2014.

Turtles had not been the only Reef symbol to derive from James Cook's Barrier Reef passage. After their five-week marooning, his crew resumed sailing the patched-up *Endeavour* in the hope of finding a northerly route through the tangle of reefs that lay in their path – a task that caused the usually phlegmatic captain to fret that he could see 'no passage to the sea, but through the *labyrinth* formed by these shoals'. Henceforth, he and Banks would often use this word, which evoked the

Heron Island.

Photograph by Frank Hurley, c. 1960, National Library of Australia

well-known classical myth of Theseus navigating through a labyrinth patrolled by a man-eating monster. Like Theseus, too, Cook risked death while trying to thread through the Reef's outer barrier. Having first reached the open sea through a break in the coral near Lizard Island, Cook proceeded, like a moth to a flame, to sail so close to the Reef edge that the *Endeavour* became caught in a powerful tidal rip that raced the ship towards the foaming rocks. Luckily, a tiny gap suddenly appeared through which he shot the barque back into the lagoon. After this, Cook ordered a sailor continually to monitor the shifting depths of the lagoon floor by casting the lead day and night.[6]

Cook's image of the Reef as a voracious underwater labyrinth preying on ships and drowning their sailors would persist throughout the nineteenth century, being modified only by a popular conviction that any shipwreck survivors would be murdered by Reef 'cannibals'. Colonists busily engaged in dispossessing Aboriginal peoples of their lands were only too ready to equate Indigenous maritime clans with the man-eating Minotaur. Exaggerated tales from shipwreck 'victims' like Eliza Fraser became colonial gospel, while stories of the clans' compassionate treatment of young castaways like Barbara Thompson, Narcisse Pelletier, Jem Morrill, John Ireland and William D'Oyley went largely unheard until a century later.[7]

A tropical paradise

By the twentieth century, the association of the Reef with gothic terrors began to give way to more benign images (Fig. 44). A Townsville journalist, Ted Banfield, was the main instigator of this change. Having suffered a health and work breakdown, Ted leased a block of land in 1896 on deserted Dunk Island, halfway between Townsville and Cairns. Mountainous, forested and well watered, Dunk had once been the home of Djiru people who called it Coonanglebah, but surviving inhabitants had mostly been gathered into a mainland mission. Fortunately for Ted and his wife, Bertha, two former Djiru inhabitants, Tom and Nellie, were keen to live and work on the island. They and their relatives helped build the Banfields' first cottage, cleared the surrounding jungle, planted vegetables and fruit trees, provided a daily catch of fresh fish and ferried supplies to and from the mainland. Ted's initial ambitions were commercial – he intended to use cheap Aboriginal labour to farm tropical fruits, eggs, honey and oysters, for sale on the mainland. By 1903, thanks to the labour and skills of his workers, Ted boasted all the trappings of an island viceroy – a substantial new bungalow, a sweeping formal avenue with flagpost, a boathouse, a suspension bridge and a storage tank with pump. One day, however, Ted discovered that two species of local birds had destroyed all his beehives. Having to choose between killing the birds or relinquishing his produce, he decided to give up commerce and turn Dunk Island into a bird sanctuary.

This decision started a revolution in Ted's self-identity. Inspired partly by Henry Thoreau's American nature writings, but, still more, by Aboriginal ecological knowledge, Ted began to fashion for himself a new image as a Reef island philosopher. His bestselling *Confessions of a Beachcomber* (1908–09) denounced the evils of modern civilisation in favour of 'the closest possible return to nature' – a rapturously free and healthy life as a 'beachcomber' on a paradise island. The book and its sequels turned him into a modern-day Robinson Crusoe along the lines of Robert Louis Stevenson and Paul Gauguin. Dunk Island, he wrote, offered a magical human tonic of sunshine, crystal seawaters, tropical scents and sounds, and the sublime aesthetic pleasure of viewing submarine coral gardens. After he died in 1923, this sensuous symbol lived on. An explosion of reef tourism during the 1950s and 1960s would disseminate countless images of his tropical Reef paradise via postcards, photographs, posters, magazines and films.[8]

Banfield might have idealised his beachcomber lifestyle, but his commitment to bird preservation had been genuine. He persuaded the Queensland Government to appoint him as an official Ranger to Dunk and neighbouring islands; and he collaborated with the conservationist Alec Chisholm to gain legal protection for the Torres Strait nutmeg pigeon which was being decimated by shooters. From the 1920s to this day, Banfield's example has continued to inspire generations of aspirant beachcombers, artists, writers and scientists, including well-known novelists like Jean Devanny, Frank Dalby Davison, Vance and Nettie Palmer and John O'Grady, as well as popular science writers like Theodore Roughley, William Dakin, Elizabeth Bennet and Len Zell.

Vance and Nettie Palmer were among the most perceptive and influential of these early Reef writers. In 1932 they spent 12 months on the coral cay of Green Island, north-east of Cairns, investigating both the positive and negative aspects of Reef island life. Nettie worried initially that the fantasy of living on an island was 'too virginal, too far from all problems, too inhuman, and therefore unreal,' but she and Vance worked hard to dispel such escapist myths by exploring local ecologies, seascapes and fishing cultures. Green Island, they learned, was 'part of the Reef intermittent', a honeycomb of fringing reefs, volcanic islands and sand cays sitting on separate coral reefs, each with their own lagoons, shallows and channels. All of these elements seemed holistically connected, though the couple noticed some disturbing tensions and disparities between white and black luggermen.[9]

A larger artist island community also grew up during the 1930s on the three major Family Group Islands of Dunk, Bedarra and Timana. Pioneered by Melbourne artists Noel Wood, Bruce Arthur and John Busst, it included Fred Williams for a time, as well as two talented sisters, Yvonne Cohen and Valerie Albright, who painted island landscapes in a lush quasi-primitive style reminiscent of Paul Gauguin. Remnants of this movement eventually shifted to the mainland town of Mission Beach, where former island artists like Deanna Conti and Liz Gallie continue to craft Reef-inspired textiles, jewellery and rattan work. Liz Gallie and Sandal Hayes also became catalysts of a vigorous local environmental movement to protect endangered communities of cassowaries – so much so, that these magnificent flightless birds have now become emblematic of the 'Cassowary Coast region' from Innisfail to Mission Beach, Tully, El Arish and beyond.[10]

Some Reef artists also gravitated from paintbrush to camera, though early photographers struggled to capture the riotous colours of a coral reef because of the technical challenges posed by filming underwater and having to use black and white film. A talented English scientist and photographer, William Saville-Kent, overcame this limitation in 1893 by including sixteen gorgeous hand-drawn and coloured chromolithographic plates in his book on the Reef and its products (Fig. 43). The reviewer of the *West Australian* newspaper was typical in declaring that Saville-Kent's 'submarine chromatic effects are ... more brilliant than the most gorgeous transformation scene conceived; one could scarcely believe that the bright greens, reds, pinks, blues and yellows are the actual colour of forms'.[11] Through the 1920s and 1930s, even famous coral reef photographers like JE Williamson and Frank Hurley were still fabricating underwater scenes using disguised aquaria and a variety of optical tricks.[12] However, an amateur biologist and musician, Noel Monkman, who moved to Green Island in 1929, managed to build a hand-pumped diving suit and modified movie camera that enabled him to produce the first vivid underwater films of Reef fish and corals.[13] Five of his documentaries were later distributed worldwide, helping to initiate the tradition of coloured coral cinematography that reached its apotheosis in January 2016 with David Attenborough's poignant BBC documentary, *Great Barrier Reef*.

The Reef in peril

Monkman's films depicted Green Island as an unspoiled paradise, but by the 1960s the island was being overwhelmed by an airline-stimulated influx of Reef tourists. Some visitors to the island's popular observatory in 1963 happened to be the first to sight the voracious coral-eating Crown of Thorns starfish in action. Within a decade, this creature had become the first widespread symbol of the Reef's fragility. Though a native species, the starfish was reported to be spreading in plague proportions. As one of the animal's earliest analysts, Noel Monkman became so worried that he urged the setting up of a national marine park.[14]

The starfish's science-fiction-like properties gripped the popular imagination. Large and menacing with thorny venomous spines, it seemed almost impossible to kill because broken-off pieces simply spawned new animals. A single large starfish could consume up to ten square metres of coral polyps per year, leaving behind a huge white scar that turned dirty-brown with algae. Each large female also spawned 47–53 million eggs, and the resulting swarms of larvae were surviving in alarming proportions. Some scientists, including Monkman, attributed these outbreaks to Taiwanese boatmen having overfished the starfish's main predator, the giant Triton. Others argued that warming waters and chemical pollution were providing a perfect incubator for the larvae, which were flourishing by feeding on phytoplankton blooms. Several books stoked alarm with sensational titles like *Crown of Thorns: the Death of the Reef* and *Requiem for the Reef*, but the panic gradually lessened with the discovery that bisulphate injections could kill individual starfish and, still more, because of the emergence of new human-driven threats to the Reef's survival.[15]

In 1967 John Busst, a longtime Mission Beach artist and the leader of a local chapter of the Queensland Wildlife Preservation Society (QWPS), lost an initial appeal against a sugarcane farmer who had lodged a proposal to the state government to mine the nearby Ellison coral reef for cheap limestone fertiliser. Refusing to give up, Busst mobilised the national president of the QWPS, poet Judith Wright and a body of Queensland University student divers led by Eddie Hegerl. Together they managed to halt the coral mining by using an underwater survey to prove that Ellison Reef was in no way 'dead', as had been claimed.[16]

Unfazed by this defeat, the Queensland Government's crafty populist premier, Joh Bjelke-Petersen, proceeded to zone 80 per cent of the Great Barrier Reef for oil and gas mining. He and his ministers, having invested heavily in oil mining shares, had every reason to ignore warnings that widespread industrial development and the associated risk of oil spills could potentially destroy every living thing within the Reef and its waters. The Queensland minister for mines, Ronald Camm, even claimed that oil, being protein, would be good for fish. For the next eight years, Busst, Wright and a forestry scientist, Len Webb, threw all their energies into gaining popular support to halt the mining and persuade the federal government to institute a marine park. Scientists, trade unionists, politicians, academics and citizens from all over Australia contributed to the subsequent political and media storm that resulted in the legal formation of the Great Barrier Reef National Marine Park in June 1975. Six years later, the Reef gained UNESCO World Heritage listing as 'the most impressive marine area in the world'. Though the Reef appeared to have been saved, Judith Wright's *Coral Battleground* (1996) warned that commercial onslaughts could resume at any time.[17]

And so they have. Since 2015 the familiar red-and-black 'Save the Reef' sign of the 1970s has reappeared in a new battle to prevent the establishment of the large-scale Adani Carmichael coalmine, which threatens the Reef in multiple ways. But this time popular resistance has been unable to stop Australian governments from fostering the mine. On 8 February 2017 the then federal treasurer even fondled a lump of coal in parliament in a gloating symbol of the triumph of coalmining over conservation. In vain, scientists warned that the mine would accelerate global greenhouse gas emissions and harm the Barrier Reef's corals directly. Dredging of the shallow Reef lagoon to facilitate Adani's huge fleet of container ships would disperse coral-smothering sand over a large area and encourage coral bacterial disease. Adani's victory also emboldened other coal tycoons to lodge new mining proposals. Even so, many Reef-loving Australians regard the Treasurer's lump of coal as a symbol of the reckless sacrifice of one of the world's greatest natural treasures to short-term political expediency and corporate greed.[18]

An ailing scientific wonder

The earlier 'Save the Reef' campaign had also revealed the scantiness of Great Barrier Reef marine research. In 1928 the first sustained biological expedition to study the Reef was undertaken by Cambridge biologists because no qualified Australians could be found. Not until 1972 was a full-time professional scientist, Dr John 'Charlie' Veron, hired to undertake the systematic taxonomic mapping of the Reef's hundreds of coral species. Fortunately, the threat of oil mining spurred the establishment in Townsville of the Australian Institute of Marine Science (AIMS) in 1972 and of the marine-oriented James Cook University in 1970. Charlie Veron, who worked for both, would go on to describe and analyse more than 15 per cent of the world's reef-growing corals. Today, specialised and internationally famous marine research stations operate across the full length of the Reef.[19]

During the 1970s coral scientists finally unlocked the complex biological process that creates a coral reef. Tiny coral polyps establish a symbiotic partnership with microscopic plants in their cells, as well as with hundreds of bacteria. The corals then use photosynthesis to generate the supercharge of energy needed to lay down limestone exoskeletons fast enough to resist the destructive forces of oceans and weather. Yet soon after the discovery of this wondrous partnership, scientists also began to see signs of its impending breakdown. Human-stimulated greenhouse gases of CO_2 and methane were causing bouts of extreme ocean warming that forced the polyp hosts to expel their plant superchargers. Vivid-coloured corals transmuted into bleached and starving skeletons. Any recurrence or intensification of the warming killed the corals altogether, turning them into rotting mounds of green-brown algae.

Scientists also discovered that Reef corals were being simultaneously harmed by alterations in the chemistry of their surrounding seawaters. Atmospheric CO_2 was being absorbed by the salt water to create carbonic acid, which was giving the oceans severe indigestion.

Like humans, they responded to this 'acidification' by dissolving alkaline calcium to re-balance their pH. Gradually, the Reef's millions of limestone coral skeletons were being stricken with a type of osteoporosis that slows their growth, generates birth defects and makes them too brittle to resist weather events. No longer can we represent the Reef with the ravishing symbol of a submarine coral garden. A grim new Reef symbol has taken its place – acre upon acre of ghostly bleached corals.[20]

During the most recent bout of warming in 2016–17, intensive scientific monitoring revealed that three-quarters of the Reef's corals were bleached – many fatally. Australians face the possibility of losing the most beautiful and bio-diverse marine habitat in the world and, with it, a substantial percentage of our oceanic food resources, as well as the enormous economic benefits that the Oxford Economics Report of 2009 estimates at $51.4 billion tourist dollars.[21]

Since 2015 the Australian federal government has been lobbying intensively to head off threats from the World Heritage Committee of UNESCO to place the Great Barrier Reef on their 'in danger' list, because of the impacts of poor water quality and land management as well as climate change. When in 2021 UNESCO threatened to formalise the 'in danger' listing, the government claimed to have been 'blindsided', despite the 2019 report of its own Great Barrier Reef Marine Park Authority that downgraded the Reef's long-term outlook to 'very poor.' After an extraordinary lobbying effort, the World Heritage Committee was persuaded to postpone its decision. The future outlook for the Reef appears grim.[22]

Still, there remains a chance that the sad prospect can be halted to some degree by restorative human ingenuity combined with nature's proven resilience. If the world's governments will act decisively to stabilise the climate by reducing greenhouse gas emissions, and if the Barrier Reef's scientists can succeed in their current attempts to develop resistant strains of corals, some form of the Reef might still be saved.[23] We would then see the resumption of an ancient partnership between two of the tiniest organisms in the sea that have created the largest and most beautiful piece of natural architecture on our planet. Should this happen, future editions of this book could include a celebratory new symbol of Great Barrier Reef resilience.

SYDNEY HARBOUR BRIDGE

Peter Spearritt

Australia has only two city structures that are immediately recognised around the world: the Sydney Harbour Bridge and the Sydney Opera House. Their fame depends on a combination of built majesty and geographical setting. Melbourne houses Australia's most magnificent nineteenth-century structure – the Exhibition Building – but it is set in a flat, parklike landscape, and few Australians recognise it.[1] Brisbane, Adelaide and Perth have nondescript skyscrapers and are continually searching for a unique and marketable symbol, without success. Hobart has a spectacular setting but no structure to take advantage of it. Canberra might be a city of symbols, as befits a purpose-built national capital,[2] but not one of its overweening structures has any real claim to symbolic status.

The Opera House and the Harbour Bridge are in an entirely different category. They share the most spectacular urban site in Australia at Circular Quay, dubbed by one journalist in 1927 'the chief theatre of Australian life'.[3] Its harbour setting, with Circular Quay, the Botanic Gardens and the large land areas under the bridge, offers mass assembly spaces unmatched by any other Australian city. Only in Sydney can the 'nation' gather in celebratory mode, as was demonstrated to marked effect in the Bicentennial celebrations in 1988.[4] It is a matter of envy and immense irritation in the other capital cities that they cannot muster or create grand sites to compete with Sydney's symbolic ceremonial space. The two structures help make Sydney Australia's only recognisable 'world' city, so these symbols of Sydney also serve as symbols of the nation.

Melbourne and the Gold Coast have pinned their hopes on building taller and taller skyscrapers, but the results are never distinguished enough to achieve symbolic status.[5] Even though it has long been superseded by taller buildings around the world, the Empire State Building (1931) will always remain the skyscraper with symbolic power, representing not only New York but the American way.

Symbols do not have to be innovative in design or even necessarily have grand settings. Other structures that have come to symbolise nations – Egypt's Pyramids, Britain's Big Ben, France's Eiffel Tower, India's Taj Mahal – work not only because they become must-see tourist sites, presumed to sum up the essence of a culture, but also because they are distinctive enough that even stylised representations of them are instantly recognisable.

Building a symbol

Some structures assume symbolic status even before they are built, the case with both the Opera House and the Harbour Bridge. Both structures were the subject of well-publicised international tenders, and in the case of the Opera House, a design competition as well. The Harbour Bridge had its share of innovations, but the arch design had a number of precedents, most notably the Hell Gate railway bridge in New York. The Opera House, on the other hand, being a unique design, provided many construction challenges. The older structure is grand and majestic in scope and function, the newer elegant and inventive, but both ultimately made the most of their enviable setting.

When the Sydney Harbour Bridge Bill passed in the New South Wales Parliament in 1922, Australians saw it as an opportunity to demonstrate the modernity and progress of a newly industrialising nation. The few doubters included some country members of parliament who acknowledged it as a great work but thought the money would be better spent in their electorates. Hundreds of owners and tenants saw their businesses and houses resumed to make way for the bridge approaches, but the catchcry of the age, 'progress cannot be stayed', swept all before it.[6]

The adoption of the arch design meant that Sydneysiders were in for a construction treat, with the two sides being built out over the harbour simultaneously from Milsons Point at North Sydney and Dawes Point in the Rocks. As the half arches, secured into bedrock by steel cables, crept out over the harbour, the wonder of the structure struck home. People even took bets on whether the two sides of the arch would meet. They did, amid great publicity, in August 1930. For five years residents and visitors to Sydney had seen the great work underway. On 50 million ferry trips a year, commuters travelling to work and families on outings to Manly saw the construction at firsthand. Once the arch was complete, hangers were installed to support the railway and road deck below.

One reason the bridge became an instantaneous symbol was that Sydneysiders had seen it grow. Its construction gave hope in a city which by 1930 was in the grip of the Great Depression. The bridge provided thousands of jobs and in Percy Trompf's 1930 poster the completed arch was a backdrop for his bold message, 'Still building Australia' (Fig. 46). The bridge proved beyond doubt that in this 'new country', the great building and architectural feats of the United States, Britain and Europe could be matched.

People elsewhere in Australia and in many parts of the British Empire got regular updates on the bridge, especially at photographically notable moments in its construction. *The Times* (London) ran a large format photograph of the arches meeting. The bridge was becoming familiar around the world as a symbol of Australia. Shipping line posters aimed at the British travel market almost invariably featured the bridge.

It also held out promise to intending migrants who were reassured that Australia not only offered sunshine, beaches and agricultural land aplenty but a city of great presence and a skilled workforce who could build with the world's best. At that time the main marketing posters for Melbourne depicted sedate images of the city centre, combining a nineteenth-century town hall with art deco buildings. Nothing that Melbourne could do matched the grandeur of the new Sydney bridge.[7] At last, Australia had a structure of which all Australians could be proud. Even Melbourne newspapers were prepared to admit it.[8]

Two openings, many roles

The power of the bridge as a symbol was demonstrated on the day it opened, 19 March 1932. Labor premier Jack Lang insisted that he, representing the people of New South Wales, rather than the state governor, representing the British crown, should open the bridge. When horseman Captain de Groot of the New Guard, a right-wing para-military organisation, beat Lang to the ribbon during the opening ceremony, de Groot gave the bridge an extraordinary symbolic fillip. Newsreel-maker Ken Hall sent the only image of de Groot cutting the ribbon, caught by one of his cameramen, free-by-wire service to newspapers around the world. It still ranks as one of the great upset openings in world history, reported with amusement by the *New York Times* and many other major newspapers. It put the bridge doubly on the map as both an engineering triumph and a media circus. In a typically Australian note, the policemen who had been rostered to shadow de Groot – a known troublemaker – refused to believe his bold boast that he would beat the premier to the ribbon, and went to the pub for a beer instead.[9]

There were other disputes about what the bridge represented. For the British press, the opening was hailed not as a symbol of Australian progress but as a triumph of British engineering, because the English

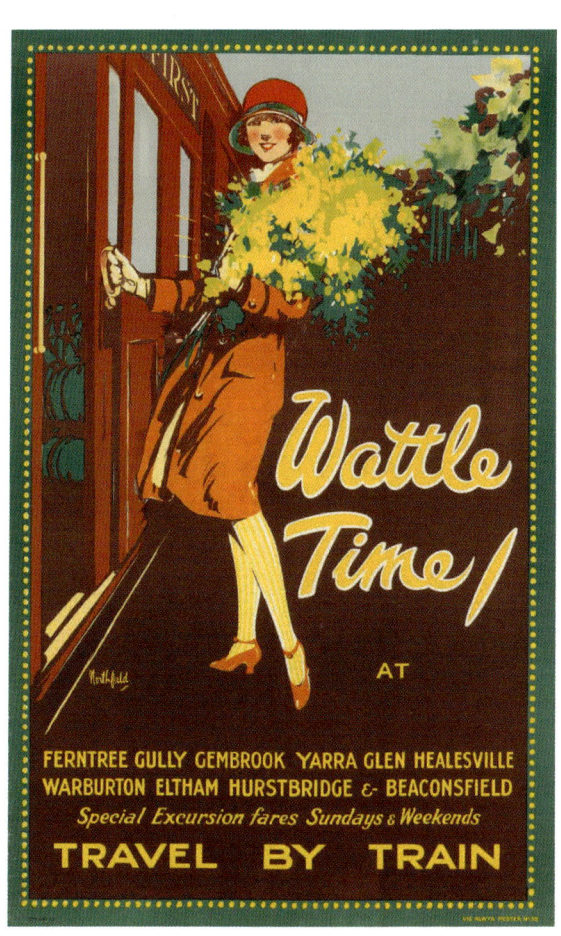

32 'Wattle time' poster advertising 'Travel By Train', c. 1927.

National Library of Australia

33 The first Australian depiction of what would become Australia's floral emblem, the golden wattle (*Acacia pycnantha* Benth.) in John E Brown, *The Forest Flora of South Australia*, 1882.

Courtesy Special Collections, University of Melbourne Library

34 In 1908, controversy erupted around the first coat of arms, featuring the kangaroo and emu and the old motto of the popular colonial arms, 'Advance Australia'.

State Library of South Australia

35 The 1912 Australian coat of arms.

National Archives of Australia

36 A 1969 sculpture inspired by the Australian coat of arms in the grounds of the Australian Embassy in Washington DC, 2009.

Photograph by Richard White

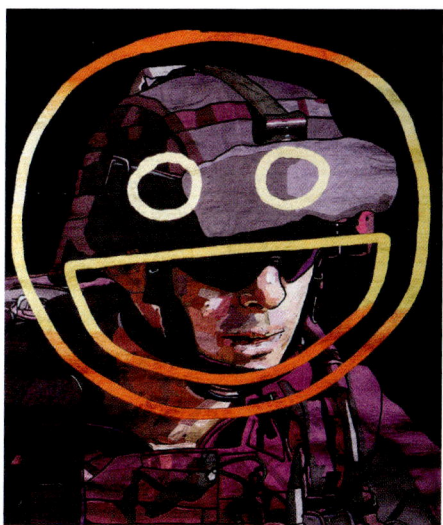

37 The digger ideal. *Corporal Jim Gordon*, 1941, by William Dargie.

Australian War Memorial

38 *For we are Young and Free*, 2017. One of the works removed from ArtSpace, Mackay, Queensland, on the grounds they were disrespectful to soldiers.

Manual embroidery by Abdul Abdullah

39 A home away from home in Australia House, London, 1979.

National Archives of Australia

40 Australia House as a site for protest: the Red Rebels of Extinction Rebellion highlighting Australia's lack of action on climate change during the Black Summer of bushfires, 10 January 2020.

Photograph by Jonathan Brady, Alamy

41 Vegemite wartime advertisement, c. 1942. When Vegemite became essential to the war effort, Kraft Walker felt the need to explain to civilians why supplies were low.

Courtesy Bega Cheese Limited

42 In 2015, creative director Darren Fishman conceived a five-storey high 'Big Vegemite' tourist attraction on top of the Port Melbourne Vegemite factory. Vegemite was sufficiently significant in Australian culture that a number of media outlets published the news, not noticing the press release was embargoed for 1 April. The factory and its Vegemite aroma now have state heritage listing.

Courtesy of Darren Fishman

43 The first published colour images of the Reef appeared as colour lithographs in William Saville-Kent's ground-breaking book, *The Great Barrier Reef of Australia*, 1893, based on his watercolour sketches.

Wikimedia Commons

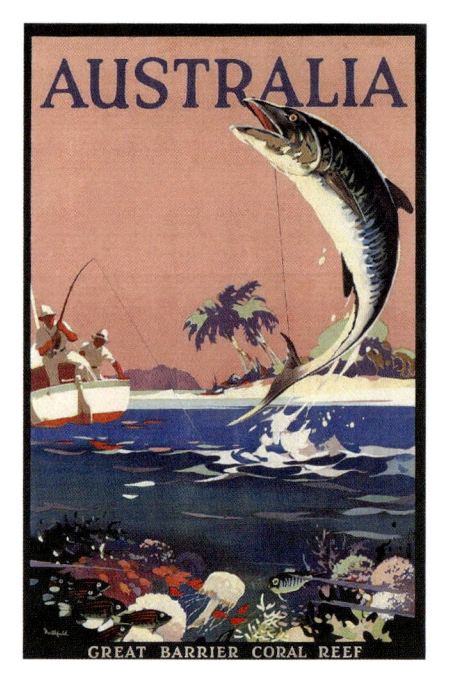

44 James Northfield poster for the Australian National Travel Association, c. 1932.

© James Northfield Heritage Art Trust, National Library of Australia

45 *Reef Wonderland*, 2018.

Melanie Hava

46 The Harbour Bridge as a symbol of industrial progress.

Poster by Percy Trompf, courtesy Josef Lebovic

47 From one symbol to another: tourists on the BridgeClimb adventure pause to take in the view of Sydney's other national symbol.

Courtesy of BridgeClimb, Hammons Holdings

48 (*Left*) 'The royal wave': surf lifesavers were regularly put on display for royal visits. Diana, Princess of Wales, meets lifesavers at Terrigal, New South Wales during her Bicentennial tour, 1988.

Mirrorpix, Alamy

49 (*Right*) In the International Year of the Surf Lifesaver, 2007, efforts were made to give the traditional image more relevance. Mecca Laalaa Hadid wearing a 'burqini', designed by Ahiida Burqini Swimwear.

Courtesy of Aheda Zanetti and Mecca Hadid

50 (*Below right*) For her 'national costume' in the 2007 Miss Universe competition, Kimberley Busteed, a competitive swimmer, chose a lifesaver themed outfit, attracting both criticism and praise, as Australian 'national costumes' typically did.

Thanks to Kimberley Busteed and photographer Geoff McLachlan, News Ltd/Newspix

51 *Anna Pavlova: The Dancing Revelation of the Age*, 1912. The dainty Russian ballerina was the dessert's inspiration – or at least its name.

National Library of Australia

52 In 2017–18, 15 sitting members of parliament were ruled ineligible by the High Court or resigned pre-emptively because they held dual citizenship – like the pavlova.

Matt Golding, The Sunday Age

53 Billboard poster advertising the FJ Holden Sedan, 1953–55.

National Museum of Australia

54 Workers at Holden's Elizabeth plant, South Australia, photograph the last Holden as it rolls off the assembly line.

Courtesy of GM Holden

55 Tourists capturing the standard image of Uluṟu, 2016.

Directphoto.bz, Alamy

56 Back of a bus in Oxford, England, 2009. By the twenty-first century Uluṟu was an internationally recognised tourist destination (though the kangaroo symbol helped).

Photograph by Richard White

57 (*Above*) In 2010, 5200 people posed naked for US photographer Spencer Tunick's *The Base*, one of his series of nude installations at significant sites around the world.

Photograph by Heidy Elainne

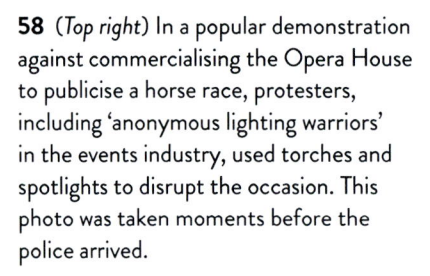

58 (*Top right*) In a popular demonstration against commercialising the Opera House to publicise a horse race, protesters, including 'anonymous lighting warriors' in the events industry, used torches and spotlights to disrupt the occasion. This photo was taken moments before the police arrived.

Thanks to Nino Pace

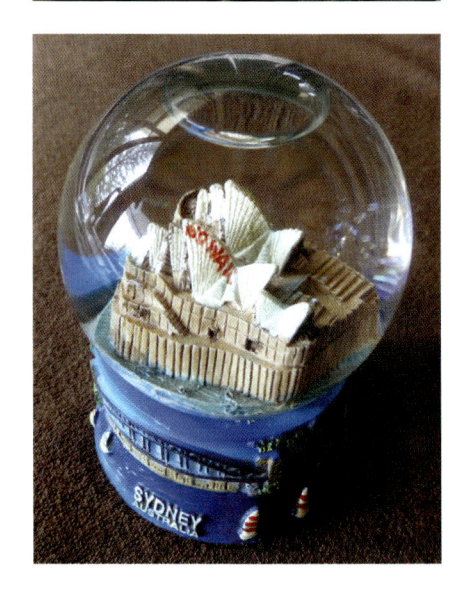

59 (*Bottom right*) Snow globes of the Opera House, complete with graffiti, helped pay off a compensation bill of $151,000 resulting from an anti-Iraq War protest.

Courtesy of Dave Burgess

60 Poster advertising Akubra hats, 1930s, designed by Walter Jardine. Akubra's strong association with the bush in the 1930s was recycled in the 2000s.

© Walter Jardine Estate, Akubra Hats Pty Ltd

61 At Tim Fischer's state funeral in 2019, his signature Akubra took pride of place on the coffin.

Photograph Alex Ellinghausen, Fairfax

62 (*Top*) Dick Roughsey's picture books retelling his traditional Mornington Island stories for children helped popularise the rainbow serpent. Illustration from *The Rainbow Serpent* by Dick Roughsey, 1975.

National Museum of Australia

63 (*Above*) Inflatable Rainbow Serpent on display at Floriade festival, Canberra, Australian Capital Territory, 2001.

Photography by Vicki Munday, Australian Capital Tourism

64 (*Right*) Ngalyod – The Rainbow Serpent, 1974, by Nabegeyo.

National Museum of Australia

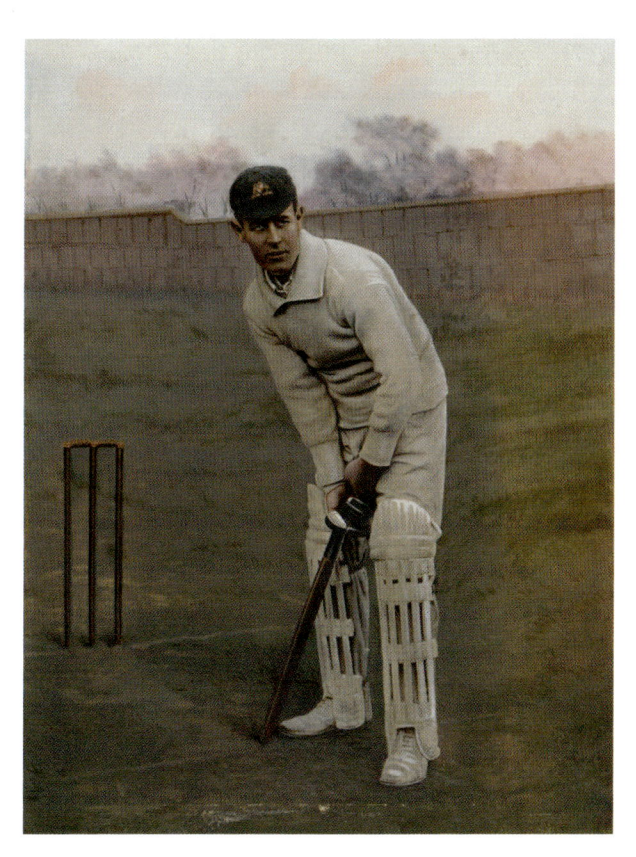

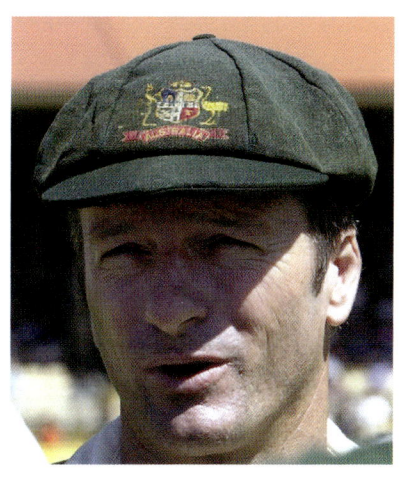

65 (*Above*) Australian cricket captain Steve Waugh wearing his original cap, newly renovated, at Adelaide Oval, 2002.

Photograph by Rebecca Naden, Alamy

66 (*Left*) Victor Trumper, 1902.

State Library of New South Wales

67 The 'Baggy Green Room' in the National Sports Museum, Melbourne Cricket Ground, Victoria. A statue of Don Bradman by Mitch Mitchell takes pride of place in a secular shrine to the baggy green.

National Sports Museum and John Gollings

68 On election day 2016, Opposition Leader Bill Shorten was widely derided for eating a 'democracy sausage' the wrong way, from the side. During the 2019 election, he and wife, Chloe, ensured they got the etiquette right.

AAP

69 Australian high commissioner in London, George Brandis, brandishing the tongs at Australia House during the 2019 election.

Photograph by Latika Bourke

firm Dorman Long and Co. had won the tender to build it against worldwide competition. Before the opening there had already been a well-publicised stoush between the British engineer Ralph Freeman and the Brisbane-born engineer John Job Crew Bradfield as to who could claim to be the designer of the bridge. In the end they both shared the credit, Bradfield for the overall conception and Freeman for the implementation and detailed calculations. The bridge featured in a number of front cover stories in the *Meccano* magazine and the popular *Wonders* books. British boys could hardly avoid reading about the bridge: engineering books produced for boys in Britain from the 1930s to the 1950s portrayed the bridge in their endpapers as one of the wonders of the world.[10]

The bridge endeared itself to Sydneysiders and visitors, for both practical and symbolic reasons. Train travellers from the northern suburbs in newly electrified trains no longer had to get out at Milsons Point and catch a ferry to the city. Suddenly they could be delivered to the city centre in about half the time. The bridge meant efficiency and speed, especially for the growing number of motorists who happily paid a toll to go into the city centre, rather than spend another half an hour or more going via the Gladesville Bridge, the only nearby route. Vehicular ferries disappeared from the main harbour and Sydney took on the mantle of modernity.

The bridge had been a local tourist site even before its completion, with many souvenirs, brochures and postcards documenting every stage of construction. Bradfield, the chief engineer for Public Works, planned the pedestrian walkway on the eastern side and the bicycle way on the western side to cope with thousands of visitors, and each of the pylons included stairways from ground level to their uppermost point, again for public purposes. The Pylon Lookout in the south-east pylon, easily accessible from Circular Quay and Milsons Point station, became one of Australia's most popular tourist attractions. In 1935 Luna Park opened on the northern side of the harbour, on the site of the Dorman Long workshops. Hundreds of thousands of children and adults visited

War memorial constructed by patients of B Ward,
Callen Park Mental Hospital, 1931.
Photograph by Catherine Bishop

the park in the late 1930s and during the war years, all to the mighty backdrop of the bridge. Swimmers and spectators using the North Sydney Olympic Pool, opened for the Empire Games in 1938, were likewise in its shadow. From visiting Britons in the 1930s to American troops in the 1940s, the bridge symbolised not just Sydney, but Australia. Hardly a novel set in Sydney after the 1920s failed to mention the bridge: under construction in Eleanor Dark's *Waterway* (1938), metaphorically centrestage in Sumner Locke Elliott's *Water under the Bridge* (1978), and central to the plot of Peter Corris's detective novel *Wet Graves* (1991). The bridge found its way into both plays and films, as subject and metaphor. In the film *The Squatter's Daughter* (1933), a sheep station owner, coming home from two years in England, tells an associate as their ship nears Circular Quay, 'When I left here two years ago, Cartwright, I never thought I'd see that bridge finished'.

During construction, amateur and professional photographers captured it from every angle and in many lights. Artists, from Grace Cossington Smith to Roland Wakelin and Dorrit Black, painted it in every imaginable style, from pictorial landscape to cubist abstraction. Because it was so well known and so recognisable, many cartoonists delighted in playing with the bridge in a variety of allegorical forms, from Jack Lang's teeth to a coathanger.[11]

In the late 1940s and 1950s the bridge featured in much of the Australian Government's promotional imagery designed to attract migrants. Books of advice for potential British migrants often had the bridge on the front cover, as did many of the books about Australia and the Australian way of life aimed at the British market. Encyclopaedia entries on Australia, from *Chambers* to the *Britannica*, invariably included a photograph of the bridge, often an oblique aerial shot showing how it linked the two sides of the city. For thousands of migrants, the bridge was not only the one man-made structure they were familiar with before they left, it was also what greeted them if they arrived in Sydney, and so came to have a very personal symbolic meaning as the start of a new life. In the rash of guidebooks to Sydney and Australia that appeared in the lead-up to the 2000 Olympics, the bridge often played second fiddle to the Opera House on book covers, though the single most common cover shot featured both structures.[12]

The depiction of the bridge by filmmakers, photographers, artists and cartoonists continued throughout the twentieth century. Max Dupain photographed it in the 1930s and 1940s, David Moore from the 1940s to the 1990s. The bridge simultaneously entered popular folklore and popular art in the work of Martin Sharp and Peter Kingston, both of whom campaigned to save Luna Park when it was threatened with closure. Even Melbourne cartoonists, most notably Michael Leunig, simply could not ignore the bridge. Cartoonists turned to the bridge when they needed an Australian symbol that worked in an international context. When Bill Leak sought to satirise Pauline Hanson's racist views on immigration, he drew Hanson in the Statue of Liberty's guise, with the bridge standing as the entry point to Australia. The inscription under the Hanson statue reads: 'Welcome to Australia – the land of the fair go – ... now bugger off'.[13]

By the beginning of the twenty-first century, Sydney airport accounted for half of all international arrivals in Australia. Many of the flights arrive at dawn. The experience might not be as emotional as it was for migrants arriving by ship in the 1950s, but weary air travellers from all over the globe, spying the Harbour Bridge and the Opera House, know that they are about to land not just in Sydney, but in Australia. No other Australian capital city offers a landing trajectory as an unmistakeable symbol of itself let alone the nation.

Appreciating the bridge: first Sydney, then the world

While the bridge has been ever-present in most attempts to depict Sydney, it has not always been revered either by the public or by its government owners, originally the Department of Main Roads, then the Roads and Traffic Authority (and now Transport NSW). With the coming of mass car ownership after World War II, the bridge became synonymous with traffic jams. Trains on the western side and trams on the eastern side continued to cope well, but the roadway simply could not meet the growing demand from commuters for car travel. In the 1950s and 1960s any cartoonist needing an image of congested Sydney would pick on the bridge, as did photographers and pictorial editors in magazines and newspapers.

At the same time the Department of Main Roads, while making sure that the painting crews continued to eradicate rust, left the Moruya granite pylons to suffer the effects of Sydney's polluted atmosphere. They became dirtier and dirtier as the fumes from lead-based petrol and pollution from the nearby Ultimo and Pyrmont power stations covered the pylons in grime. Postcards and brochures for the Pylon Lookout in the 1950s show just how dirty the pylons were.

Sydney rediscovered its early affection for the bridge in 1982, on the 50th anniversary of the opening. For the first time since 1932, the roadway was opened to pedestrians and over half a million walked across it – from both sides. While only half the number that had walked at its opening, nonetheless, in a car-based society, this proved a moment of reawakening. If only for a few hours, the people reclaimed the roadway. In the 1930s many people walked across the bridge to work, simply because they could not afford the train or tram fare. By the 1950s walking across the bridge had fallen away, but in the 1980s it became more common again for joggers, workers and tourists.

The popularity of the 50th anniversary celebrations caught authorities by surprise, and mounted police had to be called in to control the crowd. Some people wanted to sit in the middle of the bridge and savour the occasion. In May 2000, the bridge again fulfilled a symbolic role when the organisers of the People's Walk for Reconciliation persuaded the state government to close it to traffic, so the walk could symbolise a bridge between Indigenous Australians and the white majority. The spontaneity and hope that marked that occasion was completely lost at the 75th anniversary, when the troubled Labor government led by Maurice Iemma, beset by public transport woes, fearful of terrorist attack and facing an election just six days later, implemented an absurd level of control. People had to register to walk, were only allowed to walk from north to south, and weren't even allowed to walk back over the pedestrian walkway, which remained closed to the public on the day. This politically motivated attempt to limit the numbers walking received almost no press comment in either the *Sydney Morning Herald* or the local ABC radio station because both were locked in as 'sponsors' of the event.[14] Such was the power of the bridge's symbolism that a government going to the polls could not risk

268 SYMBOLS OF AUSTRALIA

The bridge gained renewed symbolic life as it became the centrepiece of Sydney's New Year's Eve fireworks.

Thanks to Michael Leunig

any images of broken-down or overcrowded trains or broken-down buses on its most visible and recognisable public structure.

World tourist icon

The opening of the Sydney Harbour Tunnel in 1992 lessened traffic congestion and the bridge continued to be an accepted part of Sydney life, but the Pylon Lookout lost popularity as a tourist attraction. In such circumstances, tourist attractions either reinvent themselves or fade away.[15] There is no better example of reinvention than BridgeClimb, an enterprise established by a commercial consortium in October 1998 to allow people to pay for the privilege of walking over the arch, capitalising on the combination of thrill, spectacle and symbolism (Fig. 47). Dogged by difficulties in getting insurance coverage, it took years of negotiation before the company was able to lease climbing rights to the bridge from the (then) Roads and Traffic Authority. In its first twenty years, the BridgeClimb company attracted over four million customers, but in 2018 Transport NSW, the state government authority now responsible for the bridge, awarded the next 20-year contract to Hammons Holdings, the proprietors of the Scenic Railway in the Blue Mountains.[16] The first such climb in the world, it spawned pale imitations in Brisbane and Auckland, and received more free advertorial in the Australian and international press than any other high-cost tourist activity. Timing was crucial. Had the entrepreneurs tried to get permission to walk fee-payers over the bridge after the terrorist attack on the World Trade Center they would have got nowhere with nervous government bureaucrats. BridgeClimb closed for some months during the COVID-19 pandemic, even though with only ten climbers in a party it could practise 'social distancing' much more readily than almost any other organised tourist attraction. BridgeClimb is one of the great international success stories of twenty-first-century adventure tourism, a success yet to be replicated anywhere else in the world.[17] Climbing the Harbour Bridge combines thrill, spectacle and symbolism. Climbers cannot avoid appreciating its organic structure, especially if their guide points out that the millions of steel rivets were heated on site and hammered in by hand.

The bridge's international status was further guaranteed by its starring role in television coverage of New Year's Eve, particularly the celebrations of the new millennium. Because of Sydney's fortuitous time zone, its fireworks display appears on prime-time television in Europe and the Americas. And the bridge is the heart of the celebration. From 1988 the fireworks were fired from the bridge itself, rather than from barges in the harbour. This broadcast coverage, along with Sydney's hosting of the 2000 Olympics, reinvigorated the bridge as an instantly recognisable symbol of Australia. Given its peerless setting, the bridge will remain a national symbol for as long as it stays up.

LIFESAVER

Caroline Ford

The figure of the lifesaver has been fought over for a century and on occasion has fought back. The broad term 'lifesaver' can encompass members of the Royal Life Saving Society which was represented in Australia from 1894. What Australians popularly regard as the 'lifesaver', and what has become a national symbol, is strictly the *surf* lifesaver, who appeared on Australian beaches over a decade later. Although many clubs have claimed to have invented the movement, its origins can be found at the Bondi Hotel on 21 February 1907: an appropriate venue given lifesavers' later association with Australia's masculine drinking culture.[1] The formation of the Bondi Surf Bathers' Life Saving Club, though dealing with a local issue of beach safety, would spawn one of Australia's most potent national symbols.

The club was quickly replicated on a number of other Sydney beaches within a year, and spread along the New South Wales coast within two years. At a national level, the surf lifesaving movement had reached Western Australia, Queensland and Tasmania by the 1920s, and Victoria and South Australia, where the older traditions of the Royal Life Saving Society had had more influence, shortly after World War II. A century after the first club was formed on Bondi Beach, more than 37,000 surf lifesavers patrolled in 305 clubs, with a total volunteer membership of the movement of more than 130,000.² The symbolic power of lifesavers lies in their close association with another Australian symbol: the beach. Australians have been described as 'a coastal people', 'the world's greatest beachgoers'.³ They consider their beaches to be a national asset, and imagine themselves in the reflection of the sun and surf. A fundamental characteristic of Australia's twentieth-century surf culture was that the beaches were free: they cost nothing to enter and access was unrestricted. Free access was considered to be an Australian 'right', and set Australian beaches apart from those of much of Europe and even parts of North America.⁴ The lifesaver came to be seen as an embodiment of this spirit of the Australian beach and was internationally recognised as a symbol of Australia's beach culture.

The beach emerged as a 'symbol of Australia at pleasure', in the interwar period. Tied with this was a celebration of the surf lifesaver – a 'super-fit, bronzed, able-bodied, muscular, controlled man' – as the embodiment of the ideal 'national type', which was especially prominent during the same period.⁵ However, despite his endurance, the extent to which the lifesaver actually represented the nation has been contested. To many Australians, the lifesaver is not a symbol of the nation but of Sydney, where Bondi and Manly, Australia's most famous ocean beaches, are within easy reach and going to the beach is an everyday summer recreation. Internationally too, it is the 'Bondi lifesaver' that most often symbolises Australia's beach culture.

The strength of the lifesaver as a national symbol was also undermined by the movement's lack of ethnic diversity, as we will see, and by the fact that women were unable to become full patrolling members until 1980. Forty years later they made up around 45 per cent of total membership.⁶ Although women were involved with surf life saving clubs in varying capacities, and in some cases even formed their own,⁷ the lifesaver was always male in the popular imagination.

Nationalising the surf lifesaver

Legalisation of all-day bathing on Sydney's coast between 1902 and 1905, the result of changing moral values, created a new form of popular coastal recreation virtually overnight. In its special 'Seaside number' in March 1906, the *Sydney Mail* captured this rapid transformation:

> We are beginning at last to wake up in earnest to our good fortune in having the Pacific at our doors and such a long spell of warm sunny weather in which to play in it or on it ... thousands now find their way where hundreds only went a few years ago. To-day every curving crescent of white sea sand is crowded by visitors, and every acre of surf is alive with bathers fascinated by this healthy and invigorating exercise.[8]

The grim reality of this collective dive into the surf was that most new bathers could not swim or were not familiar with the conditions of the surf. From 1907 regular surf bathers organised themselves to curb the frequency of drownings and near-drownings on Sydney's most popular beaches. In the face of sensationalised press reports of the dangers of the surf, opposition by moralists to daylight bathing, and a refusal by either the state or local governments to take responsibility for surf bathing, the first surf lifesavers also consciously positioned themselves as a lobby group. They won public and political support by volunteering their services and introducing formal training and qualifications. But despite lifesavers being heralded in the press as saviours of healthy and wholesome beach recreation, moralists continued to campaign against surf bathing. In response, as lobbyists for the benefits of surf bathing, the new clubs drew from an emerging discourse that constructed surf bathing as an inherently healthy activity.

In the search for a 'distinctively national culture' around Federation, many Australians looked to the bush, a romanticised natural setting whose shearers and drovers represented an idealised national type.⁹ For many residents of coastal cities the beach offered a similarly idealised landscape – a healthy, open space where fresh air and sunshine could be enjoyed in abundance, and hard-working residents could escape the emotional and physical burdens of their daily lives in the congested cities. At the start of the twentieth century, regular beachgoers were seen to embody the goodness of the beach. Like the bushman, the surf bather was strong and sun-browned; but unlike the bushman, the surf bather's contribution to national fitness was a healthiness built on leisure and the sun, ozone and salt water of the beach.

Eugenicists and surf bathing promoters drew on the healthy qualities associated with the beach to credit the surf with the creation of a new, healthy and superior generation, or 'race', of Australians. Surf bathing, it was claimed, was 'helping to build up a fine vigorous race from amongst the young people who live in the cities bordering our shores'. It was therefore described as a 'national recreation', a 'national pastime', even a 'national instinct'.¹⁰ Lifesavers, as the most regular beachgoers, became the exemplars of the healthiness associated with surf bathing. More importantly, they were also active in consciously promoting a positive image based on the physical strength of their bodies and generosity of their spirit, emphasising these as 'national traits'.

The first suggestion that lifesaving, as distinct from beach-going, was a symbol of Australia and Australianness was made in 1908 by Charles Oakes, vice president of the Surf Bathing Association and assistant minister in the New South Wales government. The government had sent film of 'scenes of Australian life' to the Franco–British Exhibition in London. Oakes announced at a social function for surf lifesavers that it was 'an important omission' not to include footage of surf lifesaving activities to advertise New South Wales abroad.¹¹ Soon lifesavers were popping up in any national publicity meant for international consumption.

Two years later, in 1910, Manly lifesaving pioneer, Arthur Relph, was confident enough to argue that surf bathing was contributing to the decline in cricket's popularity: 'are not those young men better employed in forming life saving clubs, competing one with the other for supremacy, with keen enthusiasm, developing their bodies, and helping to build up a fine race of young Australians' than in 'loafing' on the cricket field? The usually conservative *Sydney Morning Herald* typified the support lifesavers enjoyed from the Sydney press, praising their 'alertness, the patient watchfulness, and the complete disregard of self in the moment of emergency'. With no desire for reward, they represented 'nationality in the making'.[12] Lifesavers represented all that was good about 'Young Australia' because they were associated with the healthy beach, and because of their attitude to their work: a complex combination of physical and mental superiority that meant surf lifesavers were feted and adored as ideal Australians.

The appearance of lifesavers was also crucial to their appeal, and within a year of their arrival at the beach, surf lifesavers were said to be recognisable by their tanned skin. The tanned body was a fundamental component of the mythology of the surf lifesaving movement: they were the 'brown men' of the surf, an attribute actively promoted in their 'brown man' competitions. Whereas the tanned body of the bushman simply implied that he worked outdoors, the sun-browned skin of regular surf bathers, a very physical marker of leisure time spent on the beach, was celebrated as a symbol of the health, vitality and youth of Australia. Surf lifesavers themselves emphasised the supposed healthiness of skin browned by exposure to the sun, as if oblivious to generations of ingrained racial prejudice that denigrated anyone with darker skin. It was on the beach, and through the surf lifesavers specifically, that the tanned body became something to aspire to.[13]

Between the wars

While World War I interrupted the rapid growth of surf lifesaving clubs along the east coast and in Western Australia, the high rate of enlistment among lifesavers enhanced perceptions of their strength and valour, now increasingly prominent as 'national' characteristics, in the public mind.[14] Upon return to peace, the lifesaver resumed his position on the mantle of Australian masculinity, but with increased emphasis on his quasi-military discipline and sacrifice.

Between 1920 and 1940, the number of clubs in Australia jumped from 25 to 130. The innovation of the red and yellow flag in 1935 and cap in 1939 to signify patrolling lifesavers increased the visibility of the movement, and would become central to the symbol of the Australian lifesaver. While some lifesavers had always portrayed themselves as symbolising the national character, by the 1930s it was evident that the rest of Australia saw them in this light too. Advertising images of the bronzed, fit, disciplined surf lifesaver adorned beer posters in hotels and sold swimwear. He was a central figure in the posters celebrating the opening of the Sydney Harbour Bridge in 1932 and was prominent in international promotions of Australia. Campaigns aimed at tourists and potential immigrants both promoted the national characteristics of the surf lifesaver and used the figure to allay fears about some of the dangers of living in Australia.

The appeal of the lifesaver to interwar Australians lay in his physical fitness, which was particularly important in an era when eugenics was a guiding principle. He provided a contrast to the crippled bodies of the most recent national heroes, the Anzacs.[15] His urban location was also appealing. The bushman was nostalgically linked with an idealised bush life that most Australians had not experienced; the lifesaver, in contrast, represented the modern city lifestyle. He was a part of everyday life, of the summer leisure enjoyed by coastal-dwelling Australians. But, as always, his volunteer status was essential to his appeal – he represented the resourcefulness, ingenuity and generosity of character Australians liked to think applied to them.[16] And, exclusively male, he represented another characteristic associated with Australianness – 'mateship'.

A dramatic episode early in 1938 cemented the lifesaver's claim to be an instantly recognisable 'national symbol', both domestically and abroad. On 6 February, over 70 Bondi lifesavers performed the largest mass rescue in Australian surf history, when several hundred bathers were swept off a sandbank and into a strong rip. Within 20 minutes, over 200 people had been rescued, and around 60 lay unconscious on the sand. The lifesavers managed to successfully resuscitate all but four; a fifth body was found later.

The media reports of what was dubbed by one lifesaver 'Black Sunday' emphasised the selfless heroism and professionalism of Bondi's surf lifesavers. In refusing to single out any heroes, the club captain unwittingly contributed to the mythologising of the movement, reinforcing an Australian habit of valorising anonymous collective identities such as the pioneer, the bushman and the Anzac. Black Sunday was the high water mark of the lifesaver's career as a national symbol.

This was confirmed by international attention when a visiting American doctor who assisted with the resuscitations praised the rescues as 'the most incredible work of love in the world'. In a country hungry for international notice, this independent corroboration of the superhuman qualities of Australian lifesavers, cited in Australian and international newspapers, allowed their symbolic role to cross the border from internal to external significance.[17]

Raising the heat

The outbreak of another war in 1939 again created turmoil as thousands of club members enlisted and juniors were called on to patrol the beaches. Testament to the importance of lifesaving to a pervasive sense of 'Australianness', clubs were formed where Australian soldiers were based.[18] Lifesaving carnivals were held from Palestine to Cornwall, with equipment supplied by the Australian Armed Services, as a way of increasing the morale of Australian servicemen and helping them to feel 'at home' in a foreign land.

Following the end of the war, lifesavers returned to Australian beaches but they were never again as central to national identity. A surf carnival held on Bondi Beach for the enjoyment of Queen Elizabeth on her 1954 coronation tour marked perhaps the last truly glorious moments of surf lifesaving on the national stage. The Australian press delightedly reported the fascination the Queen and Prince Philip showed in the lifesaving display, both edging forward in their seats to watch the surfboat race. Despite a very tight and exhaustive schedule, the Queen overstayed her visit to Bondi by 45 minutes, witness to the spectacle that Australian lifesaving could provide (Fig. 48). Once again Australian newspapers boasted that the lifesaver had been recognised overseas, with the English press describing the carnival as 'the most novel, interesting, and exciting show they had seen ... to the Queen, as to themselves, the show was entirely new. Nowhere in the world was there anything exactly comparable.'[19]

As Australians settled into post-war affluence and the new generation of baby boomers set out to differentiate themselves from their conventional, staid parents, lifesaving lost its cachet as the embodiment of what it was to be Australian. It was contested as a national symbol. The first challenge came from the unrestricted, undisciplined hedonism of surfers, who claimed a monopoly of the waves. The 1960s marked an important transition in Australian beach culture, with sometimes violent territorial clashes between surfers and surf lifesavers. The new generation of surfies challenged old ways of using the beach, and resented their activities being policed and curtailed by surf lifesavers, who maintained an authoritative role forged decades earlier. In their turn, many surf lifesavers resented their authority being undermined by predominantly young men who, a generation earlier, might well have been lifesavers themselves. The sight of one national symbol (the lifesaver) fighting over another (the beach) was a potent image of Australian tribalism.[20]

In the 1970s, the rules restricting women from becoming surf lifesavers were seen as evidence that the surf lifesaver could only represent half the nation, and social and political pressure soon forced the organisation to rethink the gender restrictions of their membership. At around the same time, the overwhelmingly Anglo–Celtic makeup of most surf lifesaving clubs in an increasingly ethnically diverse society began to be seen as a physical reminder that lifesaving was a relic of a past world. The lifesaver had emerged as an appropriate national symbol in the early twentieth century particularly because he was a white, albeit tanned, Anglo–Celtic male. By the close of the century, these fundamental characteristics meant he was overwhelmingly seen as non-representative of what it was to be 'Australian'.

The Cronulla riots in December 2005 highlighted the extent to which the lifesaver had become a contested symbol of 'Australianness'. Their catalyst was an altercation between surf lifesavers and beachgoers, which some in the media portrayed in an inflammatory light as a 'bashing' of lifesavers by young Middle Eastern men. There was outrage in the popular press and on commercial radio and once again lifesavers were in the international news. Sydney's *Daily Telegraph* was particularly indignant that 'innocent' lifesavers had been victims of an attack, interpreting the incident as an attack on the nation:

> Going to the beach on a summer's day is a tradition in this country – as Australian as a slouch hat, the Melbourne Cup, a sprig of wattle, the scent of eucalyptus smoke in the air. And there's an aspect of the tradition we have all been taught to respect – that's the role of the volunteer army of surf lifesavers who stand guard while we enjoy ourselves. That in this country we have bred a strain of selflessness so ennobling and so constant is something which every decent Australian regards as a stamp of quality on our national character. And every day at the beach – if we are

smart – we breathe a silent prayer of thanks for the lifesavers' work.[21]

In a new manifestation of the territorial clashes of the 1960s, the war of words quickly escalated and became more about perception of ethnic difference and 'ownership' of the beach than about lifesaving. In the context of the 'culture wars' and a concerted attempt to retrieve 'traditional' symbols such as Anzac and the flag, an apparent attack on lifesavers could be used to incite mass violence. The *Daily Telegraph* suggested that 'in attacking our lifesavers, they attack us all'.[22] However, the Cronulla riots also reminded others why the lifesaver in the early twenty-first century was a problematic symbol – not culturally inclusive,

The lifesaver ideal: surf carnival at South Curl Curl Beach, Sydney, 1935.
Image courtesy of Northern Beaches Council Library Local Studies

but almost exclusively associated with his Anglo heritage. The culture wars had drawn blood. When lifesavers and lifeguards were involved in enforcing 'social distancing' during the pandemic in 2020, there was some initial harassment that then seemed to ease off.[23]

The inclusion of the red-and-yellow-clad 'Bondi' lifesaver as one of the many Australian 'icons' represented in the closing ceremony of the Sydney 2000 Olympic Games might suggest his continued relevance as a national symbol. But it wasn't the modern, mixed-gender lifesavers in sun-protective clothing who were depicted on this international stage; rather it was an idealised, masculine version of the surf lifesaver in his march-past costume of the 1930s. The lifesaver had become part of a nostalgic national past along with the Hills hoist, the Victa lawnmower and the FJ Holden.[24]

Although his resonance has declined since the interwar period, continued marketing campaigns which use images of modern lifesavers to promote Australian values are evidence that the figure retains some value as a national symbol. Certainly the red and yellow flags associated with surf lifesaving remain a symbol of the Australian beach (Fig. 50). The declaration of 2007 as the Australian Year of the Surf Lifesaver suggested that an Australian government keen to promote traditional symbols saw the centenary of surf lifesaving as worthy of national celebration.

But the danger for the movement was that the figure of the lifesaver would become nothing more than a nostalgic hangover from an exclusive, homogenised past. Programs were established to encourage culturally and ethnically diverse communities to join the ranks of surf lifesaving clubs (Fig. 49), and a surf lifesaving float joined the Sydney Gay and Lesbian Mardi Gras in 2007. The organisation was working towards creating an image which could maintain its relevance as a 'national symbol'. It supported *Surf Patrol*, a reality television show based on real-life rescues by volunteer surf lifesavers around Australia, reaching an average audience of 1.45 million per episode in 2007. But significantly it was displaced by *Bondi Rescue*, a similar show based on paid *lifeguards* employed on Bondi Beach, which began in 2008 and continues to have an even greater international reach. Tensions between volunteer lifesavers and paid lifeguards are rarely admitted but do simmer below the surface.

The strength of the surf lifesaver as a symbol of Australia lay in his association with the beach. He drew his health and vitality from the surf and sun, and his endearing nature from his role as protector of beach recreation and his volunteering spirit. Ultimately, he was the most easily and instantly recognisable beachgoer, and it was this that made him so inherently 'Australian'. Since the mid-twentieth century, the lifesaver has gradually become a less prominent figure on – and off – the beach. He, and now she, occupies far more sand than a century ago, but no longer occupies the national imagination in quite the same way.

PAVLOVA

Michael Symons

If people are what they eat, then Australians are sweet, creamy and fluffy. For their proudest claimant to a national dish is the pavlova. This is a large, single-layered meringue dessert of sugar and whipped egg whites, retaining a marshmallow centre and topped with whipped cream and fresh fruit, preferably passionfruit.

New Zealanders, too, claim this as their national dish. They too view it nostalgically as a grandmotherly accomplishment. They too associate it with heartfelt celebrations that include birthdays, weddings and family get-togethers. The only material difference is that it has become more often decorated with sliced kiwifruit.

Given the importance of foods for a sense of identity, reminding us of the intimate geographical, cultural and social links that make us who we are, the pavlova has become a beloved, too often overlooked symbol of nation. But which nation? The rival claims have stimulated considerable research into the pavlova's origins. Trawling through hundreds of old cookery books, scholars have reached a consensus that its creation is far too complex for ownership of the pavlova's intellectual property ever to be settled.[1]

This might disappoint fervent nationalists, but cooks are gentler and more generous than rugby teams, who prefer a clear-cut contest with a definite result. The more interesting reality is that the pavlova is a social invention – not created in one kitchen, but devised by numerous hands, working independently and yet together. It is the peoples' pavlova, the peoples of more than one country, an instance of the surprising degree of cross-Tasman interaction.

In the early decades of the twentieth century, domestic cooks baked a huge variety of large meringue cakes and desserts. The recipes acquired various forms and toppings. People used many names, including 'meringue cake', 'meringue pie', 'marshmallow meringue' and 'fairy pie'. Contributing to the confusion, the name 'pavlova' was also used from the late 1920s for other concoctions: two-layered meringue cakes, small meringues and, seemingly earliest, a four-layered jelly.

Despite the plethora of names and recipes, most Australians and New Zealanders came to know their pavlova when they ate one; they learned to recognise its puffed exterior, caramelised sweetness and powdery crunch. The conclusion reached here is that, working together even without knowing one another, ordinary cooks adapted and improved large meringues, were praised for exceptional results, strove to win prizes with them, and handed on recipes. In this way, cooks and eaters invented a relatively stable recipe by the early 1940s.

Simultaneously, the pavlova was socially constructed as an idea or, more accurately, a cluster of representations and meanings eventually held together by an agreed name. Cooks chatted while they beat the egg whites, suffered feedback from eaters and obliged with the cake for special occasions. In such ways, people developed a consensus – or apparent consensus – about the 'correct' pavlova. During an upsurge in nationalism in the 1960s and 1970s, the mass media in both countries helped elevate the pavlova to the hallowed status of a 'national dish' and later 'icon'. The trick is that it became such a definite entity that it seemed to require one specific, physical birth with a precise location.

Extensive research has located no single moment of creation for any one of three dozen other characteristically Antipodean cakes and biscuits: not only the pavlova, but also lamingtons, Anzac biscuits, Louise cake, Afghans, neenish tarts, Maori kisses, jubilee cake and so on.[2] That is, the twin processes of amorphous recipe invention and symbolic construction – inventing a tradition with a specific origin myth – turn out to be typical of popular food creations.

Concocting a recipe

In Australia, the oldest published pavlova recipes located so far are two separate versions entitled 'Pavlova cake', ascribed to Miss Elizabeth Laidlaw and Mrs B Lee Archer, published in *275 Choice Recipes: In Aid of Hamilton Red Cross Funds* from Hamilton (Victoria) in 1940, and two further recipes called 'Marshmallow meringue' and 'Pavlova' in Ethel Wald's *Empire Cookery Book: Containing 500 Selected Choice Recipes* from Adelaide in the same year. That two Red Cross fundraising books picked up four versions suggests that many recipes were circulating person-to-person before World War II. Ethel Wald's recipes were 'tried either by me or by friends who have been kind enough to pass them on.'[3]

A genuine and independent renaming of the meringue cake appears to have occurred earlier in Perth. The chef at the Esplanade Hotel, Herbert Sachse, refined the recipe in 1935, and either the hotel's owner or manager named it to commemorate the earlier 1929 visit of Russian ballerina Anna Pavlova (1881–1931). Sachse recalled this for a magazine interview nearly four decades after the event,[4] and the tradition is still stoutly defended by members of the families involved, unfortunately without documentary evidence, such as a menu.

Researchers in New Zealand discovered an earlier date.[5] Helen Leach and her colleagues found a large 'Pavlova cake', although of two layers, contributed under the nom de plume 'Festival' to the *New Zealand Dairy Exporter Annual* in 1929. The *Rangiora Mother's Union Cookery Book*, seemingly in 1933, recorded a 'Pavlova cake' contributed by Mrs WH [Laurina] Stevens, and other recipes popped up soon after.

While these might seem to suggest an earlier emergence in New Zealand, the hunt for 'firsts' opens up problems of definition. Can a 'true' pavlova have two layers? Can it lack one or both of vinegar and cornflour, which are said to be the 'secret' of the marshmallow centre? Can it be called a 'pavlova cake' (rather than simply 'pavlova')?[6] Should we look for the oldest large cream-and-fruit-covered meringue?

As an example of the tangle, one of New Zealand's leading food historians found a recognisable pavlova recipe published as 'Meringue with fruit filling' in *Home Cookery for New Zealanders* in 1926. Unfortunately for Kiwi honour, the book was actually a repackaging of Emily Futter's *Australian Home Cookery* from perhaps 1924. Further demonstrating that relevant recipes flitted back and forth across the Tasman, Mrs C Cooper of Sydney contributed a two-layered dessert entitled 'Meringue cake' to the *Ideal Cookery Book* in Wellington (New Zealand) in 1929.

The idea of large meringues would seem to have thrived in Australia. 'Large meringues' appeared in the *Goulburn Cookery Book*, which commenced its long run in New South Wales in 1899. The dimensions of a 'large' meringue were not specified, so it is not clear whether we might recognise the result as more like a meringue or pavlova. Confusingly, as well as requiring six egg whites, the recipe included the ambiguous instruction, 'then with a tablespoon lay the meringue on the paper'. That is, the title anticipated plural 'meringues', while the recipe might require a single and therefore pavlova-like 'meringue'.

The popularity of the concept is demonstrated by the *Coronation Cookery Book*, published by the Country Women's Association of New South Wales in 1937. Discussing meringues, it advises, 'Large meringues may be piled one on top of the other and joined with cream, flavoured to taste (passionfruit cream and strawberry cream are delicious)', although the book again did not specify the meaning of 'large'. As to recipes, the *Coronation* included two different types of 'Marshmallow cake', one of which was a large, two-layered meringue cake. Also coming close to a conventional pavlova, a recipe called 'Meringue gateau' required piped meringue, 'leaving the centre plain … to be filled with whipped cream, flavoured and sweetened and decorated to taste'. Finally, the book's

'Meringue cake or fairy pie' was anybody's idea of a pavlova, even to the passionfruit on top.

Another embarrassment is that pavlova look-alikes were employed elsewhere, notably in the United States, although often with two layers, under such names as 'Meringue torte (Schaum torte)', 'Angel pie (Lemon schaum torte)' and 'Meringue tart or Pinch pie'. The seventh edition of *Joy of Cooking* (1997) claimed to have traced schaum torte ('foam cake') back to the 1870s in Wisconsin.

Numerous examples, some from the same publication, demonstrate that the recipe was a social invention created by innumerable hands. It was reliant, in the words of early Australian cookery writer Mina Rawson, on the 'cleverness of the whole number'.[7]

Modernity and kitchens

Such cakes were an inevitable outcome given the prevailing culinary circumstances. While the temptation might be to view the large meringue as old-fashioned, it was the height of modernity, the product of the brand-new mass kitchens.

Britain colonised Australia and New Zealand just as industrialised agriculture boosted the world trade in raw commodities, especially sugar, worked by African slaves shipped across the Atlantic, making a former luxury more widely accessible in Europe. The extension of capital-intensive farming in late nineteenth-century Australia provided not only the sugar, but the other pavlova necessities. The arrival of the cream separator and refrigeration enabled the rapid expansion of dairying. The passionfruit soon became such a speciality of Australian growers that this (rather than South America) seemed like the fruit's original habitat, just as 'kiwifruit' became identified with New Zealand during the 1970s.

As a further aide, factories mass-produced the iron stove, reliant on the seemingly endless energy from wood, coal, gas and, finally, electricity. The *Coronation Cookery Book* advised to bake its 'Marshmallow cake' in a 'meringue oven', which meant 'to make meringue at night after the dinner is over and allow to stay in the oven when fire is out, until morning, but do not forget to remove it before the fire is lighted in the early a.m.'[8]

The modern kitchens were equipped with sugar, vinegar, refrigerated cream, an exciting fruit crop, the iron stove, and a further mechanical foundation of the pavlova – the hand-cranked, counter-rotating, geared egg-beater. Older books spoke of whisking with a knife on a plate, and other equally laborious ways. But literally hundreds of patents were taken out from the late nineteenth century, as recorded by enthusiastic collector Don Thornton, in *Beat This: The Eggbeater Chronicles* (Sunnyvale, California), in 1994. His cover proclaims: 'The stirring story of America's greatest invention'. Other patents were taken out in Australia and New Zealand.

Mina Rawson recommended a 'Patent egg-beater' among 11 'labour-saving machines' in her *Antipodean Cookery Book and Kitchen Companion* in 1907, and yet she remained of the old school: 'A patent egg-beater is merely optional; for my part, I much prefer a fork.' The *Coronation* still advised 'whip with an egg whipper' in 1937, but added in brackets 'use rotary egg beater for preference'. By then, the almost universal command was no longer 'whip' but 'beat'. The mechanical egg-beater liberated cooks from servant drudgery, while encouraging clouds of snows, fluffs, flummeries, angel cakes (without yolks), sponge cakes (with) and meringues, replicating to some degree the refinements of great households with their hordes of servants. Fluffed-up egg whites and cream were triumphs of the modern housewife.

The 'marshmallow' centre was such an attractive feature that 'marshmallow meringue' was a frequent early title in Australia. Proponents have traditionally – though mistakenly – credited this soft centre to the addition of vinegar and cornflour. Meringue's foam composition is such an excellent insulator that even baking a bombe Alaska protects its ice-cream centre: the centre of a large meringue simply won't cook. Indeed, softness has usually been regarded as a fault with meringues, so that experienced cooks made them small and, even then, painstakingly scooped out their tacky insides. Making a large meringue was thus another streamlining of the once fiddly cooking that large households with servants could provide. The modern cook claimed the marshmallow's gooiness as a deliberate effect, and constructed the myth that vinegar and/or cornflour were necessary to achieve it.

Given its easily recognised, lavish appearance once it was decorated, the cake tended to take centrestage. Furthermore, unlike other notable Australian and New Zealand creations from around the same period (lamingtons, Anzac biscuits and so on), which could be eaten in the fingers, the pavlova was sticky, creamy and falling to pieces and so required a plate and eating implement. It suited formal occasions, and so competed as a lighter alternative to a rich fruit cake for birthdays, weddings and Christmases. That gave it the necessary gravitas to stand as a symbol of nation.

While the rationing of eggs and cream cut the dish's urban opportunities during World War II, the subsequent consumer boom included the opulent sweet at family meals. When a Hobart woman won a prize from the *Australian Women's Weekly* in 1948 for her week-long family menu plan, she served 'Banana pavlova cake with fruit-salad sauce' for Monday's evening meal. Emerging so spectacularly after the war, the pavlova might be considered the equivalent of Christian Dior's 'Corolle' style in his first collection in 1947: that is, as a 'New Look' dessert, extravagant, prodigal, sophisticated and a triumph of femininity.

Modern daintiness

Thus far this has been a sketch of the pavlova's material invention; but it became a symbol, too. Bringing the various large meringues together and celebrating their particular qualities was a name. Once named, the pavlova accrued multiple meanings. The first was daintiness.

'Leave acrobatics to others, Anna', an early teacher admonished the Russian ballerina. 'You must realize that your daintiness and fragility are your greatest assets.'[9] Anna Pavlova, well into her forties and an international celebrity, toured her dainty art to the furthest reaches of European colonisation in 1926 and 1929 (Fig. 51).

Pavlova's sophisticated, fragile image was frequently appropriated. As husband Victor Dandré noted:

> Trading interests, always eagerly on the look-out for anything that a gullible public will greedily take up, made an extensive use of Pavlova's name – 'Pavlova Perfume', 'Pavlova Powder', 'Pavlova Fashions for the year 1925', high 'Pavlova boots' in America, 'Pavlova Ices' in London, 'Pavlova Cigarettes'.[10]

Her Sydney souvenir program 'Her Majesty's, week commencing Saturday, 24 April, 1926' carried glamorous advertisements for wine, whisky, beer, hotels, motor vehicles, cruises to Japan, women's stockings and hairstylists, and a 'Special Announcement' from chocolate manufacturers, MacRobertson:

> By arrangement with J.C. Williamson Ltd. Madam Pavlova will autograph the covers of the Special Pavlova Boxes of de luxe Old Gold Chocolates.
>
> Obtainable at all Sweet Stores within the vicinity of this Theatre.

As an even better contender for Australia's first pavlova foodstuff, that same year the Davis Gelatine company promoted a 'pavlova' recipe with four layers of jelly in a mould (using sap green colouring, milk, orange and cochineal) in its *Davis Dainty Dishes* Sydney edition.[11]

While the Davis company had started in New Zealand, its Botany

(Sydney) gelatine works were already boasted as the British Empire's largest. The company published many tens of thousands of copies of the recipe and its watercolour depiction, both in its own booklets and as inserts in other publications.

Pavlova's name became associated with meringues by 1929, although only slowly replacing others, especially 'meringue cake' in New Zealand, which lasted until about 1960. The *Green and Gold* still used the hybrid 'marshmallow meringue (pavlova)' in Australia in the 1950s. This shift from a variant description (e.g., meringue cake) to a proper name is not unusual, and contributed to recipe success – for example, 'raspberry short cake/slice' did not last as well in Australia as similar recipes named 'Louise cake' in New Zealand.

While 'pavlova cake' remained common in New Zealand until 1960, Australians quickly settled on a single noun, perhaps in association with their earlier placing of the dish in the cold desserts (rather than large cakes) category. The even shorter 'pav' was in affectionate use in one or both countries by 1966, according to GW Turner, *The English Language in Australia and New Zealand*. Here again, any rivalry becomes thwarted, because Turner did not clarify where he heard this, and was a New Zealander resident in Australia.

The settling on the dancer's name, then its contraction to 'pavlova' and even 'pav' and its eventual modification (e.g., 'pavlova roll'), charts a strengthening identity.[12] Increasing familiarity would have snowballed. One person might correct another along the lines, 'Oh, that's not a meringue cake, that's a pavlova.' Equally, a singular name promoted recipe comparisons, and so social pressure built up to use the 'best' or the 'right' recipe. That is, the recipe's form and title reinforced each other – an increasingly accepted name holding together an increasingly standardised recipe. As a social *invention*, large marshmallow/meringue cakes came in innumerable versions. As a social construction, the emerging consensus was that there was just one 'true' pavlova.

Demonstrating the power of social construction, the concept soon seemed both eternal and yet to have required a definite invention. That

Pavlova

Ingredients.

3 dessertspoons Davis Gelatine
1½ cups (¾ pint) hot water
1 cup (½ pint) orange juice
½ cup (¼ pint) milk
6 dessertspoons sugar
Flavouring
Cochineal—sap green colouring

Directions.

Dissolve all but a teaspoonful of gelatine in the hot water, and all the sugar except a dessertspoonful. Take half a cup of the mixture and add to the orange juice; of the remainder flavour with essence of lemon and divide and colour one portion with a few drops of cochineal and the other with sap green. Wet a mould and pour in the green mixture. While it is setting dissolve the teaspoonful of gelatine and dessertspoonful of sugar in a little hot water; when it is cool stir into the milk, add a few drops of flavouring essence. If the green layer is quite firm, pour over. When the milk layer is set, arrange orange circles (or any fruit in season) round the mould and add the orange jelly, which should be thickening, a little at a time. When this layer is firm, pour over the red jelly and leave to set. Serve with cream or custard.

A 'pavlova' recipe, from *Davis Dainty Dishes*, first published in 1926. The first pavlova recipe? Not a pavlova at all.

Davis Gelatine (Australia) Limited

is, on the one hand, the power of the idea added to an illusion that the pavlova, while thoroughly modern, originated in some indeterminate past, a process examined by Eric Hobsbawm and Terence Ranger in *The Invention of Tradition* (1983). On the other hand, the reverse illusion was that such a distinct dish must have had a distinct birth, and so to have clearly originated in either Australia or New Zealand. This is the 'intelligent design' fallacy that a clearly recognisable form should have an intentional maker rather than emerge out of complex interactions.

This creative process involved a strengthening of symbolic content. By the mid-1950s, the pavlova was well recognised as a particular local favourite. A Victorian rural newspaper affirmed that the 'pavlova tart is certainly one of the most popular of all fancy sweets'.[13] New Zealand cookery writer Helen M Cox told British readers: 'This is like a large meringue-cake with a soft inside. In New Zealand it is the hostess's favourite dessert (and the guest's too)'.[14] During the 1960s, people on both sides of the Tasman Sea elevated the dish to not just a local favourite but a national creation. This was helped by overseas travel when Antipodeans, isolated from their own culture, rediscovered food favourites, which also included the commercial spread, Vegemite. The *Margaret Fulton Cookbook* observed in 1969 that 'the famous Australian Pavlova is to be enjoyed in places as far flung as San Francisco and Hong Kong'.

Male writers confirmed the pavlova's national importance in the early 1970s. Sydney journalist Ross Campbell found 'Pavlova Cake – 20p a slice' in Harrods food hall in London in 1971, along with a sign: 'Pavlova Cake was created in New Zealand as a tribute to the dancer Anna Pavlova'. Irritated by the misattribution and also the 'cake' label, Campbell wrote to the manager, complaining that 'the Pavlova – "Pavlova Cake" – was believed in Australia to be an indigenous creation', and was normally topped with passionfruit. The store's response was 'conciliatory', saying that they had removed the placard, but noting, presumably to Campbell's chagrin, that sales had trebled when they switched from passionfruit to strawberries.[15]

Across the Tasman, social commentator Austin Mitchell contributed the epithet 'Pavlova Paradise' to describe the suburban New Zealand home in *The Half-gallon Quarter-acre Pavlova Paradise* in 1972. Hugh Schmitt's aforementioned article on Bert Sachse, the former chef at the Esplanade Hotel, Perth, appeared in *Woman's Day* in 1973.

This public attribution of a national meaning came when home cooking was undergoing a further fundamental change. Manufacturers now 'liberated' the modern, mass kitchen of iron stoves and sugar canisters, admitting women into the paid workforce and men into the previously female domain. Pushing a vast range of ready-made, quickly prepared meals and snacks, as well as fast-food options outside the home, marketers reconfigured food's meanings, playing up dietary fads and scouring the world's cuisines for selling points, so launching a cacophony of brand names, logos and celebrity chefs.

During an early stage in this cultural turmoil, the pavlova offered nostalgic security. It belonged to a nationalist revival in the 1960s, when culture seemed threatened by the 'Americanisation' of Coke, sitcoms and the Vietnam War. The pavlova belonged to grandmothers, yet was appreciated by urban sophisticates, hence satirist Barry Humphries' mock complaint in *Dame Edna's Coffee Table Book*: 'Many young lasses couldn't run up … a decent Pavlova these days.'[16] Humphries sniped at the pettiness of the mass kitchen expert, but with some fondness. The upshot was that a heartfelt creation of cooks proud of their modernity was commemorated nostalgically and somewhat ironically by postmodernity.

By the twenty-first century the pavlova's homely appeal was being submerged by the rise of the commercial product, with nationalism as a marketing angle. Supermarkets sold packaged pavlova bases, and mini-pavlova bases, merely requiring whipped cream and fruits (available on other shelves). White Wings continued to market a 'Pavlova magic' dessert mix in an egg-shaped container. Scores of Cheesecake Shop franchisees provided pavlovas. Soon, 'Green and Gold Pavlova' recipes displayed Australian national colours with kiwifruit or mint leaves, pineapple or mango, and a scattering of passionfruit pulp. Television cookery judge Matt Preston enthused: 'I love Australia Day because that's the day when having a second serving of the pav is actually the patriotic thing to do. And hey, it's mostly air and fruit anyway, isn't it?' That quote was among pavlova's 25.2 million search engine hits, which also showed internationalisation working both ways, so that recipes popped up around the world, crediting one country or the other, or 'friendly rivalry'. Personal investigation confirms the deliciousness of Wasabi Pavlova at the S.O.G. (Sanctuary of God) Korean-fusion restaurant in Abbotsford (Sydney).

Creating symbols

While the pavlova is shared with New Zealand, the story shows national boundaries are as socially constructed as the pavlova itself; nations might seem fixed, but are, in Benedict Anderson's memorable term, 'imagined communities'. As Richard White put it in 1981, 'There is no "real" Australia waiting to be uncovered. A national identity is an invention.'[17] Like the pavlova, nations are surprisingly modern constructions. Until the twentieth century, Australia and New Zealand were hardly more than a cluster of colonies, but were linked so effectively by sea transport that the Australian Constitution left room for New Zealand's participation. Such considerations support a case that the pavlova, while seeming frivolous, could yet be a powerful uniting force showing, on the basis of its collective creation, these two lands are really one (Fig. 52). It was called on to do that symbolic work when, with the return of quarantine-free flights across the Tasman in April 2021, Air New Zealand chief Greg Foran sent a pavlova smothered in kiwi fruit to Qantas chief Alan Joyce, presumably unaware he was highly allergic to the fruit. In return, and maintaining the genial pavlova rivalry, Joyce sent Foran a pavlova with passionfruit 'so he can taste the best … and the original'.[18]

The English word 'symbol' derives from the ancient Greek *sym-* (together) and *ballo* (throw) to mean a 'coming together'. Not the least of its original senses was a contribution meal, which might in the Antipodes be called 'bring a plate'. Each food contribution to a 'symbolic' meal was also a *symbolon*. According to the *Oxford English Dictionary*, 'symbol' was still used in the seventeenth century for a 'contribution (properly to a feast or picnic), a share, portion'. That is, the word 'symbol' refers both to a gathering to which participants bring a contribution and to the contribution, so that the contributed 'symbol' represents the whole. No better example of a symbol can thus be given than the pavlova, which has typically been whipped up as a gift for a community supper or extended family celebration. In that context, the pavlova makes an attractive national symbol, contrasting more than favourably with its most conventional contender, the flag. The Australian flag is largely symbolic, barely grounded in material reality and obsessively protected from desecration. By contrast, the pavlova is meant to be eaten, and its rich and attractive symbolism is grounded in common experience – belonging to the senses, affective occasions and the everyday cornucopia of sugar, eggs, cream, stoves and egg-beaters.

Flags originated in the battlefield and Australia's bristles with Christian crosses, as does the confusingly similar New Zealand flag. The flag has been imposed from above. It has flown on the top of buildings, in parade grounds and behind politicians. Against this, the pavlova has gained its national connotations from below, in hard work and heartfelt festivities in many homes. The pavlova's association with domestic kitchens makes it more feminine, secular and generous. The pavlova is the people's symbol.

If the pavlova has seemed almost forgotten in recent flag-waving times, this is because these two national symbols represent opposite sides of the 'culture wars'. Let us not forget that the flag perpetuates a view of human existence as continuous warfare. Instead, let us celebrate the pavlova, which is domestic, peaceful and admitting of irony.

HOLDEN

Robert Crawford

'She's a Beauty', Prime Minister Ben Chifley famously declared in 1948, admiring the first Holden as it rolled off the production line. More than a mere car, Holden became a national symbol, a status that General Motors-Holden took care to cultivate. While their advertising 60 years later claimed that 'Holden means a great deal to Australia', things had changed. Declining sales coupled with Prime Minister Tony Abbott's cessation of subsidies for the manufacturer in 2013 revealed that Holden no longer meant the same thing to Australians. The rise and fall of this Australian symbol tells us as much about Australia as it does about Australia's relationship with the broader world – notably the United States. So how did an American-owned company manufacture an Australian national symbol? The answer lies in a combination of international connections, fortuitous timing and, above all, shrewd marketing.

An international Australian

Holden's roots date back to 1856 when James Holden established a saddlery in Adelaide. It slowly branched out into carriage repairs and rebuilding before merging with Henry Frost's carriage building and trimming firm. The Boer War (1899-1902) provided the impetus for Holden & Frost to establish its brand and acquire national significance. The firm expanded rapidly to become the Australian military forces' major supplier and, in turn, the nation's leading saddler.[1] When World War I broke out in 1914, it was well placed to re-equip the nation's horsemen. However, horses and saddles were soon overwhelmed by the new mechanised warfare.

The company's first foray into automotive production occurred just prior to World War I when it began producing sidecars in partnership with American motorcycle manufacturer Harley-Davidson.[2] Reconfiguring imported cars for local conditions was another lucrative sideline. However, when the government temporarily banned car imports and only allowed the import of chassis, Holden & Frost gave priority to automotive production. The firm's fully established manufacturing plant was perfectly poised to become the nation's leading car producer.

After the war, the increased tariff enabled Holden (having discarded Frost) to expand further and to compete directly with international manufacturers. Having invested heavily in its manufacturing operations, the firm hoped that closer links with an international firm would safeguard its future. By 1924 Holden had become Australia's sole manufacturer of General Motors (GM) cars. Its relationship strengthened when GM established assembly plants across the nation to attach Holden bodies to GM chassis. While difficulties arose (GM was upset that Holden was not directly copying American plans), the partnership proved successful.

But then the Great Depression crushed Australia's fledgling automotive industry. Cars were still luxuries and sales duly plummeted when the crisis hit. In 1931 the company sold out to GM, becoming General Motors-Holden Ltd (GM-H). Laurence Hartnett, an Englishman with a broad automotive background, was appointed head of GM-H with the aim of ensuring that the Australian branch was conforming to GM's global strategy. In 1936 a new production plant was opened at Fishermans Bend in Melbourne and smaller plants followed in the other states. By facilitating its distribution, GM-H inadvertently established itself as a national brand.

War again proved to be a catalyst in the company's history after 1939. As a leading industrialist, Hartnett offered GM-H's facilities to the war effort and was himself appointed Director of Ordnance Production for the Commonwealth. While Hartnett's offer angered GM heads in the still neutral US, he had few alternatives. Hartnett had recognised that government contracts were now much more lucrative than the stagnant consumer market – a point not lost on the manufacturers of other symbolic wares such as Akubra and Vegemite. Other unforeseen benefits also emerged from GM-H's wartime service. A diversification of outputs – from trucks to aeroplanes – provided GM-H the wherewithal to develop new manufacturing processes, while Hartnett had intimate access to key political figures.

Immediately after World War II GM-H held a unique position. Although it was an international firm, it was still regarded as a pioneering Australian company that had developed alongside the nation and served it in its hour of need. Its international ties reinforced the success of this Australian venture. Deft use of history and its political and financial connections would become integral to the production of 'Australia's own' car and, indeed, its emergence as a national symbol.

She's a beauty

Although the Americans had initially raised the concept of producing an Australian-made car, it was Hartnett who firmly placed it on the agenda when he visited Detroit in 1944. His plan was coolly received but his persistence and confidence in the post-war demand for cars in Australia eventually won out. The Americans questioned whether GM would recoup an investment in an Australian car given the size and wealth of the market. Detroit was also concerned by what they perceived to be the socialist agenda of Australia's Labor government. For these businessmen, Australia's wartime alliance with the United States counted for nothing. Ironically, fears about government intervention ultimately prompted GM to give the project the green light. According to Hartnett, the Minister for Postwar Reconstruction Ben Chifley demanded that Australia produce its own car:

> What about this car business? ... I know we must make cars ourselves and I don't think these people out here in the car game will do it. They're foreign: they're not us; they represent foreign interests. Australia needs a car of her own. We must have it.[3]

Given Chifley's interest in manufacturing a car, GM reasoned that it was better to have government support than to compete against it and finally agreed to the project. Delighted with the coup, Chifley promptly lent GM-H £2.5 million to launch Australia's own car. It was, as Shane Birney notes, 'one of the more unusual corporate deals', bringing together the American manufacturing giant, its local subsidiary and a 'socialist' government.[4] But this collaboration between the state and private enterprise gave the car a national significance that it wouldn't have had if it had simply been GM's baby.

The project soon ran into difficulties over a familiar dispute. Although Detroit was happy for GM-H to manufacture and assemble the vehicle, it wanted to control design. Hartnett was adamant that the entire project be undertaken in Australia by Australians. A compromise saw the mechanical and chassis components designed by Americans, while the majority of the body structure, packaging and trim development were designed by Australians.[5] The initial model was built in Detroit and then shipped to Australia for testing. Hartnett's insistence had further strained his relationship with GM. Feeling that his stance 'had made me too much of an Australian' in the eyes of his American bosses, he angrily left GM-H long before the project's completion.[6]

With the new vehicle performing well in Australian conditions, an extensive public relations campaign was launched. An early target was GM-H's own staff. Labour shortages meant that workers were a highly prized commodity. GM-H hoped to minimise staff losses by encouraging workers to take pride in the project. Workers rubbed shoulders with politicians (the company's other vital supporters) at an advance viewing of the prototypes. Wooing the media was the next step. Journalists were given tours of the manufacturing plants and a sneak peek at the new car. GM also hoped to establish the car's 'Australianness' by naming it the 'Holden', in honour of the company's Australian founder. Carefully managed reports subsequently appeared in the press, supplemented by press advertisements and brochures for future Holden dealers. The public relations campaign sought to generate excitement while assuring consumers that the project was more than hot air. As one advertisement explained:

> *There's a new look in cars* … It's Holden – General Motors new Australian car … the real beauty of Holden is that it is the one car made in Australia especially for Australian conditions … When you buy Holden you buy the engineering experience and know-how behind all General Motors cars. You get the dependability which stands behind such famous G.M. cars as Cadillac … [and] Chevrolet … Holden is Australia's own car. Australia's biggest car value.[7]

This advertisement suggested some initial ambivalence in the Holden's promotion as a national symbol. Tested in Australia's unique conditions by Australians for Australians, the modern car was clearly identified as Australia's own from the very outset. However, references to the world-class company backing the project sought to ameliorate any scepticism about Australia's ability to produce its own car.

In the weeks before the car's public release, GM-H's publicity campaign shifted up another gear with events organised for employees, distributors and community leaders.[8] The campaign reached its

'She's a beauty': Prime Minister Ben Chifley at the launch of the first mass-produced Australian car at the General Motors-Holden's factory, Fishermans Bend, Melbourne, 1948. Although the Holden was created under the Chifley Labor government, it would be Menzies' Liberals who were more closely aligned to the relaxed consumerist Australia it symbolised.

National Archives of Australia

crescendo on 29 November 1948 when the nation's politicians and dignitaries attended the final public launch. Like the car itself, the launch was a curious amalgam of American and Australian cultures. Hollywood came to Fishermans Bend as glamorous hostesses ushered VIPs to their seats. Yet there were clear references to national symbolism. The Australian flag stood by the Union Jack and the American flag on the speaker's lectern. Chifley's speech likewise reiterated Holden's significance to the nation:

I am not here on a political but on a national mission to thank General Motors-Holden's ... I already view with pride the possibilities of Holden, not only in its own country but also for export to countries beyond our borders ... I look too on this project as another link in the warm human relationship that the war proved so essential between this country and the American people. I offer my warmest congratulations on the consummation of this national project.[9]

This was not just a commodity; it was in the interests of both the government and the advertising campaign that it be a national enterprise.[10]

The modern Australian

For the first generation of Holden owners, their purchase symbolised the dreams and hopes that they had fought for during the war. Throughout the conflict, the advertising industry had continually promised a postwar age of affluence.[11] Modern, individualistic and available, the Holden signalled the beginnings of this new consumer age. Ironically, Chifley – who never held a driver's licence – fell victim to this symbolism. His reintroduction of petrol rationing in 1949 was taken as an affront to the very values that the Holden celebrated. This point was captured by a famous *Bulletin* cartoon published during the 1949 election campaign. Depicting Chifley in a decrepit old car, it featured his opponent, Robert Menzies, ushering a young female voter into his gleaming new Holden, named *Free Enterprise*.

Modernity was an integral part of Holden's symbolism, although as Mick Taussig noted, this celebration of 'the transition from the bush to the modern urban and mechanical age' also linked contemporary Australia to its past.[12] Its suitability for 'Australian conditions' tended to be proclaimed on the rough roads of the outback – most notably in the popular Redex car trials of the 1950s – even though most of its drivers were modern suburbanites. While the motor car had long been identified with modernity and progress, the Holden had a particular impact as a national symbol in identifying these qualities with Australia itself.[13] In *Land of Australia: Roaming in a Holden*, Frank Clune celebrated this modernity:

> Today, Australian secondary industry is in every way as important as primary industry, and must become more and more important as the Australian nation further expands in population, power and influence. The Holden car is a symbol of Australia's maturity and ever growing self-dependence.[14]

Clune began his journey around Australia by watching a single screw transform into a Holden at the Fishermans Bend works. The car that rolled off the production line became his touring vehicle. Naming it Miss Icy Blue, Clune described his new model as 'a prim and proper person, stylish and fast, but reliable, and she knows how to keep out of trouble'.[15] Appearances were important; the assumption that the car had a five-year shelf life demanded that new models be designed to maintain a modern feel. When the FJ Holden replaced the original model, the major point of difference was the grille, which had been updated to look more modern and, significantly, more American (Fig. 53).

Although advertisements emphasised the Holden's value for money, the car was originally costly, largely limiting its ownership to middle-class men. However, the 1950s economic boom broadened the car's market. During the decade, the cost of a car only climbed by a third while male wages almost quadrupled.[16] As it became accessible to working-class Australians, the Holden could also embody the nation's claim to an egalitarian ethos – it truly was Australia's own car. Surprisingly, this affordability did not dent the Holden's prestige. While marketing certainly helped uphold this image, consumers also did their bit. As a symbol of personal status and success, proud owners lavished attention on their Holdens, which were regularly washed, polished and housed in a protective garage.

The Holden owner's pride also reflected the prevailing political climate. Menzies' Liberal Party had come to power in 1949 promising to assist the nation's 'forgotten people' realise their ambitions. Facilitating home ownership was the first priority, but further consumption was encouraged to simultaneously stimulate the economy and promote the Liberals' individualist ideology. The Holden's affordability was also a healthy advertisement for liberal democracy. Of this democracy of consumption, Graeme Davison observes: 'Rather than fretting about the gulf between boss and worker, the suburban family man was offered a new dignity based upon his status as defined by the style of his own home, car and repertoire of consumer goods.'[17] With social success being measured by the ability to consume, the Holden both promoted and symbolised Australia's post-war affluence.

Post-war demographic shifts and social trends contributed to the car's popularity. Australians were moving to the cities' outer fringes to realise their suburban dreams, and out there life demanded automobility. Suburban family life and rituals and a new economy of leisure came to revolve around the car. Not surprisingly, it would be a common motif in family snapshots.[18] With the dearth of alternative forms of entertainment, the Sunday drive offered a new form of escape that enabled Dad to spend quality time behind the wheel – and with the family. Holidays provided another opportunity for the family to jump into the car. Caravans facilitated even longer journeys while campers used their cars to venture further into the countryside.[19] For the less adventurous, newly built motels accommodated both family and car. Together with the incessant 'are we there yet?' from the back seat and the hot sticky leather (and later vinyl) seats in summer, such rituals placed the car at the centre of family life. And Holdens were the most popular cars in Australia throughout the 1950s, although they were closely challenged by Ford, whose larger cars appealed to increasingly affluent families. The division between Holden families and Ford families was almost tribal. Not everyone was moved by national symbolism.

The family's love affair with the Holden cooled in the 1960s. GM-H began to produce a variety of models to cater for a more segmented market. Three new models were produced in the 1950s; the 1960s saw nine. Catering for specific markets reduced the car's universal appeal and its iconic symbolism dissipated. Old Holdens frequently became 'the wife's car', providing women with a new degree of freedom. It was used to do the shopping, to run errands or to pick the kids up from school. Such mobility irrevocably altered shopping practices, causing the demise of home deliveries and increasing the popularity of 'one-stop shopping'.[20] The children who had grown up on the Holden's back seat also yearned to take their place behind the wheel, boys especially. As young adults, they hungered for the freedoms that the car promised. Borrowing the family Holden for a night out freed them from embarrassing dependence on public transport and facilitated social life, whether with a bunch of mates or a special friend at the drive-in. By this stage, the original FX and FJ models began to look old-fashioned.

The times are a-changing

The freedoms that the car and nation offered to young Australians were not absolute. Michael Thornhill's 1978 film, *FJ Holden*, pointed to significant shifts in the Holden's symbolism. Set in working-class Parramatta in Sydney's outer west, this was a road movie about being trapped – culturally, politically and economically. Although the Holden still represented the dreams and hopes of the post-war generation, they were shown to be things of the past, no longer relevant to their children. The FJ itself was already into its third decade when the film was released, the Liberals were back in power and life in the outer suburbs remained difficult for anyone without a car.

FJ Holden appeared as GM-H's market dominance was under challenge. Ford's new larger vehicles appealed to Holden's traditional family market and also affluent rev-heads. Japanese cars posed another threat (Hartnett wrought revenge on GM-H by bringing

Nissan to Australia). Anxiously looking to its parent company, GM-H increasingly used American designs and the claim to be Australian looked more spurious. Even American commercials were 'translated' for Australian audiences. The advertising campaign around 'football, meat pies, kangaroos and Holden cars', which attempted to reinforce the brand's Australianness, was a direct copy of GM's American jingle extolling 'baseball, hotdogs, apple pies and Chevrolet'.

The lifting of government tariffs in the 1980s exposed Australia's car industry to greater international competition. Local manufacturers such as GM-H were encouraged to increase output by producing fewer models. The Nissan Pulsar hatchback, for example, was rebadged as the Holden Astra. Reduced to a simple badge, Holden was losing its identity. Popular culture references also hinted that Holden's aura was fading. Taking its name from a more recent model of the Holden, the early 1980s television program *Kingswood Country* revolved around Ted Bullpit, whose bigotry, racism, and one true love in life – the Holden Kingswood – were pilloried as aspects of Australia's past.[21] Holden was becoming shorthand for the bland Australia in the 1950s. The vacuous protagonist in Murray Bail's 1987 novel *Holden's Performance* critiqued the mechanicalness and dull conformity of Australian society. Like his namesake, Holden Shadbolt is described as 'responsive to instructions in all weathers, all conditions. Predictable, matter-of-fact.'[22]

GM-H marketing sought to overcome these negative connotations while maintaining the key strengths of the Holden brand. Although Australianness remained important, advertisements attempted to give it a more sophisticated, cosmopolitan edge. Advertisements from the late 1980s alluded to the fact that Holden was competing on the international stage. 'Drive the world class Australian' declared a 1987 Commodore advertisement. Like Alan Bond and *Crocodile Dundee*, Australia's car was taking on the world. But the very success of the early campaigns identifying the original models as Australia's own, along with the nostalgia beginning to accumulate around them, meant that they, rather than later models, remained the focus of national symbolism. Nostalgic pride in the 'little Aussie battler' underpinned an advertisement for the flavoured milk brand, Big M. In it, a group of yuppies watch a weathered FC Holden pull up to a milk bar. 'How quaint, an Australian car', sneers Brad, a Porsche owner, before letting its tyres down. Discovering their flat tyre, the Holden's passengers cheerfully replace it together and drive off, one of them realising he has left his carton of Big M behind. The final shot shows an opened carton of flavoured milk about to fall through the Porsche's opening sunroof. Holden might be old, the advertisement implied, but it was still 'Australia's own' car – associated with real Australian values rather than shallow cosmopolitanism.[23]

From the 1990s onwards, the company's fortunes improved. Renamed Holden Limited, it regained much of the ground that it had lost and was also exporting more cars than ever before. While marketing continued to highlight its Australianness, this link became more tenuous with each new model. By the new century Holdens were indistinguishable from German Opels and South Korean Daewoos, and no more Australian than locally built Fords or Toyotas.

The Holden's absence from the opening of the Sydney Olympics in 2000 revealed its changing status. With cars being made from imported parts, the 'Australia's own' tagline sounded increasingly hollow. Growing competition in the Australian market coupled with the economic realities of operating in a global market meant that Holden's ongoing presence in Australia as a manufacturer was becoming dependent on government support. When Holden asked about the Commonwealth Government's financial support beyond 2016, Treasurer Joe Hockey offered nothing, bluntly declaring 'Either you're here, or you're not.'[24] Without the Commonwealth's support, Holden's bosses in Detroit opted for the latter. As the final Holden rolled out of the firm's Elizabeth production line in 2017, no politicians were in sight (Fig. 54). Media commentary focused on job losses and the end of Australia's automotive manufacturing sector.[25] This emphasis on practical concerns over the symbolic encapsulated Holden's significance to twenty-first century Australia – a nostalgic symbol of a bygone age.

ULU_RU_

Roslynn Haynes

From a distance it looks like some great prehistoric animal crouching, belly to the ground. Close up, it towers majestically above the surrounding plain, its crevices and indentations suggestive of mystery. Depending on the time of day and the weather conditions it can dramatically change colour, from deep purple to fiery, volcanic red to pale mauve, with waterfalls gushing silver down its sides. This kaleidoscopic light show is particularly vivid at sunrise and sunset when visitors line up in their thousands to take their souvenir photos as proof that they have witnessed the spectacle. The Rock seems, today, an inevitable symbol for the power and immensity of Australia's Red Heart, one that is embraced by both Indigenous and non-Indigenous Australians.

However, although known for over a century to non-Aboriginal Australians as Ayers Rock, Ulu_ru_[1] was, until the 1970s, of little or no interest to the vast majority of Australians. It achieved the status of a national symbol partly in response to the need for a distinct, visual image that would be as instantly recognisable on travel posters as the Pyramids, the Eiffel Tower, the Kremlin, or St Peter's (Fig. 56), one able to satisfy the need for tourists to photograph as evidence of their visit and one that implicitly suggested an inherent connection with ancient Aboriginal cultures. But the reasons for the elevation of Ulu_ru_/Ayers Rock to a symbol, perhaps the symbol, of Australia are complex and cross-cultural.

The Centre

By the mid-nineteenth century, locating the precise geographical centre of Australia and erecting a cairn with the British flag on it were obsessive national desires, indicating both imperial conquest and colonial optimism. Edward John Eyre and Charles Sturt tried and failed. When on 22 April 1860 John McDouall Stuart declared that he had reached the geographical centre of Australia (an assessment not shared by modern geographers), his sense of the gravitas of the situation and the need for appropriate theatre and symbolism required that due ceremony be performed on the nearest mountain top. His description of the elaborate ritual attending the event expressed both the imperial rhetoric and the paternalistic assumptions that were invoked to justify such expeditions:

> Built a large cone of stones, in the centre of which I placed a pole with the British flag nailed to it ... We then gave three hearty cheers for the flag, the emblem of civil and religious liberty, and may it be a sign to the natives that the dawn of liberty, civilization and Christianity is about to break upon them.[2]

Since then the geographical centre of the continent has ceased to generate much interest. 'The Centre' now signifies a vast area identified by a particular kind of landscape, epitomised by the red dunes of the Simpson Desert. Yet the nineteenth-century explorers of these regions seemed oblivious to the glowing colour that enchants modern tourists. Fixated on their search for green pastures they never mentioned the word 'red'.

The first to enthuse in print about the intense colours was the biologist HH Finlayson, whose book *The Red Centre* (1935) initiated a new symbolic focus. 'It might well be known as the Red Centre. Sand, soil, and most of the rocks are a fiery cinnabar.'[3] His words were made visible in the paintings of Hans Heysen, Albert Namatjira and

(Top left) Ayers Rock, Central Australia, 1873, by William Gosse. The first readily available image of Ayers Rock was a long way from modern conceptions of Uluṟu.

State Library of South Australia

(Top right) Uluṟu, Northern Territory, 2019.

Photograph by Martin Bass, courtesy of Bronwyn Hanna

later Russell Drysdale and Sidney Nolan, who showed Australians a brilliance and vividness that were not only visually stunning but which also challenged the whole tradition of European landscape art. The Red Centre now came to symbolise not imperial possession but, on the contrary, a nation intent on liberating itself from England and declaring its independent identity. Travellers, writers, photographers and artists discovered and portrayed a new kind of beauty in the desert's starkness and primary colours. By the 1980s ever-growing numbers of ordinary Australians and tourists, armed with colour film, were negotiating the dangers and monotony of the desert, transforming the nightmare journeys of the explorers into a safe, aesthetic and significantly a *limited* engagement with the sublime.[4]

The Red Centre has been embraced so warmly by popular culture that it has become the best-known Australian landscape, displacing even sheep and gum trees and the scenes depicted by the Australian Impressionists. Yet desert vastness is not immediately marketable in terms of the visual criteria that govern publicity. It requires a specific iconic object, an explicit and instantly recognisable image. In response to this need Uluru/Ayers Rock, sufficiently close to the centre of the continent, has become *the* symbol of Australia's heart.

Origins

This great inselberg, the largest monolith in the world, rises 348 metres above the surrounding plain. Its immense mass and sense of permanence belie its cataclysmic origins some 550 million years ago when the Australian landmass lay nearer to the equator. Layers of sediment, formed beneath the shallow, inland Eromanga Sea, were thrust up higher than the Canadian Rocky Mountains, to form towering, jagged fold mountains whose weathered remnants are the Musgrave, Mann and Petermann ranges to the south and west. The silt produced from this weathering process was carried north and east as an alluvial fan. Subsequently, these layers of sediment were submerged and compressed for millions of years to form arkose, a coarse-grained sandstone which was again exposed some 300 million years ago when these strata were forced up and tilted almost vertical (85°). This deviation from the horizontal is clearly visible in any aerial view of Uluru and from the ground in the deep crevices running down its sides.

The Anangu people, traditional owners of Uluru (and of the neighbouring geological structure, Kata Tjuta) have different accounts of the origin and structure of the Rock, arising from their *Tjukurpa*, a Pitjantjatjara term which, at one level refers to the creation period or Dreaming, when Ancestral beings, by their actions, brought the world as we know it into existence.[5] One creation account ascribes the clefts in the rock to a battle between Ancestral Serpents. Another describes how two tribes of Ancestors were invited to a feast but failed to arrive because they were diverted by the Sleepy Lizard Woman. Their aggrieved hosts made a mud figure of a dingo and sang it to life to punish their guests, but the Earth rose up in grief at the bloody battle, creating Uluru.[6]

The Mystique of the Rock

Despite the aura of dignity and mystery that Uluru has subsequently acquired, the early explorers were more impressed by its sheer size. Even though in 1872 Ernest Giles, the first European to see the Rock from a distance (he was prevented by Lake Amadeus from reaching it) called it with characteristic flippancy 'the remarkable pebble', he came to a different appreciation of it a year later when he finally reached the Rock, describing it in Romantic terms as 'ancient and sublime'. He felt moved to quote, with a minor variation, from Percy Shelley's poem 'Ozymandias': 'Round the decay of that colossal rock, boundless and bare, the lone and level sands stretch far away.'[7]

Western Australian surveyor William Christie Gosse, who reached the monolith on 19 July 1873, described it as a 'hill [that] presented a most peculiar appearance, the upper portion being covered with holes or caves ... what was my astonishment to find it was one immense rock rising abruptly from the plain ... I have named this Ayers Rock, after Sir Henry Ayers'. Having climbed to the summit with an Afghan camel driver Kamran, Gosse reflected: 'This rock is certainly the most wonderful natural feature I have ever seen. What a grand sight this must present in the wet season; waterfalls in every direction.'[8] Gosse's sketch of the rock may perhaps strike us as humorous, suggesting a ghost-like sphinx covered in a sheet with eye-holes; but it does indicate his impression of immense size and height and convey a sense of mystery. Photos taken today from this same aspect confirm Gosse's eye for perspective and detail. The disparity with the modern Western conventional image of Uluru indicates how readily we have been 'managed', as visitors, to see it from the angle prescribed by the tourist industry (Fig. 55).

Giles's term 'sublime' fell out of fashion but Ayers Rock continued to evoke a sense of wonder, even of numinous power. In 1935 the anthropologist Charles Mountford wrote in his diary, 'the lure of the great rock was upon me, calling me back to wander round its base, to look up at its mighty walls, to explore its numberless caves, and to hear the strange creation legends from its Aboriginal owners'.[9] In the same year, another anthropologist TGH ('Ted') Strehlow described his first sight of the Rock in similar terms:

> The Rock was reached at last, the goal of my boyhood dreams – the shadow of a great rock in a weary land, and how welcome it was. All hushed tonight, only the moon is shining down upon the great black walls of the rock – and one feels that the Land of God is indeed near. It is like the great silence of eternity.[10]

The Rock's mystique has not always been benign. Mountford and Strehlow had been sent there to investigate a police killing in one of its caves[11] and one of Australia's most notorious tabloid mysteries occurred here in 1980 when nine-week-old Azaria Chamberlain disappeared from the family's tent at a camping ground near Uluru. Her parents and others present asserted that a dingo had seized the baby. Her body was never found but two years later her mother, Lindy Chamberlain was convicted of murder and given a life sentence amid wild rumours in the media of devil worship and ritual sacrifice. In 1986 the chance finding of a piece of Azaria's jacket in an area with numerous dingo lairs led to Lindy Chamberlain's release and finally, after four more inquests, it was declared in 2012 that Azaria Chamberlain had indeed been taken and killed by a dingo. The sensationalism of the case gave rise to a book, a feature film and an opera, all of which drew on and promoted the mysterious ambience of Uluru.[12]

From Ayers Rock to Uluru

The political history of Uluru since Federation has been fraught with controversy. As long as it was regarded as commercially useless much of Central Australia was considered by Anglo–Australians an appropriate location for the Indigenous peoples. In 1920 the Petermann Reserve, which included the sites of Ayers Rock and Mount Olga, was established as a so-called 'refuge' or 'sanctuary' where 'the Aboriginal may ... continue his normal existence until the time is ripe for his further development'.[13] Many senior Anangu still recall being 'herded' into 'The Reserve'. For a decade the reserve was forgotten by the authorities but, with the growth of pastoral and mining interests, roads and infrastructure were pushed into this area and with them came the potential for a lucrative tourist industry. Renewed interest in the outback coincided with greater ease of travelling there and the Rock acquired iconic status as a symbol of the rugged and uncompromising environment that had supposedly forged the unique 'characters' of 'the outback'. Under pressure from business interests, Ayers Rock was declared a national park in 1950, though by 1956 there were still only a hundred visitors per year. Gradually tourism was established as the new, above-ground goldmine of the Centre, whereupon it was conveniently assumed that the Anangu had no legitimate claim on the site. In 1958, without any consultation with the traditional owners, both Ayers Rock and Mount Olga were excised from the reserve to form the Ayers Rock–Mount Olga National Park controlled by the Northern Territory Parks and Reserves Board, but available for use by tour companies.[14]

By the 1970s Ayers Rock and Mount Olga were the focal points of desert tourism but waves of unmonitored visitors camping indiscriminately in the area were clearly destroying the environment. The Northern Territory government decided to amalgamate accommodation facilities at a single new site and in 1984 Yulara, 18 kilometres from Uluru, was created as the infrastructure hub for all tourism to the national park. The Anangu, traditional owners, were not welcome in the area as their 'unsightly' camps spoiled tourists' photos of the pristine Rock.

The Anangu continually requested that sacred sites be protected from tourism and that respectful information about their culture be circulated to visitors, but they were ignored. Their successive land claims were unsuccessful, largely because of fears that they might close the Rock to tourism. The stalemate continued until the Australian Government announced in November 1983 that it would return the title for the national park, renamed in 1993 as the Uluru-Kata Tjuta National Park, to the traditional owners on condition that they would immediately lease the land back to the Australian Parks and Wildlife Service.

Originally Uluru was pivotal only to the Dreaming of Aboriginal peoples in its vicinity but the 'Handover' (as it was called) of Uluru became a symbolic high point for First Nations peoples across Australia in their tortuous journey towards land rights. On 26 October 1985, the Rock was the site of a staged ceremony when hundreds of Aboriginal and non-Aboriginal people watched Governor-General Sir Ninian Stephen pass the title deeds to the traditional owners in an elaborate ritual strangely reminiscent of Stuart's planting the British flag at the 'centre' of Australia as described on page 309. Five minutes later, a 99-year lease was signed with the Australian Parks and Wildlife Service which would jointly manage the park with the Anangu. Yet the Handover was not without controversy, eliciting such comments in parliament as 'Ayers Rock is part of Australia's heritage. It is part of our nationhood and it is a symbol to all Australians' and 'It is part of our psyche, because Australians feel deeply about it and love it'. The Anangu, on the other hand, claimed that not only had they 'owned' Uluru from the time of Dreaming but it continued to be essential to their spiritual traditions, their *Tjukurpa* and their culture. There are few more pointed examples of a contested national landscape where different ethnic groups claim emotional possession.[15]

Place as a symbol

As an Aboriginal place name 'Uluru' acknowledges the Indigenous history that has been integral to this place for thousands of years before

Europeans sighted it. As such it has become a focus for First Nations peoples across Australia. Bundjalung writer Ruby Langford Ginibi, who was born at Box Ridge Mission on the north coast of New South Wales in the mid-1930s, described her surprise at the unexpected emotional rapport she experienced on her first visit to Uluru:

> It was like a huge animal that was asleep in the middle of nowhere. We came closer and I could feel the goosebumps and the skin tightening at the back of my neck. Everyone else was quiet. It made me think of our tribal beginnings, and this to me was like the beginning of our time and culture. Time was suddenly shortened to include all of history in the present, and it was stretched to a way of seeing the earth that was thousands of years old.[16]

It has also come to represent for many non-Indigenous peoples not just a dramatic landform but an alluring place, resonating with spiritual power, and white Australians have attempted to engage with this sacred relationship with the land. Members of the Jindyworobak Club, founded in 1938, endeavoured to assimilate Aboriginal myths of the Dreaming into their poetry by investing visible landscapes with mystical and totemic presences and by importing Aboriginal words. In 'Uluru, An Apostrophe to Ayers Rock', Rex Ingamells celebrates his empowerment at 'Uluru of the eagles':

> Arrival is more than physical: it is
> the dreaming at the inner shrine,
> with sun and star, sun and star,
> moon after moon,
> message-stick and *tjurunga*,
> rock-hole and dune ...
> As I stepped out from one of your Caves of Paintings,
> I knew myself forever part of you

...
yesterday, today and ever after
eternal Dreaming in your heart, Uluru.[17]

The desire for a spiritual encounter centred on Uluru emerged in a more popular vein in the 1980s in conjunction with the growth of interest in Indigenous cultures and New Age cults that attempted to appropriate Uluru.[18] In 1985, the traditional owners received a request from a group of cosmic believers calling themselves Harmonic Convergence, intent on staging an international event on 16 August 1987, with a scenario not dissimilar to the revelations presented in Steven Spielberg's film *Close Encounters of the Third Kind* (1977):

> They would lay down their bodies in circular formation, heads towards a fire, feet outward, gazing skyward.
> They would surrender control to the Earth, allowing the forces of Life to use them as channels for the purification of the planet.[19]

A second cosmic gathering was planned for Easter, 1990. This request was refused but a 2020 Cosmic Consciousness Conference was held at Uluru as the flagship event of International Earth Chakra Day, from 11–13 January to coincide with a lunar eclipse and a rare Saturn–Pluto conjunction.[20]

Climbing Uluru

By the end of the twentieth century Uluru, then part of the tourist catalogue of 'must see' natural wonders, was being visited by more than 250,000 people annually[21] and approximately one-sixth of those undertook the physical challenge of climbing the steep track to the top. Whether as a personal fitness test or a declaration of conquest, the modern equivalent of colonial mastery of the continent, the climb became a central feature of the packaged tourist experience and tour operators were adamant that they would never support a total ban, despite continued Anangu requests not to climb the Rock. In Aboriginal culture, it was never a place to be climbed, least of all as a challenge or conquest, but a sacred place to be respected and cared for. In addition, the Anangu feel responsible for the safety of those visiting their Country. Many tourists suffered heat stress or heart attacks, either during the climb or soon afterwards, became lost and died from exposure, or fell to their death. There have been 37 confirmed deaths of people climbing the monolith and each year another 30 or so people needed to be rescued from the site. Many of those who climbed the Rock claim to have had a psychically disturbing experience and there are accounts of those who, having souvenired a stone from its surface, later felt an inner compulsion to return it to its original location.[22]

Alternatives to 'the climb', such as the *Mala* and *Mutitjulu* guided walks around the base of Uluru, dance performances and bush tucker trips with Aboriginal women into the surrounding desert were actively promoted by the Anangu as replacement experiences and became an increasingly important part of the tourist itinerary. There has also been a growing acceptance that some areas, such as particular waterholes and caves, may not be viewed or photographed by visitors because they are specifically men's or women's sacred sites. These prohibitions emphasise the spiritual significance of Uluru and respect for Aboriginal law and suggest that Indigenous symbolic meanings are displacing colonial attitudes. Finally, on 1 November 2017 the Uluru-Kata Tjuta National Park Board of Management, comprising eight traditional owners and four government officials, voted unanimously to close Uluru to climbers. The ban finally took effect on 26 October 2019, 34 years after the Handback to the traditional owners, and with relatively little protest, although just prior to the ban taking effect, there was a rush of visitors desperate to climb, some insisting on a 'right to climb'.[23]

Alternative tourist attractions had already been set in place. As well as opportunities to engage with Aboriginal culture, tourist operators have catered for more Western tastes with helicopter flights over Uluru at sunset and sunrise, Uluru camel tours, the Sounds of Silence dinner under the stars, astronomy lectures, and Bruce Munro's vast, spectacular installation, Field of Light Uluru, featuring 50,000 swaying spindles of light that change through a spectrum of desert colours – ochre, deep violet, blue and white.

Uluru has become a unique example of cultural convergence between Aboriginal and non-Indigenous Australians. This relationship was enacted with international exposure on 8 June 2000 when the Olympic torch was flown to Yulara to begin its 100-day journey around Australia. The first runners were Indigenous Olympic gold medallist Nova Peris-Kneebone and a group of traditional owners who carried it on the nine-kilometre circuit of Uluru. Explaining the choice of venue, Michael Knight, the NSW Minister for the Olympic Games, announced:

> Uluru is not only known worldwide but is also a place of immense historical and cultural significance. It is in the geographical heart of Australia, is of great spiritual significance to many Australians and is part of the outback character of Australians. The Sydney 2000 Olympic Torch Relay is a national event designed to showcase Australia's history, diverse culture and geography and there is no better way to highlight Australia's unique cultural history than to start at Uluru.[24]

Indigenous Australians saw an added significance for the future. In her Australia Day Address in 2000, Pitjantjatjara elder and Chair of the Aboriginal and Torres Strait Islander Commission Dr Lowitja O'Donoghue said she hoped the ceremony would 'celebrate cultural diversity, unity and reconciliation'.[25]

This hope was given physical form in the architecture of the

National Museum of Australia, Canberra, opened in 2001. Externally this postmodern structure is dominated by the Uluṟu line, which begins at the entrance canopy and loops upwards in a 30-metre high curve, symbolising Uluṟu, before becoming a wide, red footpath leading past the Australian Institute of Aboriginal and Torres Strait Islander Studies and continuing conceptually 2055 kilometres north-west to Uluṟu.

Uluru Statement from the Heart

In December 2015 a sixteen-member Referendum Council was appointed to advise the federal government about a referendum to recognise Aboriginal and Torres Strait Islander peoples in the Australian Constitution. After six months of travelling to 12 different locations around Australia and meeting with 1200 Indigenous representatives, they delivered the Uluru Statement from the Heart, acknowledging the symbolic potential of Uluṟu as a site of reconciliation. It was released on 26 May 2017 by 250 delegates to an Aboriginal and Torres Strait Islander Referendum Convention held near Uluṟu. Unlike previous Indigenous petitions to parliament, the Uluru Statement was directed to the Australian public and asked for a change in the constitution to allow Indigenous Australians a voice in the laws and policies that are made about them. It called for a 'Makarrata Commission' to supervise a process of agreement-making between governments and First Nations and truth-telling about our history'. See also Henry Reynolds' *Truth-Telling: History, sovereignty and the Uluru Statement*, published by NewSouth Publishing in 2021.[26]

The Statement was inscribed at the centre of an artwork, surrounded by the signatures of the 250 delegates and framed by depictions of two Aṉangu creation stories. One depicts the fight to the death at the Mutitjulu Rockhole between Kuniya the woma python from the north-east and Liru the poisonous snake from the south-west; the other tells of the Mala people, represented by the Rufous hare-

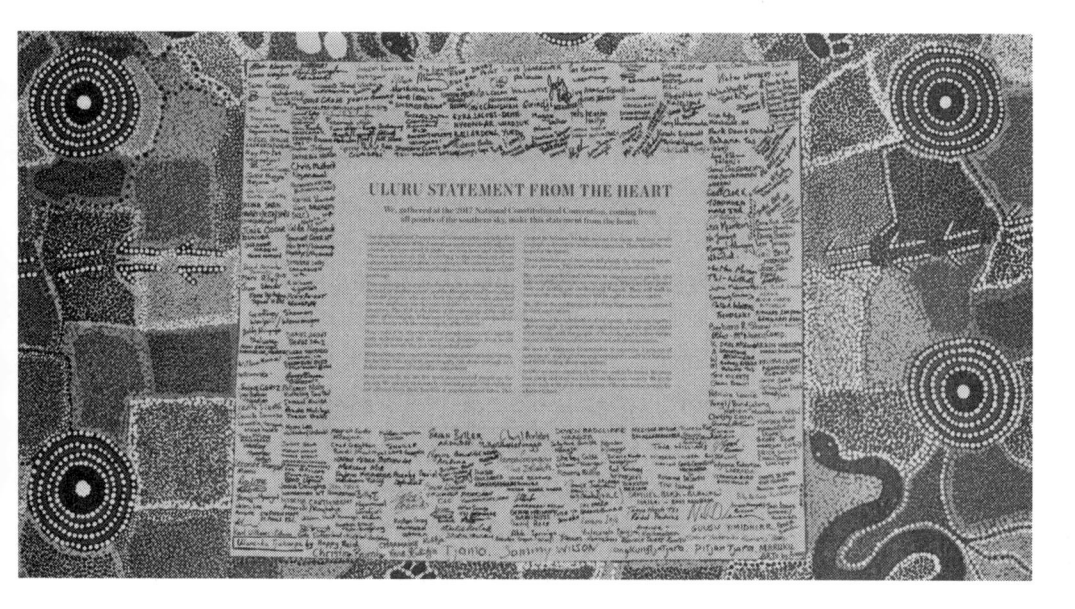

The Uluru Statement from the Heart.
Issued to the Australian people on 26 May 2017.

UluruStatement.org

wallaby, who entered into a dispute with men from the west. The men left and created Kurpany, the devil dingo, represented by dog prints.

The call for an Indigenous voice to parliament included in the Statement was endorsed by the UN Committee on the Elimination of Racial Discrimination, meeting in Chile in December 2017, but was summarily rejected by the then prime minister, Malcolm Turnbull and, at the time of writing, it has still not been accepted by the Australian Parliament. Australia remains the only Commonwealth nation without a treaty with its First Peoples.[27]

Despite this, non-Indigenous Australians need Uluru as a symbol because it aligns them with Aboriginal Australia, providing them internationally with a unique cultural identity and nationally with the hope of resolving longstanding guilt and social discord. It is their cathedral, their palace, their history, their antiquity, performing the ideological work of 'making things mean'.[28]

SYDNEY OPERA HOUSE

Richard White and Sylvia Lawson

Around the globe, the image of the Sydney Opera House is taken to represent both the city and Australia. The profile, rendered as a flowing scribble and seen in bunting all over the city, was the motif for the Sydney Olympics in 2000. Lonely Planet tells its readers that the building is 'Australia's most recognisable icon and essential site', while for the chair of the Sydney Opera House Trust it 'is core to our national cultural identity and ... the most globally recognised symbol of our country'. According to architect Frank Gehry, it 'changed the image of an entire country'; for the *New York Times*, reviewing Kristina Olsson's 2018 novel *Shell*, it was 'a reach for greatness'. In 2013 it joined the Taj Mahal and Tower Bridge in the Lego Creator Expert range. On the government's portal to Australian culture, it has shifted from being 'as representative of Australia as the Pyramids are of Egypt and the Colosseum of Rome' in 2010, to being 'synonymous with Sydney and Australia's independent cultural spirit'.[1] It's there on endless thousands of T-shirts, tea-towels, postcards, tourist promotions of every description; it is the place where visitors to the city want to go first, to be photographed on the great open stairway, or on the Broadwalk, with the building's high vaults soaring behind them. From there they can look across to that other symbol of city and nation, the Harbour Bridge. As Randy Randall of the touring noise-punk band No Age put it in 2009, 'It really does feel like you are hanging out in a postcard.'² It is famous for being famous, probably Australia's most photographed symbol, images multiplying around the world (Fig. 57). Only the kangaroo is as well known internationally as a symbol of Australia.

The Opera House, however, is represented not only by a vast array of visual images and commercial branding; it is always a story, to be written again and again, as perspectives change with time. While a symbol can mean different things to different people, those meanings are the products of a specific history. Its echoes reach all those who use and enjoy the building; from tourists visiting once in a lifetime, reading the guidebook version, to older Sydneysiders who lived through the controversy, many still maintaining the rage. The images multiply endlessly, but it is in the history, particularly in its controversial elements, that the complex symbolism of the building has been developed and contested over time.³

Sophistication and hope

The campaign for an opera house in Sydney was initiated by the conductor and composer Eugene Goossens, imported at great expense in 1947 to enrich Sydney's musical culture. Goossens wanted a brilliant musical centre on a brilliant site; a sympathetic Labor premier, JJ Cahill, duly committed Bennelong Point to the project. There the old tram-sheds, redundant when the city switched to bus transport, were demolished, and in 1955 the government launched an international competition for the design – to the chagrin of some local architects, who wanted the contest limited to Australian entrants. From the start, the project was meant to make a statement about Australia's progress; with all its material prosperity, the country was often accused of being a cultural desert. While the proposal was always for a multi-purpose venue, the emphasis on opera – one of the most expensive art forms to produce and also, conventionally, a kind of cultural apex – was central to its symbolism. It would signal that a new, more sophisticated Australia had arrived. Cahill recognised that 'the worldwide interest … would be a good advertisement for Australia'.[4] At the same time opera singing had a considerable following; apart from Don Bradman, the most famous Australian internationally was Dame Nellie Melba, even after her death in 1931. Popular eisteddfods and the Sydney and Melbourne Sun Aria competitions produced such new stars as Joan Sutherland and June Bronhill, winners of the Sydney competition in 1949 and 1950. Goossens, who had been enthralled by the evident wealth of singing talent in the country, did not live to see his dream realised: in the wake of scandal, he was driven from Australia in May 1956. Seven months later the Danish Jørn Utzon's radically modern scheme won the competition.

The boldness of his vision captured the popular imagination. Scandinavian design, with its clean flowing lines, was widely seen as the benchmark of post-war modernity. Utzon's opera house was indisputably avant-garde and there was just enough criticism to confirm its modernism, at a time when other Australian symbols, if they were not being given a modernist makeover, were looking old-fashioned and crude. The estimated cost of £3.5 million caused some censure, especially from rural interests: should governments be spending taxes on elite culture? But the fact that it would be paid for by gambling in the form of an Opera House Lottery helped convince the voters. High and popular culture were, for the moment, happily reconciled. In March 1959, Cahill and Utzon together laid a ceremonial foundation stone. The serious work of designing and contracting had barely begun, and there was no realistic estimate on costs; but had the audacious project not commenced then the building might not have happened at all. Cahill, whose determined support had been crucial, died only seven months later.

The podium, with the giant outdoor stairway, began rising. In 1960 the Opera House saw its first real musical occasion when the African–American actor, singer and civil rights activist, Paul Robeson, sang for the workers on the site, a legendary occasion crossing the old boundary lines between elite and popular, black and white. It also drew attention to a new aspect of post-war Australia: between 1959 and 1973 some 10,000 people, of 32 nationalities, worked on the site.[5] Bennelong Point, like the Snowy Mountains Hydro-Electric Scheme a decade earlier, was a place where Australians of many origins learned to live together. But, for all the diversity in its performers and audiences, the Opera House, unlike the Snowy, lost its identification with the multicultural workforce that built it.

Decades before completion, the Sydney Opera House's symbolism was effective because of its appeal to disparate groupings: an older, Anglo–Australian cultural elite, a recently arrived European population, a younger university-educated generation and sections of the working class who sought culture as a right. Though the 1950s have often been identified with an assimilationist white Australia besotted by its young English Queen, the building's emerging audiences would be multicultural, a new kind of constituency that could imagine Australia as a vibrant, cosmopolitan, intellectually sophisticated society. Even before the war Australian towns and cities had begun to benefit from the influx of Europeans, especially of Jewish families fleeing Hitler. Those immigrants set their marks on musical and theatrical life, on the worlds of bookshops and cafés and small art galleries; there was an urban intellectual life outside the universities; middle-class people began to enjoy wine, 'continental' cinema and a cautious modernism in the arts.[6]

The Sydney Opera House could stand as an aspirational symbol for this new Australia and its mix of Australian-born and new arrivals, young and old, the wealthy and the workers. But it also harked back to an older New South Wales Labor (and, further back, colonial liberal) tradition that gave the state a role in taking culture to the people. In 1915 an earlier Labor government had founded the first state-supported conservatorium of music in the Empire, along with a state orchestra. In a portent of things to come, those initiatives were later undermined by changes of government.[7]

Controversy

The great battle erupted in 1965. Once the costs began rising and the completion date was postponed, the press turned more critical. In an election year, the project became a political football. The Liberal-Country Party coalition, under Robin (later Sir Robert) Askin, depicted the Opera House as a symbol of Labor profligacy and mismanagement needing rescue by practical, down-to-earth business methods. Though the escalating costs were largely covered by the success of the lottery, for one strand of New South Wales politics – wedded to convention, economic development and small government, distrustful both of foreignness and intellectual life – culture was a costly extravagance, a waste of taxpayers' money. The battle lines were drawn.

The cost blowout had to do with the unrealistic original estimate, the time involved in the development of the design and the necessary problem-solving on the ground. Utzon's approach was based on precise geometric repetition and the industrial mass production of elements: the giant concrete ribs which form the main structure, the chevron-shaped lids which hold the tiles, the tiles themselves. Utzon, for all his own status as an artist–architect, decisively rejected expensive individual craftsmanship in favour of industrialised mass-production systems. He had said, 'I like to be very modern; I like to live on the edge of the possible.'[8] The marriage of geometry and modern technologies provided for great simplicity of manufacture and construction, and also, crucially, for economy as to costs; but that was something Utzon's political opponents refused to recognise.

Progress on the building also involved three-dimensional testing on plywood models, a necessary strategy given the difficult brief; Utzon had been asked to devise a major auditorium capable of variable acoustics, suitable for both symphonic music and opera. Working drawings were necessarily derived from, and dependent upon, such testing. From late 1964, Utzon sought funding from the government to build the essential prototypical models. He had the support of Norman

Ryan, the Labor minister for works, an unassuming former electrician who had become convinced of the soundness and practicality of Utzon's methods, unorthodox as they were in the time and place. Ryan, however, delayed approval of funding for the models until after the May 1965 state election; then, unexpectedly, Labor lost. The new minister for works, Davis Hughes, a country schoolteacher and one-time leader of the Country Party, drew on a long tradition of 'country-mindedness' which imagined the bush as moral and productive, the city indulgently extravagant.[9] It was an old and symbolic conflict: the Opera House was an unjustified city-centred luxury when the bush needed new roads, schools and hospitals.

Thus the new government's hostility had to do with politics, face-saving and money. But the symbolism went deeper. There was a clash in ways of thinking. Utzon wasn't a nine-to-five man; while he worked and planned incessantly, he was always ready to stop the work in the drafting office, take his team round the site in a boat, and think about the design of clouds. He carried with him an air of easy optimism and freedom, and his apparently casual working methods connected with an interesting moment of ideological tension. Those Labor governments that had commissioned the Opera House had also made moves to a shorter working week and longer annual holidays. By the mid-1960s some commentators were arguing that Australia, 'land of the long weekend', should work harder, pursue excellence more seriously.[10] In that context, Utzon, pursuing excellence casually, was a dangerous anomaly.

Work continued under an impossible combination of pressures. Hughes made the architect's regular payments conditional on productivity as he understood it but would not authorise the manufacture of those plywood prototypes, without which design could not proceed. By early 1966 there was no money left for the drafting office. Utzon, reaching a point of deep exasperation, wrote an ill-considered letter of ultimatum, hand-delivered late in the day on 28 February 1966. Hughes insisted on taking the letter as one of resignation, and called in the press immediately to announce that the architect had quit.

There were frantic attempts at damage control by the architect's supporters, and protesting cables from the major names in world architecture: Kahn, Candela, Gropius, Neutra, Saarinen, Arne Jacobsen, Tange and Markelius among them. To accommodate the storm of letters – most on the architect's side – the *Sydney Morning Herald* ran extra pages.[11] But the situation was irretrievable. Hughes went ahead with the installation of a panel of local architects, Hall, Todd and Littlemore (HTL), with Peter Hall in charge of design. They had in fact been lined up for months; in mid-1965 Hughes had held a meeting with some senior local architects to plan for exactly this eventuality. If the minister had been the principal agent of the crisis, its real authorship lay with the New South Wales Chapter of the Royal Australian Institute of Architects (RAIA).[12]

The protests would continue for another two years. Three days after Utzon's effective dismissal, a thousand people marched from Bennelong Point to Parliament House in support. Placards proclaimed 'WE NEED UTZON', and – showing historical sense – 'FIRST GRIFFIN NOW UTZON', harking back to 1920, when Walter Burley Griffin was forced to quit as designer of Canberra. It was the first notable public demonstration of the later 1960s in Sydney, pre-dating by several months the opening rallies of the anti–Vietnam War campaign, and radicalising some of the same people. At least one prominent architectural firm threatened its younger draftsmen with dismissal if they joined in. Professional respectability was at stake; so were major government contracts.

Utzon gave up, and left Australia with his family in late April; he and his wife would never return (though their children did). For two years, in Denmark, he continued work on the Opera House interiors, seriously believing he would be called back. Twice, with the support of several thousand supporters, he asked the state government to allow him to return and finish the building as he and his team had planned it. But the government was implacable. Although Utzon had been widely accused of tardiness, extravagance and, always, 'impracticality', HTL were allowed all the time and money they wanted for research, overseas travel and consultation.

Controversy turned into print. Three books appeared in the next two years. Michael Baume, later a Liberal Party politician, wrote a solid, conservative account which tended to favour the government's position, and included an epilogue by Peter Hall.[13] John Yeomans pitted Utzon, 'a very tall, slim, smiling, suntanned Dane ... a model of casual elegance', against Hall, whom he compared to 'an upper-crust young Italian landowner on his way to a town council meeting'.[14] The third and most important publication was little more than a pamphlet, which, in starkly simple language, explained the architect's approach, and defended him against the charges of impracticality and inattention to function and costs. It was written by the town-planner and academic Elias Duek-Cohen, assisted by Bill Wheatland, Utzon's Australian associate, and Donald Horne.[15] Australia's greatest architectural critic, Robin Boyd, wrote a fierce modernist lament for America's *Life* magazine, 'Now it can never be architecture'. Peter Hall's solutions might well:

> be more rational, more predictable, and probably much more in line with the consensus in world architecture at this time. The interiors he creates may even be to some visitors more attractive than those which Utzon might have done. Yet they may be as remote from the giant white sails above them as a Viking helmet from khaki overalls.[16]

Under the new regime the cost continued to increase: the eventual $112 million was double the estimate at the time Utzon left.[17] HTL solved Utzon's major problem, the dual-purpose auditorium, by simply abandoning it. With the government's consent, the new architects secured a change of brief, committing the major hall to the uses of symphony orchestras alone. That was the final nail in the coffin of Utzon's plans for the interiors, which were intended to work as great sound-chambers, with the forms of the plywood ceilings staggered for variable reverberation times. For opera, stage machinery would have made up for the absence of wing space, with the stage tower and machinery rising into the vault of the great central sail, thus making full functional sense of that remarkable element. The machinery, purpose-built in Vienna, was installed, torn out, and largely jettisoned. Utzon's glass walls, filling in the arches at each end, would have appeared to fall like curtains from the vaults; the ones HTL built were rigidly angled and jutting, in complete conflict with the major curves of the vaults. In the name of efficiency, some nine years' collaboration with the best acousticians and theatre designers of Europe, with extraordinary work and invention on the cutting edges of architectural, engineering and acoustic technologies, went to waste.

Ironically, both the cost and the controversy contributed substantially to the building's prominence as a national symbol. The controversy attracted international attention, and gave the building a rich and complex back-story that still stirred passionate argument in the twenty-first century. The battle itself became part of the symbolic effect; great cultural advances within modernism have always, from *The Rite of Spring* onwards, required temporary symbolic defeats by the Philistines. Cost played an important part too. Since the building was meant to symbolise Australians' commitment to high culture, the final spectacular price tag provided, to the more materialistically minded, a clear index to how cultured they were. This was the era of record prices for art: two months before the Sydney Opera House opened, Whitlam's federal government paid $1.3 million for Jackson Pollock's *Blue Poles*, provoking a similar backlash but now likewise recognised as a bargain.[18]

The world's most famous building

For the opening on 20 October 1973, the symbolism was carefully contrived by the Askin government. At that moment those who had

Dame Edna weaing her Opera House hat
at Ascot Races Ladies Day, 1976.

*Photograph by John Timbers, Australian Performing
Arts Collection, Arts Centre Melbourne*

condemned the Opera House as elitist extravagance embraced it as a popular symbol. Though Australia was moving away from the traditional relationship with Britain, the highest compliment was still to have the building opened by Queen Elizabeth II. A descendant of Bennelong, Ben Blakeney, stood at the apex of one of the shells, silhouetted against the sky. Utzon's name was not mentioned.

Once the building was a functioning reality and an established part of Sydney life, it was possible for both sides of the controversy to claim it. One side told themselves tales of how the architect wasn't really *practical*; he managed to get the famous shells into the air but then had to be replaced by sensible, realistic Australians. The other side saw the building as a ruptured object, a beautiful unfulfilled promise that flouted modernism's fundamental tenet, the harmonisation of form and function. For them it was, as a symbol of the country, only too valid: adventure on the outside, timidity within. But all agreed it was Utzon's extraordinary exterior that gave the building its symbolic power.

With genuinely international recognition – not just, as with the Harbour Bridge, recognition within the British Empire – the cost no longer mattered. Sydney's emergence as an international city depended, more than anything, on the Opera House having become one of the world's most recognisable buildings. In Iris Murdoch's 1978 novel, *The Sea, the Sea*, a postcard of the Opera House became a symbol of innocence and new possibilities, the message: 'Just arrived, I think Sydney is the most beautiful city I have ever seen, we are so happy.'[19] Even Paris acquired an Hôtel Sydney Opéra. Also in Paris, in 1998, Françoise Fromonot's *Jørn Utzon et l'Opéra de Sydney* was published by Gallimard, the definitive work, later translated into English and Italian. In 2003, Utzon was awarded the Pritzker prize, architecture's Nobel. According to the official announcement, his masterpiece had 'arguably become the most famous building in the world'.[20] Australians were flattered by the international attention, perhaps becoming even a little extravagant. The Australian architectural critic, Philip Drew, wrote that:

> Few sites make you feel you are standing at the centre of the world at the beginning of creation ... here architecture, theatre, ritual and symbol unexpectedly unite to make sacred music between sky and earth.[21]

Those who condemned the cost now embraced the building as Sydney's most valuable symbolic asset. It would become a focus for celebrations that encapsulated national meaning: for the Bicentenary in

1988, Corroboree 2000, the Olympics in 2000, APEC in 2007, World Youth Day in 2008, Oprah Winfrey's Ultimate Australian Adventure in 2010. When Kerry Packer, Australia's wealthiest and most powerful man, was offered a state funeral by John Howard's coalition government in 2006, the Opera House was the venue, as it was for Bob Hawke's state memorial service in 2019. Yet it never lost its democratic feel. Schoolchildren have outnumbered divas on the Opera House stages. Celebrations of popular culture, from *Australian Idol* to the National Poetry Slam, culminate at the Opera House. In 2016 the building was destroyed in *X Men: Apocalypse*. As a symbolic site, it attracted symbolic acts. None was more effective than Will Saunders and Dave Burgess's protest against the looming war in Iraq in 2003: they managed to climb the major sail in the early morning of 18 March, and painted the words 'NO WAR' in scarlet capitals 1.5 metres deep (Fig. 59).

The sense of popular identification with the building was demonstrated in 2018. Vituperative broadcaster Alan Jones, who has substantial horse-racing interests, called for the sacking of Louise Herron, the Opera House's chief executive, when she rejected Racing NSW's proposal to screen a promotion for The Everest horse race on the sails. Politicians on both sides in thrall to his political influence supported Jones, the premier over-ruling Herron just hours after Jones's attack. But the public was not amused: not only revering the building but feeling they owned it. Within days petitions attracted over 283,000 signatures and an opinion poll found 81 per cent of people opposed the proposal. While the promotion went ahead, spontaneously organised protests sabotaged the moment with noisy objections, torches and high-powered spotlights (Fig. 58).[22]

In 2007 the Sydney Opera House was given World Heritage listing, the expert report calling it 'one of the indisputable masterpieces of human creativity, not only in the 20th century but in the history of humankind'.[23] That year, Utzon was commissioned, with his son Jan, to redesign the interior, bringing a kind of resolution not only of the controversy but also of the building itself. Before his death in November

2008, visitors found him at peace with the past. In 2017 an episode of the ABC's *Australian Story* staged a reconciliation between the sons of Utzon and Peter Hall.[24] The Opera House's role as a national symbol will continue; but as it gradually, imperceptibly, turns into a historic monument, will it remain as meaningful as it once was, when it stood for a radical, modernist future?

AKUBRA

Philippa Macaskill and Margaret Maynard

The Akubra broad-brimmed rabbit fur hat has assumed the role of one of Australia's best-loved symbols of nation. Worn as a practical accessory on the land, a stylish item for celebrities, a gesture to constituents by politicians, and a part of popular leisure and tourist garb, the Akubra had become a virtual ambassador for 'Australianness'. In 2007, Prime Minister John Howard placed it alongside the Sydney Opera House, Uluru and Vegemite as a national icon: it 'captures Australia like no other item of clothing'.[1] Over time it had accrued a multiplicity of symbolic and national meanings from mateship and egalitarianism to outback business acumen and political activism. Yet like all national symbols, its meaning is not fixed and while its longevity showed an adaptability to change, the Akubra is perhaps no longer the symbol it once was.

Such hats are certainly not unique to Australia, but the Akubra came to be regarded as a form of quasi-national dress. Although Australia has no official national costume, the Akubra's popular endorsement, grassroots appeal and tourist usage suggests it fulfilled that role.[2] From being worn by energetic rough-riders who burst into Stadium Australia in the opening ceremony of the 2000 Olympics to being offered as a gift to Prince Harry and Meghan Markle on their marriage in 2018, the Akubra has acquired the status of Australia's own special hat.

Its national symbolism derives from the way the Akubra company capitalised on rural mythology (Fig. 60). Akubra promotes itself as synonymous with outback Australia and its popular product names have included 'Cattleman', 'Snowy River', 'Down Under' and 'Stockman'. This marketing strategy resonated with a particular view of Australian national identity, an inherently masculine one. For despite living in one of the most urbanised countries in the world, Australians have traditionally turned to bush landscapes, rather than the city, to find their national symbols.[3] But what kind of nostalgia for rural life is at work in the symbolism of this hat, now also worn by women? How has this been melded with celebrity use and clever marketing? And how have these symbolic meanings withstood or altered with shifts of time, demography and culture?

To understand some of the meanings associated with this hat we need to know a little of the company's history. The Akubra can be traced to British migrant hatter Benjamin Dunkerley, who invented a trimming machine to cut the hair tip off rabbit fur for hat-making. In Sydney in the late 1880s he set up a small hat factory, originally known as Dunkerley Hat Mills Ltd, and in 1904 was joined by young Englishman Stephen Keir who became Dunkerley's business partner, general manager and son-in-law. Apparently the trade name Akubra was registered in 1912, but there is no proof that it was used before the early 1920s.[4]

In 1921 commercial artist Isaac (James) Northfield of Armadale registered for artistic copyright a drawing of a hat with an Akubra trade symbol.[5] By 1925, all the company's hats began to be known by the name.[6] There are apocryphal claims that 'Akubra' derives from an Aboriginal word for head covering. 'Gabarra' is the Dharuk (Sydney region) word for head, and variants of this word, including 'cobbra', 'gabara', 'kubbura' and 'kubera', are recorded.[7] Regardless, the choice of name distinguished the brand from other major hat retailers of the time, such as John Bardsley & Sons, and possibly gave it a distinctly national sales edge.

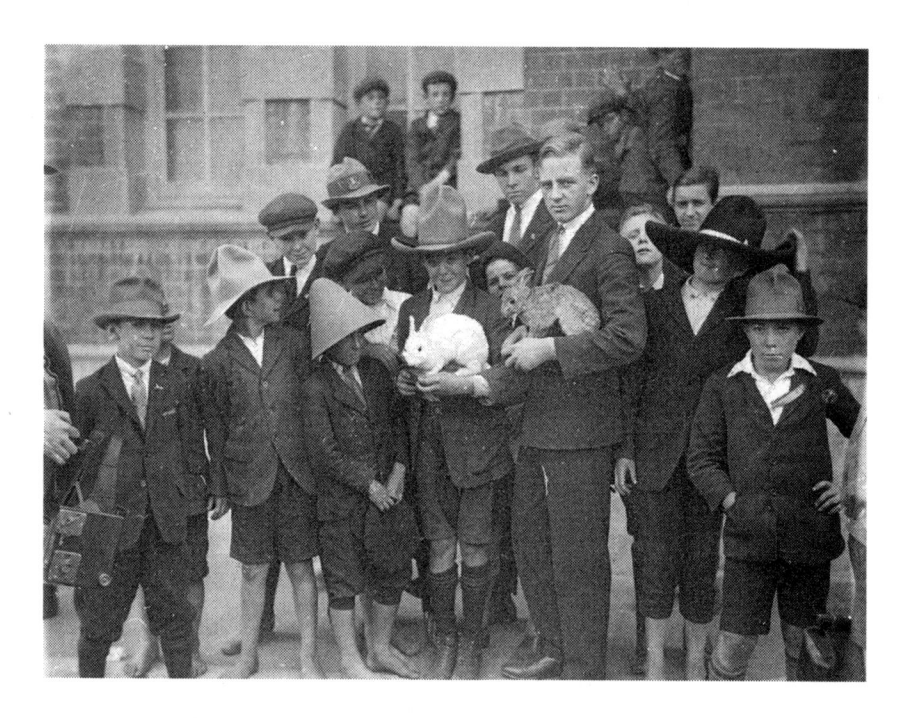

Boys from Fort Street school are initiated into the mysteries of hat-making by Akubra at the Australian Manufacturers' Exhibition, Moore Park, Sydney, 1927.

Photograph by Sam Hood, State Library of New South Wales

But a successful symbol is more than a name. The stories that accrue around a brand also determine its success, and Akubra has used its stories well. By promoting an ethos of loyalty, fair dealing, generosity, egalitarianism and integrity, the company acquired a level of respect that paid off in positive associations for the brand. When other firms were laying off staff during the Depression, Akubra's general manager Stephen Keir Senior proposed all employees should take a 10 per cent wage cut until the economy improved, enabling them to retain their jobs. The Akubra's ethos, as much as the product, contributed to its acceptability as an Australian symbol.

The bush hat

The origins of the broad-brimmed felt hat in Australia can be traced back to hats worn by early male settlers who worked the land. In rural and goldfields areas during the 1840s and 1850s European working-class dress was adapted to harsh Australian conditions. It included riding boots, bowyangs, moleskin trousers, shirts or singlets and broad-brimmed felt or palm leaf hats of various shapes and widths. Increasingly from the 1850s this durable and practical working clothing became invested with connotations of the supposed adaptability, communality and mateship of its wearers.[8]

Issues of dress were bound up with debates over Australia's national identity, which unfolded in the 1890s when urban radicals politicised egalitarianism, mateship and the figure of the working-class man. The male bush worker (not property owner), kitted out in rural dress, was nostalgically portrayed by nationalist writers and artists. Pastoral scenes by artists of the Heidelberg School included images of heroic bush workers in broad-brimmed hats. This nostalgic representation extended to literature. Steele Rudd's popular book *On Our Selection*, first published in 1899, illustrated less heroic protagonists, Dad and Dave, as quintessential Australian men of the land wearing various types of brimmed hat. Occasionally the bushman's companion, the fearless 'Australian girl', also wore a bush hat, but it was the bushman and his dress that were enshrined in national mythmaking.

This legendary rural worker took shape in the context of urban anxieties, and was the product of a romantic city-dweller's image of the bush.[9] While hat-wearing became increasingly popular for men in the cities, the rural imagery of the Akubra became less representative. It nevertheless acquired the power of nostalgia, reinforced by, from time to time, country and western music, radical historians in the 1950s and the tourism industry. Tapping into this legend, advertising for the Akubra identified it, along with a host of other products, with what were taken to be traditional male Australian characteristics such as independence, egalitarianism and doggedness.

Military headwear

A 'slouch' hat describes one with a soft floppy brim, but in Australia, colloquially, it has come to refer to a hat with its side turned up, most notably in the khaki version adopted by the army. First worn by the newly formed Victorian Mounted Rifles in 1885, it was modelled on hats worn by native police in Burma.[10] In 1889, visiting British General James Bevan Edwards urged use of what he called this 'distinctive national dress'.[11] It made its overseas debut during the Boer War and became part of Australian military uniform after the Defence Act of 1903. During World War I, when Dunkerley Hat Mills was one of the companies contracted to produce slouch hats for the Australian armed forces, symbolic national meaning became attached to the hat and, by extension, the company. Though no World War I slouch hats seem to bear the brand name Akubra, many World War II slouch hats do, along with that of the firm, Dunkerley. The company was still called by this name until the early 1970s when it was physically relocated and the owners renamed it Akubra.

After 1917 the 'digger' became a national hero who, like the bushman, embodied qualities of mateship, egalitarianism and endurance in the face of adversity. Australia's wartime prime minister, Billy Hughes, gave the slouch hat political meaning by wearing one when he visited troops in England and France. Revelling in the sobriquet 'the little Digger', he wore his hat each Anzac Day in Martin Place after 1918. So potent was this image that, after his death in 1952, Hughes's slouch hat was placed on his chair at the Anzac Day commemorations.[12]

By World War II, Dunkerley was one of two companies that continued to produce the slouch. As the company had actively promoted the values embodied in the symbol of the slouch in its own practices – namely, fairness, generosity and integrity – a measure of the hat's symbolism attached to the company itself.[13] The populist appeal of the slouch was strengthened by George Wallace's song, 'A brown slouch hat', broadcast on Australian wartime radio. Soldiers themselves were caught up in this symbolism. Tip Kelaher, of the 9th Division AIF, wrote a patriotically sentimental poem about his hat:

> It exudes the smell of gum leaves
> From crown to sweaty band,
> And often makes me homesick
> In this Palestinian sand;
> But it stands for Right and Manhood –
> And who'd want more than that?
> That's why one day in '40
> I took the digger hat.[14]

Almost 60 years later, Chief of the Defence Forces, General Peter Cosgrove (later Governor-General), maintained that the slouch hat was a legacy of all Australians, symbolising the best elements of the Australian character, including courage, sacrifice and devotion to mates and family.[15]

Marketing the brand

The 1950s and 1960s saw the gradual demise of hat-wearing in the city. But for rural men engaged in harsh, hot pursuits like droving, fencing and mustering, a brimmed hat remained a necessity. The company recognised early on the importance of this market, emphasising Akubra's durability and quality in their advertising. After the company was taken over by Mainline in 1972, Stephen Keir's two sons, Stephen and Herbert, bought back the plant for $500,000 and the trade name

A stockman tries on hats in a general store, Alice Springs, Northern Territory, 1954. Hats had status for all countrymen, Indigenous and non-Indigenous.

Photograph by Neil Murray, National Archives of Australia

Akubra for $1. In 1974 they relocated the factory to the rural New South Wales town of Kempsey. This was to prove a significant move.

Having positioned itself as a rural company, Akubra was well placed when nationalist bush mythology regained currency during the 1980s in the lead-up to Australia's bicentenary celebrations. There were calls to celebrate what was considered the nation's character and revisit symbols of national identity. At the 1984 Olympics in Los Angeles all Australian athletes were outfitted in the Akubra 'Aussie Gold' and at the Brisbane Commonwealth Games in 1986 parading athletes wore the Akubra 'Snowy River'. In 1988, two books on the Akubra were published proclaiming it a national icon and positioning it as essential to *the* Australian national dress.[16] This remained an abiding view into the twenty-first century.

Building on historic links between Australianness and the bush, and benefiting from the boom in Australian tourism and overseas marketing, the Akubra company extended internationally, with agents all over the world. In an interesting global slippage, Akubra was licensed to make and sell American Stetsons and vice versa, somewhat diluting its national symbolism. The brand's global appeal has been achieved through canny use of web and print advertising, celebrity sponsorship, cross-marketing and public relations. Along with other successful Australian clothing brands such as R.M. Williams and Driza-Bone, Akubra emphasised the various 'qualities' of its products. Their durability and practicality not only made them suitable for rough outdoor life, but identified them with traditional, practical values, rather than a passing fashion.

Akubra's most important advertising strategy from the 1980s was to either encourage endorsements by sportsmen, musicians and media celebrities or to be simply carried along by well-known personalities wearing their hats. Akubras featured prominently in the costuming of successful and nationalistically inclined movies from *The Man from Snowy River* (1982) and *Phar Lap* (1983) to *Kokoda* (2006) and Baz Luhrmann's *Australia* (2008), which used around 250 specially made Akubras.[17] But perhaps the best-known unpaid brand ambassador was Paul Hogan as Mick Dundee in the immensely popular film *Crocodile Dundee* (1986). Dundee was recognisable by his black Akubra (the 'Down Under') sporting an uncharacteristically aggressive looking crocodile hatband (crocodile skin hatbands were subsequently sold by Driza-Bone).

The film was America's highest grossing foreign film ever at the time of its release.[18] Mick Dundee transported a version of the Australian type, and his hat, to the United States, a character Hogan himself also personified. He featured in an Australian Tourism Commission television campaign, memorable for the famous line, 'Throw another shrimp on the barbie', and timed to directly precede the film's US release. Presenting Australians as a friendly, laid-back people, Hogan was described as 'one of the purest living examples of Russel Ward's "national type"', who offered his time free as an apparently patriotic gesture to develop local industry.[19]

When choosing formal, paid ambassadors for their product, Akubra sought to ensure that they aligned with the company's declared values of honesty, fairness, generosity and integrity.[20] The first formal ambassador was Greg Norman who, after admiring a friend's Akubra at the Australian Grand Prix in 1986, was signed up on a five-year agreement with the company. Norman's endorsement was crucial in promoting the brand as a national icon, particularly in the United States, where the Australianness of both hat and golfer were mutually reinforcing. Company secretary (now chief finacial officer) Roy Wilkinson attested to Norman's influence: when he wore a new hat at a tournament hundreds of orders for the same style would turn up on the fax machine the next morning. Using Norman, the company was able to extend association with the Australian bush myth to include links with Australian sporting prowess. Other paid sporting ambassadors included Australian surfer Pam Burridge, world motorcycle champion Wayne Gardner and racing driver Allan Grice.

Australia's well-loved country singer, Slim Dusty, was also an Akubra wearer. His hat, with front rim turned down over the right eye, epitomised the singer's public persona for his fans. He once quipped, 'If I don't want to be recognised in the street, I can guarantee it by leaving the hat at home, and wearing sunglasses.'[21] Endorsed by Slim, the Akubra reinforced its association with the rural community. When Sara Henderson appeared in an Akubra on the cover of her bestselling autobiography *From Strength to Strength* in 1993, telling of her business success in reviving the fortunes of Bullo River Station, the hat's meaningfulness as a masculine symbol was readily interwoven with the strength, resolution and doggedness of rural women.

From 1996 the brand sponsored Australian country singer Lee Kernaghan, who was, according to Wilkinson, 'a good fit – a loyal Australian and out there in our core market' but also a 'really down to earth honest guy'. Advertising campaigns presented Kernaghan as the 'real Australian' and the Akubra as the 'real hat', a claim to genuineness and authenticity that both company and celebrity found mutually beneficial.

Political hats

The Akubra's associations with practical bush values have been used by politicians, particularly when visiting rural electorates, where the hat seemed to act as a sort of 'bush passport'. They appear to believe that it allows them to connect better to their rural constituents but have had differing levels of success. Akubras are de rigueur in the National Party and among rural politicians but when others attempt to identify with rural values by donning one, it can backfire.

The most warmly applauded Akubra wearer was Tim Fischer, a country boy from Boree Creek, near Wagga Wagga, New South Wales. On becoming leader of the National Party in 1990, his Akubra became a self-conscious attempt to make himself recognisable to the Australian public, to foreign dignitaries and on overseas trade missions. As he explained in an interview in 2005, 'I thought it would give the cartoonists something to hang their hat on and give me an image … and a bit of notoriety. And it's worked right through to the King of Spain taking one of my Akubra hats.'[22]

The company never directly supplied Fischer with a hat during his political career though they recognised 'he certainly [did] an excellent job for us'.[23] In recognition, they assured Fischer a lifelong supply of hats following his retirement in 1999. He was still wearing his 'trademark Akubra hat' in 2008 when he met the Pope and it remained a feature of his term as Australian ambassador to the Vatican and Holy See.[24] Laudatory media reports on his death in 2019 called him 'The Man with the Hat' and his Akubra adorned his coffin at his state funeral. (Fig. 61)

During his term as Australian prime minister, John Howard was less successful when wearing an Akubra. Perhaps because his preferred style was the Pastoralist – earmarked for 'women's casual wear' – or perhaps because he appeared ill-at-ease wearing it, the Australian public's responses were not positive. It could easily be seen as a false identity, satirised in the musical *Keating!* as just one of the outfits Howard donned to prove his capacity to represent Australian values. Howard's sense of Australian mateship and national identity did not match with that of some of his predecessors and his discomfort may also have had a philosophical undertow.[25] But perhaps most importantly, he lacked bush roots. Journalist Mike Carlton succinctly summed up a common reaction:

> Akubras should be left to the National Party where they belong. Dear old Tim Fischer could wear his to the White House with aplomb, and your younger Nats like John Anderson are taught how to don them in primary school at King's; for them, they work to the manner born. For John Howard, Wollstonecraft Man, they do not. [Howard's] hat is a thing that a Shore parent might wear to a school cricket match at Northbridge, but that is all. The bush will not be fooled.[26]

The bush may not be fooled, but Howard donned the Akubra as much for urban constituents as rural ones. Urban-dwellers, too, subscribe to the notion that the bush myth reflects a more down-to-earth national identity.

This type of 'Akubra transplant' has led to cynicism about the symbol and some struggle over the right to wear it. Bill Roberts, mayor of the small town of Murgon in Queensland, told journalists in 2000: 'I get the impression that once these people put an Akubra hat on they reckon … that makes them a bushie.'[27] Those rural–urban (and conservative–liberal) tensions boiled over during Malcolm Turnbull's prime ministership, and the Akubra suffered a crisis of authenticity whenever Turnbull put one on. Significantly, Scott Morrison on replacing Turnbull as prime minister, insisted 'I don't have an Akubra, mate' in a photo op discussing the drought.[28] His preference for a baseball cap is a self-conscious rejection of the Akubra, now seen as potentially *in*authentic, though he continues the tradition of handing out Akubras on overseas trips, for example to Mike Pompeo in 2019.

But more than this, the Akubra's symbolic value is based on a fundamental irony in Australian nationalism: that is, that the enduring 'bush myth' is largely unfounded. The Akubra, like the Driza-Bone or R.M. Williams products, is symbolic of a rural myth that has very little relation to the actual experiences of most Australians.

The Akubra remains a practical garment for workers on the Australian land but the company has recognised the limitations of the rural myth and has successfully marketed the brand as an expensive lifestyle accessory for urban Australians and a favourite souvenir for tourists wanting to take home a reminder of Australia. Increasingly, Akubra has targeted women. Queensland's first woman premier, Anna Bligh, has been a regular Akubra wearer. Many Indigenous Australians adopted the Akubra: prominent Yawuru activists Mick and Patrick Dodson have made their black Akubras a political symbol, the latter wearing his during his swearing in as a federal senator in 2016.

The symbolic meanings and uses of the Akubra continue to be shaped to comply with the shifting needs and desires of both male and female consumers, and its Australianness can be sold in Australia and abroad. Akubra's ability to respond to these changes ensured that the brand remained identified with the nation, but increasingly self-consciously. Thus the Akubra has become part of a quasi-Australian national dress, even if it has been heavily diluted with American values under the umbrella of global marketing. The benefits to the company are commercial, but it provides a wider public with a ready-made and recognisable badge of Australianness.

RAINBOW SERPENT

Shino Konishi

Prior to colonisation there were approximately 250 different Aboriginal language groups, encompassing some 500 clans, throughout Australia. Each possessed numerous Dreaming stories, depicting how the land was traversed and marked by the Ancestral Beings, who created landforms, people, animals, plants and celestial stars. Their experiences, and often the consequences of their actions, formed the basis for Aboriginal kinship systems, laws, ways of caring for Country and connecting to land. These ancestors are not relegated to the past, for their presence is still felt at sacred sites, and they are still responsible for providing the resources that sustain the clan. Some Aboriginal people maintain their connection to these powerful beings by continuing to perform the songs and dances they gave them, and marking their bodies and objects with their sacred designs. Thus Aboriginal cultures are necessarily rich with symbolism.[1] Towards the end of the twentieth century Aboriginal culture was increasingly being called upon to provide a symbol of nation – representing Australia as a whole – by groups of non-Indigenous Australians who believed it offered a depth and richness of symbolic meaning that more conventional symbols had lost (or perhaps had never had).

The best known Ancestral Being is the Rainbow Serpent, or Rainbow Snake, the English names for the figure that appears in the

Dreamings of many different Aboriginal language groups across the continent. It features as an important creator figure, guardian of sacred places, bringer of monsoonal rains and storms, bestower of magical powers upon healers and rainmakers, or a dangerous creature that punishes people who violate laws, or dwells in waterholes threatening to swallow unwary passers-by, to name just a few incarnations. It is also strongly connected with fertility, both human and ecological. In all of its guises and geographies the Rainbow Serpent is associated with water, an essential resource, and the rainbow, whose shimmering light and curved form reflects the scales and body of the snake. The rainbow is also an important bridge between the water and the sky, the sky yet another resting place for the Rainbow Serpent.[2]

Just one of the many Rainbow Serpents who travelled the land is Yingarna, whose story is told by Kunwinjku-speaking people from western Arnhem Land. In one of many stories she was said to be the first Rainbow Serpent, and in the beginning swallowed all of the people, animals, landforms and so on, and held them in her body. When a hole was cut in her side by three hunters wanting to release their friend, all of creation burst from her body. The three hunters were then transformed into birds: a kookaburra, a willy wagtail and a peewee. This story is shared by all of the different clans in the Kunwinjku language group, who maintain that they are all the 'children of Yingarna', so must come together to perform various ceremonies, such as the Kunabibi, or initiation of children. Thus Yingarna represents widespread unity.[3]

The Kunwinjku also possess Dreaming stories about Yingarna's child, Ngalyod, who is associated with the 'potentially destructive power of the storms and the plenty of the wet seasons' (Fig. 64).[4] She also has the power to transform others, swallowing people and animals and regurgitating them in the form of something else, landforms for instance. The Kunabibi ceremony sees the young initiates swallowed by Ngalyod and then reborn as men. The immense power that Yingarna and Ngalyod have is both creative and destructive: these Rainbow Serpents are not simply benevolent symbols of unity, but can also be threatening,

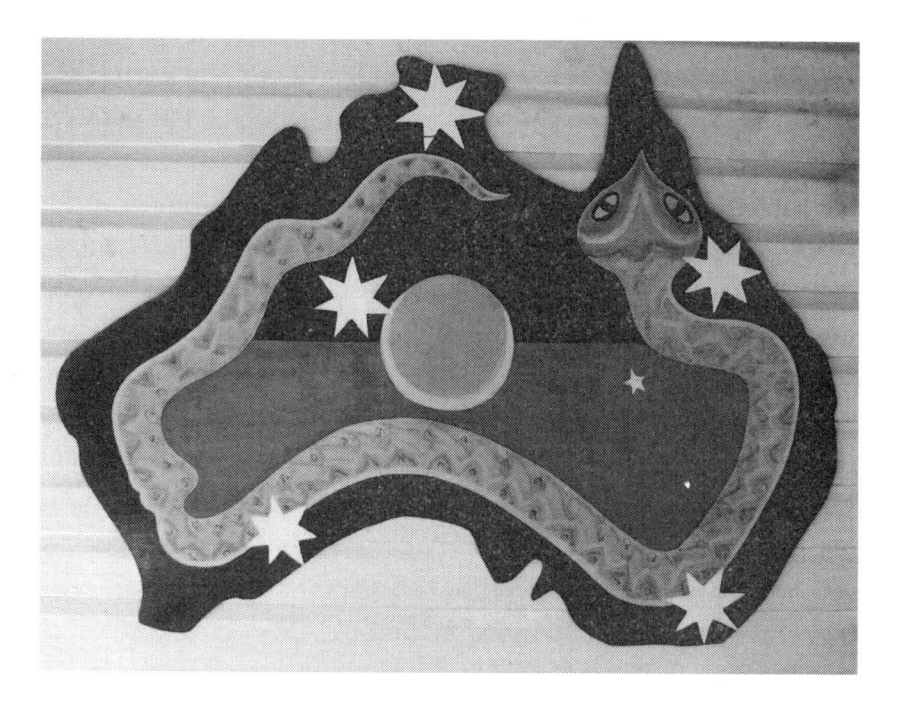

Rainbow Serpent mural created by teacher Jenny Noble and the children of Rosebank School, New South Wales, 2000.

Rosebank Public School

so their resting places should be avoided.[5] This menacing aspect has been symbolised in Dick Nguleingulei Murrumurru's painting from the National Museum of Australia's collection, which depicts Yingarna with terrible crocodile's teeth and tail, and a round emu-like body capable of holding all she has swallowed. The idea of the Rainbow Serpent as a composite of many other animals and even plants appeared elsewhere; western Arnhem Land rock paintings portray Rainbow Serpents with the head of a kangaroo, body of a snake, tail of a barramundi, and yam-shaped protrusions from the body. The oldest of these rock paintings have been dated to 6000 years, supporting the argument that Rainbow Serpent stories are among the world's oldest continuous religious traditions.[6] This makes it especially useful as a national symbol, claiming for modern Australia both universality and longevity.

Another example concerns Thuwathu, a Rainbow Serpent celebrated by the Lardil people from Mornington Island. He had been resting in his humpy when his sister came to repeatedly ask him to shelter her baby from the approaching storm. Over and over Thuwathu said no, claiming that he needed all of the space for himself. Unfortunately the baby got very wet in the storm and died. This infuriated his sister who, seeking vengeance, set fire to Thuwathu's shelter while he was asleep. He awoke on fire, and in agony tried to go to the water, pushing the ground up as he writhed and twisted in an attempt to extinguish the flames, thereby creating the Dugong River. On his journey to find water Thuwathu vomited other landforms and created new landscapes. The people watched his suffering, and were so saddened that they cut themselves in sympathy for his torment (at a place now known as Neyithalan, or 'place of burning or cutting'). Thuwathu was in such pain that he retreated to the sky where he is still seen as a rainbow. The symbolism of this story is said to be sexual, for it represents labour and birth, and establishes the appropriate relationship between brothers and sisters.[7]

For Aboriginal people the Rainbow Serpent was not just relegated to the past and time of creation, but remained an awesome source of power that shaped the contemporary world. When Cyclone Tracy devastated the city of Darwin in 1974, local Aboriginal people interpreted it as a 'warning to stop neglecting their traditional law and associated rituals', and succumbing to the temptations of 'lawless' city life. Similarly, when an elderly woman died following a car accident, her spirit was said to visit Kukatja-Wangkatjungka artist Rover Thomas who subsequently composed the 'Gurirr Gurirr' cycle, a public ceremony which 'was a reconfirmation of the law, and hence could ward off the Rainbow Serpent's anger.'[8]

Attaching meaning

Non-Indigenous Australians have known stories about other Rainbow Serpents since colonial times. Francis Armstrong, the first government interpreter of the Swan River Colony (now Perth), recorded an account of the Waugal (also spelled Wagyl), a Noongar Rainbow Serpent, in 1836, seven years after the establishment of the settlement. He observed that there were 'certain large round stones, in different parts of the Colony, which they [Noongar people] believe to be the eggs laid by the waugal ... On passing such stones, they are in the habit of making a bed for it, of the rushes of the blackboy [*balga*, grass tree or *Xanthorrhoea preissii*]'.[9] This was because, according to Noongar elder Clarrie Isaacs, the Waugal had created the Swan River and all its associated waterholes, and 'has the power of life and death over Aborigines and demands the respect due to it'.[10] However, despite noticing the reverence that the Noongar paid these stones, the settlers still removed them from their place, indicating that they accorded them no significance. This instance suggests the difficulty of translating the symbolic significance of an object and story across cultures, especially when there is such disparity in cultural power. But in addition it reveals the way the very land contained symbolic meaning for Indigenous people, whereas for the increasingly utilitarian colonisers the land was reduced to little more than an economic resource.

The Rainbow Serpent, then, means different things for Indigenous and non-Indigenous Australians. Armstrong's example demonstrates that in the early period it was considered a mere curiosity and disregarded, for the colonists were busy transforming and re-purposing the land. Conflicting attitudes about the Waugal arose again in the 1980s when the state government wanted to redevelop the site of the Old Swan Brewery, also known as Goonininup, a resting place of the Rainbow Serpent.[11] Again, a century and a half later, few non-Indigenous Western Australians sympathised with Noongar protests, and received the idea of the Waugal with great scepticism. Isaacs attempted to find equivalences in European systems of belief:

> They say because when they drive past the site that because they cannot see some sort of ridiculous fire breathing dragon like creature poking its Loch Ness Monster like head from the waters that it does not exist. It is as ridiculous as myself making an assertion that God is actually a large white man sitting on a throne atop some puffy clouds.[12]

But the developers ignored inconvenient arguments about religious symbolism, preferring a more self-interestedly rational interpretation which, according to John Fielder, 'demonstrates the imperial nature of Western rationality, where our logic renders all other logics as essentially illogical, irrational – not to be thought of as logic at all'.[13] The Noongar saw the Waugal as a 'spiritual being', while their opponents saw the Waugal as 'some wildly primitive superstition' and the Noongar themselves as troublemakers.[14]

However, non-Indigenous Australians have attached a range of other meanings to the Rainbow Serpent, for the most part far from hostile. This is partly due to the influence of anthropologists who, in the early twentieth century, became interested in what they called 'myth'. Anthropologist AR Radcliffe-Brown compiled a survey of stories from different Aboriginal language groups across Australia, and concluded that the Rainbow Serpent occupied 'the position of a deity'.[15] Despite noticing many differences in these stories, Radcliffe-Brown assumed that there was just a single Rainbow Serpent, and that it was akin to a god, 'the most important nature-deity'.[16] It was a view that greatly influenced non-Indigenous Australian understandings.[17]

Taken out of the particular contexts of each language group's Dreamings, the Rainbow Serpent has been stripped of its numerous ambivalent symbolisms and iconographic forms, and frequently reduced to a singular entity – a benevolent mother/creator-figure in the form of a brightly coloured snake. Perhaps this is in part due to the snake's particular morphology; it is easy to imagine its enormous sinuous body carving out the rivers and creeks in the ancient

'Dreamtime' (as it used to be described), whereas the meaning of the multiple symbolisms and composite form of Yingarna, Ngalyod and other Rainbow Serpents discussed by Aboriginal clans eludes outsiders. It could be argued that this new rendering as a benevolent snake is a process of intellectual colonisation, for the settlers have domesticated the Rainbow Serpent, making it comprehensible and palatable to Western ideas. It was a case of non-Indigenous Australia connecting to Aboriginality only on a disembodied and superficial aesthetic level rather than at a level of deep understanding.[18] In the 1970s celebrated Australian artist Sidney Nolan painted two large murals depicting Rainbow Serpents. 'Snake', a 45 metre long by 9 metre high mosaic comprising 1620 panels was completed in 1971 and was said to be Nolan's 'homage to Australia's Aborigines'. This work was not displayed until 2011, when it was hung at the Museum of Old and New Art, Hobart. The second work, 'Little Snake' comprised 324 individual paintings displayed as two large mosaic panels for the Adelaide Festival Theatre in 1973. Inspired by the sight of the Central Australian desert blooming after years of drought, Nolan used the Rainbow Serpent to represent 'the magical power of water that brings life from a state of stasis'.[19] Unsurprisingly, it is this 'domesticated' image of the giant brightly coloured snake with which Australians are probably most familiar and which would prove most suitable for representing the Australian nation as a whole.

A commonplace symbol

Since then, images of the Rainbow Serpents have slithered across school walls and community murals in suburbs and towns throughout the nation, at least those with large Indigenous or left-leaning populations. The education system has taken the Rainbow Serpent to its widest audience. For many young Australians the Rainbow Serpent has been packaged as a simple Indigenous fairytale. From the 1970s Australian children have read illustrated books depicting the life and adventures of the Rainbow Serpent (Fig. 62).[20] By the 1990s children could paint their own Rainbow Serpent designs during NAIDOC Week, Harmony Day, or other events celebrating Australia's multiculturalism.

For adult Australians, the Rainbow Serpent has a number of other connotations. Tourists have been able to buy prints, T-shirts, books and jewellery or even underpants decorated with the great snake's sinuous form, as an exotic souvenir of Australia. Walkers and leisure-seekers can photograph, sit on or picnic by large public sculptures of the snake in public spaces, where it was intended to acknowledge and commemorate Aboriginal people.[21] And since 1997 New Agers, ravers and eco-tourists can come from 'across the globe to dance a common dream' at the annual Rainbow Serpent Festival in Lexton, central Victoria, to camp, dance and learn from local Dja Dja Wurrung and Wadawurrung peoples and other Indigenous people from the Pacific and north America.[22] Here festival-goers 'connect with like minded individuals and celebrate nature, community and harmony' through music, dance, and performance art. Following the disastrous fires of 2019–20, there was speculation it may no longer be held there in summer.[23] The New Age market has been one of the most avid consumers of the Rainbow Serpent symbol, reading in it positive messages about the earth and people's spiritual relationship with it. Sallie Anderson has noticed that:

> The authors of many New Age books on Aboriginal culture and spirituality pick and choose characteristics from ethnographic descriptions of various rainbow serpent myths that seemingly support their comparisons with the Kundalini, electromagnetism, Vishnu, fertility and death, vibration and energy sources and various other themes.[24]

The Rainbow Serpent's winding form and brilliant colours have become a commonplace symbol within Australian pedagogical, cultural, economic and built environments. This widespread familiarity with the image, and the apparent tangibility of the concept in its domesticated and aestheticised form, has led to it being understood as the pre-eminent symbol of Aboriginal identity, especially apparent in public events celebrating the centenary of Federation.

The turn of the century saw a groundswell of interest in Aboriginal people and their place in Australia. The first year of the new millennium was supposed to mark the end of the ten-year journey towards reconciliation between black and white Australia. In June 2000 hundreds of thousands had participated in the 'Walk for Reconciliation' and in September Australians cheered for Indigenous athlete Cathy Freeman at the Sydney Olympics. These milestones meant that a feel-good emblem of the newly reconciled nation was needed for 2001, when Australia's national identity was celebrated in the centenary of Federation. The Rainbow Serpent was called into service.

On 1 January 2001 the 'Journey of a Nation – Centenary of Federation' parade through the streets of Sydney included a float shaped like a huge coiled snake, with dancers wearing costumes decorated with Rainbow Serpents designed by Bundjalung artist Bronwyn Bancroft. Then, at Canberra's 2001 Floriade festival, the Rainbow Serpent again appeared, this time in the 'Century in bloom' display (Fig. 63). On this 'floral walk through the decades', viewers passed through plantings of humble vegetables representing the hardships of the Depression and beds of flowers planted in the shapes of the German Iron Cross and the Japanese Rising Sun, indicating World War II. The 1970s were represented by a display of tulips and native flora planted in the design of the Rainbow Serpent, ostensibly symbolising 'Australia's Aboriginal heritage'. These examples suggest that the Rainbow Serpent was used by the event organisers as a metonym for Aboriginality, so audiences could embrace Aboriginal peoples' place within Australia's national identity.

However, the Rainbow Serpent was also used to symbolise Australia as a whole, and not just its Indigenous peoples. In Sydney's annual New Year's Eve fireworks display, the grand finale is always the lighting of the mystery symbol that adorns the eastern side of the city's beloved Harbour Bridge. In 2001 that symbol was the Rainbow Serpent, depicted alongside the Federation Star. The maxim of that year's show was '100 years as a nation, thousands of years as a land'. Thus the Rainbow Serpent was used to give modern Australia an ancient past, and, in conjunction with the star, was appropriated to represent Australia. The use of the Rainbow Serpent was no doubt well intentioned, but this plainly benevolent and amorphous meaning was far removed from that connoted by the original, highly ambivalent Rainbow Serpents of the Dreaming, such as Yingarna and Ngalyod.

Aboriginal people themselves, however, have not always retained the original multiple symbolic meanings of the Rainbow Serpents. Due to the history of colonisation and the emergence of Indigenous political organisations and media, Aboriginal societies have become more mixed and cosmopolitan, and a pan-Aboriginal identity has emerged. Instead of identifying solely with one's clan or language group, Aboriginal people have formed a community that encompasses the entire continent. As such, they have needed to develop their own symbols to represent this new pan-identity, and the ubiquity of the Rainbow Serpent in both Indigenous and non-Indigenous societies makes it well placed to act as 'a symbol of unity … amongst urban Aborigines'.[25] This has manifested in a number of ways. The Rainbow Serpent has provided a logo for Aboriginal corporations such as the Northern Land Council. Victoria's Rumbalara Oral Health Centre depicted the Rainbow Serpent as dental floss, 'twisting through an orange tangled web, which represents plaque on teeth'.[26] For the Aboriginal community of Moree, it was a symbol of unity when they constructed a 17 metre long Rainbow Serpent for the 'Black + White + Pink Reconciliation Float', entered in the 1999 Mardi Gras parade.[27] Following its seeming overuse as a national symbol during the Federation centenary, some Aboriginal people began to question its appropriateness. In 2003 the Rainbow Serpent was suggested as a motif for the then-proposed Stolen Generations memorial at Reconciliation Place, Canberra. However, National Sorry Day members ultimately rejected this suggestion because the non-Indigenous appropriation of the Rainbow Serpent motif, especially by New Agers, had 'diminished' its potency as a symbol for representing both 'Stolen Generations and Indigenous groups right across Australia'.[28]

Inscribing new meaning

The Rainbow Serpent has been an important symbol in Aboriginal societies for thousands of years, and by the start of the twenty-first century it was also a recognised symbol for the wider Australian society. In making that transition it lost its particular 'traditional' meanings of creation, water and fertility, and its ambiguous combination of creative and destructive forces. Although it has not featured much on the national stage as a symbol since the Federation centenary in 2001, it remains a potent symbol of local Aboriginal community spirit and reconciliation. For example, Bundjalung artist John Robinson's Rainbow Serpent artwork was installed at a shopping centre in East Maitland, New South Wales to celebrate 2018's Reconciliation Week. In 2019 a Rainbow Serpent water feature designed by a collective of Kamilaroi women artists was commissioned for the Gunnedah Civic Centre, and the Perth Royal Show showcased a public performance by Noongar man Walter McGuire, featuring a '35m long Wagyl inflatable creation … illuminated by the colours of the rainbow'.[29] It is evident then, that the supple skin of the Rainbow Serpent continues to provide an ideal canvas for inscribing new meanings and symbolisms for both Indigenous and non-Indigenous Australians.

BAGGY GREEN

Gideon Haigh

To solve the mystery of the 'blue carbuncle', Sherlock Holmes has a solitary clue: an old trilby hat recovered from an affray. He encourages Dr Watson to look upon it as an embodiment of the wearer. 'What can you gather from this battered old felt?' protests his friend. 'I can see nothing.' The great detective reassures him: 'On the contrary Watson, you can see everything. You fail, however, to reason from what you see.'[1]

The battered old felt perched atop Steve Waugh's head on the cover of his autobiography *Out of My Comfort Zone* seems likewise pregnant with meanings. The baggy green cap is as battered and faded as the face is leathery and lined. With the wary eyes and weary stubble, it completes the mighty cricketer's image as a slouch hat completes an Anzac. Nor is it there for effect. Waugh, the most taciturn of cricketers, becomes positively effusive where his cap is concerned: it is 'almost mythical', has 'almost a power to it', and positions cricketers as heirs to 'the Anzac spirit' of 'fighting together and looking after your mates' (Fig. 65).[2]

Yet what you see with the baggy green – or, at least, what Steve Waugh sees – is not necessarily what you get. Many common assumptions nurtured about the Australian cricket cap are erroneous. It is far from eternally unchanging, having been extensively modified over time. It has not always been baggy or even green; the Australian coat of arms it features is redundant. Its presentation to newly minted international players was not ritualised until the late 1990s; indeed, it used to be distributed quite liberally to players on non-Test match occasions. Even the phrase 'baggy green cap' is of relatively recent usage. What is paraded as fact is often arrant nonsense.[3] Sometimes memory itself plays false. When Waugh introduced the custom of the whole Australian team taking the field together beneath their caps during the Gabba Test of December 1996, he was lavishly praised by the venerable Neil Harvey, a member of Sir Donald Bradman's Invincibles:

> It was a wonderful sight. I'm pleased to see Steve Waugh is an old traditionalist, although sometimes you wonder if he's the last of them. In my day the baggy green was much more publicised. The papers in England would make a fuss of it and any new player wearing it. I just hope they never change the shape of it. Baggy is exactly how it should stay.[4]

Yet you will search in vain for a photograph of Harvey wearing a baggy green cap on the cricket field. His view that the brim was distracting was embraced by a number of teammates: Richie Benaud and Alan Davidson, for instance, always played bare-headed, while the most magnetic cricketer of his generation, Keith Miller, was famous for a mane of hair that no cap ever tamed. In short, we are moving in the realm of Eric Hobsbawm's concept of 'invented tradition'. And sorting fact from fancy where the baggy green cap is concerned is what Holmes would classify a 'three-pipe problem', at least one pipe of which would need to involve an amalgamation of the surprisingly little we know of the headgear's origins.

Not baggy, not green

In the pioneering days of touring, agreement about uniform was chiefly a matter of aesthetics. Australia's first team abroad, the Aboriginal XI mustered by Charles Lawrence to tour England in 1868, took the field resplendent in a uniform of white trousers and maroon shirt with a cream sash. Dave Gregory's team a decade later wore a blazer of white and azure blue stripes, topped with a matching brimless cap. A peaked cap had come into vogue by the time Billy Murdoch's team toured again in 1880, playing Australia's first Test in England, but this time in magenta and black. When Australia won the Test that inaugurated the Ashes tradition at the Oval in August 1882, it bore the colours of the Sydney-based 96th Regiment: red, black and yellow.

If Australian cricket had a colour at all in the first quarter century of international competition, it was blue. Murdoch's 1884 Australian team wore a fetching navy jacket with gold piping. The team that toured two years later were blazered in blue, red and white: the colours of the Melbourne Cricket Club who were the tour's organisers and underwriters. In Australia, meanwhile, there was not even this level of cohesion. Teams played in the colours of the colonial association hosting the match, a reflection of the fact that the local body was also responsible for selecting, marshalling, accommodating and paying the team. In a way, too, this was a truer reflection of the nature of the teams themselves, uneasy coalitions sometimes riven by intercolonial jealousies.

Australia's 1893 tour of England was the first under the auspices of a national organising body, the fledgling Australasian Cricket Council, and the team's blue caps and blazer bore a shield-shaped patch enclosing the stars of the Southern Cross in a cross of St George, beneath which was the legend 'Advance Australia' – a sentiment at least 70 years old. It did not have the desired inspirational effect on the players. 'It was impossible to keep some of them straight', complained the team's manager, Victor Cohen. 'One of them was altogether useless because of his drinking propensities ... Some were in the habit of holding receptions in their rooms and would not go to bed until all hours.'[5]

Green and gold's sudden primacy is mysterious. Initially it found no favour: at a meeting of the council in Adelaide in January 1895, the motion of John Portus from New South Wales that 'the Australian XI's colours be olive green with the Australian coat of arms worked into the cap and coat pocket' lapsed without a seconder; the team that toured England the following year did so again, at the players' instigation, in 'dark blue caps and gold binding'. A plausible hypothesis involves the council's dissolution. At one of the starveling body's last meetings, in January 1898, South Australian delegate Mostyn Evan suggested 'a very attractive arrangement of green and gold colours' for the forthcoming 1899 tour of England. By the time it came for the tour to be arranged, the council was in its death throes and the Melbourne Cricket Club moved in to provide financial support for the venture. But the club's shrewd and ambitious secretary, Major Ben Wardill, was sensitive to whispered criticisms that his institution was too rich and influential in the local game, and insufficiently representative of the country to perform the role it had arrogated to itself. It would have been with his approval that the team in London outfitted itself in blazers and caps of 'sage green and gold', and also hoisted a flag in those colours above their headquarters at Holborn's Inns of Court Hotel, as a means of reinforcing the point that the team represented Australia rather than the interests of a private club.[6]

In hindsight, the circumstances of the 1899 tour were ideal for the establishment of a tradition. It was the first in England to span what became the traditional five Test matches; it provided also the first Australian victory over the course of an away series. Above all, the coincidence of the triumph with the country's last wranglings over the form of its federation earned the cricketers favourable comparison with Australia's bickering politicians.[7] Had they lost, the green and gold might never have caught on; as it was, success against strong opposition on this and the next tour three years later lent the colours and cap a talismanic quality. Cricketers are superstitious; they stick to teams, routines and gear that they associate with success. Victor Trumper was the foremost batsman of his generation but a man of ingrained habits: the sight of a clergyman on game day, for instance, filled him with foreboding. So it was, noted a teammate, that he clung to the cap in which he first dazzled audiences (Fig. 66):

> Trumper always wore an old Australian XI cap when batting. It was bottle green. He was wearing it when he made 135 not out at Lord's in 1899, and he continued wearing it until he retired from Test cricket in 1912. It was faded but he would not give it up for the many new ones he had. There was a row if one of the other humourists [sic] of the side took his cap and hid it.[8]

If the colours were condoned as politically expedient, they deceived nobody. The state associations regathered their forces to originate the Australian Board of Control for International Cricket in May 1905 and, within three years, had not only usurped the Melbourne Cricket Club but successfully hosted their first inbound tour by an English team. With this authority came control of uniform, and the new body resolved again a South Australian motion that the colours for Australia be '"gum tree" green and gold'. The coat of arms with the 'Advance Australia' motif was also confirmed, having just three weeks earlier become official on the grant of King Edward VII.[9]

There remained ambiguity about the entitlement to these colours: at the same meeting, Queenslander Joseph Allen asked that full caps be awarded to those who had played in a non-Test 'Australian XI' match in Brisbane a few months earlier. His plea was ignored, and Australian cricketers themselves would almost certainly have disapproved. A letter from Wardill to Frank Laver, manager of the 1909 Australian team, suggests an already marked degree of proprietorship about the XI's colours:

> A man I don't know called on me just now and wanted to know where he could get the Australian XI uniform and colours for a friend of his in Montevideo (South America). I told him he couldn't get them, he was not entitled to wear them. He has been in South

America for 8 years, is not even a member of any Australasian club, and his friend thought he could wear them to show off his loyalty to Australia!!![10]

Another feature set in stone from the first was the cap's bestowal on every team member, regardless of seniority or social status. Australian players had always looked askance at divisions between amateur and professional in English cricket, whereby 'gentlemen' and 'players' changed, travelled and were accommodated separately, and even emerged from different gates at the ground. They thought it savoured of class distinction, too, when amateurs affected the caps of their schools and clubs (most famously Douglas Jardine, who favoured the multicoloured cap of the Harlequins CC during the unruly Bodyline series). That the Australian cap has been worn alike by cricketers in their first Test and their hundredth is not a triviality.

But if this has not changed, much else has. For the 1909 Ashes tour, the cap was augmented by a telltale year beneath the coat of arms; the blazer pocket showed the kangaroo on the left and the emu on the right. For the 1921 Ashes tour, the previously tight-fitting cap became baggy, in deference to the fashion of the times, and the fauna were reversed, where they stayed. Somehow, too, it escaped the board's attention that a new Australian coat of arms had come into being in 1912, so the Australian cap continued to bear the symbol that had officially been retired. This hybrid antique character was reinforced in 1931–32 when the legend 'Advance Australia' was finally replaced by 'Australia' – the formation still in use.

Where the Australian uniform was concerned, the board had periods of both great restrictiveness and uncharacteristic liberality. In September 1931, the board agreed that blazers and caps 'only be given to those who had not previously represented Australia'.[11] Yet if this prohibition was ever enforced, it cannot have been for long, as the evidence of memorabilia auctions is that players who played over extended periods usually acquired multiple caps and blazers, and sometimes swapped the ones they received for the better-fitting items of teammates.

On their 1948 trip to England, each Australian player received two caps, as well as an official blazer, sweater and tie. Bradman's caps from this, his valedictory tour, suggest that even he wasn't impervious to superstition: one, on loan to the Melbourne Cricket Club from the private collector who acquired it in June 2003, shows wear; the other, in the collection of the State Library of South Australia, is in pristine condition. Interestingly, too, for Bradman a cap was chiefly functional. He ended his career having given all his baggy greens away, and his collected works contain no emotional tributes to what it signifies.[12] It was a much later and very different generation that erected the baggy green idol, and fashioned it in its own image (Fig. 67).

Valuing the baggy green

In hindsight, Australian cricket administrators took a long time to realise the value locked up in their national cap. While the board was loath to sully its own hands with matters commercial, it looked on mutely as players wore the cap freely in advertisements and in their books; nor did it concern itself when England's Derbyshire County Cricket Club in 1970 adopted a baggy green cap apparently patterned on the Australian item.[13]

By the early 1970s, the term 'baggy green cap' had acquired a low-level recognition worthy of remark. In 1971 Englishman Alan Hewitt lauded the 'baggy green Australian caps' which 'appear to underline the formidable nature of those broad and tall young cricketers, who offer relentless challenge to English cricket'. Australian cricket writer Ray Robinson in his canonical text *On Top Down Under* stated that 'Under their green caps, their forces have been harder to repel than the Spanish armada.' Journalist Ian Brayshaw entitled his eulogy for Australian teams of the 1970s *Warriors in Baggy Green Caps*. Even

Kerry Packer deferred to it, having the Australians who appeared in his breakaway World Series Cricket troupe between 1977 and 1979 play in tight-fitting yellow caps. When his general manager suggested the use of green headgear, Packer snapped: 'You've got to earn those, son.'[14] Yet in a period of cricket upheaval, the Australian cap seemed to embody cricket traditions more often under threat – from the enticements of commercialisation, the demands of television, the deterioration of on-field behaviour and the private incursions of Kerry Packer, to the political perplexities of the excommunication of South Africa. The board itself was in one of its none-too-fussy stages about the cap's distribution. In the 1980s it was handed out to players picked for Australia B teams, for the Prime Minister's XI and even Australian Under-19s. 'I'm not sure why we were given the real thing, but I couldn't believe I had that almost mythical possession in my hands,' noted one player. His name: Steve Waugh.[15]

If any individual is responsible for the cap's latter-day iconic status it is Waugh: its ultimate elevation to a national symbol dates from his captaincy. Quite why is almost worthy of psychoanalytic scrutiny, although at one level it is probably as simple as Trumper's attachment to *his* cap: he made runs and won games wearing it. Like Trumper, Waugh was a disarmingly superstitious cricketer, who never played without his lucky red rag, and regarded ladybirds as a good omen; the cap, likewise, became part of his psychological armour. As he gradually made a publishing fetish of his growing millinery obsession, through the media and his successful series of tour diaries, he became Australian cricket's glass of fashion and mould of form. After Australia's victory in the Worrell Trophy in May 1995, for example, Waugh noted the conspicuousness of the cap in the dressing room celebrations:

> Lang [Justin Langer] retained that Australian flag draped over his shoulders all night while Heals [Ian Healy], Slats [Michael Slater], Lang and I kept the baggy green on until we were told the festivities were over.[16]

The 1868 Aboriginal Australian cricketers in England, wearing a uniform of maroon shirt with cream sash. The team consisted of Bullocky (Bullchanach), Mosquito (James Couzens, Grougarrong), Charley Dumas (Pripumuarraman), Peter (Arrahmunijarrimun), Dick-a-Dick (Yangendyinanyuk), Red Cap (Brimbunyah), Jim Crow (Lytejerbillijun), Sundown (Ballrinjarrimin), Johnny Cuzens (Zellanach), Tiger (Bonnibarngeet), Johnny Mullagh (Unaarrimin), Twopenny (Jarrawuk/Murrumgunarrimin), King Cole (Bripumyarrimin), with Charles Lawrence (captain, coach) and William Shepherd (manager) in front.

National Library of Australia

Wearing the cap for as long as possible after a victory became a competition. Western Australian Langer, known as 'Mini-Tugga' in the Australian team for his almost slavish devotion to Waugh, won:

> They said it couldn't be done. Well, they didn't count on the love affair Lang has had with his cherished baggy green cap. To everyone's astonishment, some four days after the Southern Comfort had done the talking in our victorious dressing room celebrations at Trent Bridge, Lang is still proudly sporting his cap, a fact which wins him a bet neither Slats nor I could fulfil. But at

least we didn't have an odour any skunk would have been proud of, or a permanent red ring around our melons from the elastic band inside the rim of the cap. This was another morale boosting effort from Lang, who always does these little things that help bond a side together.[17]

Respect for an imagined past became a motif of Waugh's captaincy when he assumed the role in February 1999. In Hugh de Selincourt's 1924 classic *The Cricket Match*, the Tillingfold secretary rejoices in his team's sky-blue caps: 'If we all wears 'em, lord bless my soul, it'll fair put the wind up those Raveley chaps. We'll have them beat before the coin's tossed.'[18] Waugh regarded the baggy green in similar light, and insisted on all his players wearing it in the first session of a Test. He inaugurated the custom of Test debutants being presented with their caps by a distinguished ex-player; he commissioned replicas of the turn-of-the-century Australian cap to be worn in the Sydney Test of January 2000; he led the team on a pilgrimage to Gallipoli in May 2001 en route to England, inspired by a conversation with Lieutenant General Peter Cosgrove in which they 'compared cricket and the army, especially things that are important in both endeavours – such as camaraderie, discipline, commitment and the importance of a plan'. On the visit, explicit connections were drawn between representing Australia in war and in sport; the slouch-hatted cricketers even attempted to re-enact the famous cricket game played on Shell Green to cover the Anzac evacuation on 17 December 1915. There was conjecture that Waugh was trying to shore his team up from recent criticism of its on-field behaviour, and the views solicited from the players afterwards suggest fairly superficial, bemused and self-conscious experiences. Steve Waugh's twin brother, Mark, tried to extract a sporting lesson ('We underestimated the Turks … Plan to know your opposition and what they do'). The captain, however, felt it had 'a profound effect on most of the squad', and Cosgrove himself probably reflected a fair proportion of public opinion when he paid the cricketers cheerful homage:

They're our sporting Anzacs. We want that cricket team to embody all those marvellous Australian characteristics we prize; you know, fair play, good humour, toughness, success. They represent all Aussies, just as the Anzacs who fought in those trenches represented all Australians.[19]

For Waugh and his administrators, the baggy green was a brand name ripe for celebration, precisely because it had been so relatively little exploited before. The board had always received legal advice that the Australian Trade Marks Office would not consent to trademark protection for an item involving a coat of arms. But various annoyances – including an advertisement by the brewer Coopers Brewing Company in which baggy green caps replaced the lids on stubbies – led to chairman Denis Rogers approaching the devoutly cricket-loving prime minister, John Howard. A legal adviser to the Prime Minister's Department helped the board prepare registrations across several trademark categories, which were then expeditiously approved. Thus did the baggy green become an asset beyond value in the board balance sheet, advertised by the launch of the official Australian cricket website, www.baggygreen.com.au (run by Channel Nine), and tapped by licensed merchandise. Its History of the Baggy Green was marketed as the 'consummate Australian cricket collectable, taking you through an authoritive [sic] journey exploring the history, tradition and pride of the coveted baggy green' and featured 'an actual green flannel swatch as used … in the crafting of the baggy green'.[20] To protect what was now a commercial asset, the board restricted the production and distribution of the baggy green more than it had ever done before. As the national women's cricket team became increasingly professionalised, its players too embraced the baggy green, although there is some lingering resentment that its badge remains subtly different from the men's.[21]

A number of reasons can be advanced for the baggy green exhibitionism around the turn of the millennium – a hankering for continuity in a period of change, the recrudescence of Australian conservatism, the desire for values transcending the shallow materialism of modern sport. But one factor shouldn't be overlooked: there was no stakeholder it did not suit. Players building private *esprit de corps* and public reputations, administrators striving to generate brand value and to control intellectual property, Channel Nine trying to engender viewer loyalty and extend their reach to new technologies, sponsors anxious to identify with a premium product, fans and sports journalists seeking symbolic embodiment of their allegiance.

The attachment of that last group, however, involves some unexamined assumptions. It is commonly repeated that the baggy green is essentially held in trust for the public of whom the Australian team are representative. Waugh did not feel that way: 'The players "own" the Australian team traditions and to be able to partake of these rituals and traditions has meant you have been awarded the highest honour in Australian cricket – you have been selected to play for your country.' In other words, it was the current players who defined the baggy green, not the public, and as its 'owners' they defined appropriate behaviour. For instance, when ex-players criticised the methods of former Australian coach John Buchanan in December 2007, Adam Gilchrist jumped to his defence:

> I guess one of the traits that we have a lot of pride in, in wearing the baggy green, is that we show a lot of respect. It seems some guys in retirement have lost that ... [The Australian team] is an elite club and we've always felt a major characteristic of being in that club is to show respect.

In an allegedly egalitarian country, this could be seen as a strangely inegalitarian remark, an assertion of caste and status, a claim to be beyond criticism. When players were tempted by the hearty cash incentives of the Indian Premier League, Cricket Australia's public affairs manager Peter Young stated optimistically: 'The status of the baggy green is more powerful than cash for any red-blooded Australian and cricketers will tell you that themselves.' Volatile all-rounder Andrew Symonds, however, implied that loyalty had its price: 'For me, there's no question the baggy green cap is still the jewel in the crown of Australian cricket. But the way things are heading, loyalty is going to become a major issue, particularly when you can make more money in six or eight weeks than you can in a season.'[22]

When Steve Smith, David Warner and Cameron Bancroft were arraigned in March 2018 on charges of aiding and abetting ball tampering in a Test in Cape Town, it shattered the players' claim that they could define appropriate behaviour and the public issued a stern verdict: 'Not in our name.' Smith and Bancroft wore their caps to the press conference where their equivocations and evasions deepened their plight; their caps accentuated their disgrace. All three were unceremoniously stripped of their uniforms before returning home to lengthy suspensions. Part of the restoration of Australia's fortunes and reputation was a new coach, Justin Langer, who employed his old mucker Steve Waugh as a muse and guru during the 2019 Ashes.

The cap's redemptive powers were put to a further test in January 2020 when, in the aftermath of the summer's calamitous bushfires, fundraising initiatives included the auction of the baggy green owned by Shane Warne. Warne had been a noted agnostic where the cap's properties were concerned ('There was too much verbal diarrhoea about the baggy cap, it was a bit too over the top for me') but grasped its magic in the eyes of others. The purchaser, for a record $1,007,500, was another Australian icon: Commonwealth Bank. Reputation tarnished by the Hayne Royal Commission into the banking industry, which had resulted in the departure of its CEO, the bank was seeking the burnish of sporting and charitable associations – it announced plans for the cap to go on display at Bowral's Bradman Museum.[23] Sherlock Holmes was right. About the headgear's new owner you could tell a lot.

THE DEMOCRACY SAUSAGE

Judith Brett

Mention the democracy sausage and Australians smile.[1] Since the term was coined in 2012 it has taken off to become a symbol of the egalitarian good nature of Australian elections and Australians' pride in their democratic tradition (Fig. 52). Buying and eating a sizzled sausage at the polling booth and, especially for younger voters, tweeting a photo of same have become acts of communal participation in the Australian nation almost as significant as filling out the ballot paper and a lot more fun; a jokey accompaniment to the serious act of choosing the government, celebrating what we all share no matter which side wins.

It was not always so good-natured. Early elections were riotous affairs as candidates plied electors with food and drink, mostly alcoholic, and rival teams of supporters sang songs, cheered, booed and sometimes fought. At the first elections held in New South Wales in 1843 two men were killed in rioting and many more injured. Once the colonies had self-government, and most men the right to vote, elections become much more orderly. Candidates were prohibited from bribing voters, including with food and drink, and alcohol was banished. When a voter arrived at the polling booth a government official handed him a ballot paper bearing the candidates' names which he marked in the privacy of a compartmentalised polling booth. This was an Australian invention which ensured the secrecy of the vote and so prevented intimidation. Known as the Australian ballot, it spread quickly through the democratic world and is now the standard format for elections. The orderliness of Australian polling booths also contributed to the early granting of women's suffrage, first in South Australia in 1894 and then for the Commonwealth in 1902, neutralising the objection that polling booths were too disorderly for respectable women to attend.

It is not clear when food and drink reappeared at polling booths: a photo of the 1928 polling day at the Atherton courthouse shows women standing behind a stall serving refreshments.[2] Crucially, they were volunteers raising funds for worthy causes, not party supporters trying to entice the voters. Because many polling booths were located in schools, kindergartens and other community halls, election days were opportunities for fundraising. These began with stalls offering cakes, jams and crafts, but since the advent of the portable gas barbecue in the 1980s, voters and their families have also been able to buy a barbecued sausage in a roll or piece of white bread, with mustard or tomato sauce, and sometimes fried onion, especially at primary schools where parents' groups are well used to running sausage sizzles at school events and where funds are always needed.

Sausages are an egalitarian food of humble origin. For centuries, thrifty butchers have salted and minced offcuts of meat, including organs, and stuffed them into a cleaned intestine, perhaps adding blood, bread, herbs and spices. The resulting sausage could be cooked or dried. Like the meat pie, in days before rigorous food laws one could never be quite sure what was in them, rats' tails or the minced body of a murder victim perhaps. The nineteenth century German Chancellor, Otto von Bismarck, captured something of this suspicion in his aphorism, 'Laws are like sausages. It is better not to see them being made.' Sausages were cheap lower-class food. My downwardly mobile maternal grandmother, hanging on to her caste identity by her fingernails, prided herself on never serving them. In mid-twentieth century Australia they were also identified with wartime rationing. Prime cuts of meat were rationed, but sausages were not.[3]

Bring along some cash!

DEMOCRACY TASTES BETTER WITH A SAUSAGE!

ELECTION DAY SAUSAGE SIZZLE AND CAKE STALL

Democracy sausages
Baked goodies
Entertainment Books
Eco shopping bags, tea towels

Saturday, May 18
9am-2.30pm

Raising funds for playground improvements

Wembley Primary School
41 Grantham St, Wembley

Wembley Primary School (WA) P&C sausage stall poster, 2019.
Courtesy of Tiffany Fox

By the 1960s the status of the sausage was on the rise. For an affluent population which could afford better cuts of meat, the sausage lost its association with poverty. Improved national food safety standards removed the suspicion, post-war migrants introduced new versions like bratwurst and salami, and the sausage suited the new vogue for outdoor living centred round the backyard barbecue, supplementing the lamb chops and easier for children to eat. During the 1970s local councils began to install electric barbecues in parks with picnic tables conveniently nearby. These facilities for large social gatherings were especially welcomed by migrants who were often from the Mediterranean and well used to cooking and dining al fresco.

Community and service groups soon began to acquire portable gas barbecues and the volunteer-run sausage sizzle became a fundraising fixture at Australian outdoor community events. They suited the easygoing sociability Australians pride themselves on and provided a focal point for the men. Unlike the traditional fundraising street stalls, sausage sizzles – for service clubs like Rotary and Lions for instance – are mostly run by men. Throughout Australia on a Saturday morning, groups of men can be found turning the sausages outside the stores of the dominant hardware chain Bunnings which provides this fundraising facility to local community groups. It is also of course enhancing its egalitarian credentials as the go-to store for Australia's legions of DIY practitioners.

Back to the polling booth. How does a hungry young voter rolling out of bed on Saturday morning know where they can grab breakfast? To help them out, at the 2010 federal election some Brisbane friends set up a website for groups to register their election day fundraising offerings to enable voters to locate them. Calling itself Snagvotes, according to founder Grant Turner, the group's underlying objective was

> to celebrate our democracy, encourage participation in the democratic process and offer support for community groups and volunteers that run sausage sizzles and stalls on election day. There is

humour involved, people tweet their pictures, give reviews via social media, and most importantly for a lot of these volunteers doing the cooking it's their biggest fundraising venture of the year.

The message is 'Get together with your community and enjoy a sausage on election day – a great Australian tradition'.[4]

Perhaps it was from this initiative that the term was born, as the Australian National Dictionary Centre's earliest recordings of 'democracy sausage' are Twitter messages from the 2010 election day: 'Voted too early for a democracy sausage. Bought homemade cake and jam instead.'[5] There are a number of social media mentions up until the 2013 federal election when another group of social media savvy friends set up Twitter, Facebook and Instagram accounts using the phrase, with crowd-sourced maps to help voters decide where to vote. They did it again for the 2016 double dissolution election and the term took off: 'Hey everyone, let us know where you find your sausage sizzle tomorrow #democracy sausage.'[6]

At the end of that year the Australian National Dictionary Centre at the Australian National University selected 'democracy sausage' as the word of the year. Its popularity was boosted, said Centre Director Dr Amanda Laugesen, 'when Opposition Leader Bill Shorten bit awkwardly into the middle of his sausage in a roll rather than tackling it end on'.[7] He was at the Strathfield North Public School polling booth and photographer Alex Ellinghausen captured the moment. Clearly he had never grabbed his weekend breakfast at Bunnings was the conclusion on social media (Fig. 68).[8]

It is even more dangerous to refuse one, as Malcolm Turnbull learned a year later. He was visiting Lismore to inspect flood damage when a kind old lady from the Country Women's Association offered him a sausage on bread on a paper plate. 'That's lovely, that's very kind of you', he said, 'but I think I am running around a bit much to be eating that,' and he awkwardly put it back on the table.[9] He too had shown himself to be no ordinary bloke.

For election day 18 May 2019 more than two thousand stalls registered for the Democracy Sausage website and #Democracy Sausage was tweeted 2.2 million times. Democracy sausage social media sites which began to support fundraising have enabled the social media generation to engage with the electoral process in their own way, using the online maps to choose where to vote, and sharing photos on Instagram. Many election day stalls have since expanded their offerings beyond the basic sausage, to include vegan and halal options, additional extras, higher-grade sausages and more. Cake stalls can also be included on the website, and fundraising committees have fun with names and signage. In 2019 Camdenville Public School offered the Josh Fried'n'burg, the Barnaby (Joyce) Pulled Pork Barrel Roll, and the Pauline (Hanson) Plain White Roll.[10] The punning and jokester possibilities are endless. In London, new high commissioner, George Brandis, wielded the tongs outside the Australia House polling booth to raise money for the Royal Flying Doctor Service and so that expats and travellers could feel at home (Fig. 69).[11]

As a symbol of the nation the democracy sausage is a popular, bottom up creation, invented and spread by groups of friends,[12] and cooked and eaten in their hundreds of thousands on election day. But it is a symbol that is only possible because of Australia's distinctive electoral practices. Many of us vote in community halls rather than in government buildings, such as town halls or electoral offices. We vote on Saturdays. We can choose where we vote. And voting is compulsory.

Australia is one of only a handful of countries to hold elections on Saturdays. Most countries go to the polls on Sundays, except in the Protestant-dominated Anglosphere where public activities on the Sabbath other than attending church have historically been severely restricted. Canada, Ireland, the United States and the United Kingdom all vote on weekdays: Canada, Monday; Ireland, generally Friday; the United States, Tuesday (though some states declare a public holiday); and the United Kingdom, Thursday.

Australians have been voting on Saturdays federally since 1913,

A new coat of arms. Logo of the group of volunteers
mapping sausage stalls on social media during elections.

Thanks to democracysausage.org

and since the end of the nineteenth century in Queensland and South Australia. In Australia in the nineteenth century, and for much of the twentieth, Saturday was a half day for most workers and the weekly shopping day for many farmers. Some arguments were put against Saturday election days when Labor proposed to introduce it in 1911, chiefly on religious grounds, but these gained no traction. The advantages were too many. No one needed to take time off work to vote and lose pay. More people could participate in electioneering. Husbands could accompany their wives to the booths or mind the children while they slipped out. Polling hours were extended beyond sunset so that Jews could vote, and Seventh Day Adventists shunned voting on religious grounds. The Melbourne *Age* described the atmosphere at the larger booths on the first Saturday federal polling day in June 1913 as like 'some huge bazaar'.[13] And turnout improved, over 73 per cent compared with 62 per cent in 1910.[14]

Australia is also distinctive in the freedom it gives to voters as to where they vote. Since the Commonwealth's 1902 Electoral Act, Australians have been able to vote at any polling booth in their state, rather than being registered to a particular polling booth and required to vote there as is the case in the United Kingdom and Ireland, unless they apply for a postal vote, or arrange for a proxy.

Australia's greater flexibility is largely the result of Labor's determination to make voting easily accessible to the nomadic rural workforce. Western Australia, Victoria and South Australia all introduced postal voting in the nineteenth century for people away from home on business and to economise on the provision of polling booths in the sparsely settled districts. This was an obvious way to accommodate absentee voters, but Labor feared postal voting would compromise the secrecy of the ballot: employers could oversee the votes of their servants, squatters their men and doctors their housebound patients. After Labor won government in 1910, it abolished postal voting. This didn't last. Postal voting was reintroduced by a later Liberal government, but the flexibility of voting locations remained.

So we can choose where to vote. What we cannot choose – again unusually – is whether or not to vote. Since 1924 it has been compulsory for us to vote at federal elections, when a private members Bill passed through both houses in a single day with scarcely any debate. Since then the states have all followed suit. As the pedants will point out, we are really only compelled to attend the polling booth and have our names crossed out. Once in the polling booth, what we do is secret and the ballot put in the box can be blank or defaced with a message or an obscene drawing. Even so, we are all legally obliged to turn up or face a small fine if we don't.

Only eighteen other countries compel their citizens to vote.[15] None of the countries in the mainstream of Australia's political development have compulsory voting, not the United Kingdom from which Australia drew its parliamentary institutions and traditions, nor the United States, Canada, New Zealand or Ireland. People from these countries are generally astonished that we are compelled to vote. To them it seems an affront to democracy. We embrace it, with most opinion polls putting support in the 70 per cent range.[16] There is some opposition, mainly from the right of the Liberal Party, but nothing has come of it and Australian turnouts are consistently above 90 per cent.

Not only are we compelled to vote, we are also compelled to register to vote. This too is unusual. Compulsory registration was introduced by Labor in its 1911 revision of the Electoral Act, in this instance on the recommendation of the Chief Electoral Officer, Ryton Campbell Oldham. The Electoral Office was responsible for the electoral roll and went to great lengths to ensure it was as complete as possible. With voluntary enrolment, Oldham believed, there were too many errors and omissions, with many people believing that 'it is the duty of the electoral administration to follow them from place to place, and relieve them of the obligation of taking action in the preservation of their electoral rights'. Australia's exceptionally large migratory population, with at least 20 per cent of city electors changing houses each year, placed an unreasonable burden on government officers responsible for the roll, he said.[17]

Caucus accepted Oldham's recommendation. King O'Malley, who was the minister responsible for introducing the revised Electoral Act to parliament, suggested that this was the first instalment towards compulsory voting in a society in which the government already visited a good deal of compulsion on its citizens: compulsory vaccination, compulsory military service, compulsory census and statistical returns by individuals, compulsory education in every state and so on.[18] How, then, he asked, under these circumstances, can anyone object to compulsory enrolment?

Indeed few in the parliament did, except to ask why the government wouldn't go the whole way and introduce compulsory voting. The answer was that compulsory voting would require Labor to drop its opposition to postal voting. It could hardly make voting compulsory and not enable the house-bound to vote. There were also some practical problems raised. How much should people be fined? Wouldn't there be too many miscreants? What were acceptable excuses?

By 1924 when a private members Bill to make voting compulsory was introduced Labor had given up opposing postal voting and supported the Bill. So did the Nationalist Party (the major non-labour party) and the newly formed Country Party. Debate on the bill was minimal and it passed through all stages in a single day. Queensland had made voting compulsory for state elections in 1915 and turnout had increased significantly. It was hoped the same would now happen for federal elections where turnout was sliding.[19] Striking in the parliamentary debate and in the newspaper coverage is the absence of any sustained objections on the grounds of liberty.

Geoffrey Sawer, doyen of Australia's legal historians, famously wrote 'No major departure in the federal political system had ever been made in so casual a fashion'.[20] Sawer was wrong; the ease of the Bill's passage was not because of lack of attention. Rather it was uncontroversial because it expressed deep currents in Australia's political culture.

Liberal democracies are hybrid political systems which combine the rule of law and commitment to civil rights with popular elections and majority rule. There are obvious tensions here, and different polities find their own balance. In Australia we tilt towards majoritarian democracy. We want our governments to be elected by the majority of voters, not just the majority of those who turn up, and are not much bothered by the resort of compulsion to achieve this end.

Before voting was made compulsory Australians' majoritarian preferences were already apparent, in Saturday voting, in the flexible voting arrangements, and in another of our distinctive features, preferential voting for Lower House seats. This began in 1918 at the insistence of the new Country Party to avoid splitting the non-labour vote. With first-past-the-post voting it was possible for a candidate to win who was not supported by the majority of voters. With preferential voting if no candidate received more than 50 per cent of first preference votes, then second preferences were distributed, until one candidate had more than 50 per cent of preferences. The majority thus elected the candidate who was least disliked.

Majoritarian democracy is a close companion of egalitarianism. If government is to deliver the greatest happiness to the greatest number then the greatest number need to vote. Every one counts as one and property has no special claims. We know from voluntary systems that the poor and marginalised are least likely to vote, but with compulsory voting no political party can afford to ignore a substantial group of voters. Policies pitched only at the comfortable just won't fly.

Compulsory voting and registration also foster political engagement, compelling new citizens and young people who come of voting age into the polity and forcing them to pay at least minimal attention to parties, leaders and issues and ensuring that the polity includes us all. It also lowers the political temperature, ensuring that moderate citizens, with no axes to grind, turn out to balance the zealots of both right and left.

In his 1998 Boyer Lectures David Malouf said that 'The spirit of Holiday hovers over our election boxes'.

> Voting for us is a family occasion, a duty fulfilled, as often as not, on the way to the beach, so that children early get a sense of it as an obligation, but a light one, a duty casually undertaken. And it can seem casual. But the fact that voters so seldom spoil their vote, either deliberately or by accident, in a place where voting is compulsory and voting procedures are often extremely complicated, speaks for an electorate that has taken the trouble to inform itself because it believes these things matter, and of a citizenship lightly but seriously assumed.[21]

Although Malouf's is a Queensland perspective, where there are many more beach days than, say, in north-west Tasmania, his description captures well the mildness of our political culture. On election days we shrink from overt expressions of hostility, chit-chatting in the queue with people who may well be voting to put back a government we abhor, and perhaps buying a sizzled sausage to support a worthy local cause.

Observing the 2016 presidential election in the United States, Dennis Altman commented that 'there was no sense of the community that Australians associate with elections, no enthusiasts handing out election materials, no sausage sizzle or school fetes'. Similarly, Bevan Shields described Britain's voting in the 2019 General Election as 'an entirely grim affair'. 'You can forget that tasty democracy sausage. Or any shred of community spirit, really.'[22]

The democracy sausage is a recent symbol, created by the social media generation, but its rapid spread is due to the way this humble, egalitarian, no-fuss meat condenses the majoritarian accessibility of Australia's electoral system. The democracy sausage tells us that despite the many reasons to be cynical and frustrated by our politics, there is also much to celebrate.

NOTES

Preface
1. Michael Dawson, Catherine Gidney & Donald Wright (eds) (2018) *Symbols of Canada*, Between the Lines, Toronto, 238.
2. National Museum of Australia, *Annual Reports*, 2010–12.

Land of symbols
1. Joseph Furphy (1903) *Such Is Life*, Bulletin Newspaper Co., Sydney, 117.
2. CJ Dennis (1916) *The Moods of Ginger Mick*, Angus & Robertson, Sydney, 131.
3. Victor Turner (1967) *The Forest of Symbols: Aspects of Ndembu Ritual*, Cornell University Press, Ithaca, NY, 28. Turner goes on to note a symbol's 'juxtaposition of the grossly physical and the structurally normative, of the organic and the social', so that 'norms and values, on the one hand, become saturated with emotion, while the gross and basic emotions become ennobled through contact with social values', 29–30.
4. Cf. Philip J Deloria (1999) *Playing Indians*, Yale University Press, New Haven; Dawson, Gidney & Wright (eds) (2018), *Symbols of Canada*, Between the Lines, Toronto; Roger Blackley (2018) *Galleries of Maoriland: Artists, Collectors and the Māori World, 1880–1910*, Auckland University Press, Auckland.
5. Jan Kociumbas (2003) Performances: Indigenisation and postcolonial culture. In Hsu-Ming Teo & Richard White (eds) *Cultural History in Australia*, University of New South Wales Press, Sydney; see also Boomerang chapter, 128, Crown chapter, 53 and Rainbow Serpent chapter, 347; cf. Dawson, Gidney & Wright, 5–7.
6. Richard White (1994) The outsider's gaze and the representation of Australia. In Don Grant & Graham Seal (eds) *Australia in the World: Perceptions and Possibilities*, Black Swan Press, Curtin University of Technology, Perth, 22–8.
7. Interview, ABC radio, 20 November 2008.
8. John Rickard (2017) *Australia: A Cultural History*, Monash University Publishing, Melbourne (though it should be noted in this case an Aboriginal bicentennial protest is foregrounded); Mark Peel & Christina Twomey (2011) *A History of Australia*, Palgrave Macmillan, London; also 2nd edition, 2018; Stuart Macintyre (2020) *A Concise History of Australia*, Cambridge University Press, Melbourne, 5th edition; Alison Bashford & Stuart Macintyre (eds) (2015) *Cambridge History of Australia*, vol. 2, Cambridge University Press, Melbourne.
9. Comparisons inevitably depend on what geographical area is counted. Matt Wade (2017) Is Melbourne already bigger than Sydney, 22 September, viewed 21 January 2020, <https://www.SMH.com.au/opinion/is-melbourne-already-bigger-than-sydney-20170922-gyn2k4.html>.
10. Raymond Williams (1980) *Problems in Materialism and Culture*, Verso, London, 40.
11. Trevor Howells & Michael Nicholson (1989) *Towards the Dawn: Federation Architecture in Australia 1890–1915*, Hale & Iremonger, Sydney.

12 WS Ramson (ed.) (1988) *The Australian National Dictionary: A Dictionary of Australianisms on Historical Principles*, Oxford University Press, Melbourne, 535.
13 *Australian Women's Weekly*, 8 March 1941, 16. Thanks to Louise Prowse for this reference.
14 *The All Australian Flag*, <www.allaustralianflag.com.au>, and thanks to James Parbery.
15 David Vines White, Somerset Herald (2008) Of sheep and emus, lions and kangaroos: 19th and early 20th century grants of arms to Australians, unpublished lecture, 8 November 2008, State Library of New South Wales.
16 Cited in James Curran (2004) *The Power of Speech*, Melbourne University Press, Melbourne, 79.
17 See the prime minister's official website, viewed 10 December 2008, <www.pm.gov.au/australia/symbols/icons.cfm>. Now available at Australian Web Archive, NLA; email communication from Michael Parry, National Symbols Officer, Department of the Prime Minister and Cabinet, 29 October 2019.
18 Samantha Hutchinson & Stephen Brook (2021) PM has mansplaining down to a fine art, says Banks, *Sydney Morning Herald*, 5 July, viewed 11 July 2021, <https://www.SMH.com.au/national/pm-has-mansplaining-down-to-a-fine-art-says-banks-20210705-p5871a.html>.
19 Alison Holland & Fiona Paisley (2005) Fernando, Anthony Martin (1864–1949) *Australian Dictionary of Biography*, Supplementary Volume, Melbourne University Press, Melbourne, 127–8; Fiona Paisley (2012) *The Lone Protestor: AM Fernando in Australia and Europe*, Aboriginal Studies Press, Canberra, 99–100.
20 Mimmo Cozzolino (1980) *Symbols of Australia*, Penguin Books, Melbourne.
21 On banal nationalism, see Michael Billig (1995) *Banal Nationalism*, Sage, London; Tim Edensor (2002) *National Identity, Popular Culture and Everyday Life*, Berg, Oxford.
22 See AustralianPhotographers.org, Hou Leong, viewed 28 March 2021, <http://www.australianphotographers.org/artists/hou-leong>.
23 For jocular popular outrage on this phenomenon, see *Sydney Morning Herald*, 21 October 2006, 24; 24 October 2006, 20; 25 October 2006, 22.
24 See Paige Murphy, Creatives review Australia's new brand, viewed 28 March 2021, <https://www.adnews.com.au/news/creatives-review-australia-s-new-brand>.
25 When we sought permission from Kraft to use an image of theirs in the 1st edition, the company wanted the right to vet the text. We found other images.
26 See Matesong (Official Video) Tourism Australia Ad 2019, viewed 20 January 2020, <https://www.youtube.com/watch?v=QMAq8F8N2Fg>; Ricki Green (2019) Kylie Minogue invites Brits Down Under in new Tourism Australia campaign via M&C Saatchi, 26 December, viewed 20 January 2020, <https://campaignbrief.com/kylie-minogue-invites-brits-down-under-in-new-tourism-australia-campaign-via-mc-saatchi/>.
27 Carole Pateman (1988) *The Sexual Contract*, Polity Press, London; Marilyn Lake (1992) Mission impossible: How men gave birth to the Australian nation: Nationalism, gender and other seminal acts, *Gender and History*, 4(3), 305–22.
28 Maria Nugent (2011) 'You really only made it because you needed the money': Aboriginal Women and Shellwork Production, 1870s to 1970s, *Labour History*, 101, 71–90.
29 KS Inglis (1997) Men, women and war memorials: Anzac Australia. In Richard White & Penny Russell (eds) *Memories and Dreams: Reflections on Twentieth-Century Australia: Pastiche 2*, Allen & Unwin, Sydney, 44–5.
30 See the proliferation of national symbols in Jennifer Isaacs (1987) *The Gentle Arts: 200 Years of Australian Women's Domestic and Decorative Arts*, Lansdowne Press, Sydney.

31　Anthony D Buckley (ed.) (1998) *Symbols in Northern Ireland*, Institute of Irish Studies, Belfast, 2; for battles around Irish symbols, see Ewan Morris (2005) *Our Own Devices: National Symbols and Political Conflict in Twentieth-Century Ireland*, Irish Academic Press, Dublin.

32　John Howard's term, used in a speech to the Queensland branch of the Liberal Party, September 1996; Andrew Marcus (2001) *Race: John Howard and the Remaking of Australia*, Allen & Unwin, Sydney, 99. On 'sentimental nationalism', see Mark McKenna & Stuart Ward (2007) 'It's really moving mate': The Gallipoli pilgrimage and sentimental nationalism in Australia, *Australian Historical Studies*, 38, April, 129.

Southern Cross

1　Vivian Robson (1969) *The Fixed Stars and Constellations in Astrology*, Weiser, New York, 40; Elly Dekker (1990) The light and the dark: A reassessment of the discovery of the Coalsack Nebula, the Magellanic Clouds and the Southern Cross, *Annals of Science*, 47, 555–7.

2　Frank Cayley (1966) *Flag of Stars*, Rigby, Adelaide, 15.

3　Quoted in Luciano Formisano (ed.) (1992) *Letters from a New World: Amerigo Vespucci's Discovery of America*, Marsilio, New York, 6–7 (reference omitted). For academic debates concerning the discovery of the Southern Cross, see Pierre Chaunu (1979) *European Expansion in the Later Middle Ages*, trans. Katharine Bertram, Elsevier North Holland, New York, 254; Anne McCormick & Derek McDonnell (1989) *Letter of Andrea Corsali 1516: With Additional Material*, Hordern House, Potts Point, 8; Dekker (1990), 533–5; Joaquim Bensaude (1967) *L'Astronomie Nautique au Portugal à l'Epoque des Grandes Découvertes*, Meridian, Amsterdam, 252–4.

4　Cayley (1966), 15–16.

5　EGR Taylor (1956) *The Haven-Finding Art: A History of Navigation from Odysseus to Captain Cook*, Hollis & Carter, London, 8; Patricia Seed (1995) *Ceremonies of Possession in Europe's Conquest of the New World, 1492–1640*, Cambridge University Press, Cambridge, 105.

6　Maria Seta Guiseppe (1992) *The Glorious Constellations*, trans. Karin H Ford, Abrams, New York, 299; Richard Feinberg (1988) *Polynesian Seafaring and Navigation: Ocean Travel in Anutan Culture and Society*, Kent State University Press, Kent, 101; Seed (1995), 105; Raymond Haynes, Roslynn Haynes, David Malin & Richard McGee (1996) *Explorers of the Southern Sky: A History of Australian Astronomy*, Cambridge University Press, New York, 17.

7　Jorge Canizares Esguerra (1999) New world, new stars: Patriotic astrology and the invention of Indian and creole bodies in colonial Spanish America, 1600–1650, *American Historical Review*, 104, 50–1.

8　See Wattle chapter, 14 and Pavlova chapter, 282.

9　John Bingle (1996) *The Illustrated Retrospect of the Present Century*, quoted in Carol A Foley (1996) *The Australian Flag: Colonial Relic or Contemporary Icon?*, Federation Press, Leichhardt, 37.

10　Raffaello Carboni (1855) *The Eureka Stockade: The Consequence of Some Pirates Wanting on Quarter-Deck a Rebellion*, JP Atkinson, Melbourne, 50, 68; Deborah Wickham (2000) *The Eureka Flag: Our Starry Banner*, Ballarat Heritage Services, Ballarat, 13–17; *Ballarat Times*, 30 November 1854; see also Claire Wright (2013) *The Forgotten Rebels of Eureka*, Text, Melbourne, 381–6.

11　David Day (2005) *Claiming a Continent*, Harper Perennial, Pymble, 215; Letter, Sir Charles Hotham to Sir G Grey, 20 December 1854, quoted in Bob O'Brien (1998)

Massacre at Eureka: The Untold Story, Sovereign Hill Museums Association, Ballarat, 110; Letter, Captain Thomas to Major-General Sir Robert Nickle, 3 December 1854, reprinted in O'Brien (1998), 112; SDS Huyghue, *The Ballarat Riots*, manuscript reprinted in O'Brien (1998), 19; Transcript of Eureka Trial (1855), quoted in *Eureka: The First Australian Republic?*, Ballarat Fine Art Gallery, Ballarat, 3; *Ballarat Times*, 30 November 1854; *Age*, 3 January 1855.

12 Charles S Blackton (1955) The dawn of Australian national feeling, 1850–1856, *Pacific Historical Review*, 24, 128; Cayley (1966), 61, 92.

13 Helen Irving (1999) *To Constitute a Nation: A Cultural History of Australia's Constitution*, Cambridge University Press, Melbourne, 32; *Naval and Military Gazette*, 30 April 1870; Cayley (1966), 37, 66; Foley (1996), 38–9.

14 *Argus*, 11 July 1874, quoted in CMH Clark (1962–99) *A History of Australia*, vol. 5, Melbourne University Press, Melbourne, 130–1; Cayley (1966), 61.

15 Quoted in Foley (1996), 65.

16 Haynes et al. (1996), 2.

17 Graeme MacLennan (2008) Australia's Christian heritage, viewed 29 July 2008, <www.cdp.org.au/vic/australiaschristianheritage1.asp>; I am grateful to Michael Symons for this reference.

18 Karen Fox (2022) *Honouring a Nation: A History of Australia's Honours System*, ANU Press, Canberra (forthcoming).

19 Michael Willis & Geoffrey Gold (1976) Eureka, our heritage. In Geoffrey Gold (ed.) (1976) *Eureka: Rebellion beneath the Southern Cross*, Rigby, Adelaide, 91–2; Len Fox (1973) *Eureka and its Flag*, Mullaya Publications, Canterbury, 33.

20 *Hummer*, 13 February 1892, quoted in Willis & Gold (1976), 94.

21 Willis & Gold (1976), 91; Richard White (2005) Symbols of Australia. In Martyn Lyons & Penny Russell (eds) *Australia's History: Themes & Debates*, University of New South Wales Press, Sydney, 121.

22 Alice Brennan (2006) Southern Cross tattoos (transcript), *Triple J Hack*, 27 April, <www.abc.net.au/triplej/hack/notes/s1625883.htm>; Annalise Walliker (2008) Young Aussies flag favourites, *Herald-Sun*, 26 January; Such is life for proudly inked Aussies, *Northern Territory News*, 27 January 2008.

23 Luke Wong (2018) Southern Cross tattoos losing their lustre, leaving many bearers opting to cover up, 26 January, viewed 21 March 2021, <https://www.abc.net.au/news/2018-01-26/trend-of-covering-up-and-removing-southern-cross-tattoos/9360746>; WANTED: Southern cross tattoo cover up suggestions, viewed 21 March 2021, <https://www.reddit.com/r/australia/comments/5451p0/wanted_southern_cross_tattoo_cover_up_suggestions/>.

Kangaroo

1 Jerry Seinfeld (2007) Three questions, *Sydney Morning Herald*, 26 November, 28; Jeremy Berlin, *National Geographic Magazine*, Australia's beloved kangaroos are now controversial pests, February 2019, viewed 21 March 2021, <https://www.nationalgeographic.com/magazine/2019/02/australia-kangaroo-beloved-symbol-becomes-pest/>; Marcus Clarke cited in Bernard Smith (ed.) (1975) *Documents on Art and Taste in Australia: The Colonial Period 1770–1914*, Oxford University Press, Melbourne, 135; Pelsaert quoted in Terence J Dawson (1995) *Kangaroo: Biology of the Largest Marsupials*, Cornell University Press, New York, 139; William Dampier (1939) *Voyage to New Holland &c. in the Year 1699*, (ed.) JA Williamson, Argonaut Press,

London, Volume 1, Chapter 3; Diary entry for 26 August 1770. In JC Beaglehole (ed.) (1962) *The 'Endeavour' Journal of Joseph Banks 1768–1771*, Angus & Robertson, Sydney; Captain WJL Wharton (ed.) (1968) *Captain Cook's Journal During his First Voyage Round the World made in H.M. Bark Endeavour, 1768–71: A Literal Transcription of the Original Mss*, Libraries Board of South Australia, Adelaide, Chapter 8.

2 HJ Frith & JH Calaby (1969) *Kangaroos*, Cheshire Publishing, Melbourne, Plate 1.
3 Dawson (1995), 4.
4 Frith & Calaby (1969) *Kangaroos*, 5–6; Terence Lane (1979) *The Kangaroo in the Decorative Arts: Exhibition Catalogue for the National Gallery of Victoria, 18th December 1979–3rd February 1980*, Gardner Printing, Victoria, 2; Ken Gelder & Rachael Weaver (2020) *The Colonial Kangaroo*, Miegunyah, Melbourne, 16; John Simons (2013) *Kangaroo*, Reaktion Books, London.
5 Gelder & Weaver (2020), 3.
6 Dawson (1995), 141; Michael Archer, Tim Flannery & Gorden Grigg (1985) *The Kangaroo*, Weldons, Sydney, 106.
7 Gelder & Weaver, Chapter 3; Bill Hornadge (1972) *If It Moves, Shoot It: A Squint at Some Australian Attitudes towards the Kangaroo*, Review Publications, Dubbo, 20–4.
8 Beth Hatton (1997) Handmade, underfoot. In *Floorcoverings in Australia 1800–1950*, Historic Houses Trust of NSW, Sydney, 29.
9 Martin Denny (1981) Kangaroos: An historical perspective. In *Kangaroos and Other Macropods of New South Wales*, NSW National Parks and Wildlife Service, Sydney, 43.
10 Dawson (1995), 147–8; Denny (1981), 42.
11 Lane (1979), 2–4; Mimmo Cozzolino (1980) *Symbols of Australia*, Penguin Books, Melbourne.
12 Description of the 1912 Commonwealth Coat of Arms, viewed 23 January 2008, <www.itsanhonour. gov.au/coat-arms/index.cfm#significance>.
13 Hornadge (1972), 20–4.
14 George Stubbs' kangaroo and dingo paintings to stay in UK, 6 November 2013, viewed 22 February 2021, <https://www.bbc.com/news/entertainment-arts-24826579#>; also, viewed 22 February 2021, <https://www.bbc.com/news/av/entertainment-arts-24839551>.
15 Steele Rudd (1998 [1899]) *On Our Selection*, University of Sydney, Sydney, 84.
16 Episode 233, 'Eight Misbehavin', aired 21 November 1999.
17 Barron Field (1819) The kangaroo. In *First Fruits of Australian Poetry*, George Howe, Sydney, 7–8.
18 *Table Talk*, 7 September 1888, 1; *Table Talk*, 3 April 1891, 13; *Table Talk*, 10 April 1891, 16; *Table Talk*, 17 April 1891, 13.
19 Margaret Williams & Hilary Golder (2000) Fighting Jack: A brief Australian melodrama, *Australasian Drama Studies*, 36, 120.
20 *Newcastle Morning Herald*, 3 November 1891; *Table Talk*, 26 March 1891.
21 Lindy Kerin (2010) Gloves off over boxing kangaroo dispute, ABC News, 5 February, accessed 21 November 2019, <https://www.abc.net.au/news/2010-02-05/gloves-off-over-boxing-kangaroo-dispute/2568738>; Decision on boxing kangaroo 'ridiculous', news.com.au, 5 February 2010, accessed 21 November 2019, <https://www.news.com.au/breaking-news/decision-on-boxing-kangaroo-ridiculous/news-story/2e14526d7e4b7c2303c33c14a0b914f1> and Australian Olympics Committee, The Boxing Kangaroo 1 AOC, accessed 21 November 2019, <https://www.olympics.com.au/the-boxing-kangaroo/>.

22 Julie McNamara (2007) Media sinks teeth into kangaroo shark attack, *Geelong Advertiser*, 14 December.
23 Michaela Farrington (2007) Kangaroo killing shark strikes again, *Daily Telegraph*, 12 December.
24 In the remake the kangaroo does not possess 'Superskippy' powers. Ironically, however, considering the wild flights of fancy in the original series, the *New Adventures* were heavily criticised by the Australian Broadcasting Tribunal as 'insufficiently factual' for children. See Shelley Dempsey (1991) Skippy's back, *Sun Herald*, 8 September, 18; Broadcasting authority slams Skippy (1992) *Broadcast*, 20 March.
25 Tom O'Regan & Susan Ward (2006) Experimenting with the local and transnational: Television drama production on the Gold Coast, *Continuum: Journal of Media and Cultural Studies*, 20(1), 20.
26 Ulla Rahbek (2007) Revisiting *Dot and the Kangaroo*: Finding a way in the Australian bush, *Australian Humanities Review*, 41, 3.
27 Marcie Muir (1994) Stirring of the gum leaves, *Voices*, 4(3), 87.
28 *Australian War Memorial Collection* (2008) MEA0597, viewed 10 January 2008, <http://cas.awm.gov.au/photograph/MEA0597>.
29 *Australian War Memorial Collection* (2008) UK0396, viewed 13 February 2008, <http://cas.awm.gov.au/photograph/UK0396>.
30 *Royal Australian Airforce* (2008) 'Air Force roundel', viewed 17 October 2008, <www.airforce.gov.au/aboutus/roundel.htm>.
31 Annette Carter (ed.) (2005) *I Still Call Australia Home: The Qantas Story 1920–2005*, Focus Publishing, Sydney, 9, 116, 117.
32 Qantas media release, 27 October 2016, <https://www.qantasnewsroom.com.au/media-releases/flying-kangaroo-receives-an-update-as-qantas-prepares-to-welcome-dreamliner/?print=1.>
33 Tourism Australia (2007) Brand Australia industry toolkit, viewed 10 January 2007, <www.tourism.australia.com/Marketing.asp?sub=0413&al=2119>; Qantas Corporate Communication (2007) 'New logo takes Qantas into the A380 era', 24 July, viewed 15 January 2007, <www.qantas.com.au/regions/dyn/au/publicaffairs/details?ArticleID=2007/jul07/3621>; Horizon Research Corporation for Australian Made (2007) Australian Made consumer study, 6, 5 January, viewed 10 December 2007, <www.australianmade.com.au/objectlibrary/260&filename=Australian%20Made,%20Australian%20Grown%20in%20LA%202005.pdf>, 16; Morgan Research for Australian Made (2006) Australian Made report: Australian Made logo awareness and perceptions, Morgan Research, Victoria, viewed 19 December 2019, <https://www.australianmade.com.au/why-buy-australian-made/about-the-logo/>.
34 Simons (2013), 183.
35 For Darwin's objections and later concern at lack of control over killing see Dawson (1995), 141, 143, 145; RSPCA (2008), viewed 29 February 2008, <www.rspca.org.au/about/history_foundation.asp>; for a discussion of the Wildlife Preservation Society see Vincent Serventy (1988) The history of kangaroo conservation since human settlement of Australia, *Australian Zoologist*, 24(3), 180–1; Australian Wildlife Protection Council (2008), viewed 29 February 2008, <www.awpc.org.au/newsite/about/about.html>.
36 MA Burgman & DB Lindenmayer (1998) *Conservation Biology for the Australian Environment*, Surrey Beatty & Sons, Sydney, 172–3.
37 Ingrid Witte (2005) Kangaroos – misunderstood and maligned reproductive miracle workers. In *Kangaroos: Myths and Realities*, Australian Wildlife Protection Council,

	Melbourne, 188–207; David Croft (1999) When big is beautiful. In *The Kangaroo Betrayed*, 2nd edition, Australian Wildlife Protection Council, Melbourne, 70–3.
38	For example, VIVA! (2008) Australia massacres its national symbol on the capital's doorstep, viewed 29 February 2008, <www.savethekangaroo.com/newsarchive/20040722.shtml>; Maryland Wilson (ed.) (1999) *The Kangaroo Betrayed*, Australian Wildlife Protection Council, Melbourne, cover.
39	VIVA! (2008) Exotic meat campaign, viewed 29 February 2008, <www.viva.org.uk/campaigns/exoticmeat/index.htm#Kangaroo>; VIVA! (2008) Adidas: Keep the kangaroo boots off Beck's feet, viewed 29 February 2008, <www.savethekangaroo.com/adidas/beckham.shtml>; PETA (2008) Save kangaroos —Please stop SB 880!, viewed 29 February 2008, <http://getactive.peta.org/ campaign/ca_kanga_commerce_p>; VIVA! USA (2008) Kangaroo victory in California, viewed 29 February 2008, <www.vivausa.org/campaigns/ kangaroo/kangaroo.html>; John Kelly (2004) *Selling the Kangaroo Industry to the World*, Rural Industries Research and Development Corporation, Canberra, 1; <https://www.congress.gov/bill/117th-congress/house-bill/917/text>.
40	M Archer & B Beale (2004) *Going Native*, Hodder, Sydney, 139–53; Gordon Grigg (1988) Kangaroo harvesting and conservation of the sheep rangelands, *Australian Zoologist*, 24(3), 124–8; Archer, Flannery & Grigg (1985), 236–54.
41	Des Purtell (1997) *Improving Consumer Perceptions of Kangaroo Products*, RIRDC, Canberra, i–x; Archer & Beale (2004), 149; James Woodford (2008) Worth two in the bush, *Sydney Morning Herald*, 26–27 January, 28–9; Malcolm Fisher (2008) Leave our hunted national symbol off the menu, *Sydney Morning Herald*, 28 January, 10.
42	Nancy Cushing (2019) To Eat or Not to Eat Kangaroo: Bargaining over Food Choice in the Anthropocene, *M/C Journal*, 22(2), <https://doi.org/10.5204/mcj.1508>.
43	Archer, Flannery & Grigg (1985), 252.

Crown

1	Tohby Riddle (1993) *The Royal Guest*, Hodder and Stoughton, Sydney.
2	Anne Twomey (2006) *The Chameleon Crown: The Queen and her Australian Governors*, Federation Press, Annandale.
3	Frank Bongiorno (2000) 'Commonwealthmen and Republicans': Dr H.V. Evatt, the Monarchy and India, *Australian Journal of Politics and History*, 1, 33–50, 42.
4	Law Reform Commission New South Wales (1997) Circulation of legal advice to government, Issues paper 13, <www.lawlink.nsw.gov.au/lrc.nsf/pages/IP13CHP3>.
5	James Cook (2003) *The Journals*, Penguin Classics, London, 170–1.
6	For more on the relationship between Aboriginal people and the crown, see Mark McKenna (2004) *This Country: A Reconciled Republic?*, University of New South Wales Press, Sydney.
7	Herman Merivale (1870) The colonial question, *Fortnightly Review*, February.
8	Letter, Lyons to Baldwin, 5 December 1936, M2270/1 National Archives of Australia.
9	Menzies in Mark McKenna (2004), 98–101; Queen Elizabeth II (1954) Queen's farewell broadcast, 1 April 1954. In 'The Queen's speeches 1954–1992', MS 9174 National Library of Australia. The Queen's speech in Parliament appears in Rod Kemp & Marion Stanton (eds) (2004) *Speaking for Australia: Parliamentary Speeches that Shaped our Nation* (2004), Allen & Unwin, Sydney, 156–8.
10	Alan Atkinson (1993) *The Muddle-Headed Republic*, Oxford University Press, Melbourne, 29.

11 Samuel Pepys (2003) *The Diaries of Samuel Pepys: A Selection*, Penguin Classics, London, 130–2.
12 Martyn Lyons (2021) *Dear Prime Minister: Letters to Robert Menzies, 1949–1966*, Univerity of New South Wales Press, Sydney, 133.
13 *Daily Telegraph*, 24 June 1920, 1; *Sydney Morning Herald*, 24 June 1920, 6.
14 Coronation celebrations in immigration centres, A445/1 National Archives of Australia, 1953.
15 Quoted in Rex Ingamells (1954) *Royalty and Australia*, Hallcraft, Melbourne, 81.
16 New Australian coins may depict King bareheaded, *Sydney Morning Herald*, 15 October 1936, 1.
17 Marc Bloch (1973) *The Royal Touch: Sacred Monarchy and Scrofula in England and France*, Routledge & Kegan Paul, London, 223.
18 David Flint (1999) *The Cane Toad Republic*, Wakefield Press, Adelaide, 49; Tony Abbott (1995) *The Minimal Monarchy and Why it Makes Sense for Australia*, Wakefield Press, Adelaide, 137.
19 Paul Hasluck (1979) *The Office of the Governor General*, Melbourne University Press, Melbourne, 8; David Leach (2003) Crown as a symbol of unity in the Australian Defence Forces and as a non-political source of allegiance, Address to the 2003 ACM national conference, <www.norepublic.com.au/index.php?option=com_content&task=view&id=176& Itemid=24>. For further discussion of the referendum, see also Dennis Altman (2021), *God Save the Queen: The Strange Persistence of Monarchies*, Scribe, Melbourne, 72–7.

Map
1 John Forrest (1889) Lecture to the Geographical Section, 30 August 1888, *Report of the First Meeting of the Australasian Association for the Advancement of Science*, Sydney, 352.
2 Alan Atkinson (2005) Tasmania and the multiplicity of nations, *Tasmanian Historical Research Association*, 52, 189–200.
3 Elizabeth McMahon (2001) Tasmania: Island or archipelago, trinket or chain. In Susan Ballyn et al. (eds) *Changing Geographies: Essays on Australia*, University of Barcelona, Barcelona, 115–16 (citing Maturin Ballou & Hume Nisbet).
4 Islandhopping, viewed 29 January 2008, <www.islandhopping.com>; Holiday wizard, viewed 29 January 2008, <www.holidaywizard.co.uk/seeinsidebrochure/Kuoni-Travel>.
5 Eugen Weber (1977) *Peasants into Frenchmen: The Modernization of Rural France*, Stanford University Press, London, 334–6 (thanks to Richard White for this reference); Benedict Anderson (1991) *Imagined Communities: Reflections on the Origin and Spread of Nationalism*, Verso, London, 171–4; see also Robert Dixon (2014) 'A Nation for a Continent': Australian Literature and the Cartographic Imaginary of the Federation Era, *Antipodes: A North American journal of Australian literature*, 28(1), 141–54.
6 Anon. (1986) New colony of South Australia. In Brian Dickey & Peter Howell (eds) *South Australia's Foundation: Select Documents*, Wakefield Press, Adelaide, 59–60 (original emphasis).
7 Anne Coote (2004) Space, time and sovereignty: Literate culture and colonial nationhood in New South Wales up to 1860, PhD thesis, University of New England, 125–40, 160–1, 167–93.
8 Anon. (1986), 59–60.
9 Alan Atkinson (1997) *The Europeans in Australia: A History*, vol. 1, Oxford University Press, Melbourne, 188, 248–50, and Atkinson (2004) *The Europeans in Australia: A History*, vol. 2, Oxford University Press, Melbourne, 87–8.

10   Ernest Giles (1889) *Australia Twice Traversed: The Romance of Exploration* (two vols), Sampson Low, London, vol. 1, lv.
11   John Updike (2008) The clarity of things, *New York Review of Books*, 26 June, 11.
12   Emil Jung (1874) Report of the Central Board of Education, 13. In *Parliamentary Papers of South Australia*, vol. 2, no. 44, Govt Printer, Adelaide, 1875, 13.
13   Edward Dewhirst (1876) Report of the Council of Education, 11. In *Parliamentary Papers of South Australia* (1877), vol. 2, no. 44, Govt Printer, Adelaide, 1877; Edward Dewhirst (1880) Report of the Minister controlling Education, 4. In *Parliamentary Papers of South Australia*, vol. 3, no. 44, Govt Printer, Adelaide, 1880.
14   Jules Michelet (1869) Preface to his *Histoire de France*, quoted in Paul Ricoeur (2006) *Memory, History, Forgetting*, trans. Kathleen Blamey & David Pellauer, University of Chicago Press, Chicago, 380 (my emphasis).
15   Edmond Marin la Meslée (1883) Speech at 'Preliminary Meeting to Establish a Geographical Society', 2 April. In AC Macdonald, JH Maiden & JH Myring (eds) (1885) *Special Volume of the Proceedings of the Geographical Society of Australasia*, Government Printer, Sydney, 4; E Marin la Meslée to Harrie Wood, 26 April 1883, and to John Shillinglaw, 28 April 1883, Mitchell Library ML A2664, ff. 5–6, 8–9; Jules Michelet (1844) *The History of France*, trans. Walter K Kelly, two vols, Chapman & Hall, London, vol. 1, 264, 331, 336; Edmond Marin la Meslée (1973) *The New Australia*, trans. and ed. Russel Ward, Heinemann, London, 32, 33.
16   Minutes of Proceedings of the Intercolonial Meteorological Conference (1879). In *Parliamentary Papers of South Australia*, vol. 3, no. 32, Govt Printer, Adelaide, 1880.
17   *Advertiser*, 9 August 1905; *Sydney Morning Herald*, 2 November 1907; *Age*, 28 November 1910.
18   Salman Rushdie (2008) *The Enchantress of Florence*, Jonathan Cape, London.

Cooee
1   Peter Bromley Maling (1960) *Samuel Butler at Mesopotamia, Together with Butler's 'Forest Creek' Manuscript and his Letters to Tripp and Acland*, Government Printer, Wellington, 45–6.
2   Richard White (2001) Cooees across the strand: Australian travellers in London and the performance of national identity, *Australian Historical Studies*, 32(116), April, 109–27; see also Geoffrey Blainey (2003) *Black Kettle and Full Moon: Daily Life in a Vanished Australia*, Penguin/Viking, Melbourne.
3   Paul Carter (1992) *The Sound In-Between: Voice, Space, Performance*, University of New South Wales Press, Sydney; John Hunter (1793) *An Historical Journal of the Transactions at Port Jackson and Norfolk Island*, John Stockdale, London, 149.
4   The classic is Marcus Clarke's short story, Pretty Dick (1896). In *Australian Tales*, A & W Bruce, Melbourne.
5   [JC Hotten] (1864) *The Slang Dictionary; or, The Vulgar Words, Street Phrases and 'Fast' Expressions of High and Low Society*, John Camden Hotten, London, 107.
6   White (2001), 112–16; see also Angela Woollacott (2001) *To Try Her Fortune in London: Australian Women, Colonialism and Modernity*, Oxford University Press, Oxford, 175–6.
7   Ernest William Hornung (1908 [1890]) *A Bride from the Bush*, John Murray, London, 184.
8   According to Iain Aitch (2008) *We're British, Innit? An Irreverent A–Z of All Things British*, HarperCollins, London, the cooee is 'uniquely British'.
9   DH Lawrence (2005 [1928]) *Lady Chatterley's Lover*, Collector's Library, London, 259.

10   Justin McCarthy MP & Mrs Campbell-Praed (1888) *The Ladies' Gallery*, Richard Bentley & Son, London, 1.
11   Henry Lawson, The southern scout or, the natives of the land. In Colin Roderick (ed.) (1967) *Henry Lawson: Collected Verse*, vol. 1, Angus & Robertson, Sydney, 224; Henry Lawson (1924) Jack Cornstalk. In Henry Lawson, *Humorous Verses*, Cornstalk, Sydney, 106.
12   I Nathan (1848) *The Southern Euphrosyne and Australian Miscellany*, Whittaker, London, 103–4.
13   Richard White & Emily Pollnitz (2006) Cooee music, *This Century's Review: A Privileged Source of Information*, special issue 'Tuning', 3, <www.thiscenturyreview.com/history0.html?&L=0>.
14   Kenneth Mackay (1887) Bushed. In *Stirrup Jingles from the Bush and the Turf and Other Rhymes*, Edwards, Dunlop, Sydney, 22–3.
15   Mimmo Cozzolino (1980) *Symbols of Australia*, Cozbook/Penguin, Melbourne, 33–4, 106, 148, 172; *Aussie*, 15 November 1921, 49.
16   CMH Clark (ed.) (1955) *Select Documents in Australian History 1851–1900*, Angus & Robertson, Sydney, 787.
17   An Australian [Maude Wordsworth James] (c. 1917) *The 'Coo-ee' Call*, Sands & McDougall, Adelaide, 30; News report cited in Justine Greenwood (2008) The 1908 visit of the Great White Fleet: Displaying modern Sydney, *History Australia*, 5(3), 77.
18   Phyllis (1913) In the looking glass, *British-Australasian*, 31 July, 20.
19   Julia Dean (2006) Along the scouting trail: The development of the boy scouts in Australia, History IV thesis, Department of History, University of Sydney, 28–9.
20   An Australian [Maude Wordsworth James] (c. 1917), 4.
21   White (2001), 125–6.
22   Land of symbols, 22–3.
23   Maude Wordsworth James (1897–1907) Scrapbooks, State Archives of Western Australia, MN 1499, 295–8.
24   An Australian [Maude Wordsworth James] (c. 1917), 5.
25   Athol Lewis (1917) Diary entry for 10 March 1917, La Trobe MS10863. Cited in Bart Ziino (1999) Journeys to war: Experience of Australian recruits in the Great War, MA thesis, University of Melbourne, 49.
26   A Matchett (c. 1916) Coo-ee Australia. In *Coo-ee: Gift Souvenir Dedicated to the Australian Imperial Forces*, Norman Bros, Melbourne, 1.
27   *The Times* (London), 14 November 1957, 17.
28   Graeme Smith (1994) Australian Country Music and the Hillbilly Yodel, *Popular Music* 13(3) 297–311, 306; Toby Martin (2015) *Yodelling Boundary Riders: Country Music in Australia since the 1920s*, Lyrebird Press, Melbourne, 119.
29   James Curran (2006) *The Power of Speech: Australian Prime Ministers Defining the National Image*, Melbourne University Press, Melbourne, 78.
30   James Valentine, ABC radio 702, 27 July 2021.
31   Helen Thomas (1956) *As it Was and World Without End*, Faber & Faber, London, 182; Coo-ee! The echo of a poignant First World War parting rings out in Glasgow Cathedral, *The Telegraph*, viewed 20 January 2020, <https://www.telegraph.co.uk/history/world-war-one/11012568/Coo-ee-The-echo-of-a-poignant-First-World-War-parting-rings-out-in-Glasgow-Cathedral.html>.

Stamps

1 For an overview of relevant literature see Phil Deans & Hugo Dobson (2005) East Asian postage stamps as socio-political artefacts, *East Asia*, 22(2), 1–7. There are several authoritative catalogues of world stamps, of which those produced by Stanley Gibbons are best known in Australia. See also Dennis Altman (1991) *Paper Ambassadors: The Politics of Stamps*, Angus & Robertson, Sydney.
2 See House of Representatives debates, 21 August 1913.
3 Humphrey McQueen (1988) The Australian stamp: Image, design and ideology, *Arena*, 84.
4 Anne-Marie van de Ven (2002) Clients and designers: Australian stamps 1930–1960. In Michael Bogle (ed.) *Designing Australia: Readings in the History of Design*, Pluto Press, Sydney, 141.
5 Dennis Altman (1993) *The Comfort of Men*, Heinemann, Melbourne, 75.
6 For the controversy, see Lenore Nicklin (1988) Elusive stamp of approval, *Bulletin*, 22 March, 52–5.
7 See Jillian Barnes (2002) Resisting the captured image: How Gwoja Tjungurrayi, 'One Pound Jimmy', escaped the 'Stone Age'. In Ingereth Macfarlane & Mark Hannah (eds) *Transgressions: Critical Australian Indigenous Histories*, special issue of *Aboriginal History*, Monograph 16, ANU E Press, Canberra; and more generally Chris Healy (2008) *Forgetting Aborigines*, University of New South Wales Press, Sydney.
8 Hugo Dobson (2005) The stamp of approval, *East Asia*, 22(2), summer, 67.

Gum tree

1 A Gum Tree Guide, Centre for Plant Biodiversity Research, Canberra, viewed 1 February 2008, <www.chah.gov.au/cpbr/gum-tree/gum-tree.html>.
2 For a comprehensive manual on the botany and classification of the gum tree, see MIH Brooker & DA Kleinig (2006) *Field Guide to Eucalypts*, 3rd edition, Bloomings Books, Melbourne.
3 Rumours of the eucalypt's effectiveness as a cure for malaria were a major reason for its exportation overseas in the nineteenth century. In fact, the gum tree's greatest use was in preventing, rather than curing malaria: it dried up the swamps that bred mosquito larvae, thus helping to stop the spread of the disease. For a discussion of the history of exportation of the gum tree and its various uses overseas, see Ashley Hay (2002) *Gum*, Duffy & Snelgrove, Sydney.
4 The term 'gumsucker' refers to the shoots, known as 'suckers', which sprout from the rootstock of mature gum trees. In the Australian nationalist vocabulary 'gumsucker' describes the Australian-born, or, more specifically, those born in Victoria.
5 For further reading on gum leaf painting, see Sophie C Ducker (2001) *Story of gum leaf painting*, School of Botany, University of Melbourne.
6 Steve Parish (2006) *Gum Tree: An Australian Icon*, Steve Parish Publishing, Archerfield, Queensland.
7 Richard White (2005) Symbols of Australia. In Martyn Lyons & Penny Russell (eds) *Australia's History: Themes and Debates*, University of New South Wales Press, Sydney, 124; cf. Michael Dawson, Catherine Gidney & Donald Wright (eds) (2018) *Symbols of Canada*, Between the Lines, Toronto, 86–95; Claudia Bell (1996) *Inventing New Zealand: Everyday Myths of Pakeha Identity*, Penguin, Auckland, 38.
8 For a discussion of the role of the concept of Britain in Anglo–Australian identity, see NK Meaney (2001) Britishness and Australian identity: The problem of nationalism in Australian historiography, *Australian Historical Studies*, 32(116), 76–90.

9   Nathan Spielvogel (1913) Our gum trees. In *Our Gum Trees and Other Verses*, DW Paterson, Melbourne.
10 Baron Ferdinand von Mueller, author of the seminal gum tree catalogue, *Eucalyptographia*, claimed this in his (1889) *Second Systematic Census of Australian Plants*, printed by McCarron, Bird & Co. for the Victorian Government.
11 For further detail on the 'world's biggest tree' competition, see Geoffrey Edwards (2003) *Giant: Ancient and Historic Trees*, Geelong Gallery, Geelong. See also Tom Griffiths (2001) *Forests of Ash: An Environmental History*, Cambridge University Press, Cambridge & New York, for a comprehensive cultural and environmental history of *E. regnans* forests.
12 Barron Field (1822) 'Journey of an Excursion across the Blue Mountains of New South Wales, October 1822'. In George Mackaness (ed.) (1978) *Fourteen Journeys over the Blue Mountains of New South Wales, 1813–1841*, Review Publications, Dubbo, 120. Also Barron Field (1825) *Geographical Memoirs on New South Wales*, John Murray, London, 423.
13 Quoted in Elizabeth Johns, Andrew Sayers & Elizabeth Mankin Kornhauser, with Amy Ellis (1998) *New Worlds from Old: Nineteenth Century Australian and American Landscapes*, National Gallery of Australia, Canberra, 59. For more on the history of Australian landscape painters and their treatment of gum trees, as well as colonial relationships with, and uses for, gum trees generally, see Tim Bonyhady (2000) *The Colonial Earth*, Miegunyah Press, Carlton.
14 Richard White (1981) *Inventing Australia: Images and Identity 1688–1980*, George Allen & Unwin, Sydney, 85.
15 Quoted in Julian Howard Ashton (1929) Australia beautiful. In *Australia Beautiful: The Home Pictorial Annual*, 3.
16 Dorothea Mackellar (1930) Australia beautiful (editorial). In *Australia Beautiful: The Home Pictorial Annual*, 4.
17 (Beryl) Llywelyn Lucas (1927) To the gums, *Bulletin*, 3 November.
18 For further detail, see LJ Kaldor (2006) 'Hideous fidelity': Gum tree photography in Australia 1850–1950, Honours thesis, University of Sydney.
19 WK Hancock (1930) *Australia*, Ernest Benn, London.
20 Marjorie Barnard (1938) A mask of Australia for inaudible voices, *The Home*, 1 March, 25–27, 71.
21 Cazneaux first published this photograph in the *Home Annual*, 1 October 1938, under the name *Giant Gum from the Arid Land of the North, Wilpena, SA*. Ashley Hay notes that Cazneaux exhibited this photograph under a couple of different names in the late 1930s, including *A Mighty Gum* and *A Giant of the Arid North*. See Hay (2002), 138. In 1941, Cazneaux doubled the impact and the fame of this image by publishing a slightly different version of the same picture under the name *The Spirit of Endurance*.
22 Quoted in Hay (2002), 137.
23 Alison French (2003) *Seeing the Centre: The Art of Albert Namatjira 1902–1959*, National Gallery of Australia, Canberra.
24 Kath Walker (Oodgeroo Noonuccal) (1966) *The Dawn is at Hand*, Jacaranda, Brisbane, 10.
25 George Johnston (1964) *My Brother Jack*, Collins, London, 287–92.

Shark

1. A further elaboration of this argument can be found in Helen Tiffin (2009) Sharks and the Australian imaginary. In Susan Hosking, Rick Hosking, Rebecca Pannell & Nena Bierbaum (eds) *Something Rich and Strange: Sea changes, beaches and the littoral in the Antipodes*, Wakefield, Adelaide.
2. Michael Sturma (1986) The great Australian bite: Early shark attacks and the Australian psyche, *Great Circle*, 8(2), 78.
3. Sturma (1986), 78.
4. Nino Culotta [John O'Grady] (1957) *They're a Weird Mob*, Ure Smith, Sydney, 65.
5. Bill Bryson (2001) *Down Under*, Black Swan, Reading, 29.
6. Bryson (2001), 32.
7. See for example the advertising posters for the film *Jaws* and the cover of the *Australian Magazine*, 6–7 January 2001.
8. M Price (2001) Something out there, *Australian Magazine*, 6–7 January, 16.
9. D Richards (1992) Sharks, *Overland*, 128, 76.
10. See for example the *Weekend Australian*, 18–19 November 2001, 1. (Although the caption states that the shark has 'a doomed bull seal' in its jaws, the 'victim' is in fact an offal-filled plastic bag.)
11. Steve Baker (1993) *Picturing the Beast: Animals, Identity and Representation*, Manchester University Press, Manchester, 28–9.
12. *Jaws*, dir. Steven Spielberg, 1975.
13. The voice was that of *Peyton Place* star, Percy Rodrigues.
14. For an extended commentary on the uses of cannibalism in 'othering' human groups, see FP Barker (1998) *Colonial World*, Cambridge University Press, Cambridge. An 'othering' is to represent such humans as 'beastly', moving them to the 'animal' side of the species boundary, even though the act which precipitates this is the alleged *human* consumption of *human* flesh.
15. Price (2001), 16.
16. Nick Fiddes (1991) *Meat: A Natural Symbol*, Routledge, London.
17. Peter Matthiessen (1997) *Blue Meridian: The Search for the Great White Shark*, Penguin, New York, 5.
18. Tim Winton (1995–96) Blue water, dark shadows, *Independent Monthly*, December–January, 29.
19. Noel McLachlan (1989) *Waiting for the Revolution: A History of Australian Nationalism*, Penguin, Melbourne, 326.
20. Cited in Baiba Berzins (1988) *The Coming of Strangers: Life in Australia 1788–1822*, Collins/State Library of New South Wales, Sydney, 54.
21. Berzins (1988), 54; Russel Ward (1965 [1958]) *The Australian Legend*, Oxford University Press, Melbourne, 202.
22. Advertisement, *Sydney Gazette and New South Wales Advertiser*, 1(49), Sunday, 5 February 1804.
23. Paradoxically, while the shark is imaged as a threat to women – as in the famous poster for the film *Jaws* – it is also represented as 'female', its maw a *vagina dentata*. See for example, Jane Caputi (1987) *The Age of Sex Crime*, Popular Press, London, 147.
24. For details of this story, salaciously recounted, see *Famous Detective Stories*, 4(7–8), June and July 1950; also Vince Kelly (1963) *The Shark Arm Case*, Angus & Robertson, Sydney.
25. Dean Crawford (2008) *Shark*, Reaktion, London, 13.

26 For example, Raffaella Ciccarelli, prod., (2018) Great white shark attack victim hits out at use of drumlines, 9News, 30 September, viewed 24 January 2020, <https://www.9news.com.au/national/great-white-shark-survivor-drumline/a154b747-91f5-453e-9f34-5e43bcc66452>; Shark attack survivors unite to save sharks (2010) *Australian Geographic*, 14 September, viewed 27 January 2020, <https://www.australiangeographic.com.au/news/2010/09/shark-attack-survivors-unite-to-save-sharks/>; Blake Chapman (2017) *Shark Attacks: Myths, Misunderstandings and Human Fear*, CSIRO, Melbourne, v, 87.

Boomerang

1 Herb Smith (1975) *Boomerangs: Making and Throwing Them*, Littlehampton Printers, Sussex, 2.
2 See Michael Hitchcock & Ken Teague (eds) (2001) *Souvenirs: The Material Culture of Tourism*, Ashgate, Aldershot, 1.
3 Roland Barthes (1979) *The Eiffel Tower and Other Mythologies*, trans. Richard Howard, Hill & Wang, New York, 3–7.
4 For a discussion of the first Europeans in Australia as 'tourists' see Richard White (2005) *On Holidays: A History of Getting Away in Australia*, Pluto Press, Melbourne, 1–40.
5 See Philip Jones (2007) *Ochre and Rust: Artefacts and Encounters on Australian Frontiers*, Wakefield Press, Adelaide.
6 JC Beaglehole (ed.) (1963) *The Endeavour Journal of Joseph Banks 1768–1771*, Angus & Robertson, Sydney, vol. 2, 53.
7 See Keith Vincent Smith (1992) *King Bungaree: A Sydney Aborigine Meets the Great South Pacific Explorers, 1799–1830*, Kangaroo Press, Kenthurst, 67–8.
8 Traveller and journalist James St John wrote in the *Westminster Review* in 1830 that most of the writers 'who, in their reasonings on human nature, have had occasion to allude to the aboriginal inhabitants of Australia, appear to have delighted in representing them as the last link in the chain of humanity'. James St John (1830) Aboriginal natives of Australia, *Westminster Review*, 12, 166–86. In Judith Johnston & Monica Anderson (eds) (2005) *Australia Imagined: Views from the British Periodical Press 1800–1900*, University of Western Australia Press, Crawley, 71.
9 Philip Jones (1992) The boomerang's erratic flight: The mutability of ethnographic objects, *Journal of Australian Studies*, 35, 64.
10 Phillip Parker King (1827) *Narrative of a Survey of the Intertropical and Western Coasts of Australia: Performed between the Years 1818 and 1822*, John Murray, London, vol. 2, 137.
11 Roslyn Poignant (2004) *Professional Savages: Captive Lives and Western Spectacle*, Yale University Press, New Haven & London, 77–8, 87, 91, 123, 164, 169, 215.
12 Maria Nugent (2005) *Botany Bay: Where Histories Meet*, Allen & Unwin, Crows Nest, 76.
13 Sianan Healy (2006) 'Years ago some lived here': Aboriginal Australians and the production of popular culture, history and identity in 1930s Victoria, *Australian Historical Studies* 37: 128, 18–34; Ian Clark (2015) *'A Peep at the Blacks': A History of Tourism at Coranderrk Aboriginal Station, 1863–1924*, De Gruyter Open, Warsaw; Baiba Berzins (2007), *Australia's Northern Secret: Tourism in the Northern Territory, 1920s to 1980s*, Baiba Berzins, Sydney, 28, 73.
14 Nugent (2005), 72–7.
15 Valda Blundell (1994) Take home Canada: Representations of aboriginal peoples as tourist souvenirs. In Stephen Harold Riggins (ed.) *The Socialness of Things: Essays on the Socio-Semiotics of Objects*, Mouton de Gruyter, Berlin and New York, 252.

16 Jan Kociumbas (2003) Performances: Indigenisation and postcolonial culture. In Hsu-Ming Teo & Richard White (eds) *Cultural History in Australia*, University of New South Wales Press, Sydney, 127.
17 Sydney launches Games with wit, flair and symbolism (2000) *Guardian*, 15 September, viewed 10 December 2019, <https://www.theguardian.com/sydney/story/0,,368825,00.html>.
18 Harris, Kerr, Forster & Company (1966) *Australia's Travel and Tourist Industry*, Harris, Kerr, Forster & Company and Stanton Robbins & Co., Sydney, 281, 283.
19 Jon Altman (1988) *Aborigines, Tourism and Development*, Australian National University North Australian Research Unit, Casuarina, 33, 36; Toby Martin (2014) 'Socialist paradise' or 'inhospitable island'? Visitor responses to Palm Island in the 1920s and 1930s, *Aboriginal History*, 38, 131–53, 136.
20 Arthur Groom (1950) *I Saw a Strange Land*, Angus & Robertson, Sydney, 76.
21 Stephen Alomes (1988) *A Nation at Last?*, Angus & Robertson, Sydney, 156.
22 Mimmo Cozzolino (1980) *Symbols of Australia*, Penguin Books, Melbourne, 48, 95, 97, 105, 152; Alomes (1980), 107.
23 Philip Jones (1996) *Boomerang: Behind an Australian Icon*, Wakefield Press, Adelaide, 106.
24 Jones (1996), 104.
25 ibid., 109.
26 ibid., 111.
27 Liz Connor (2017) The politics of Aboriginal kitsch, *Conversation*, 3 March, viewed 10 December 2019, <https://theconversation.com/friday-essay-the-politics-of-aboriginal-kitsch-73683>.
28 Adrian Franklin (2011) Aboriginalia: Souvenir Wares and the 'Aboriginalization' of Australian Identity, *Tourist Studies* 10(3) 195–208; Kerry Reed-Gilbert (2018) A response to 'The politics of Aboriginal kitsch', 15 July, viewed 1 December 2019, <https://theconversation.com/friday-essay-the-politics-of-aboriginal-kitsch-73683>. See also Gina Fairley (2014) A Dark Heart with a Difference: Tony Albert. In Nick Mitzevich (ed.)(2014) *2014 Adelaide Biennial of Australian Art: Dark Heart*, Art Gallery of South Australia, Adelaide.
29 Jones (1996), 111, 123.
30 Boomerang Association of Australia, viewed 4 March 2008, <http://www.boomerang.org.au/>.
31 Jim Davidson & Peter Spearritt (2000) *Holiday Business*, The Miegunyah Press at Melbourne University Press, Melbourne, 210.
32 Author's notes, 2/11/2005; see Australian Government (2019) Digital Labelling to Promote Authenticity Trialled at Alice Springs Indigenous Art Fair 'Desert Mob', media release, viewed 10 December 2019, <https://www.indigenous.gov.au/news-and-media/announcements/digital-labelling-promote-authenticity-trialled-alice-springs>.
33 The Australian Council for the Arts defines authentic Aboriginal art as 'that which is attributed to the creativity and the output of an Aboriginal or Torres Strait Islander person … or persons'. (Inquiry, 14); House of Representatives Standing Committee on Indigenous Affairs (December 2018), 'Report on the impact of inauthentic art and craft in the style of First Nations peoples', Commonwealth of Australia, 5.
34 ibid., 9.
35 Australian Competition & Consumer Commission (2004) ACCC concludes aboriginal-style souvenir proceedings, media release, viewed 4 March 2008, <www.accc.gov.au/content/index.phtml/itemId/526357>.

36 Lorena Allen (2019) Birubi Art fined $2.3m for selling fake Aboriginal art made in Indonesia, *Guardian Australia*, 26 June, viewed 10 December 2019, <https://www.theguardian.com/artanddesign/2019/jun/26/birubi-art-fined-23m-for-selling-fake-aboriginal-art-made-in-indonesia>.
37 Jones (1996), 71.
38 Dean MacCannell (1992) *Empty Meeting Grounds*, Routledge, London & New York, 168.
39 Nelson Graburn (ed.) (1976) *Ethnic and Tourist Arts*, University of California Press, Berkeley, 6. Philip Jones could be seen as taking this view.
40 Blundell (1994), 274–6.

Billy
1 Edward S Sorenson (1911) *Life in the Australian Backblocks*, Whitcombe & Tombs, London, 276–7.
2 Geoffrey Blainey (2003) *Black Kettle and Full Moon: Daily Life in a Vanished Australia*, Viking, Melbourne, 357; Bill Wannan (1987) *A Dictionary of Australian Folklore: Lore, Legends, Myths and Traditions*, Viking O'Neil, Melbourne, 54–5; Russel Ward (1972) An early tribute to royalty? The probable derivation of 'billy', *Meanjin*, 31(3), September, 324–9.
3 Cash cited in Ward (1972) 328; Davenport in Lucy Frost (ed.) (1984) *No Place for a Nervous Lady: Voices from the Australian Bush*, McPhee Gribble, Fitzroy, 258; George B Wilkinson (1849) *The Working Man's Handbook to South Australia*, John Murray, London, 79; HW Orsman (ed.) (1997) *The Dictionary of New Zealand English: A Dictionary of New Zealandisms on Historical Principles*, Oxford University Press, Auckland, 51.
4 John Rochfort (1853) *Adventures of a Surveyor in New Zealand and the Australian Gold Diggings*, David Bogue, London, 63. Geoffrey Blainey inexplicably attributes the switch from the quart pot to the billy around this time to the availability of 'cheap iron rather than dear tin' but the billy was also made of tin, not iron. See Blainey (2003), 357.
5 For a summary of the debate, see Wannan (1987), 54–5.
6 Ward (1972), 324–9. Ward was not the first to suggest that billy came from William but he went further in linking it to the king. In 1898 Edward E Morris traced the origin of billy to William: see Morris (1972) *A Dictionary of Austral English*, Sydney University Press, Sydney, 30.
7 Sorenson (1911), 278–81; Anne Gollan (1978) *The Tradition of Australian Cooking*, Australian National University Press, Canberra, 25–6.
8 James Lister Cuthbertson (1912) *Barwon Ballads and School Verses*, Melville & Mullen, Melbourne, 240–1; Edward Harrington (1957) *The Swagless Swaggie and Other Ballads: Selected Verse*, Australasian Book Society, Melbourne, 34; Louis Esson (1910) *Bells and Bees: Verses*, Lothian, Melbourne.
9 Cited in Ward (1972), 328.
10 Michael Farrell (2007) The billycan in Australian poetry, MA thesis, University of Melbourne, 33–5, 43–7.
11 Sorenson (1911), 276.
12 Matthew Richardson (2006) *Once a Jolly Swagman: The Ballad of Waltzing Matilda*, Melbourne University Press, Melbourne, 18, 65–80; National Library of Australia, Who'll come a waltzing Matilda with me? , viewed 27 January 2008, <www.nla.gov.au/epubs/waltzingmatilda>; Richard Magoffin (2001) *The Provenance of Waltzing Matilda: A Definitive Exposition of the Song's Origins, Meanings and Evolution from a Pivotal Episode in Australian History*, Matilda Expo Publishers, Kyuna.

13   Christopher Kelen (2005) His masterpiece, our haunting: Banjo Paterson's nation-making artefact, *Nebula*, 2(3), September, 6.
14   Martha Rutledge (1972) Inglis, James (1845–1908). In *Australian Dictionary of Biography – Online Edition*, viewed 15 January 2008, <www.adb.online.anu.edu.au/biogs/A0404517b.htm>.
15   Richardson (2006), 124–5, 131–4; National Library, Who'll come a waltzing. John Safran describes the association between billy tea and 'Waltzing Matilda' as an early version of product placement. See Safran (2002) Waltzing Matilda, courtesy of a tea-leaf near you, *Sydney Morning Herald*, 20 December.
16   Henry Tompkins (1906) *With Swag and Billy: Tramps by Bridle Path and the Open Road*, NSW Government Tourist Bureau, Sydney; Melissa Harper (2007) *The Ways of the Bushwalker: On Foot in Australia*, University of New South Wales Press, Sydney, 141–67.
17   See Harper (2007), 292–4; Julia Bowes (2012) Playing with fire: the place of campfires in nature tourism. In Richard White and Caroline Ford (eds) *Playing in the bush: recreation and national parks in New South Wales*, Sydney University Press, 100–5, 118–19; Bill Garner (2013) *Born in a Tent: How Camping Makes Us Australian*, NewSouth Publishing, Sydney.

Miss Australia
1   *Sydney Punch*, 14 July 1864, in Margaret Anderson (ed.) (1998) *When Australia Was a Woman: Images of a Nation*, Western Australian Museum, Perth, Plate 22, 62. This chapter draws extensively on the images shown in this catalogue and on Anderson's illuminating discussion of their significance.
2   Marina Warner (1996) *Monuments and Maidens: The Allegory of the Female Form*, Vintage, London, 49–51.
3   Maurice Agulhon (1981) *Marianne into Battle: Republican Imagery and Symbolism in France, 1789–1830*, trans. Janet Lloyd, Cambridge University Press, Cambridge.
4   This discussion draws on Anderson (ed.) (1998), 9–13.
5   *Illustrated Sydney News*, 25 March 1868, in Anderson (ed.) (1998), Plate 26, 63. Cindy McCreery has discussed the controversy that followed the first appearance of this cartoon, in *Sydney Punch* on 21 March, with commentators deploring the 'vile caricature' and her brutal, 'fiendish' expression: Cindy McCreery (2013) Rude interruption: colonial manners, gender and Prince Alfred's visit to New South Wales, 1868, *Forum for Modern Language Studies* 49(4) 437–56.
6   Anderson (ed.) (1998), 6–7.
7   John Hirst (2000) *The Sentimental Nation: The Making of the Australian Commonwealth*, Oxford University Press, Melbourne, 19.
8   See Richard White (1981) *Inventing Australia: Images and Identity 1688–1980*, Allen & Unwin, Sydney, 110–24.
9   Anderson (ed.) (1998), Plates 16–19, 56–7.
10   Invitation to the opening of Parliament, 1901, Anderson (ed.) (1998), Plate 16, 56.
11   Rudyard Kipling (1903) The Young Queen. In *The Five Nations*, Methuen, London, 100–3.
12   Joan B Landes (1988) *Women and the Public Sphere in the Age of the French Revolution*, Cornell University Press, Ithaca and London; Warner (1996).
13   John Farrell (1883) No. Cited in Hirst, *Sentimental Nation*, 21.
14   Josie Castle & Helen Pringle (1993) Sovereignty and sexual identity in political cartoons. In Susan Magarey, Sue Rowley & Susan Sheridan (eds), *Debutante Nation: Feminism Contests the 1890s*, Allen & Unwin, Sydney, 140–1; Anderson (ed.) (1998), 21–2.

15 Anderson (ed.) (1998), 22.
16 Castle & Pringle (1993), 148; Anderson (ed.) (1998), Plate 48, 70.
17 Anderson (ed.) (1998), Plate 57, 74.
18 For example ibid., Plate 52, 73.
19 ibid., Plate 46, 70.
20 ibid., Plate 66, 79.
21 See Castle & Pringle (1993); Penny Russell (1994) Recycling femininity: Old ladies and new women, *Australian Cultural History*, 31–51.
22 See the brief but illuminating discussion of this point in Anderson (ed.) (1998), 75.
23 On the figure of Uncle Sam, see Alton Ketchum (1990) The search for Uncle Sam, *History Today*, 40; Thomas Bivins (1987) The body politic: The changing shape of Uncle Sam, *Journalism Quarterly*, 64(1).
24 For an account of the Pacific tour of the United States fleet, see Marilyn Lake & Henry Reynolds (2008) *Drawing the Global Colour Line: White Men's Countries and the Question of Racial Equality*, Melbourne University Press, Melbourne, Chapter 8; for Sydney, see Justine Greenwood (2008) The 1908 visit of the Great White Fleet: Displaying modern Sydney, *History Australia*, 5(3), December, 78.
25 Deakin final draft, 1540/15/3912, Deakin papers, National Library of Australia; *Age*, 24 August 1908.
26 *Age*, 27 August 1908.
27 *Age*, 17 August 1908.
28 *Age*, 21 August 1908.
29 *Bulletin*, 20 August 1908, in Anderson (ed.) (1998), 64.
30 See *Review of Reviews of Australasia*, June–December 1908, 232, 429.
31 See Ketchum (1990); Thomas Bivins (1987).
32 *Review of Reviews of Australasia*, June–December 1908, 323.
33 Kristin Hoganson (1998) *Fighting for American Manhood: How Gender Politics Provoked the Spanish-American and Philippine-American Wars*, Yale University Press, New Haven; Gail Bedermann (1995) *Manliness and Civilization: A Cultural History of Gender and Race in the United States 1880–1917*, Chicago University Press, Chicago. American historian Joan Scott has argued that the constitutive relations of gender and power were reciprocal: that the meaning of gender was constructed in terms of power relations and that power was often signified in terms of gender. See Joan Scott (1986) Gender: A useful category of historical analysis, *American Historical Review*, 91, December.
34 Alfred Mahan quoted in Hoganson (1998), 10.
35 Alfred Mahan (1895) *The Influence of Sea Power upon History 1660–1783*, 10th edition, Little Brown, Boston.
36 See Judith Smart (2001) Feminists, flappers and Miss Australia: Contesting the meanings of citizenship, femininity and nation in the 1920s, *Australian Studies*, 71.
37 Julia Baird (2004) *Media Tarts: How the Australian Press Frames Female Politicians*, Scribe, Melbourne.
38 The damaging impact of misogyny in Australian public culture during the Gillard era drew much attention. See for example Marilyn Lake, 'How the PM's gender took over the agenda', *Age*, 25 June 2013, and 'Women's vote in play even after Gillard demise', *Age*, 10 September 2013, as well as Anne Summers (2013) *The Misogyny Factor*, NewSouth Publishing, Sydney.

Flag

1 James Purtill, (2015) Meet the man who wants to celebrate the Cronulla riots, podcast, 9, 10 December, <https://www.abc.net.au/triplej/programs/hack/meet-the-nick-folkes-who-wants-to-celebrate-the-cronulla-riots/7014848>; Supreme and Federal Courts rule against Cronulla riots memorial rally (2015) ABC News, 11 December, viewed 25 June 2021, <https://www.abc.net.au/news/2015-12-11/courts-rule-against-cronulla-riots-memorial/7020282>; Cronulla protesters kept apart as 'halal-free' memorial barbecue held (2015) ABC News, 12 December, viewed 26 June 2021, <https://www.abc.net.au/news/2015-12-12/cronulla-protesters-kept-apart-as-halal-free-bbq-held/7023304>; United Patriots Front want Cronulla rally (2015) *St George and Sutherland Shire Leader*, 28 July, viewed 7 July 2021, <https://www.theleader.com.au/story/3238870/united-patriots-front-want-peaceful-cronulla-rally/>.

2 Elizabeth Kwan (2006) *Flag and Nation: Australians and their National Flags since 1901*, University of New South Wales Press, Sydney, 139–41. Refer to this source for further details on this chapter.

3 *Commonwealth Parliamentary Debates* (CPD) (1953), 368, 367.

4 Kwan (2006), 24, 31.

5 *Commonwealth of Australia Gazette* (CAG), 29 April 1901, 89; Judges' Report, 2 September 1901, National Archives of Australia (NAA): A461, B336/1/1 Part 1.

6 Secretary, Defence Department, to Secretary, External Affairs Department, 22 September 1903, NAA: A461/A336/1/1 Part 1.

7 Atlee Hunt (1932) Federal memories, *Sydney Morning Herald*, 18 June; *Sydney Morning Herald*, 24 May 1898; CPD, 26 May 1904, 1609, 1610.

8 CPD, 2 June 1904, 1913–14; CAG, 7 March 1908, 589.

9 Saluting flag, NAA: MP84/1, 1874/1/28.

10 *Argus* (Melbourne), 10 May 1920; Secretary, Education Department to Premier, 21 May 1920, Victoria Public Record Office: Series 1163, box 513, file 1675; Elizabeth Kwan (1994) The Australian flag: Ambiguous symbol of nationality in Melbourne and Sydney, 1920–21, *Australian Historical Studies*, October, 103, 280–303.

11 Circulars, prime minister to state premiers, 31 January, 3 May 1924, NAA: A461, A336/1/1 Part 1.

12 John Ross Matheson (1986) *Canada's Flag: A Search for a Country*, Mika Publishing Company, Belleville, 82–3; Australian flag – flying of at funerals, NAA: A705, 85/1/158; Elizabeth Kwan (1995) Which flag? Which country? An Australian dilemma, 1901–1951, PhD thesis, Australian National University, 359–64; James Curran (2004) *The Power of Speech: Australian Prime Ministers Defining the National Image*, Melbourne University Press, Melbourne, 22–7.

13 Necessity of an Australian National Flag, c. 1949, NAA: A462, 828/1/1 Part 1.

14 CPD, 20 November 1953, 368.

15 Arthur Smout (1968) *The Flag Book: Australia*, Lions International Australia, Brisbane, 23.

16 Matheson (1986); Michael Dawson, Catherine Gidney & Donald Wright (eds) (2018) *Symbols of Canada*, Between the Lines, Toronto, 86–95.

17 Extract, minutes of meeting, ANFA steering committee, 21 April 1983, from John Vaughan, national spokesman, ANFA, 2004.

18 Quoted in Don Watson (2003) *Recollections of a Bleeding Heart: A Portrait of Paul Keating*, Random House, Sydney, 123.

19 The two proclamations of the flags of 'the Aboriginal peoples of Australia' and of 'the Torres Strait Islander people of Australia', referred to them also as flags 'of significance

to the Australian nation generally'. *Commonwealth of Australia Gazette*, Nos 258 & 259, 14 July 1995.
20 Farewell to icon of Australian sport (2003), 16 July, viewed 23 March 2021, < https://www.abc.net.au/news/2003-07-16/farewell-to-icon-of-australian-sport/1449838>.
21 Key Recommendations, *Select Committee on the Aboriginal Flag Report*, 13 October 2020; Company that owns rights to Aboriginal flag in the spotlight at Senate inquiry, viewed 11 July 2021, <https://www.theguardian.com/australia-news/2020/sep/14/company-that-owns-rights-to-aboriginal-flag-in-the-spotlight-at-senate-inquiry>; Fiona Harari (2020) Tears in the Fabric, *The Weekend Australian Magazine*, 30 October, viewed 11 July 2021, <https://www.theaustralian.com.au/subscribe/news/1/?sourceCode=TAWEB_WRE170_a&dest=https%3A%2F%2Fwww.theaustralian.com.au%2Fweekend-australian-magazine%2Floyalties-versus-royalties-the-battle-over-the-aboriginal-flag%2Fnews-story%2Fa1666b6dc86cb2f891f38a1a9dbb84a2-&memtype=anonymous&mode=premium>; The Torres Strait Island Regional Council, which holds copyright in the Torres Strait Islander Flag, directs requests for permission to reproduce the Torres Strait Islander Flag to the Records Officer of the Island Regional Council. Department of Prime Minister and Cabinet, viewed 11 July 2021, <https://pmc.gov.au/government/australian-national-symbols/australian-flags>.
22 Special access files re flag video and flagpoles, as cited in Kwan, *Flag and Nation*, 142–7.
23 ibid., 142.
24 James Jupp (2004) *The English in Australia*, Cambridge University Press, Cambridge, 191; Malcolm Knox, The Nation Reviewed. Comment: Cronulla five years on, *Monthly*, December 2010–January 2011.
25 Amelia Johns (2005), *Battle for the Flag*, Melbourne University Press, Carlton, 229, 236.
26 *Sydney Morning Herald*, 31 January 2009; Malcolm Knox, The Nation Reviewed. Comment: Cronulla five years on, *Monthly*, December 2010 – January 2011.
27 Morgan Poll, Finding No. 4495, 13 May 2010, surveyed 652 Australia-wide people aged over 14 by telephone.
28 New Australian flag backed by 64% in university survey on alternative designs (2016) *Guardian Australia*, 26 January, viewed 27 January 2020,< https://www.theguardian.com/australia-news/2016/jan/26/new-australian-flag-backed-by-64-in-university-survey-on-alternative-designs>; Poll finds Australian flag out of favour (2016) *Mercury*, 26 January, viewed 27 January 2020, <https://www.themercury.com.au/news/tasmania/poll-finds-australian-flag-out-of-favour/news-story/da14855e3e428308066b55ee6044f4b6>.
29 Luritja linguist Lance McDonald, quoted by Emily Napangarti Butcher in What Central Australia's remote Aboriginal communities think of Australia Day (2018) ABC News, 26 January, viewed 29 November 2019, <https://www.abc.net.au/news/2018-01-26/what-do-remote-aboriginal-communities-think-of-australia-day/9363470>.
30 Elizabeth Kwan (2008) *Celebrating Australia: A History of Australia Day*, National Australia Day Council, 15, quoting *Australian*, 15 August 1994, viewed 29 November 2019, <https://www.australiaday.org.au/storage/celebratingaustralia.pdf>.
31 Scott Morrison pushes to make citizenship ceremonies compulsory on Australia Day (2019) *Sydney Morning Herald*, 13 January, viewed 29 November 2019, <https://www.SMH.com.au/national/scott-morrison-pushes-to-make-citizenship-ceremonies-compulsory-on-australia-day-20190113-p50r2o.html>.
32 Phillip Adams (2015) Advance Australia Fair is lamentable, unmemorable and offensive, *Weekend Australian*, 9 May; Warwick McFadyen (2018) Advance Australia Fair is an

anthem that is racist at so many levels, *Sydney Morning Herald*, 16 September, viewed 24 January 2020, <https://www.SMH.com.au/national/advance-australia-fair-is-an-anthem-that-is-racist-at-so-many-levels-20180916-p5043s.html>.
33 Emma Kemp (2020) Wallabies sing Indigenous language Australian anthem before Tri-Nations draw with Argentina, *Guardian Australia*, 5 December, viewed 28 March 2021, <https://www.theguardian.com/sport/2020/dec/05/wallabies-sing-indigenous-language-australian-anthem-before-tri-nations-draw-with-argentina>.
34 Sarah Elks & Sean Parnell (2018) Indigenous flags flown lower at parliament, *West Australian*, 27–28 January.
35 Kieran Finnane (2019) Aboriginal woman, Councillor Satour, in report of Alice Springs Town Council meeting of 25 August 2019, *Alice Springs News*, viewed 24 January 2020, <https://www.alicespringsnews.com.au/2019/08/26/aboriginal-flag-year-round-on-anzac-hill/>.
36 See Australia Day, Reconciliation, viewed 26 January 2020, <https://www.australiaday.org.au/about/reconciliation/>.
37 Ken Wyatt, We're united as one in Oz, *NT News*, 25 January 2020, 12; cf. Paul Kelly (2018) We need to embrace our two truths, *West Australian*, 27–28 January, 29; Paul Kelly (2018) Australia Day: we must face the two truths about January 26, Eric Löbbecke illustration, 26 January, viewed 26 January 2020, < https://www.theaustralian.com.au/nation/inquirer/australia-day-we-must-face-the-two-truths-about-january-26/news-story/29e7490c91e7911adc6245d8ecb42199>.

Wattle
1 See Australian Floral Emblem, Department of Prime Minister and Cabinet, <https://pmc.gov.au/government/australian-national-symbols/australian-floral-emblem>. The Palawa people are an example of the many different Aboriginal nations still using wattle for cultural business: Phoebe Hosier (2019) Tasmanian Aboriginal bush tucker business winning hearts via the stomach, ABC News, 17 March, viewed 22 June 2021, <https://www.abc.net.au/news/2019-03-17/tasmanian-aboriginal-food-business-spreading-culture/10903856>.
2 Green and gold were officially proclaimed national colours on 19 April 1984, but had been used for many years before this: Australian symbols website, Office of the Prime Minister of Australia, viewed 13 February 2008, <www.pm.gov.au/australia/symbols/symbols.cfm>.
3 Quoted by Mary Grant Bruce (1916), *Jim and Wally*, Ward Lock, London, 43.
4 James O'Connell, Peter Latz & Peggy Barnett, Traditional and Modern Plant Use among the Alyawara of Central Australia, *Economic Botany*, vol. 37, No. 1 (January–March, 1983), 80–109, <https://www.jstor.org/stable/4254460>.
5 *Acacia aneura*, viewed 18 February 2008, <http:// asgap.org.au/APOL16/dec99-5.html>.
6 Suzette Searle (1991) *The Rise and Demise of the Black Wattle Bark Industry in Australia*, CSIRO Division of Forestry, Canberra.
7 Maria Hitchcock (1991) *Wattle*, Australian Government Publishing Service, Canberra, 1; AJ Campbell (1921) *Golden Wattle, Our National Floral Emblem*, Osboldstone, Melbourne, 62; Frances J Woodward (1996) Franklin, Jane (1791–1875), *Australian Dictionary of Biography*, vol. 1, Melbourne University Press, Melbourne, 411–12.
8 'Objects' of the ANA as published in 1938–39. In John E Menadue (1971) *A Centenary History of the Australian Natives' Association 1871–1971*, Horticultural Press,

Melbourne. Also John Hirst (2001) *The Sentimental Nation: The Making of the Australian Commonwealth*, Oxford University Press, Melbourne, 36–9.

9   Quote from *Register*, 26 August 1912, NLA MS 9650, Cutting in the AJ Campbell archives; Wattle memorabilia, in Campbell (1921), 62; Menadue (1971), 307 (my emphasis); Michael Dawson, Catherine Gidney & Donald Wright (eds) (2018) *Symbols of Canada*, Between the Lines, Toronto, 86–95.

10 RT Baker (1915) *The Australian Flora in Applied Art: Part I. The Waratah*, Technological Museum, Sydney, fig. 26; *Cabinet Timbers of Australia*, Government Printer, Sydney, 1913.

11 Letter, RT Baker to RC Dixson, 31 May 1933, National Museum of Australia Library [0080323// VS/GS/ 99999801. IRN 3701].

12 On bushwalking, see Melissa Harper (2007) *The Ways of the Bushwalker: On Foot in Australia*, University of New South Wales Press, Sydney; Genevieve Brunet (2008) Mimosa: Une route et des fêtes, *Nice Matin*, 30 January, 36–7.

13 Edwin Ride (2007) Wattle days: From Adam Lindsay Gordon to Ginger Mick, *NLA News*, August, viewed 26 January 2020, <http://www.wattleday.asn.au/about-wattles/EdwinRide2007WattledaysfromAdamLindsayGordontoGingerMick.pdf >. See also Ride (2007) Wattle – a changing symbol for a changing nation, viewed 16 October 2008, <http://wattleday.asn.au/wattle-day-events-1/edwinridewattledayforumspeech07.pdf/view>.

14 Hitchcock (1991); Campbell (1921), 62; *West Australian*, 2 September 1912; *Argus*, 11 September 1912; *Daily Express* (London), 27 January 1913, 7.

15 Tullie C Wollaston (1916) *Our Wattles*, Lothian, Melbourne, 11–13.

16 Bruce (1916), 43; Baker to Dixson, 31 May 1933.

17 *Adelaide Observer*, 18 July 1896, 43.

18 Douglas Sladen (1934) *Adam Lindsay Gordon: The Life and Best Poems of the Poet of Australia*, Hutchison, London, 192, 269; AJ Campbell archives, NLA MS 9650.

19 Libby Robin (2002) Nationalising nature. In *The Dog of War*, special issue of *Journal of Australian Studies*, 73, 13–26.

20 *Register*, 22 May 1911.

21 ibid; cf. attitudes to the Southern Cross, 26.

22 Protea was official in South Africa in 1975, and wattle in Australia in 1988.

23 Anthony Orchard & Bruce Maslin (2005) The case for conserving *Acacia* with a new type, *Taxon*, 54, 509.

24 Eugene Moll (2005) Acacia for Africa! *Veld & Flora*, December, 178. This argument was rather unhelpful, as the *Senegalia* group did not include the type; see also Libby Robin & Jane Carruthers (2012) National identity and international science: the case of *Acacia*, *Historical Records of Australian Science* 23(1): 34–54; Jane Carruthers et al., (2011) A native at home and abroad: the history, politics, ethics and aesthetics of *Acacia*, *Diversity and Distributions* 17(5) September: 810–21. DOI: 10.1111/j.1472-4642.2011.00779.x.

25 Maria Hitchcock (ed.) (2004) Editorial, *Australian Plants*, 22 (180) September, 290; ibid., A is for Acacia …, 291.

26 Advance Acacia Fair, *Weekend Australian*, Saturday, 26 August 2006; Acacia Appreciation Club of Hiroshima, Japan, Hitchcock (ed.) 2004 (180), 299.

27 National Library of Australia [Wattle Day: Programs and invitations ephemera material collected by the National Library of Australia]; Katy Cronin (1999) Swiss memorial, transcript ABC Archive, viewed 13 September 2019, <www.abc.net.au/am/stories/s41943.htm>.

28 Prime Minister's Office (2002) A national day of mourning, media release, viewed 13 September 2019, <http://pandora.nla.gov.au/pan/10052/20021121-0000/www.pm.gov.au/news/media_releases/2002/ media_release1923.htm>.

Coat of arms

1 Conrad Swan (1977) *Canada: Symbols of Sovereignty: An Investigation into the Arms and Seals Borne and Used from the Earliest Times to the Present in Connection with Public Authority in and over Canada, along with Consideration of some Selected Flags*, University of Toronto Press, Toronto, see especially Chapter 1 *passim*.
2 Prime Minister's Department (1906–18) Requests for Commonwealth Coat of Arms (in Colour), 1906–18, National Archives of Australia, Series A462, Control symbol 828/3/8 PART 1, viewed 30 January 2008, <http://naa12.naa.gov.au/scripts/imagine.asp?B=98430&I=1&SE=1>, Harcourt to Governor-General, 13 February 1912.
3 Charles Hasler (1980) *The Royal Arms: Its Graphic and Decorative Development*, Jupiter Books, London, 9, 53–5, 67. Mantling refers to the long flowing material often depicted around a coat of arms representing a knight's cloak.
4 Vane Lindesay (1988) *Aussie-ossities*, Greenhouse Publications, Melbourne.
5 Charles Low (1971) *A Roll of Australian Arms: Corporate and Personal Borne by Lawful Authority*, Rigby, Adelaide.
6 David Kaus (2005) Aboriginal Breastplates, National Museum of Australia, viewed 30 January 2008, <www.nma.gov.au/exhibitions/past_exhibitions/captivating_and_curious/the_stories_behind_the_objects/aboriginal_breastplates/>.
7 Hasler (1980).
8 Department of External Affairs (1907–11) Commonwealth mottoes. In Commonwealth Coat of Arms, 1907–11, National Archives of Australia, Series A63, Control symbol A1910/3923; viewed 30 January 2008, <http://naa12.naa.gov.au/scripts/ Imagine.asp>; also Prime Minister's Department (1906–18), Dobbs to Hunt, 30 September 1907.
9 See papers in Prime Minister's Department (1906–18), especially Eyre-Dodd & Dunlop to Hunt, 6 May 1908; Collins to Hunt, 15 May 1908; Milligan to Hunt, 13 May 1908; Burridge to Hunt, 24 January 1908; Collins to Hunt, 27 February 1908; Scott-Gatty to Colonial Office, 27 February 1908; Wilson Dobbs to Hunt, 13 February 1908; Mulligan to Hunt, 25 March 1908; Gullick to Hunt, 10 July 1908; Gullick to Hunt, 24 June 1910.
10 Sir Thomas Innes of Learney (1934) *Scots Heraldry: A Practical Handbook*, Oliver and Boyd, Edinburgh, 78–80. Borders are used in Scottish heraldry to indicate blood relations between the descendants of an armiger (a person entitled to a coat of arms).
11 Prime Minister's Department (1906–18) Woodrow to secretary, Post-Master General's Department, 4 May 1915.
12 ibid., Shepherd to Oxenham, 12 May 1915.
13 ibid., Circular 15/1999, from secretary Shepherd to all departments, 24 May 1915.
14 ibid., acting secretary Bingle to secretary, Prime Minister's Department, 12 July 1915; and secretary, Prime Minister's Department to Government Printer, 27 September 1918.
15 Susan Bures (1987) *The House of Wunderlich*, Kangaroo Press, Kenthurst.
16 Heraldry is not referred to in Part V, or anywhere else, in the *Commonwealth of Australia Constitution Act 1900* (Cth); some states have made a very limited patriation of heraldic authority, but only with regard to their state arms. See for example the *State Arms, Symbols & Emblems Act 2004* (NSW) or the *Armorial Bearings Protection Act 1979* (WA).
17 Prime Minister's Department (1954–56) Commonwealth coat of arms – proposed redesign, 1954–1956, National Archives of Australia, Series A463, Control symbol 1956/219 PART2, viewed March 2008, <http://naa12.naa.gov.au/scripts/ imagine.

asp?B=727358&I=1&SE=1>, Minutes, Commonwealth Art Advisory Board, 11 October 1954.
18 ibid., especially Cumming to Morrison, 2 May 1956; Cumming to Ashton, 9 March 1956; Timbs to Cumming, 23 May 1956; Cumming to Beadle, also to Morrison, 17 August 1956; Minutes, Commonwealth Art Advisory Board, 3 September 1956.
19 ibid., Wagner, Richmond Herald to Timbs, 10 August 1956.
20 See Eileen Mayo, Design for a coat of arms, National Gallery of Australia, Accession number: 93.2381.

Digger
1 See Graham Seal (2004) *Inventing Anzac: The Digger and National Mythology*, University of Queensland Press, Brisbane, 18–22.
2 Russel Ward (1958) *The Australian Legend*, Oxford University Press, Melbourne.
3 Quoted from a New Zealand soldier's letter home in John Robertson (1990) *Anzac and Empire: The Tragedy and Glory of Gallipoli*, Hamlyn Australia, Port Melbourne, 43–4; see also Amanda Laugesen (2015) *Furphies and Whizz-Bangs: Anzac Slang from the Great War*, Oxford University Press, Melbourne.
4 H Diddams (1921) *Anzac Commemoration 1921*, Brisbane, 3.
5 David Kent (1985) The Anzac Book and the Anzac legend: C.E.W. Bean as editor and image-maker, *Historical Studies*, 21(84), April.
6 CEW Bean (ed.) (1916) *The Anzac Book*, Cassell, London, 23.
7 Robin Gerster (1987) *Big-Noting: The Heroic Theme in Australian War Writing*, Melbourne University Press, Melbourne, 1987.
8 Lloyd Robson (1970) *The First AIF: A Study of its Recruitment 1914–1918*, Melbourne University Press, Melbourne.
9 For example, Can Anzac Day Survive? Fifty Years After Gallipoli a Panel Debates, *Sydney Morning Herald*, 17 April 1965; Robyn Mayes and Graham Seal (2014) Anzac Day media representations of women in Perth 1960-2012, in Bobbie Oliver & Sue Summers (eds) *Lest we forget?: Marginalised aspects of Australia at war and peace*, Black Swan Press, Perth, 117–36. For a history of Anzac remembrance, see Carolyn Holbrook (2014) *Anzac: The Unauthorised Biography*, NewSouth Publishing, Sydney.
10 Suzanne Gillham (2001) From Memory to Myth: The Resurrection of Anzac 1960–2000, History Honours thesis, University of Sydney.
11 Bruce Scates (2006) *Return to Gallipoli: Walking the Battlefields of the Great War*, Cambridge University Press, Cambridge.
12 Christina Twomey (2013) Trauma and the Reinvigoration of Anzac: An Argument, *History Australia*, 10(3) 85–108.
13 David Stephens (2015) Why is Australia spending so much more on the Great War centenary than any other country?, *Pearls and Irritations*, 20 June, viewed 13 January 2020, <https://johnmenadue.com/david-stephens-why-is-australia-spending-so-much-more-on-the-great-war-centenary-than-any-other-country/>; Carolyn Holbrook (2016) Anzac Offers a New Way to Join Team Australia, *Age*, 19 April, viewed 12 January 2020, <https://www.SMH.com.au/opinion/anzac-season-turning-war-memory-into-a-nationalist-festival-is-wrong-20160418-go8uhe.html>.
14 Carolyn Holbrook (2019) Making Sense of the Great War Centenary, in Carolyn Holbrook & Keir Reeves (eds), *The Great War: Aftermath and Commemoration*, University of New South Wales Press, Sydney, 244–53; on commercialisation, see Jo Hawkins (2018) *Consuming Anzac: The History of Australia's Most Powerful Brand*, UWA Publishing, Perth.

15 Alkira Reinfrank & Clarissa Thorpe (2015) Anzac Day 2015: Record crowd of 120,000 attend dawn service, 31,000 attend National service and march in Canberra, ABC News, 25 April, viewed 13 January 2020, <https://www.abc.net.au/news/2015-04-25/record-crowd-of-120,000-people-attend-dawn-service-in-canberra/6420536>.
16 Romain Fathi (2021) Crowds at dawn services have plummeted in recent years. It's time to reinvent Anzac Day, *Conversation*, 21 April, viewed 14 July 2021, <https://theconversation.com/crowds-at-dawn-services-have-plummeted-in-recent-years-its-time-to-reinvent-anzac-day-157313>.
17 See for example Marilyn Lake et al. (2010) *What's Wrong with Anzac? The Militarisation of Australian History*, NewSouth Publishing, Sydney.
18 Thomas Keneally (1979) *The Chant of Jimmie Blacksmith*, Australian Classics Edition, Angus & Robertson, Sydney, 178.
19 Bridget Judd (2020) Australia's bushfire crisis in pictures, 3 January, viewed 23 January 2020, <https://www.abc.net.au/news/2020-01-03/australia-bushfire-crisis-in-pictures/11838792>; Graham Seal (2011) '... and in the morning': Adapting and Adopting the Dawn Service, *Journal of Australian Studies*, 3(1) 49–63.

Australia House
1 National Archives of Australia (1914) New government offices: Naming of building, Memorandum, Commonwealth Building London to the Secretary, Department of External Affairs, 16 January, NAA: A2911 200/1914. For further reading on the history of the building see Olwen Pryke (2006) Australia House: Representing Australia in London, 1901–1939, PhD thesis, University of Sydney; John Thompson (1972) The Australian High Commission in London: Its origins and early history, 1901–1916, MA thesis, Australian National University; Eileen Chanin (2018) *Capital Designs: Australia House and Visions of an Imperial London*, Australian Scholarly Publishing, Melbourne.
2 Isabel Edgar (1930) Is it fair?, *British Australian and New Zealander*, 30 October, 8.
3 Senator Edward Findley, *Commonwealth Parliamentary Debates* (CPD), Senate, 25 November 1908, 2165 and also Senator James Charles Stewart, 2193.
4 Alfred Deakin, CPD, Representatives, 12 December 1911, 4124.
5 Senator Colonel John Neild, CPD, Senate, 25 November 1908, 2180 and also Senator Edward Pulsford, 2169, 2163 ff.
6 Australian negotiations in London (1907) *British-Australasian*, 26 September, 3.
7 Sir William Lyne (1907) Memorandum reproduced in *Sydney Morning Herald*, 25 September, 10. Lyne, the acting prime minister, 'had a conviction that the London County Council was very anxious that Australia should secure this block of land' see CPD, Representatives, 24 September 1907 condensed in *Sydney Morning Herald*, 25 September 1907, 10; see also Jonathan Schneer (1999) *London 1900: The Imperial Metropolis*, Yale University Press, New Haven, 26–7.
8 Senator Edward Pulsford, CPD, Senate, 25 November 1908, 2169, 2183; also Senator James MacFarlane, 2174; Alfred Deakin, CPD, Senate, 12 December 1911, 4126.
9 Australia in London (1911) *Sydney Morning Herald*, 19 June, 8.
10 CPD, Senate, 12 December 1911, 4114 ff.
11 Corporate Property Committee Report, tabled at London County Council meeting 26 May 1903, cited in Charles Gordon [1903] *Old Time Aldwych, Kingsway and Neighbourhood*, T Fisher Unwin, London, 38–9.
12 Australia House archives, newspaper clippings file: Australia in London, a costly enterprise (1912) *Age*, 18 March; William Oliver Archibald in CPD, Representatives, 12 December 1911, 4134; Senator Josiah Symon, in CPD, Senate, 25 November 1908, 2478.

13 See Australia House archives, Envelope 1: The site, George Reid to Bertram Mackennal, 6 February 1912.
14 Arthur Atlee Hunt (1912) Letter to Captain Robert Collins, 11 September, Arthur Atlee Hunt Papers, NLA, MS 52, item 843. Hunt's political allegiances were regarded with suspicion by the Fisher Labor ministry, who disassociated themselves from the Department of External Affairs and eventually established an autonomous Prime Minister's Department in 1913, appointing Malcolm Shepherd permanent head. See Helen Davies (1983) Hunt, Atlee Arthur (1864–1935), *Australian Dictionary of Biography*, vol. 9, Melbourne University Press, Melbourne, 403–4.
15 National Archives of Australia (1912) Construction of high commissioner's new offices, NAA: A2911, 362/1912; Australia House (1918) *Architectural Review: A Magazine of Architecture and the Arts of Design*, 44, July–December, 50; Australian High Commission (1918) *Australia House*, London, August, 4.
16 Commonwealth House, Australian stone admired (1914) *Argus*, 3 January, 11; Australia House, nearing completion: 'A fine landmark' (1916) *Argus*, 10 November, 8; National Archives of Australia, The Australia House story, NAA: A463/32, 1966/2350, 24–6; see also Alexander Marshall Mackenzie, Collection of perspective drawings of furniture for Australia House, held in State Library of Victoria, Pictures collection.
17 National Archives of Australia, Statuary and decorations for Australia House, NAA: A458, O370/1. Acting Official Secretary, Australia House (1920) Memorandum to the Secretary, Prime Minister's Department, 13 July; Mackennal's masterpiece, group for Australia House (1924) *Argus*, 24 May, 10, cited in Ken Scarlett (1980) *Australian Sculptors*, Nelson, Melbourne, 405.
18 The builders estimated they had used over a million bricks and a hundred thousand cubic feet of Portland stone, see Australia House, nearing completion; National Archives, Australia House story. Apparently the government briefly considered importing Australian stone for the exterior of the high commission also, but the cost was found to be prohibitive. See David Braithwaite (1981) *Building in the Blood: The Story of the Dove Brothers of Islington, 1781–1981*, Godfrey Cave Associates Ltd and Dove Brothers, London, 69.
19 Eileen Chanin (2018) *Capital Designs: Australia House and Visions of an Imperial London*, Australian Scholarly Publishing, Melbourne.
20 Australia House (1918) *Architectural Review: A Magazine of Architecture and the Arts of Design*, 44, July–December, 49; Australia House (1918) *Builder*, 12 July, 19.
21 Here and there by Rollingstone (1918) *British-Australasian*, 8 August, 4–5.
22 *Evening Standard* (London) cited in Aust. House home from home (1966) *Mirror*, 4 March; Peter Cole-Adams (1971) Canberra-on-the-Thames, *Sydney Morning Herald*, 17 July, 21; John Haskell (1981) Architecture: Hodge-podge haven for visitors, *Sydney Morning Herald*, 29 October.
23 Secretary of State for the Environment (c. 1992) Department of Environment, list of buildings of special architectural or historical interest, City of Westminster, Greater London, Part 1, 39. It achieved Grade II status.
24 Hans Van Leeuwen (2019) Gringotts Bank: Magic overseas polling booth, *The Australian Financial Review*, Melbourne, 10 May, 13

Vegemite
1 Mark Scott (2006) Getting serious about any bias, *Australian*, 17 October, 12. There is not a large amount of information to be found in books and journals, and to my knowledge the only academic article is my own, A brief cultural history of Vegemite,

reproduced in Ian Craven (ed.) (1994) *Australian Popular Culture*, Cambridge University Press, from *Australian Studies*, 7, 1993, 15–21. However, the internet has given Vegemite a new kind of life by allowing easy access to newspaper reports, the main reference source for this subject. Some of the main historical facts are found in the official Vegemite site at <http://www.vegemite.com.au>. I am grateful especially to Chris Pratt, and also Kirsten Wehner of the National Museum of Australia, and to other contributors to this book for generously sharing their knowledge.

2   Vegemite Timeline, viewed 17 March 2021, <https://vegemite.com.au/heritage/vegemite-timeline/>.
3   As an added twist, Kraft was up until 2007 a subsidiary of tobacco giant, Philip Morris Companies Inc.
4   Reid Sexton (2007) Mite not right – in prison, *Sunday Age* (Melbourne), 14 October, 10.
5   Information from Powerhouse Museum, Sydney.
6   Michael Symons (1982) *One Continuous Picnic: A History of Eating in Australia*, Duck Press, Adelaide 165.
7   See Simon Canning (2007) Modern tots replace the veteran happy Vegemites, *Australian* (Media Supplement) 15 March, 13.
8   Biographical note for Dr Keith Farrer, website of the Australian Academy of Technological Sciences and Engineering, viewed 10 May 2009, <www.atse.org.au/index.php?sectionid=648>.
9   Colin Campbell & Jerry Coleby-Williams (2006) Rooting out the rot for green thumbs, *Sun-Herald* (Sydney), 15 January, 60.
10 Dina Rosendorff (2007) Cure rises in the yeast, *Herald Sun* (Melbourne), 3 July, 9.
11 Mark Leggett & Susan Leggett (1989) *The Australian Food Report*, S&W Info Guides, Melbourne, 190.
12 Concern over Aussie icon (2007) *Townsville Bulletin*, 15 March, 28.
13 DD McNicoll (2008) Vegemite the new whales, *Australian*, 'Strewth' column, 14 April, 10.
14 *Toledo Blade*, 23 January 1987.
15 Kelvin Healey (2006) Our Vege might, *Sunday Times* (Perth), 29 October, 33.
16 Danny Lannan (2006) Vegemite ban anger spreads, *Geelong Advertiser*, 25 October, 3.
17 Sweden's Disgusting Food Museum to challenge perception of disgust with polarising dishes (2018) ABC News, 31 October, viewed 19 September 2019, <https://www.abc.net.au/news/2018-10-31/disgusting-food-museum-to-challenge-perception-of-disgust/10425446>.
18 Vegemite Recipes, viewed 17 March 2021, <https://vegemite.com.au/recipes/>.
19 Lauren Novak (2007) Chocolate, footy and photos, *Sunday Mail* (Adelaide), 20 May, 2; see also Father on way to Hicks' hearing (2007) *Northern Territory News*, 25 March, 9.
20 Vegemite spreads some rare happiness (2005) *Daily Telegraph* (Sydney), 3 May, 6.
21 Bruce Beresford & Barry Humphries (1972) *The Adventures of Barry McKenzie*, dir. Bruce Beresford, DVD Longford Productions Pty Ltd.
22 Examples cited from Who owns what and where (2007) *Sunday Times* (Perth), 21 January, 57.
23 Bega's $530m deal brings iconic brands back into Australian hands (2021) 9News, 27 January, viewed 17 March 2021, <https://www.9news.com.au/national/bega-brings-iconic-brands-back-into-australian-hands/a98a8d04-f2d6-4d0b-b1c2-6d82baf37d6a>; Making news: how Bega bought Vegemite (2017) *IntheBlack*, 1 November, viewed 17 February 2021, <https://www.intheblack.com/articles/2017/11/01/how-bega-bought-vegemite>.

24 Julian Croft (1991) *Confessions of a Corinthian*, Collins and Angus & Robertson, Sydney.
25 Georgia Savage (1981) The spider, *Bulletin Literary Supplement*, 30 June, reprinted in Geoffrey Dutton (ed.) (1986) *The Illustrated Treasury of Australian Stories*, Nelson, Melbourne.
26 On their album, *Business as Usual*, originally released in 1982.
27 Vegemite leaves 'em cold (2007) *Herald Sun* (Melbourne), 26 January, 8.
28 Michael Sarah designed the poster in the late 1980s for a term assignment. He then submitted it in a TAFE competition to design posters promoting multiculturalism. Sarah's teacher contacted the Office of Multicultural Affairs about the poster, and they decided to publish and distribute it. The office printed several thousand and distributed them free to government departments, community organisations, overseas missions, etc.
29 Annabel Crabb (2007) You're toast, says one happy little Vegemite to the PM, *Sydney Morning Herald*, 20 November, 6.
30 Meraiah Foley, Vegemite Contest Draws Protests (2019) *New York Times*, 2 November, viewed 10 January 2020, <https://www.nytimes.com/2009/11/03/business/global/03vegemite.html>; How not to re-create another Vegemite iSnack 2.0 branding disaster (2016) 17 May, viewed 10 January 2020, <https://www.thebrandingjournal.com/2016/05/vegemite-isnack-2-0-branding-disaster/>.
31 Paige Murphy, Vegemite spreads support for Australian tennis player Ash Barty (2019) *AdNews*, 14 October, viewed 22 January 2020, <https://www.adnews.com.au/news/vegemite-spreads-support-for-australian-tennis-player-ash-barty>.
32 Greg Jericho, Marmite for Vegemite? Australia's trade deal with the UK really is rather small beer (2021) *Guardian*, 20 June, viewed 29 June 2021, < https://www.theguardian.com/business/commentisfree/2021/jun/20/marmite-for-vegemite-australias-trade-deal-with-the-uk-really-is-rather-small-beer>.
33 Darren Fishman, Vegemite 'April Fools', viewed 23 March 2021, <https://darrenfishman.com/home/vegemite-april-fools/>.

The Great Barrier Reef
1 Iain McCalman (2013) *The Reef – A Passionate History. The Great Barrier Reef in Twelve Extraordinary Tales*, Penguin, Melbourne, 14–16.
2 Great Barrier Reef Foundation (2019) The Reef – The Great Barrier Reef is Australia's unique living icon. Facts, viewed 8 December 2019, <https://www.barrierreef.org/the-reef>.
3 McCalman (2013), 15–34.
4 James Bowerb & Margarit Bowen (2002) *The Great Barrier Reef – History, Science, Heritage*, Cambridge University Press, Melbourne, 283–4.
5 This grotesque entertainment was popularised by a fraudulent Australian castaway, Louis de Rougemont [Henry Louis Grin], who wrote a spurious memoir of 1898 in which he claimed to have ridden Reef turtles by steering them with his toes. BG Andrews, Louis de Rougemont (1847–1921), *Australian Dictionary of Biography*, vol. 8, Melbourne University Press, Melbourne, 8; Rod Howard (2006) *The Fabulist: The Incredible Story of Louis de Rougemont*, Random House, Sydney, 224–36.
6 JC Beaglehole (ed.) (1955) *The Journals of Captain James Cook on His Voyages of Discovery*, vol. 1, Cambridge University Press for the Hakluyt Society, 387–1, 387–8.
7 McCalman (2013), 64–90, 117–67.
8 EJ Banfield (1908) *The Confessions of a Beachcomber*, Five Mile Press, Melbourne; Michael Noonan (1986) *A Different Drummer. The Story of E.J. Banfield, Beachcomber of Dunk Island*, University of Queensland Press, Brisbane.

9   Deborah Jordan (2010) Environment and Colonial Shadows Green Island 1932, *Literature in North Queensland*, vol. 37, 142–58.
10 See the excellent catalogue (2013) To The Islands. Exploring works created by artists on Dunk, Bedarra and Timana Island between the 1930s and 1990s, curated by Ross Searle, Perc Tucker Regional Gallery, Townsville City Council, Queensland.
11 William Saville-Kent (1893) *The Great Barrier Reef of Australia: Its Products and Potentialities*, facsimile edition, Melbourne, 1972, and William Saville-Kent (1897) *The Naturalist in Australia*, 'Extracts from Opinions of the Press', Chapman and Hall, London.
12 Ann Elias (2019) *Coral Empire: Underwater Oceans, Colonial Tropics, Visual Modernity*, Duke University Press, Durham and London.
13 Noel Monkman (1956) *Escape to Adventure*, Halstead Press, Sydney, chapters 9–10.
14 McCalman (2013), 281.
15 Bowen & Bowen (2002), 322–5.
16 McCalman (2013), 276–81.
17 Judith Wright (2014) *The Coral Battleground*, 'Finale Without an Ending', Spinifex, Melbourne, 186–90.
18 David Ritter (2018) *The Coal Truth: The fight to stop Adani, defeat the big polluters and reclaim our democracy*, UWA Publishing, Perth.
19 Bowen & Bowen (2002), 357–78; Charlie Veron (2017) *A Life Underwater*, Penguin Australia, Melbourne, esp. 72–103.
20 JEN Veron (2009) *A Reef in Time: The Great Barrier Reef From Beginning to End*, Harvard University Press, Cambridge, Massachusetts, 56–65, 89–112, 200–20.
21 James Woodford (2010) *The Great Barrier Reef*, Macmillan, Sydney, 53.
22 Jon Day, Scott Heron & Terry Hughes (2021) Australian Government was 'blindsided' by the UN recommendation to list the Great Barrier Reef as in-danger. But it's no great surprise, *Conversation*, 23 June, viewed 11 July 2021, < https://theconversation.com/australian-government-was-blindsided-by-un-recommendation-to-list-great-barrier-reef-as-in-danger-but-its-no-great-surprise-163159>.
23 Irus Braverman (2018) *Coral Whisperers: Scientists on the Brink*, University of California Press, Berkeley, 109–38; 231–44.

Sydney Harbour Bridge
1   David Dunstan (ed.) (1996) *Victorian Icon: The Royal Exhibition Building Melbourne*, Exhibition Trustees, Melbourne.
2   KS Inglis (1985) Ceremonies in a capital landscape. In SR Graubard (ed.) *Australia: The Daedalus Symposium*, Angus & Robertson, Sydney. There is a vast literature on Canberra's monumental architecture and its claims to national symbolism, but most of it is of the booster variety, including the websites for all of the major political and cultural institutions.
3   Charles Whitham, a Tasmanian journalist and author, made this remark in his unpublished manuscript, Book of the North Shore, 1927, held by the Mitchell Library.
4   Peter Spearritt (1988) Celebration of a nation: The triumph of spectacle. In S Macintyre & S Janson (eds) *Making the Bicentenary, Australian Historical Studies*, Melbourne, 3–20; the only possible rival would be the Olympic Games at the Melbourne Cricket Ground in 1956, but it was more a celebration of Melbourne than Australia.
5   See the website of the Council on Tall Buildings and Urban Habitat, which keeps up-to-date entries on both skyscrapers and observation towers, <www.ctbuh.org>.
6   Analysis of the Harbour Bridge in this chapter is drawn from Peter Spearritt (2007) *The Sydney Harbour Bridge: A Life*, University of New South Wales Press, Sydney; see also

C Mackaness (ed.) (2007) *Bridging Sydney*, Historic Houses Trust, Sydney, for a detailed account of the planning and building of the bridge.
7   For a historical analysis of Sydney–Melbourne rivalry, including imagery, see Jim Davidson (ed.) (1986) *The Sydney Melbourne Book*, Allen & Unwin, Sydney. On war memorials see KS Inglis (2008) *Sacred Places: War Memorials in the Australian Landscape*, 3rd edition, Melbourne University Press, Melbourne.
8   See the extensive coverage in the Melbourne press, including the *Age* and the *Argus* of March 1932.
9   Andrew Moore (2005) *Francis de Groot: Irish Fascist, Australian Legend*, Federation Press, Sydney and *New York Times* online index.
10 Illustrations and the bibliography in Peter Spearritt (1982) *The Sydney Harbour Bridge: A Life*, 1st edition, Allen & Unwin, Sydney; front covers of the widely circulated *Meccano Magazine*, December 1926, October 1927; front cover of *Building in Steel*, from *The Modern How it Works Series*, Wells Gardner, Surrey, 1950.
11 On textual, artistic and photographic representations see the chapter on the bridge in Laurie Duggan (2001) *Ghost Nation: Imagined Space and Australian Visual Culture, 1901–1939*, University of Queensland Press, Brisbane.
12 See the books produced by all the major guidebook publishing houses, including Lonely Planet, Rough Guide and Frommer's.
13 Cartoon published in the *Australian*, 10 July 1998, reproduced in Spearritt (2007), 148.
14 The lack of coverage of the issue is evident in the *Sydney Morning Herald* in the days leading up to the 75th anniversary walk on Sunday 18 March. The *Australian*, which was not a sponsor of the event, did cover the measures to keep numbers down.
15 John Urry's (1995) *Consuming Places*, Routledge, London and New York, remains the most important study of how places are promoted and reinvented. See also RW Butler (1980) The concept of a tourism area cycle of evolution, *Canadian Geographer*, 24, 5–12; Gordon Waitt (2001) The city as tourist spectacle: Marketing Sydney for the 2000 Olympics. In David Holmes (ed.) *Virtual Globalization*, Routledge, London.
16 Hammons Holdings (2018) Hammons Holdings says returning Sydney Harbour Bridge to the people will be a priority following its appointment as new operator of Bridge tourism, viewed 29 January 2020, <http://hammonsholdings.com.au/wp-content/uploads/2018/06/HH-MediaRelease.pdf>.
17 See BridgeClimb's regularly updated website, <www.bridgeclimb.com>, with the slogan 'For the climb of your life'. The bridge climbs in Brisbane and Auckland do not attract anywhere near the same number of climbers, not least because their landscape settings and the views are neither as thrilling nor as awe-inspiring.

Lifesaver
1   I would like to thank Ed Jaggard and Sean O'Connell for providing thoughtful comments on early drafts of this chapter, as well as input from the editors and other contributors to this book.
2   By 2019, the number of clubs had grown to 314, with more than 176,000 members, Surf Life Saving Australia (SLSA), *Annual Report 2018–19*, 21.
3   Tim Winton (2003) *Land's Edge*, Pan Macmillan, Sydney, 37; Robert Drewe (ed.) (1993) *The Picador Book of the Beach*, Pan Macmillan, Sydney, 7.
4   Caroline Ford (2014) *Sydney Beaches: A history* NewSouth, Sydney, esp. 29–47.
5   John Rickard (1996) *Australia: A Cultural History*, Longman, London, 192; Kay Saunders (1998) 'Specimens of superb manhood': The lifesaver as national icon, *Journal of Australian Studies*, 56, March, 96–105.

6 SLSA, 21.
7 For more on women and surf lifesaving, see Ed Jaggard (1999) Australian surf life-saving and the 'forgotten members', *Australian Historical Studies*, 30(112) April, 23–43.
8 The summer seaside carnival, *Sydney Mail*, 7 March 1906, 604.
9 Richard White (1981) *Inventing Australia: Images and Identity 1688–1980*, Allen & Unwin, Sydney, 85.
10 *Sydney Morning Herald* (SMH), 11 September 1909, 5; Letter to the editor, SMH, 21 January 1902; SMH, 1 October 1909, 13; Arthur Relph (1910) Surf bathing: Influence on stamina and physique, SMH, 12 November, 10; Letter to the editor, SMH, 3 February 1911, 7; Surf bathing joys: A national pastime, SMH, 26 September 1911, 7; Surf bathing: Mr Griffith and nationalisation, SMH, 10 November 1913, 6; Toll of the surf, SMH, 6 January 1914, 8; see also Grant Rodwell (1999) The sense of victorious struggle: The eugenic dynamic in Australian popular surf-culture, 1900–50, *Journal of Australian Studies*, 62, September, 56–63.
11 Surf bathers as state advertisements, SMH, 18 May 1908, 6.
12 Relph (1910); SMH, 8 March 1910, 6.
13 See Ford (2014), 70–4; Caroline Ford (2020) Battles over Bodies on the Beach: The Origins of the Suntan, *History: Magazine of the Royal Australian Historical Society*, 146, 2–5.
14 Nancy Cushing & Leone Huntsman (2006) A national icon: Surf lifesaving and Australian society and culture. In Ed Jaggard (ed.) *Between the Flags: One Hundred Summers of Australian Surf Lifesaving*, University of New South Wales Press, Sydney, 11.
15 Saunders (1998).
16 Cushing & Huntsman (2006), 11.
17 *The Times* (London) 7 February 1938, 13. For a detailed analysis of Black Sunday, see Sean Brawley (2007) *The Bondi Lifesaver: A History of an Australian Icon*, ABC Books, Sydney, 133–9.
18 A total of 244 soldiers gained their bronze medallions at Torokina Beach, in the Solomon Islands in 1945, about 61 in New Guinea and seven in Palestine. Surf Life Saving Australia (SLSA) bronze medallion records, SLSA archives.
19 *Sun Herald*, 7 February 1954.
20 For more on surfers and surf lifesaving, see Douglas Booth (2001) *Australian Beach Cultures: The History of Sun, Sand and Surf*, Frank Cass, London.
21 Editorial, *Daily Telegraph*, 6 December 2005, 16; see also SMH, 9 December 2005, 6; Ford (2014), 202–3.
22 Editorial, *Daily Telegraph*, 6 December 2005, 16.
23 Victoria Pengilley & Sarah Thomas, Lifesavers being 'harassed' by beachgoers defying crowd bans over coronavirus fears (2020), ABC News, 22 March, viewed 22 March 2021, < https://www.abc.net.au/news/2020-03-22/appeal-to-beachgoers-defying-bondi-beach-ban-coronavirus/12078868>.
24 See Holden chapter, 296.

Pavlova
1 The author's original research has proved gratifyingly resilient despite much further work. See Michael Symons (1982) *One Continuous Picnic: A History of Eating in Australia*, Duck Press, Adelaide (enlarged edition, 2007). Further work was supported by the Marsden Fund of the Royal Society of New Zealand. With grateful acknowledgment to principal investigator, Professor Helen Leach. For a fuller account of social invention/construction, see Michael Symons (2010) The confection of a nation: The social

invention and social construction of the Pavlova, *Social Semiotics*, 20(2), 197–217. This has not dampened research on 'firsts'; Andrew Paul Wood and Annabelle Utrecht have for a few years been promising further revelations, as hinted in such teasers as a press release (2015), viewed 8 January 2020, <http://www.pavlovadoco.com/Files/Other/DocAndTheFrock_PressRelease_10_10_2015.pdf>.
2   Michael Symons (2008) The cleverness of the whole number: *Social invention in the golden age of Antipodean baking, 1890–1940*, Petits Propos Culinaires, 85, 31–60; Maurice French (2013) *The Lamington Enigma: A Survey of the Evidence*, Tabletop Publishing, Toowoomba; Allison Reynolds (2018) *Anzac Biscuits: The Power and Spirit of an Everyday National Icon*, Wakefield Press, Adelaide.
3   Ethel Wald (1940) *The Empire Cookery Book: Containing 500 Selected Choice Recipes*, South Australian Red Cross Society and Royal Naval Friendly Union, Adelaide.
4   Hugh Schmitt (1973) The man who whipped up the world's first pavlova, *Woman's Day*, 27 August.
5   Helen Leach (2008) *The Pavlova Story: A Slice of New Zealand's Culinary History*, Otago University Press, Dunedin. For an earlier excursion, see Helen M Leach (1997) The pavlova cake: The evolution of a national dish. In Harlan Walker (ed.) *Food on the Move: Proceedings of the Oxford Symposium on Food and Cookery, 1996*, Prospect Books, London, 219–23.
6   Jennifer Hillier raised this in The pavlova and the 'fate of nations'. In Arthur Grimes, Lydia Wevers & Ginny Sullivan (eds) (2002) *States of Mind: Australia and New Zealand, 1901–2001*, NZ Institute of Policy Studies, Wellington, 345–63.
7   Mrs Lance Rawson (1895) *The Australian Enquiry Book of Household and General Information: A Practical Guide for the Cottage, Villa, and Bush Home*, 2nd edition, Pater & Knapton, Melbourne, 14.
8   Jessie Sawyer & Sara Moore-Sims (1973) *Coronation Cookery Book*, Country Women's Association of NSW, Sydney, 193.
9   Quoted in Gennady Smakov (1984) *The Great Russian Dancers*, Alfred A. Knopf, Inc., New York, 4.
10 Victor Dandré (1932) *Anna Pavlova in Art & Life*, Cassell, London, 190.
11 Davis Gelatine (1926) *Davis Dainty Dishes*, 5th edition, Davis Gelatine (Australia), Sydney.
12 Publishers were still not sufficiently familiar to pick up the misspelling 'Padalova' in Elsie Gill's (1952) *New Australian Jubilee Cookery Book*, Murwillumbah, 75.
13 Anon. (c. 1950s) *Selected Recipes from The Leader: Another Spare Corner Book*, David Syme, Melbourne, 10.
14 Helen Cox (1956) *Time Saving Cooking*, London, 104–5.
15 Ross Campbell (1971) *Bulletin*, 11 December, 13–14.
16 Quoted in WS Ramson (ed.) (1988) *The Australian National Dictionary: A Dictionary of Australianisms on Historical Principles*, Oxford University Press, Melbourne, 466.
17 Richard White (1981) *Inventing Australia: Images and Identity, 1688–1980*, Allen & Unwin, Sydney, viii; Benedict Anderson (1983) *Imagined Communities: Reflections on the Origin and Spread of Nationalism*, Verso, London.
18 Samantha Hutchinson & Stephen Brook (2021) You have mail: Upton's reply all to the party of the year, *Sydney Morning Herald*, 15 April, viewed 11 July 2021, < https://www.SMH.com.au/national/you-have-mail-upton-s-reply-all-to-the-party-of-the-year-20210415-p57jm6.html>.

Holden
1   Shane Birney (1985) *Australia's Own: The History of Holden*, Golden Press, Sydney, 19.
2   ibid., 20.
3   LJ Hartnett (1965) *Big Wheel and Little Wheels*, Angus & Robertson, London, 171.
4   Birney (1985), 53.
5   Norm Darwin (2017) *Early Australian Automotive Design: The First Fifty Years*, H@nd Publishing, Mount Rowan, Chapter 7.
6   Hartnett (1965), 58.
7   *Bulletin*, 17 November 1948, 25.
8   Don Loffler (2006) *She's a Beauty! The Story of the First Holdens*, revised edition, Wakefield Press, Adelaide, 94.
9   ibid., 86.
10 Jack Fahey (2019) The cultivation of an Australian identity: New insights into public relations at General Motors-Holden in the interwar era, *Australian Historical Studies*, 50(4), 483–502.
11 Robert Crawford (2008) *But Wait, There's More … A History of Australian Advertising*, Melbourne University Press, Melbourne, 114–18.
12 Mick Taussig (1987) An Australian hero, *History Workshop Journal*, 24(1), 117.
13 John William Knott (2000) The 'Conquering Car': Technology, symbolism and the motorisation of Australia before World War II, *Australian Historical Studies*, April, 114, 7–10.
14 Frank Clune (1953) *Land of Australia: Roaming in a Holden*, Hawthorne Press, Melbourne, 5.
15 ibid., 2.
16 Graeme Davison (2004) *Car Wars: How the Car Won our Hearts and Converted our Cities*, Allen & Unwin, Sydney, 13–15.
17 ibid, 16.
18 Peter Spearritt (1987) Cars for the people. In Ann Curthoys, AW Martin & Tim Rowse (eds) *Australians: A Historical Library: Australians from 1939*, Fairfax, Syme & Weldon, Sydney, 122.
19 Richard White (2005) *On Holidays: A History of Getting Away in Australia*, Pluto Press, Melbourne, 132–3.
20 Beverley Kingston (1994) *Basket, Bag, and Trolley: A Short History of Shopping in Australia*, Oxford University Press, Melbourne, 94–6.
21 See Richard Strauss (1998) *Up for Rego: A Social History of the Holden Kingswood*, Pluto Press, Sydney.
22 Michael Ackland (2006) Murray Bail. In Selina Samuels (ed.) *Dictionary of Literary Biography Vol. 325 Australian Writers 1975–2000*, Thomson Gale, Detroit, 28.
23 Caroline Ford makes a similar point about the lifesaver, see Lifesaver chapter, 270.
24 Ben Potter (2013) Hockey dares GM to leave, *Financial Review*, 11 December, viewed 3 December 2019 <https://www.afr.com/companies/manufacturing/hockey-dares-gm-to-leave-20131211-iyoj2>.
25 Roy Green (2017) The Truth about the Holden Shutdown in Australia, *Sydney Morning Herald*, 13 October, viewed 3 December 2019, <https://www.SMH.com.au/opinion/the-truth-about-the-holden-shutdown-in-australia-20171010-gyxogj.html>; Joshua Dowling, Counting the Cost of Killing Australia's Car Industry (2017) *Advertiser*, 19 October, viewed 3 December 2019, <https://www.adelaidenow.com.au/rendezview/counting-the-cost-of-killing-australias-car-industry/news-story/

cb10862b3405a9b26ce9f4541bbdbc08>; Royce Kurmelovs (2017), *The Death of Holden: The End of an Australian Dream*, Hachette, Sydney.

Uluru

1 Uluru is a Pitjantjatjara word that 'doesn't have an English translation': see <https://parksaustralia.gov.au/uluru/about/ayers-rock-or-uluru/>.
2 Stuart's journal of the expedition shows that 'Central Mount Sturt' was the name originally given to the hill. Later it was changed to Central Mount Stuart on the suggestion of the then governor of South Australia, presumably with Stuart's consent. William Hardman (ed.) (1865) *Explorations in Australia: The Journals of John McDouall Stuart, During the Years 1858–62*, 2nd edition, Saunders, Otley & Co., London, 165. Online version viewed 26 January 2008, <http://gutenberg.net.au/ausdisc/ausdisc2-17.html>.
3 HH Finlayson (1935) *The Red Centre: Man and Beast in the Heart of Australia*, Angus & Robertson, Sydney, 8, 16–17.
4 Roslynn Haynes (1998) *Seeking the Centre: The Australian Desert in Literature, Art and Film*, Cambridge University Press, Cambridge, 262–3.
5 *Tjukurpa* is the Pitjantjatjara word for law, traditional knowledge, religion, morality and relation to country.
6 For a more detailed account of Anangu Tjurkurpa relating to Uluru see the *Uluru-Kata Tjuta National Park Knowledge Handbook*, <www.environment.gov.au/system/files/resources/d97e9851-014c-4bd0-96c8-9b05c59da72a/files/handbook.pdf>.
7 Ernest Giles (1889) *Australia Twice Traversed*, 2 vols, Sampson Low, Marston, Searle & Rivington, London, vol. 1, 210. Giles merely substituted 'rock' for 'wreck' in Shelley's poem.
8 William Christie Gosse (1973), Diary 19 July 1873 in *Report and Diary of Mr W.C. Gosse's central and western exploring expedition, 1873*, Libraries Board of South Australia, Adelaide, viewed 7 November 2019, <https://www.samemory.sa.gov.au/site/page.cfm?u=77&c=7213>. Sir Henry Ayres was the Chief Secretary of South Australia.
9 Quoted in Barry Hill (1994) *The Rock: Travelling to Uluru*, Allen & Unwin, Sydney, 4.
10 TGH Strehlow, Diary entry for 11 June 1935, quoted in Hill (1994), 4.
11 For a full account, see Mark McKenna (2021) *Return to Uluru*, Black Inc., Melbourne.
12 The 1988 film *Evil Angels* (also released as *A Cry in the Dark*) directed by Fred Schepisi was based on John Bryson's 1985 book of that name. The opera, *Lindy*, composed by Moya Henderson, premiered in 2002.
13 Annual Report of the Northern Territory 1938, quoted in Robert Layton (1986) *Uluru: An Aboriginal History of Ayers Rock*, Australian Institute of Aboriginal Studies, Canberra, 73.
14 Australian Government Department of the Environment, Water, Heritage and the Arts, Parks and Reserves: Uluru-Kata Tjuta National Park, viewed 9 November 2019, <https://parksaustralia.gov.au/uluru/discover/factsheets/>.
15 Quotations from Peter English (1986) *Storm over Uluru (The greatest hoax of all)*, Veritas Publishing, Bullsbrook, 140–1, cited in Jane Carruthers, 'Contesting cultural landscapes in South Africa and Australia', in David Trigger & Gareth Griffiths (eds) (2003) *Disputed Territories: Land, Culture and Identity in Settler Societies*, Hong Kong University Press, Hong Kong, 246–7. Jerusalem presents a similar situation of a contested location.
16 Ruby Langford Ginibi (1988) *Don't Take your Love to Town*, Penguin Books, Melbourne, 234.

17   Rex Ingamells, Extracts from 'Uluru, An Apostrophe to Ayers Rock' in Brian Elliot (ed.) (1979) *The Jindyworobaks*, Queensland University Press, Brisbane, 33–5.
18   See Rainbow Serpent chapter, 347.
19   Hill (1994), 270.
20   ibid. Hill records in detail the reasons why the second request was refused. See the program of this Conference, viewed 14 January 2020, <https://www.cosmicconsciousness.com.au/programme>.
21   This is the figure given on the Australian Government Parks website, viewed 14 January 2020, <https://parksaustralia.gov.au/uluru/discover/highlights/amazing-facts/>. The ABC records a figure of more than 300,000, viewed 14 January 2020, <https://www.abc.net.au/radionational/programs/offtrack/climbing-the-rock:-why-do-tourists-still-climb-uluru/6603640>.
22   Quoted in Hill (1994), 167–9.
23   Ann Jones interviewed a number of visitors about their imperative to climb Uluru in the ABC program 'Off Track', viewed 14 January 2020, <https://www.abc.net.au/radionational/programs/offtrack/climbing-the-rock:-why-do-tourists-still-climb-uluru/6603640>.
24   Olympic Games 2000 Sydney, Torch and Torch Relay, viewed 7 November 2019, <http://www.olympic-museum.de/torches/olympic-games-torch-2000.php>.
25   Dr Lowitja O'Donoghue (2000) Australia Day Address, 24 January, viewed 7 November 2019, <https://www.australiaday.com.au/events/australia-day-address/dr-lowitja-odonoghue-2000/>.
26   Makarrata is a Yolngu word 'describing a process of conflict resolution, peacemaking and justice'. Luke Pearson (2017) What is a Makarrata? It's more than a synonym for treaty, ABC News, 10 August, viewed 28 September 2018, <https://www.abc.net.au/news/2017-08-10/makarrata-explainer-yolngu-word-more-than-synonym-for-treaty/8790452>. Joint Select Committee on Constitutional Recognition relating to Aboriginal and Torres Strait Islander Peoples Submission 21, viewed 9 November 2019, <https://www.aph.gov.au >DocumentStore>; Henry Reynolds (2021) *Truth-Telling: History, sovereignty and the Uluru Statement*, NewSouth Publishing, Sydney.
27   Jesse John Fleay (2019) 'The Uluru statement: A First Nations perspective of the implications for social reconstructive race relations in Australia', *International Journal of Critical Indigenous Studies*, 12(1): 1–14, viewed 9 November 2019, <https://ijcis.qut.edu.au/article/view/532>.
28   Graeme Turner (1993) *National Fictions*, Allen & Unwin, Sydney, 142. Its significance has been recognised internationally since 1987 when it was World Heritage listed and said to be one of very few listed by UNESCO for both natural and cultural values. In 1995 UNESCO gave it the Picasso Gold Medal because of the Anangu control. See <https://www.environment.gov.au/system/files/resources/d97e9851-014c-4bd0-96c8-9b05c59da72a/files/handbook.pdf>.

Sydney Opera House
1   Justine Vaisutis et al. (2007) *Australia*, Lonely Planet, Melbourne, 103; House History, viewed 27 January 2020, <https://www.sydneyoperahouse.com/our-story/sydney-opera-house-history.html>; In *Shell*, Kristina Olsson Captures a City That's Reaching for Greatness, viewed 24 March 2021, <https://www.nytimes.com/2018/10/26/books/shell-kristina-olsson.html>; Ian Walker, Spectacular Sydney Opera House to be built in Lego later this year, viewed 27 January 2020, <https://www.dailytelegraph.com.au/news/nsw/spectacular-sydney-opera-house-in-lego-later-this-year/news-story/

e076c41827f3a0801cb7064cf64b1a9d>; Sydney Opera House web page, viewed 10 December 2008, Culture.Gov.Au website, <www.cultureandrecreation.gov.au/articles/sydneyoperahouse> (now available at Australian Web Archive, NLA); National Heritage Places – Sydney Opera House, viewed 27 January 2020, <https://www.environment.gov.au/heritage/places/national/sydney-opera-house>, though no longer included as a prime ministerial 'symbol of Australia'. Compare how the Eiffel Tower symbolises both Paris and France: Roland Barthes (1997) *The Eiffel Tower and Other Mythologies*, trans. Richard Howard, University of California Press, Berkeley, 3.

2 Randy Randall (2009) Update from Oz, 3 February, viewed 8 February 2009, <www.noagela.blogspot. com>.

3 The account that follows here is drawn from many sources. They include Sylvia Lawson's personal recollections and diary material generously shared by WCA (Bill) Wheatland and Oktay Nayman, former associates to Jørn Utzon; the late Norman Ryan, former NSW Minister for Public Works; the late Elizabeth Price, former clerk and acting registrar to the NSW Board of Architects; the late Ellis Ezra, formerly of Ralph Symonds and Company, plywood manufacturers; also Peter Myers, Richard le Plastier, Clive Buhrich, Peter Compagnoni, Mary Anderson, Michal Tomaczewski, all formerly of Utzon's architectural staff; GJ Zunz, John Blanchard and the late Peter Rice, of Ove Arup and Partners, London. Of numerous books on the subject, the most useful have been Elias Duek-Cohen (1967) *Utzon and the Sydney Opera House: Statement in the Public Interest*, Morgan Publications, Sydney; new edition with addenda, 1998; Anne Watson (ed.) (2006) *Building a Masterpiece: The Sydney Opera House*, Powerhouse Publishing, Sydney; and Françoise Fromonot (1998) *Jørn Utzon et l'Opéra de Sydney*, Editions Gallimard, Paris. Unpublished theses on the subject particularly include Nino Bellantonio (1998) On emergence: Designing for quality, Faculty of Environmental Design, University of Canberra; Peter Georgiades (1993) Utzon's unseen work, Department of Architecture and Building, University of Technology, Sydney; Philip Nobis (1994) Utzon's interiors for the Sydney Opera House, Department of Architecture and Building, University of Technology, Sydney.

4 George Molnar (1955) Plans for Sydney's Opera House: What comes next?, *Sydney Morning Herald* (SMH), 4 June, 2.

5 Sarah Gregson (2006) Who built the Opera House? In Watson (ed.) (2006), 122–35.

6 For the meaning of 'continental' in the 1950s, see Mischa Barr (2009) Sex, art and sophistication: The meanings of 'Continental' cinema, *Journal of Australian Studies*, 33(1), March, 1–18.

7 Diane Collins (2009) Henri Verbrugghen's auditory Utopianism: Sound, reform, modernity and nation in Australia, 1915–1922, *History Australia*, 6(2), August, 36, 11–12.

8 See the series of articles by Philip Parsons & Francis Evers (1967) The Opera House crisis, *Australian*, 11, 13 and 14 February; Philip Parsons (1967) Radical versus conservative architecture: The ruin of Utzon's audacious vision, *Meanjin*, 26(3), Spring, 339–46.

9 Don Aitken (1985) 'Country-mindedness': The spread of an idea, *Australian Cultural History*, 4, 34–41.

10 Richard White (with Sarah-Jane Ballard, Ingrid Bown, Meredith Lake, Patricia Leahy & Lila Oldmeadow) (2005) *On Holidays: A History of Getting Away in Australia*, Pluto, Melbourne, 147–52.

11 SMH, especially for 3–10 March 1966.

12 On the RAIA's dealings with government, opposition and architect, see Parsons, Duek-Cohen and the evidence of those named in Note 3, above.

13 Michael Baume (1967) *The Sydney Opera House Affair*, Nelson, Melbourne.
14 John Yeomans (1968) *The Other Taj Mahal: What Happened to the Sydney Opera House*, Longmans, London, 41, 166.
15 Duek-Cohen (1967).
16 Robin Boyd (1967) Now it can never be architecture, *Life*, 24 July, 58.
17 These estimates are from Alexander Kouzmin (1979) Building the new Parliament House: An Opera House revisited? In *Working Papers on Parliament*, Canberra Series in Administrative Studies No. 5, Canberra College of Advanced Education, Canberra, 115–71.
18 For the symbolic role of *Blue Poles* see Lindsay Barrett (2001) *The Prime Minister's Christmas Card: Blue Poles and Cultural Politics in the Whitlam Era*, Power Publications, Sydney.
19 Iris Murdoch (2001 [1978]) *The Sea, the Sea*, Penguin, London, 451.
20 Hyatt Foundation (2003) Announcement: Danish architect Jørn Utzon becomes 2003 Pritzker Architecture Prize Laureate, viewed 25 May 2009, <http://www.pritzkerprize.com/laureates/2003/announcement.html>.
21 Philip Drew (2006) Poetic paradox: Utzon's sources for the Sydney Opera House. In Anne Watson (ed.) *Building a Masterpiece: The Sydney Opera House*, Sydney, Powerhouse Publishing, 83.
22 Luke Henriques-Gomes, 'It's not a billboard': anger at use of Sydney Opera House for horse racing ads, *Guardian Australia*, 6 October 2018, viewed 27 January 2020, <https://www.theguardian.com/australia-news/2018/oct/06/its-not-a-billboard-anger-at-use-of-sydney-opera-house-for-horse-racing-ads>; Jacob Saulwick, Eight out of 10 in NSW opposed to Berejiklian's Opera House sails deal: survey, SMH, 9 October 2018, viewed 27 January 2020, <https://www.SMH.com.au/national/nsw/eight-out-of-10-in-nsw-opposed-to-berejiklian-s-opera-house-sails-deal-survey-20181009-p508oc.html>; Kevin Nguyen & Nick Dole, Sydney Opera House painted with light from torches, lamps to disrupt Everest promotion, ABC News, 9 October 2018, viewed 27 January 2020, <abc.net.au/news/2018-10-09/opera-house-everest-protest/10357074>.
23 ICOMOS (International Council on Monuments and Sites) Sydney Opera House (Australia) No. 166 rev., 92, viewed 7 June 2009, <http://whc.unesco.org/archive/advisory_body_evaluation/166rev.pdf>.
24 Helen Pitt (2018) *The House: The Dramatic Story of the Sydney Opera House and the People who Made it*, Allen & Unwin, Sydney, 362.

Akubra
1 John Howard (2007) Australian icons, viewed 20 April 2007, <www.pm.gov.au/australia/symbols/icons.cfm> (now available at Australian Web Archive, NLA).
2 For a more detailed discussion of the constructed nature of so-called 'national dress' see Margaret Maynard (2004) *Dress and Globalisation*, Manchester University Press, Manchester, 59–64; Jennifer Craik (2009) Is Australian Fashion and Dress Distinctively Australian?, *Fashion Theory* 13(4): 409–42.
3 Richard White (2005) Symbols of Australia. In Martin Lyons & Penny Russell (eds) *Australia's History: Themes and Debates*, University of New South Wales Press, Sydney, 125.
4 Jill Bowen (1988) *The Akubra Hat*, Weldon Publishing, Sydney, 13.
5 National Archives Series A 1861, lodged 19 August 1921.
6 Bowen (1988), 13.
7 RM Dixon, Bruce Moore, WS Ramson & Mandy Thomas (1990) *Australian Aboriginal Words in English: Their Origin and Meaning*, Oxford University Press, Melbourne, 196; see

also Jakelin Troy (1994) *The Sydney Language*, Australian Dictionaries Projects, AIATSIS, Canberra.
8   This myth was specifically masculine, as was the dress. For more on the masculinity of the Australian bush myth and bush dress, see Margaret Maynard (1994) *Fashioned from Penury: Dress as a Cultural Practice in Colonial Australia*, Cambridge University Press, Cambridge; Jennifer Craik (2001) Tourism, culture and national identity. In Tony Bennett & David Carter (eds) *Culture in Australia: Policies, Publics and Programs*, Cambridge University Press, Cambridge, 89–113.
9   Richard White (1981) *Inventing Australia: Images and Identity 1699–1980*, Allen & Unwin, Sydney, 85.
10 Rick Grebert (2002) *The Australian Army Slouch Hat and Rising Sun Badge*, New South Wales Military Historical Society Inc., Sydney, 17.
11 Edwards quoted in a South Australian defence report of 1889. Peter Burness (1983) New South Wales infantry uniforms 1854–1903, *Journal of the Australian War Memorial*, 3, 44.
12 Rick Grebert (1997) *Slouch Hat on the Australian Army*, New South Wales Military Historical Society, Caringbah, NSW, 32.
13 Bowen (1988), 13–25.
14 Grenville Turner (1988) *Akubra is Australian for Hat*, Simon & Schuster, Brookvale, NSW, 22–3.
15 Grebert (1997) Foreword.
16 Bowen (1988); Turner (1988).
17 Hats off to the Akubra (2019) *Chronicle*, viewed 22 October, <https://www.thechronicle.com.au/news/hats-off-to-the-akubra/2217801/>.
18 Ruth Brown (1994) *Crocodile Dundee* and the revival of American virtue. In Ian Craven (ed.) *Australian Popular Culture*, University of Cambridge Press, Cambridge, 79.
19 Graeme Turner (1994) *Making it National: Nationalism and Australian Popular Culture*, Allen & Unwin, Sydney, 108.
20 Personal correspondence from Roy Wilkinson (now Akubra's chief financial officer) to Philippa Macaskill, 4 June 2007.
21 Anthony Hoy (2003) Slim Dusty, 1927–2003, *Bulletin*, 24 September, viewed 18 April 2007, <http:// bulletin.ninemsn.com.au/article.aspx?id=134787>.
22 See transcript of the *Insiders* episode (2015) Akubra image a publicity ploy, Fischer tells, 27 November, viewed 15 April 2007, <www.abc.net.au/insiders/content/2005/s1517577.htm>.
23 DD McNicoll (1997) Wherever he lays his hat, he's home, *Australian*, 17 September, 2.
24 Linda Morris, Jonathan Dart & Mark Davies (2008) Fischer to be our man in Vatican, *Sydney Morning Herald*, 22 July, 4.
25 Nick Dyrenfurth (2007) John Howard's hegemony of values: The politics of mateship in the Howard decade, *Australian Journal of Political Science*, 42(2), 222.
26 Mike Carlton (2000) Hats off to cowpat PM, *Sydney Morning Herald*, 5 February, 38.
27 Qld — Murgon mayor slams PM's bush policies, AAP, 8 February 2000.
28 Annabel Crabb (2018) Scott Morrison is perfecting the art of Not Being Malcolm Turnbull, ABC News, 7 September, viewed 20 October 2019, <https://www.abc.net.au/news/2018-09-07/scott-morrison-not-being-malcolm-turnbull/10208598>.

Rainbow Serpent
1   See further Luke Taylor (1999) Introduction. In Luke Taylor (ed.) *Painting the Land Story*, National Museum of Australia, Canberra; David Mowaljarlai & Jutta Malnic (1993) *Yorro Yorro: Everything Standing Up Alive!: Spirit of the Kimberley*, Magabala Books,

Broome; Michael Walsh & Colin Yallop (eds) (1993) *Language and Culture in Aboriginal Australia*, Aboriginal Studies Press, Canberra; RM Berndt (1992) *The World of the First Australians: Aboriginal Traditional Life, Past and Present*, 5th edition, Aboriginal Studies Press for AIATSIS, Canberra; Max Charlesworth, Françoise Dussart & Howard Morphy (eds) (2005) *Aboriginal Religions in Australia: An Anthology of Recent Writings*, Ashgate, Aldershot; Tony Swain (1993) *A Place for Strangers: Towards a History of Australian Aboriginal Being*, Cambridge University Press, Cambridge.

2   Taylor (1999) Introduction, 5–6; Luke Taylor (1999) Rainbows in the water, in Taylor (ed.) *Painting the Land Story*, 39; Anne Marie Brodie (1984) *Kinwinjku Bim: Western Arnhem Land Paintings from the Collection of the Aboriginal Arts Board*, National Gallery of Victoria, 7 December 1984–24 June 1985, National Gallery of Victoria, Melbourne, 74; Lloyd D Graham (2003) The creation of Wilkinkarra (Lake Mackay) in Pintupi/Kukatja Dreamings, *Australian Aboriginal Studies*, no. 1; Charles E Hulley (1999) *The Rainbow Serpent*, New Holland, Sydney; A Buchler & K Maddock (eds) (1978) *The Rainbow Serpent: A Chromatic Piece*, Mouton, Paris; Oodgeroo Noonuccal & Kabul Oodgeroo Noonuccal (1988) *The Rainbow Serpent*, Australian Government Publishing Services, Canberra; Georges Petitjean (2012) 'Casting ahead serpent-fashion – the Rainbow Serpent in Australia' in Wouter Welling (ed.) *Dangerous and Divine: the secret of the serpent*, KIT Publishers/Afrika Museum, 172–81; and Susan Greenwood (2019) *Developing Magical Consciousness A Theoretical and Practical Guide for the Expansion of Perception*, Routledge, London.

3   Taylor (1999) Rainbows; Brodie (1984).
4   Taylor (1999) Rainbows, 39.
5   Taylor (1999) Rainbows; Brodie (1984).
6   G Chaloupka cited in Paul SC Taçon, Meredith Wilson & Christopher Chippindale (1984) Birth of the Rainbow Serpent in Arnhem Land rock art and oral history, *Archaeology in Oceania*, 31(3), 103; see also Bruno David (2002) *Landscapes, Rock-Art and the Dreaming: An Archaeology of Preunderstanding*, Leicester University Press, London and New York.
7   There are many versions of this story told by the Lardil people. See Thuwathu – the Rainbow Serpent, as told by Lindsay Roughsey in Amanda Ahern and the Mornington Island Elders, *Paint Up*, University of Queensland Press, Brisbane, 2002, 32; David McKnight (1999) *People, Countries, and the Rainbow Serpent: Systems of Classification Among the Lardil of Mornington Island*, Oxford University Press, New York and Oxford, 193–200.
8   Petitjean (2012), 176–7.
9   Armstrong (1836), cited in Patricia Vinnicombe (1992) An Aboriginal site complex at the foot of Mount Eliza which includes the Old Swan Brewery Building, *Historic Environment*, 9(1–2), 54.
10 Clarrie Isaacs (1992) The Great Rainbow Serpent Dreaming Track: Part of one of the great religious belief systems of the world, *Historic Environment*, 9(1–2), 52.
11 See Steven Churches (1990) Aboriginal people and government responsibility and accountability, *Aboriginal Law Bulletin*, 2(47), 6–7; Steven Churches (1992) Aboriginal heritage in the wild west: Robert Bropho and the Swan Brewery site, *Aboriginal Law Bulletin*, 2(56), 9–13; and Roy Jones & Christina Birdsall-Jones (2003) Native or manufactured? A comparison of Indigenous–industrial heritage conflicts in Perth and Ottawa, *Australian–Canadian Studies*, 21(2), 73–106.
12 Isaacs (1992), 52.
13 John Fielder (1994) Sacred sites and the city: Urban Aboriginality, ambivalence, and modernity, *boundary 2*, 21(1), 78.

14 Isaacs (1992), 52, and Fielder (1994), 78, 82.
15 AR Radcliffe-Brown (1930) The Rainbow-Serpent myth in south-east Australia, *Oceania*, 1, 342.
16 ibid., 342.
17 Ken Maddock (1978) Introduction. In A Buchler & K Maddock (eds) *The Rainbow Serpent: A Chromatic Piece*, Mouton, Paris, 3.
18 See Christine Nicholls (2000) *From Appreciation to Appropriation: Indigenous Influences and Images in Australian Visual Art*, Flinders University, Adelaide, 5.
19 Gavin Damien Francis Malone (2012) Phases of Aboriginal Inclusion in the Public Space in Adelaide, South Australia, since Colonisation, PhD thesis, Flinders University, School of the Environment, 97–8; Greenwood, Chapter 1.
20 Anthropologist Catherine Berndt was most prolific in producing such books, most notably around Australia's bicentennial celebrations. See Catherine H Berndt (1979) *Land of the Rainbow Snake: Aboriginal Children's Stories and Songs from Western Arnhem Land*, Collins, Sydney; Catherine H Berndt (1988) *When the World Was New: In Rainbow Snake Land*, Bookshelf, Gosford; Catherine H Berndt (1988) *This Is Still Rainbow Snake Country*, Martin Educational, Cammeray. For examples of books by Aboriginal elders see Dick Roughsey (1975) *The Rainbow Serpent*, Angus & Robertson, Sydney; David Gulpilil (1987) *The Rainbow Serpent*, retold by Mary O'Toole, Macmillan, Melbourne.
21 For example, a large sculpture in Townsville's Pioneer Park, developed by the Migrant Resource Centre, Townsville and Thuringowa in the name of reconciliation, and an engraving by Alice Mitchell Marrakorlorlo on a stone in honour of Aboriginal artist Robert Lee, in Canberra's Reconciliation Park.
22 Petitjean, 176; Greenwood.
23 Rainbow Serpent Festival, Philosophy, viewed 29 January 2008, <www.rainbowserpent.net/about/philosophy/>. Daniel Miles (2020) Rainbow Serpent festival too dangerous to be held in summer, landowner says, ABC News, 9 January, viewed 20 January 2020, <https://www.abc.net.au/news/2020-01-09/rainbow-serpent-festival-too-dangerous-for-summer-landowner-says/11855678>.
24 Sallie Anderson (2001) Rejecting the Rainbow Serpent: An Aboriginal artist's choice of the Christian God as creator, *Australian Journal of Anthropology*, 12(3), 297. For a typical example see Robert Coon (2000) *The Rainbow Serpent and the Holy Grail: Uluru and the Planetary Chakras*, Robert Coon, Warburton, or various New Age and pagan websites; Petitjean, 176; Greenwood.
25 Luke Taylor (1990) The Rainbow Serpent as visual metaphor in Western Arnhem Land, *Oceania*, 60, 329.
26 How the long necked turtle and the rainbow serpent are promoting oral health, *Reconciliation News*, 1(1), 2007, 7.
27 Black + White + Pink, Reconciliation 99 – Getting it right, viewed 12 March 2008, <www.queers4reconciliation.wild.net.au/mg99.htm>.
28 Fiona Murphy, 'Memorialising the story of Australian Aboriginal child removal: The story of Reconciliation Place', in Fiona Larkan & Fiona Murphy (eds), *Memory and Recovery in Times of Crisis*, Routledge, London, 2017, 32–47, 40.
29 Local Bundjalung artist John Robinson creates rainbow serpent artwork for Stockland Green (2018) *The Maitland Mercury*, 31 May, viewed 25 October 2019, <https://www.maitlandmercury.com.au/story/5441314/aboriginal-art-to-be-installed-at-green-hills/>; Gunnedah Indigenous water feature welcomed by Kamilaroi community (2019) *Namoi Valley Independent*, 17 July, viewed 25 October 2019, <https://www.nvi.com.au/

story/6277048/rainbow-dreaming-kamilaroi-women-eager-to-see-water-feature-take-shape/>; and Wagyl the Rainbow Serpent, Perth Royal Show, viewed 25 October 2019 <https://www.perthroyalshow.com.au/event/wagyl-rainbow-serpent/>.

Baggy green
1. Sir Arthur Conan Doyle (1974) The blue carbuncle, *The Adventures of Sherlock Holmes*, Pan, London, 166–7.
2. Steve Waugh (2005) *Out of My Comfort Zone: The Autobiography*, Penguin, Camberwell, 35; Steve Waugh (2001) *Never Satisfied: The Diary of a Record-Breaking Year*, HarperCollins, Sydney.
3. A good example is in Roland Perry's characteristically unreliable history of the Australian Test captaincy: Perry (2000) *Captain Australia: A History of the Celebrated Captains of Australian Test Cricket*, Random House, Sydney, 84. Perry asserts that South Australian Joe Darling responded to Federation by instructing players to wear their new 'velvet skull caps' throughout the Sydney Test of December 1901 'to present the opposition with the perception of a tight unit, truly representative of a new nation'. Perusal of photographs of the game shows this to be quite untrue: almost everyone is wearing a sunhat.
4. Jim Tucker (1997) The power of baggy green, *Inside Edge*, January, 76–7.
5. For further details of the stresses and strains of 1880s cricket in Australia, see David Montefiore (1992) Cricket in the doldrums: The struggle between private and public control of Australian cricket in 1880s, *ASSH Studies in Sports History No 8*, Australian Society for Sports History Inc., Campbelltown.
6. Gideon Haigh (2004) *Game for Anything: Writings on Cricket*, Black Inc., Melbourne, 108.
7. Peter Sharpham (1997) *The 1899 Australians*, JW McKenzie, Epsom, 149–57.
8. John Harms (1995) Cricket and Federation: A study of the 1889 Australian tour of England, paper delivered at Australian Society for Sports History Conference, Brisbane.
9. Minutes of Australian Board of Control for International Cricket, 29 May 1908, meeting at Port Phillip Club Hotel, Melbourne.
10. Letter book of Ben Wardill, secretary of Melbourne Cricket Club, 25 May 1910.
11. Minutes of Australian Board of Control for International Cricket, 10–11 September 1931, meeting at Cricket House, Sydney.
12. The section about caps in Bradman's famous instructional text *The Art of Cricket*, Hodder & Stoughton, Sydney, 1990, 16, does not mention the baggy green cap at all. Instead it contains purely basic advice such as: 'Unless the weather is dull, I think it advisable to wear a cap.'
13. At the board's meeting of 14–16 February 1962, for instance, a letter was read attached to a clipping of a food advertisement featuring an Australian player wearing his 1961 tour cap. But although Mr PA Bartlett of Brisbane's West End said he took exception to the use of the item for a 'commercial enterprise', the board took no action.
14. AJM Hewitt (1971) Cricket caps, once a symbol, are not in the fashion these days, *Playfair Cricket Monthly*, February, 13; Ray Robinson (1975) *On Top Down Under*, Cassell Australia, Sydney, 4; Ian Brayshaw (1982) *Warriors in Baggy Green Caps*, Currawong Press, Sydney; World Series Cricket general manager Vern Stone, in conversation with author, 1992.
15. Waugh (2005), 34.
16. Steve Waugh (1995) *West Indies Diary*, Harper Sports, Sydney, 141.
17. Steve Waugh (1997) *Ashes Diary 1997*, Harper Sports, Sydney, 202.
18. Hugh de Selincourt (1980 [1924]) *The Cricket Match*, Oxford University Press, London, 24.

19 Steve Waugh (2001) *Ashes Diary 2001*, Harper Sports, Sydney, 79–80; see also the remarks of Lt-Gen Peter Cosgrove, historians Chris Coulthard-Clark and Kevin Fewster in David Mark (2001) Public relations campaign for cricketers, *The World Today*, <www.abc.net.au/worldtoday/stories/s304572.htm>, 29 May; and Dennis Glover (2005) The price of forgetting, *Weekend Australian Financial Review*, 22–25 April, 2.
20 A full account of the intellectual property protection can be found in Gideon Haigh & David Frith (2007) *Inside Story: Unlocking Australia's Cricket Archives*, News Custom Publishing, Melbourne, 333–4. For further details of the 'History of the baggy green', signed inevitably by Steve Waugh, see <www.sportsonline.com.au/item.aspx?id=8103&cID=5> and <https://taylormadememorabilia.com.au/product/cricket-steve-waugh-signed-framed-history-of-the-baggy-green-print/>.
21 Fiona Bollen (2017) Women's cricketer Alex Blackwell says men's and women's teams should wear same baggy green, *The Daily Telegraph*, 7 July, viewed 6 July 2021, <https://www.dailytelegraph.com.au/sport/swoop/womens-cricketer-alex-blackwell-says-mens-and-womens-teams-should-wear-same-baggy-green/news-story/ebdc4af2eb757ea2f08cb9d480772c99>.
22 Rohit Brijnath (2001) The importance of rituals, *Sports Star*, 10–16 November, <www.hinduonnet.com/tss/tss2445/24450340.htm>; Cricinfo staff (2007) Team tired of criticism – Gilchrist, *Cricinfo*, 23 December, <http://content-www.cricinfo.com/australia/content/story/326994.html>; Lyall Johnson, Show respect – Gilly fires back at Warne, *Sydney Morning Herald*, 24 December 2007; Andrew Symonds (2008) What price the baggy green?, *Fox Sports*, 17 February, 8, <www.foxsports.com.au/story/0,8659,23224682-23212,00.html>; Sir Arthur Conan Doyle (1985) Silver blaze. In *The Memoirs of Sherlock Holmes*, Penguin, United Kingdom, 31.
23 Shane Warne slams Australian reverence for Baggy Green (2020) *Sportstar*, 11 May, viewed 22 April 2021, <https://sportstar.thehindu.com/cricket/shane-warne-slams-australian-reverence-for-baggy-green-steve-waugh/article31555587.ece>; Dave Middleton (2020) Warne's mystery $1m Baggy Green buyer revealed, cricket.com.au, 10 January, viewed 22 April 2021, <https://www.cricket.com.au/news/shane-warne-baggy-green-cap-commbank-bradman-museum-bushfire-fundraising-money-charity-jeff-thomson/2020-01-10>; Shane Warne's $1m baggy green finds permanent home next to Bradman (2020) *Guardian Australia*, 27 August, viewed 22 April 2021, <https://www.theguardian.com/sport/2020/aug/27/shane-warnes-1m-baggy-green-finds-permanent-home-next-to-bradman>.

Democracy sausage
1 This chapter draws on Judith Brett (2019) *From Secret Ballot to Democracy Sausage: How Australia got Compulsory Voting*, Text, Melbourne.
2 Polling Day at the Court House, Atherton, 1928, John Oxley Library, Queensland State Library, image number 7222.
3 Jacqui Newling, Sydney Living Museum, quoted in Mike Williams, 'From Aussie Battler to icon of democracy – the history of the sausage sizzle', ABC News, 14 May 2019.
4 Debbie Schipp (2016) Sausagocracy: The Real Burning Issue of Saturday's Trip to the Polls, news.com.au, 1 July, viewed 24 October 2019, <https://www.news.com.au/national/federal-election/sausagocracy-the-real-burning-issue-of-saturdays-trip-to-the-polls/news-story/5f18c3a8c620fb047e425d303f5e9b8d>.
5 Information provided by Dr Amanda Laugesen, 11 November 2019.
6 Kimberley Seats, cited in Hilary Whiteman, In Australia sausages are a symbol of election day. Here's why, CNN, 18 May 2019.
7 Democracy sausage wins Australia's word of the year, 14 December 2016, viewed

25 October 2019, <https://www.anu.edu.au/news/all-news/democracy-sausage-wins-australias-word-of-the-year>.
8 Simon White, Bill Shorten confounds by eating sausage sizzle from side (2016) *Sydney Morning Herald*, 2 July, viewed 25 October 2019, < https://www.SMH.com.au/politics/federal/federal-election-2016-bill-shorten-confounds-by-eating-sausage-sizzle-from-side-20160702-gpwwpi.html>.
9 Annabel Crabb (2017) Not a sausage, *Sydney Morning Herald*, 9 April.
10 Sausage analytics, <https://democracysausage.org/sausagelytics/federal_election_2019>; Adrianna Zappavigna (2019) Voters can't stop tweeting about Democracy Sausages, www.news.com.au, 18 May, viewed 22 April 2021, <https://www.news.com.au/national/federal-election/voters-cant-stop-tweeting-about-democracy-sausages/news-story/edfba554a10a4d74fbc42d23107d5197>.
11 Latika Bourke (2019) Aussie Voters in London taste first democracy sausage, *Sydney Morning Herald*, 12 May, viewed 22 April 2021, <https://www.SMH.com.au/federal-election-2019/federal-election-2019-aussie-voters-in-london-taste-first-democracy-sausage-20190512-p51mff.html>.
12 See Pavlova chapter, 282.
13 How the People Voted, *Age*, 2 June 1913, 9.
14 Australian Politics and Elections Data Base, University of Western Australia.
15 In Europe only small players compel voters to the ballot box: Belgium, Luxembourg, Lichtenstein, Cyprus, Greece, two regions of Austria and one Swiss canton. The only other ex-British colonies in the group are Cyprus, Egypt, Fiji and Singapore. Apart from Singapore the only other Asian country in the group is Thailand. In Central and South America, however, it is the norm with Argentina, Brazil, Bolivia, Chile, Ecuador, Peru, Panama, Costa Rica, and the Dominican Republic all making voting compulsory and enforcing it. There are some other countries, such as Venezuela and the Philippines, where voting is compulsory but not enforced. Lisa Hill, 'A Great Leveller' in Marian Sawer, *Elections: Full, Fair and Free*, Federation Press, Sydney, 2001, 129.
16 Ian McAllister (2011) *The Australian Voter: Fifty Years of Change*, University of New South Wales Press, Sydney, 21–3.
17 'Compulsory Enrolment', paper prepared by the Chief Electoral Officer, RC Oldham, 6 October 1911, Commonwealth Parliamentary Papers 1911, general vol. 2, no. 27. Senator George Pearce read large sections of this paper to the Senate, *Commonwealth Parliamentary Debates*, 6 October 1911, 1117–18.
18 *Commonwealth Parliamentary Debates*, 4 December 1911, 3633.
19 These figures are from the Second Reading Speech of Senator Payne who introduced the Bill. They are slightly different from those given in the Australian politics and election database, but as these are the ones believed at the time they are the ones given here, *Commonwealth Parliamentary Debates*, 17 July 1924, 2180.
20 Geoffrey Sawer (1956) *Australian Federal Politics and Law 1901–1929*, Melbourne University Press, Melbourne, 237.
21 David Malouf (1998) *A Spirit of Play: The Making of Australian Consciousness*, Boyer Lectures, ABC Books, Sydney, 111–2.
22 Dennis Altman (2019) *Unrequited Love: Diary of an Accidental Anarchist*, Monash University Publishing, Melbourne, 1; Bevan Shields (2019) In Britain, forget a democracy sausage. Or any shred of community spirit, really, 13 December, viewed 4 August 2021, <https://www.smh.com.au/world/europe/in-britain-forget-a-democracy-sausage-or-any-shred-of-community-spirit-really-20191212-p53jju.html>.

CONTRIBUTORS

Dennis Altman is currently Emeritus Professor and Professorial Fellow in Human Security at La Trobe University. He is the author of fourteen books, including *Paper Ambassadors* (1991), one of the few books to examine the politics of stamp design, and most recently *Unrequited Love: Diary of an Accidental Activist* (2019) and *God Save the Queen: The Strange Persistence of Monarchies* (2021). He has been President of the AIDS Society of Asia and the Pacific and is a patron of the Australian Queer Archives and the Pride Foundation.

Alan Atkinson writes mainly in Australian history. He taught first in Western Australian universities before spending 27 years at the University of New England in northern New South Wales, and he now holds honorary positions at Sydney University and the University of Western Australia. He has written and/or edited eleven books, including *Camden: Farm and Village Life in Early New South Wales* (1988) and the multi-award-winning *The Europeans in Australia*, in three volumes (1997–2014).

Bruce Baskerville is Associate Director of the Centre for Western Australia History at the University of Western Australia and a public historian on the Batavia Coast of Western Australia. He was previously a senior officer in the New South Wales Heritage Office where in 2006 he curated *How Brightly You Shine*, an online exhibition commemorating the centenary of the New South Wales coat of arms. He has worked on several official heraldry projects for the New South Wales Heritage Council.

JUDITH BRETT is a Melbourne-based political historian and an Emeritus Professor of La Trobe University. Her most recent books are the prize-winning *The Enigmatic Mr Deakin* (2017) and *From Secret Ballot to Democracy Sausage: How Australia got Compulsory Voting* (2019), both published by Text. She writes regularly for *The Monthly* and in 2020 published the Quarterly Essay, *The Coal Curse: Resources, Climate and Australia's Future*. A selection of her writing, *Doing Politics: Writing on Public Life* was published by Text in 2021.

ROBERT CRAWFORD is Professor of Advertising in the School of Media and Communication at RMIT University. His publications include *Digital Dawn in Adland: Transforming Australian Agencies* (2021), *Decoding Coca-Cola: A Biography of a Global Brand* (2021), *Global Advertising Practice in a Borderless World* (2017), *Behind Glass Doors: The World of Australian Advertising Agencies 1959–89* (with Jackie Dickenson, 2016) and *But Wait There's More …: A History of Australian Advertising, 1900–2000* (2008).

FELICITY ERRINGTON works to promote gender equality in the Australian Government's international aid program. She has worked for a range of NGOs including Oxfam and Transform Aid International. She completed an Honours degree in history at the University of Sydney in 2006 and a Masters in Anthropology and Development at the London School of Economics in 2010. Her research interests include the politics of cultural appropriation, gender equality and cultural change in international development, and the not-for-profit sector. She is the co-author of *Driven by Purpose* (2012), which considers the relationship between charities and Australian society.

CAROLINE FORD has a PhD in history from the University of Sydney. Her book, *Sydney Beaches: A History* (2014) explores the cultural and environmental history of Sydney's ocean coast. She worked as a research historian for Surf Life Saving Australia in the lead up to the Year of the Surf Lifesaver 2007, and was a contributor in the organisation's centenary history book, *Between the Flags: One Hundred Summers of Australian Surf Lifesaving* (2006). Caroline works in environment and heritage policy for the New South Wales Government.

GIDEON HAIGH has been a journalist for 36 years. He is the author of 35 books and has edited another seven, mainly about cricket, but also concerning business, crime, social policy and cultural history. He has contributed to more than 100 newspapers and magazines, and now works mainly for *The Times* and *The Australian*. His most recent books are *The Momentous, Uneventful Day: A requiem for the office* (2020) and *The Brilliant Boy: Doc Evatt and the Great Australian Dissent* (2021).

MELISSA HARPER is an honorary senior research fellow in Australian Studies at the University of Queensland, where she was lecturer from 2003 to 2021. Her interest in the billy was aroused when writing her book, *The Ways of the Bushwalker: On Foot in Australia* (2007, 2020), which explores how bushwalkers have engaged with the natural environment through leisure.

BETH HATTON is an artist whose work explores our place in the environment, aspects of Australian history, the meanings of materials and recycling. Her rugs, woven from kangaroo skin offcuts and wool, focus on extinct and endangered species while her sculptures from plant materials examine iconic tools of early settlement. She has exhibited across Australia and overseas (Japan, Germany, America) and received numerous awards, including two grants from the Australia Council and most recently the Greenway Art Prize (Local Award 2018). Her work has been collected by the National Gallery of Australia and many state and regional Galleries.

ROSLYNN HAYNES is Adjunct Associate Professor in the School of Arts and Media, University of New South Wales and a Fellow of the

Australian Academy of the Humanities. In 2001 she received an Australian Bicentenary Medal for cultural studies. She has been a Visiting Fellow at the universities of Leicester, Tasmania and Bremen. Her books include *H.G. Wells: Discoverer of the Future* (1980), *From Faust to Strangelove* (1994), *Explorers of the Southern Sky* (co-authored, 1996) *Seeking the Centre: The Australian Desert in Literature, Art and Film* (1998) *Tasmanian Visions: Landscapes in Writing, Art and Photography* (2006), *Desert: Nature and Culture* (2013), *From Madman to Crime Fighter: The Scientist in Western Culture* (2017) and *Under the Literary Microscope: Science and Society in the Contemporary Novel* (co-edited, 2021).

CAROLYN HOLBROOK is an ARC DECRA Fellow in the Contemporary Histories Research Group at Deakin University, and the Director of Australian Policy and History. She is the author of *Anzac: The Unauthorised Biography* (2014) and edited with Keir Reeves *The Great War: Aftermath and Commemoration* (2019).

LUCY KALDOR graduated with honours in history from the University of Sydney with a thesis on the history of photography of the gum tree in Australia. She has worked since then as a historical researcher with Clive Lucas Stapleton & Partners and is currently senior research officer at the Design Innovation Research Centre, University of Technology, Sydney, where she uses the methods of history in social design projects. She also has interests in garden history and horticulture.

SHINO KONISHI is a historian based at the Australian Catholic University and the University of Western Australia. Her research explores histories and representations of Aboriginal people and cultural practices. She is the author of *The Aboriginal Male in the Enlightenment World* (2012), and is currently leading an ARC project on Indigenous biography. She is Aboriginal and identifies with the Yawuru people of Broome, Western Australia.

ELIZABETH KWAN has been a senior lecturer in history and Australian Studies at the University of South Australia and a senior researcher in the Department of the Senate, Parliament House, Canberra. She now works as a historian in Darwin. Her interest in the politics of patriotism behind Australians' continuing transition from British to Australian national symbols led to her book, *Flag and Nation* (2006), which calls on lobby groups arguing about flag change – and the Australian public caught between them – to question the mythmaking and misinformation surrounding the flag's history. Her *Celebrating Australia: A History of Australia Day*, commissioned by the National Australia Day Council for their website, was published in 2008.

MARILYN LAKE AO is Professorial Fellow in History at the University of Melbourne. Her books include *Getting Equal: The History of Australian Feminism* (1999), the prize-winning biography *Faith: Faith Bandler, Gentle Activist* (2002), the prize-winning *Drawing the Global Colour Line: White Men's Countries and the Question of Racial Equality* (2008, co-authored with Henry Reynolds) and, most recently, *Progressive New World: How Settler Colonialism and TransPacific Exchange Shaped American Reform* (2020), recently shortlisted for the Australian Prime Minister's prize for Australian History. She was President of the Australian Historical Association from 2010 to 2014. A Festschrift celebrating her work, *Contesting Australian History*, edited by Joy Damousi and Judith Smart, was published in 2018.

SYLVIA LAWSON wrote history, journalism and fiction. Her work includes the prize-winning *The Archibald Paradox* (1983), *How Simone de Beauvoir Died in Australia* (2001), *The Outside Story* (2003), a novel centred on the early history of the Sydney Opera House, and *Demanding the Impossible: Seven Essays on Resistance* (2012). Sylvia died in 2017.

PHILIPPA MACASKILL has a keen interest in history, particularly Australian history. She completed an Honours degree in History at the University of Sydney in 2007 during which she first considered the symbolism of Australia's 'national hat'. She then moved into the field of law and continues to work as a lawyer in Sydney.

IAIN MCCALMAN recently retired from a position as Co-Founder and Co-Director of the Sydney Environment Institute at the University of Sydney where he remains a Professor Emeritus. He is a Fellow and former President of the Australian Academy of the Humanities, and a Fellow of three other Learned Academies. His recent books are *Darwin's Armada* (2009, 2010) and *The Reef – A Passionate History* (2013, 2014), both prize-winning. He is now a Professor Emeritus of the ANU's Australian Studies Institute and a Research Professor of the ACU's Institute for Humanities and Social Sciences.

MARK MCKENNA is Emeritus Professor at the University of Sydney, and is the author of several prize-winning books, including *From the Edge: Australia's Lost Histories* (2016), *Looking for Blackfellas' Point* (2002) and *An Eye for Eternity: The Life of Manning Clark* (2011), which won the Prime Minister's Literary Award for non-fiction. His latest book is *Return to Uluru* (2021).

MARGARET MAYNARD is Associate Professor and Honorary Research Consultant, School of Communication and Arts, University of Queensland. Trained at the Courtauld Institute of Art, she is one of Australia's foremost dress historians, publishing three books and numerous articles on dress and fashion. She edited Volume 7, 'Australia, New Zealand and the Pacific Islands', *Berg Encyclopedia of World Dress and Fashion* (2010), continues to contribute to the Berg Encyclopedia, writes articles for journals like *Costume* (United Kingdom) and is publishing a book centred on new approaches to methodology in dress.

OLWEN PRYKE has worked for the History Council of New South Wales, taught history at the University of Sydney and the University of New South Wales and undertaken historical research consultancies. Since joining the State Library of New South Wales, she has managed the institution's research and evaluation program and is currently engaged in strategic and audience research projects. In 2006, she was awarded a PhD for her thesis, 'A Cultural History of Australia House', Australia's High Commission in London. She remains interested in representations of Australia in Britain and the intersections between travel and identity.

LIBBY ROBIN is a historian and museum curator, who writes about the Australian environment, art and climate justice, and the humanities and planetary change. She is Emeritus Professor, Fenner School of Environment and Society at the Australian National University, Canberra and Fellow of the Australian Academy of Humanities. Her books include *The Environment: A History of the Idea* (2018) and the prize-winning *How a Continent Created a Nation* (2007).

PENNY RUSSELL is Emeritus Professor of History at the University of Sydney. Her research focuses on families, intimacy and social encounters, seeking out the intricacies of gender, culture, class, race and colonialism in nineteenth-century Australia. Her books include *Honourable Intentions?* (2016), *Savage or Civilised?* (2010), *This Errant Lady* (2002) and *A Wish of Distinction* (1994).

GRAHAM SEAL, Emeritus Professor at Curtin University, is interested in the relationship between history and myth. He has published widely on Anzac and its central role in Australian culture and society, including *Inventing Anzac: The Digger and National Mythology* (2004), as well as *The Soldiers' Press: Trench Journals in World War I* (2013). His most recent book is *Condemned: The Transported Men, Women and Children Who Built Britain's Empire* (2021).

PETER SPEARRITT has had a long fascination with Australian symbols. His *The Sydney Harbour Bridge: A life,* produced for the 50th anniversary in 1982, went into its third edition in 2012. He served as a General Editor on the ten-volume bicentennial history of Australia, published in 1987 and 1988. His latest book, *Where History Happened: The hidden past of Australia's towns and places* (2019) traverses the nation from Darwin and Cooktown to Burra and New Norcia. Peter has taught at Macquarie and Monash, and at the University of Queensland where he is now an Emeritus Professor.

MICHAEL SYMONS is the author of *Meals Matter: A Radical Economics through Gastronomy* (2020). He has been a Sydney journalist, was a partner in the Uraidla Aristologist Restaurant in the Adelaide Hills for 15 years, and gained a PhD in the 'sociology of cuisine' from Flinders University in 1992. His other works include *One Continuous Picnic: A Gastronomic History of Australia* (1982, 2007), *The Shared Table: Ideas for Australian Cuisine* (1993), and *The Pudding that Took a Thousand Cooks* (1998), republished as *A History of Cooks and Cooking* (2000).

JANE TAYLOR completed an arts/law degree at the University of Sydney with University Medals in History and Law in 2007 and an interest in Australian colonial history. She is now a barrister practising in Sydney.

LINDA THOMPSON completed an arts degree at the University of Sydney with joint honours in Art Theory and History in 2008. Her areas of interest are European art and Australian history. Her Honours thesis examined how travel to artistic 'centres' has influenced Australian art. After several years working as a lawyer in London, she returned to Sydney in 2020.

HELEN TIFFIN is an Honorary Professor at the University of Wollongong. She has degrees in Science (marine biology) and Humanities. Her most recent books are *Wild Man from Borneo: A Cultural History of the Orangutang* (2015) and *Ecocritical Concerns and the Australian Continent* (2020). She formerly held a Senior Canada Research Chair, and is a Member of the Australian Academy of the Humanities.

RICHARD WHITE taught Australian history and the history of travel and tourism at the University of Sydney from 1989 to 2013. His publications include *Inventing Australia* (1981), *The Oxford Book of Australian Travel Writing* (1996) and *On Holidays: A History of Getting Away in Australia* (2005). He has been collecting and writing about cooees for too long and in 2008 co-produced a radio documentary on its history. He is also currently working on the history of 'history tourism' in Australia.

ROBERT WHITE was Senior Lecturer at the University of Newcastle upon Tyne from 1974 to 1989 where, among other subjects, he taught Australian Literature and Film. Since then he has been Winthrop Professor of English at the University of Western Australia, Fellow of the Australian Humanities Academy, a Chief Investigator in the Australian Research Council Centre of Excellence in the History of Emotions, an Australian Research Council Professorial Fellow, and most recently Visiting Senior Research Fellow, Magdalen College, Oxford. His main research subjects are Shakespeare and Keats, and he has tried to sever links with Vegemite studies for 25 years, without success. He would prefer to be remembered for *Pacifism and English Literature: Minstrels of Peace* (2008).

INDEX

Illustrations from the photo sections are indicated by *ill*.

A
Abbott, Tony 14, 64, 296, *ill.* 29
Abdel-Magied, Yassim 24–25, 218
Abdullah, Abdul 218, *ill.* 38
Aboriginal people *see* First Peoples
Adelaide 10, 74, 188–89, 197, 259, 284, 296, 353
advertising 3, 11–12, 15–18, 34, 41, 67, 83, 86, 94, 135, 147, 152, 197, 202, 225, 233–35, 237–38, 242, 245, 273, 275, 289, 296, 300–303, 306–307, 324, 338–39, 340–44, 364, 368, *ill.* 9, 32, 41, 44, 53, 60
Aeroplane Jelly 9, 16, 242
Afghanistan, war in 179, 181, 218–19
Akubra viii, 3, 14, 16, 21, 241, 244, 298, 335–46, *ill.* 60, 61
Algeria 104
Altman, Dennis 382
Ampol 16
Anangu people 311, 314–15, 318–20
Anderson, Benedict 294
Anderson, John 345
Anderson, Margaret 157, 160–61, 399
Anderson, Sallie 354
Anmatyerre people 97
Annand, Douglas 204
Anzac 2, 9, 14, 19, 23, 24–25, 48, 99, 166, 182, 187, 206–208, 211–20, 275–76, 279, 358, 367–68 *see also* digger
  Anzac biscuits 184, 283, 288
  Anzac Day 62, 173, 180, 182, 207, 213, 214–16, 217–18, 339
APEC 333
architects and architecture 11, 203, 222, 225–26, 228–30, 261, 319, 322–34
Armstrong, Francis 351

armed forces 11, 47–48, 136, 165, 171–72, 174–75, 207, 217, 220, 222, 234, 297, 339–40, *ill.* 27 *see also* Anzac, digger, military symbolism
Arnott's biscuits 17, 242
Arrernte people 113–14, 182
art 7, 23, 33, 39, 42–43, 57–58, 89, 97, 99, 106, 109–10, 113–14, 136–40, 148, 150, 208–09, 228, 242, 248, 252–53, 265, 309–10, 349, 353–54, *ill.* 7, 10, 11, 17, 24, 37, 38, 45, 62, 64 *see also* decorative arts
Ashton, Julian 150, *ill.* 25
Askin, Sir Robert 326, 330
Attenborough, Sir David 42–43, 253
Ausflag 169, 177–79
Australia Day 24, 51, 89, 98, 115, 135–36, 180–82, 294, 319
Australia House, London 5, 11, 14–15, 84, 221–31, 376, *ill.* 39, 40, 69
Australia Post *see* postal services
Australian Broadcasting Corporation (ABC) 232, 267, 334
Australian Imperial Forces *see* Anzac, digger
Australian National Dictionary 145, 375
Australian National Flag Association (ANFA) 169, 178–79
Australian Natives Association 83, 172, 185
Australian symbols *see* national symbols
Australian War Memorial 10, 207, 211, 213, 214, 217, 218
Australian Women's Weekly 11, 288
authenticity 85, 131, 137–41, 147, 154, 344, 345–46

B
Baden-Powell, Lord Robert 84
baggy green 14, 358–70, *ill.* 65, 66, 67
Bail, Murray 115, 306
Baker, Richard Thomas 185–88

Baker, Sidney 145
Baker, Steve 120
Bali 194, 220, 240
'banal nationalism' 15
Bancroft, Bronwyn 355
Bancroft, Cameron 370
Banfield, Ted 250–52
Banks, Sir Joseph 39, 43, 129, 247–48, *ill.* 7
Banks, Julia 14
Barnard, Marjorie 112
Barthes, Roland 129
Barton, Edmund Sir 160, 171, 172
Barty, Ashleigh 21, 245
battler 43, 216–17, 307
Baume, Michael 329
Baynton, Barbara 147
beaches 22, 117, 127, 270–81, 381 *see also* Bondi, Coogee, Cottesloe, Cronulla, Curl Curl, lifesaver
Bean, CEW 211–12
beer 16, 18, 21, 136, 214–15, 232–33, 237, 241, 262, 270, 275, 289, 360 *see also* Foster's
Bellear, Sol 181
Benaud, Richie 359
Benchley, Peter 120–21
Bennelong 331
Betts, Margery Ruth 184
Bicentenary 19, 97, 178, 259, 332–33, 341
Big Day Out 24, 180
'big things' 99, 103, 108, 245, 354
Billabong (fashion wear) 242
billy 9, 89, 142–55, 398, *ill.* 25, 26
Billy Tea 16, 17, 83, 147, 148, 151–55
Bingle, Captain John 29, 31–32
Bingle, Lara 18
birds *see* black swan, emu, koel, lyrebird, kookaburra
Birney, Shane 299
Bjelke-Petersen, Joh 254–55
black swan 87, 92
Blakeney, Ben 331
Bligh, Anna 16, 346
Bloch, Marc 63
Blue Poles 330
Blundell, Valda 141
Boer War *see* South African War
Bond, Alan 45, 306, *ill.* 8

Bondi 1, 9, 270–71, 276, 277, 280
boomerang viii, 3, 6, 15, 18, 21, 23, 87, 128–41, 156, *ill.* 2, 23, 24
Borghetti, John 48
Bowman, John, Honour and Mary 22, 41, 197, 201
Boyd, Arthur 99
Boyd, Robin 329
Bradfield, John Job Crew 263
Bradman, Don 98, 324, 359, 364, 370, 423, *ill.* 67
Brandis, George 231, 376, *ill.* 69
Brazilian symbols 29
Brereton Report 219
Brexit 22, 245
BridgeClimb 268–69, 412, *ill.* 47
Brisbane 10, 93, 182, 259, 269, 341
Britain and British symbols
    Australia's political relations with ix, 29, 30–32, 50, 53–64, 67–68, 112, 168, 171, 173–75, 178, 221–22, 378
    Australia's cultural relations with 21–22, 82, 105, 109, 117, 129, 209–11, 238–39, 240–41, 261–63
    British migrants and British–Australians 6, 20, 42, 46, 59, 105, 107–08, 110–11, 129, 179–80, 185, 265, 278–80, 336
    British symbols 9, 12, 24, 41, 42–43, 47–48, 77, 94, 97, 100, 116, 145–46, 157–62, 168–82, 195–205, 260 *see also* Australia House, Brexit, coat of arms, crown, monarchy and monarchs, republicanism, flags, Union Jack
Bruce, Mary Grant 82, 188
Bryce, Quentin 167
Bryson, Bill 118
Bulletin 85, 147, 159, 160, 164, 302
Bundjalung people 181, 316, 355, 357
Bungaree 129
Burgess, Dave 333
Burridge, Pam 343
bush culture and imagery 7, 9, 77–85, 88–89, 110, 142–55, 208, 214, 237, 272, 275, 302, 318, 327, 336, 341–46 *see also* bushmen
Bushells tea 242
bushfires 15, 22, 115, 154, 220, 370, *ill.* 40 *see also* climate change

bushmen 8–9, 16, 19, 34–36, 85, 142–44, 146–55, 189, 208–14, 220, 272–76, 338–39, 345 see also bush culture and imagery, swagmen
bushrangers 69, 144, 209 see also Kelly, Ned
bushwalkers 154–55, 198
Busst, John 252, 254–55
Busteed, Kimberley ill. 50
Buy Australian campaign 6, 135

C
Cahill, JJ 323–24
Callister, Cyril 233, 235, 238
Camm, Ronald 255
Campbell, Archibald James 186–87
Campbell, Ross 292
Canada and Canadian symbols vii–ix, 17, 18, 30, 56, 107, 116, 132, 141, 158, 174–75, 177, 185, 191, 195, 205, 210, 224–25, 376, 378
Canberra 10, 13, 53, 105, 170, 174, 176, 193–94, 203, 259, 328, 355, 356, ill. 63
Carboni, Raffaello 30
Carlton, Mike 345
Carter, Paul 79
cartoons 20, 23, 94, 156–57, 159–67, 169, 234, 265–66, 268, 302, 344, 399, ill. 52
Cash, Martin 144, 150
Cassowaries 252–53
Cazneaux, Harold 113, 394, ill. 19, 20
celebrity 16,18, 44, 84, 289, 293, 335, 336, 342–44
centenaries 92, 96–97, 169–70, 217, 230, 280, 355–57 see also Bicentenary
Chamberlain, Azaria 313
Chanin, Eileen 229
Cherbourg 131
Chifley, Ben 12, 56, 296, 299, 301, 302
children 2, 5, 19–20, 45–47, 53, 62, 70, 79, 89, 100, 112, 124, 125, 161, 175, 193, 235–38, 240–41, 243, 305, 333, 348–49, 353–54, 377, 388, ill. 2, 12 see also schools, youth
China and Chinese symbols 16, 18, 21, 31, 37, 69, 101, 122, 127, 162, 241
Chisholm, Alec 252
Christianity 28, 33, 61, 295, 309
Christy, Vic 125

citizenship 24, 67, 162, 166, 171, 181, 184, 194, 378–79, 381, ill. 52
climate and climate change vii–viii, 15, 18, 49, 76, 105, 111–12, 115, 127, 254–57, ill. 29, 40
Clune, Frank 303
coats of arms 4, 8, 11, 12, 21, 22, 33, 41, 49, 63, 168, 171, 183, 195–205, 358, 361–63, 368, ill. 24, 34, 35, 36
coinage see currency
Commonwealth (and Empire) Games 99, 178, 264, 341
compulsory voting 376, 378–81, 425
conservation 47, 49–51, 127, 251–58, 314
constitution 4, 22, 33, 56–57, 64, 65, 196, 205, 294, 320
convicts 31, 66, 68, 69, 124, 156
cooee viii, 3, 4, 6, 15, 23, 77–90, 144, ill. 14, 15
Coogee 126
Cook, Captain James 38–39, 43, 58, 129, 247, 248, 250
Cook, Joseph 93
copyright 19, 87, 179, 232, 336, 402
Coranderrk 131, ill. 23
Corris, Peter 264
Corsali, Andrea 27
Cosgrove, General Peter 340, 367
Cossington Smith, Grace 265
Cottee's cordials 17
Cottesloe 119, 122
Country Women's Association 285, 375
COVID-19 pandemic viii, 14, 22, 89, 269, 280
Cowan, Marie 152–53
Crawford, Dean 127
cricket 11, 12, 14, 34, 62, 64, 98, 122, 274, 345, 358–70 see also baggy green
crocodile 2, 89–90, 100, 122, 127, 342, 349, ill. 2
Crocodile Dundee 117, 306, 342
Croft, Julian 243
Cronulla riots 24, 37, 168, 180, 278–79
Crouch, Richard 172
crown 53–64, 159, ill. 10
Cuba 164
Culotta, Nino see O'Grady, John
Curl Curl 279
currency 8, 48, 58, 62–63, 185, 248

Curtin, John 174–75
Cuthbertson, James Lister 149

D
dagginess 12, 89, 99 *see also* national symbols, falling out of fashion
Dampier, William 38
Dancey, George 161
Dargie, William *ill.* 10, 37
Dark, Eleanor 264
Darwin 350
Darwin, Charles 49, 56
Davidson, Alan 359
Davis Gelatine 289–91
Davison, Frank Dalby 252
Davison, Graeme 304
Dawson, Mike viii
De Florian, Gherardo 244
de Groot, Francis 262
Deakin, Alfred 160, 163–64, 172, 199–200, 224–25
Deane, Sir William 205
decorative arts 8, 22, 185
democracy 11, 22, 36, 56–57, 146, 150, 179, 304, 333
  democracy sausage vii, 21, 371–82, *ill.* 52, 68, 69
Denmark and Danish symbols 9
Dennis, CJ 3
Depression, Great 234, 261, 297, 337, 355
design 4, 7, 11, 12, 13, 18, 21, 22, 23, 29, 30, 33, 45, 48, 63, 87, 89, 91–95, 99–100, 131–32, 169, 171–72, 175–76, 178, 179–81, 185–86, 192, 195–205, 221, 225–26, 228–30, 242, 244, 260–61, 263, 299, 303, 306, 323–28, 333, 347, 354–55, 357 *see also* national symbols, aesthetics of
Dharug people 14–15
digger 9, 47, 105, 206–20, 339–40, *ill.* 37, 38 *see also* Anzac
Dingle, Peter 238
dingo 2, 40, 51, 311, 313, 320
Dja Dja Wurrung people 354
Djab Wurrung people 115
Djiru people 250–51
Dobbs, Wilson 187–89
Dodson, Mick 346
Dodson, Patrick 346

Dot and the Kangaroo 46–47
Drew, Philip 332
Driza-Bone 16, 342, 346
Drysdale, Russell 310
Duek-Cohen, Elias 329
Dunkerley, Benjamin 336, 339
Dunlop, Edward 'Weary' 216
Dunstan, Albert 174
Dunstan, Roy 97
Dupain, Max 265
Dusty, Slim 99, 343
Dyson, Edward 147

E
Edwards, General Bevan 339
egalitarianism 11, 36, 142, 147, 153–54, 185, 303, 335, 337–39, 369, 371, 372, 374, 381–82 *see also* democracy
Egypt and Egyptian symbols 128, 207, 214, 260, 322
Ellinghaus, Alex 375
Elliott, Sumner Locke 264
Ellyard, Peter 51
emu 1, 8, 15, 22, 41, 87, 93, 117, 131, 196–98, 201, 349, 363
environmental issues 18, 49, 50–51, 74–75, 105, 111–15, 116–17, 127, 184, 248–54, 314, 347–49 *see also* climate change, conservation
Eora people 78, 181
Esson, Louis 149
ethnic differences 19, 20–21, 46, 140, 181, 201, 243, 271, 278–80, 315 *see also* First Peoples, national symbols, exclusionary role of, race and racism
eucalyptus *see* gum tree
Eureka and Eureka flag 12, 14, 22, 26, 30–31, 34–35, *ill.* 3
Everage, Dame Edna 4, 99, 240, 293, 331 *see also* Humphries, Barry
exhibitions, international 41, 158, 171, 259, 273
Eyre, Edward John 309

F
Farrer, Keith 235–36, 238
fashion 99, 178, 242, 363, *ill.* 31, 49 *see also* Akubra, jewels and jewellery

Federation 8, 10–11, 15, 32, 57, 65–66, 75–76, 78, 83, 86, 93, 108–09, 131, 157–61, 170–72, 175, 183–85, 196, 209, 218, 221, 272, 355–57, 361
Fernando, Anthony 14–15
Fesl, Eve 90
Fewster, Kevin 43
Field, Barron 44, 108
Fielder, John 352
film 98, 253, 305, 342
Finlayson, HH 309
First Peoples
  art 7, 23, 89, 97, 113–14, 136–40, 248, *ill*. 11, 24, 45, 62, 64
  culture and symbols 5–7, 19, 28, 38, 40, 43, 67, 76, 78–79, 82, 84, 104, 115, 131–33, 135–36, 140–41, 183–84, 251, 308, 311, 313, 315–19, 347–57, *ill*. 11, 62, 63, 64
  dispossession viii, 6, 57–58, 66, 85, 104, 112–13, 136, 246, 250, 314
  flags *see* flags, Aboriginal, Torres Strait Islander
  in national symbols 6–7, 14, 19, 41, 77–90, 96–97, 128–41, 143, 145, 158, 181, 187, 198–99, 204–05, 213, 217, 308–21, 336, 347–57, 359–60 *see also* boomerang, cooee, Rainbow Serpent, Uluṟu
  politics 7, 13, 15, 57–58, 129, 178–79, 181–82, 247, 267, 320–21, 356–57, *ill*. 31 *see also* reconciliation
  missions and reserves 77, 131–33, 250–51, 314, 316, *ill*. 23, 24
Fischer, Tim 16, 344, 345, *ill*. 61
Fisher, Andrew 172, 201–02
Fishman, Darren *ill*. 42
flags 5, 11, 24, 29, 32, 86, 174–75, 177, 191, 196, 295, 301
  Aboriginal 7, 13, 19, 178–79, 182, 242, *ill*. 31
  Australasian Anti-Transportation League 31–32, 171
  Australian 2, 4, 8, 13, 14, 24, 33, 168–82, 301
  Australian flag competition 32–33, 171, *ill*. 30
  Bowman 22, 41, 197, 201
  boxing kangaroo 45, *ill*. 8
  debates about a new flag 7, 11, 12, 168–70, 175, 177–78, 180–81
  Eureka 12, 22, 30–31, 34–37, *ill*. 3
  Federation flag 170–72
  National Colonial 29, 31–32
  South Australian 6
  Torres Strait Islander 13, 178–79, 182
  Union Jack 168–77, 179–81, 301, 309
flannel flower 185
Flinders, Matthew 68, 72–73
Flint, David 64
food and foodways 9, 39, 43, 49, 51, 83, 122, 127, 151, 184, 247, 257, 318 *see also* democracy sausage, kangaroo, pavlova, shark, Vegemite
football 17, 21, 50, 89, 136, 181, 282, 306, *ill*. 2
Ford 304, 305, 307
Forrest, Sir John 66
Foster's lager 3, 17, 18, 233
Fox, Mem 243
France and French symbols ix, 18, 28, 41, 67, 71, 74, 145, 157, 177, 187, 218, 242, 260, 339
Franklin, Adrian 136
Franklin, Jane, Lady 188
Freeman, Cathy 99, 178, 355
Freeman, Nicholas 96
Freeman, Ralph 263
Fromonot, Françoise 332
Frost, Henry 296–97
Fulton, Margaret 292
Furphy, Joseph 1, 24, 82, 147

G

Gallie, Liz 252
Gallipoli 3, 94, 173, 200, 207, 209, 212, 214, 216, 217, 218, 367 *see* Anzac, digger, World War I
gambling 208, 214, 324, 333
Gardner, Wayne 343
Garigal people 129
Gay and Lesbian Mardi Gras 280, 356
Gehry, Frank 322
Gelder, Ken 39
gender *see* men and masculinity, women and femininity

General Motors 296–97, 300–02 *see also* Holden
Geographical Society of Australasia 71, 74
Germany and German symbols 18, 92, 101, 162, 164, 307, 355
Gibbs, May 112
Gidney, Catherine viii
Gilchrist, Adam 369
Giles, Ernest 69, 312
Gillard, Julia 45, 167, *ill.* 29
Gleeson, Libby 89
Glover, John 109, *ill.* 17
Gold rushes 29–30, 65–66, 68, 69–70, 86, 144–45, 207, 338 *see also* Eureka
Gold Coast 260
golf 63, 117, 343
Gompertz, Will 40
Goossens, Eugene 323–24
Gordon, Adam Lindsay 23, 189
Gosse, William 310, 312
Graburn, Nelson 141
Graham, Billy 33
Great Barrier Reef vii, 21, 66, 118, 246–58, *ill.* 43, 44, 45
'Great White Fleet' 84, 162–63, 172
green and gold *see* national colours
Gregory, Dave 360
Grice, Allan 343
Griffin, Walter Burley 328
Gubbi Gubbi people 90
Gullick, William 186, 189
gum tree 2, 3, 6, 8, 23, 81, 83, 102–15, 142, 148, 154, 310, 340, 362, 278, *ill.* 15, 17, 18, 19, 20
Guugu Yimithirr people 247

H
Hall, Ken 262
Hall, Peter 328–29
Hanson, Pauline 13, 265–66, 376
Harrington, Edward 149
Harry Potter 230
Hartnett, Laurence 297–99, 305
Harvey, Neil 359
Haskell, John 230
Hasluck, Sir Paul 64
Hava, Melanie 248, *ill.* 45
Hawke, Bob 98, 178, 333

health ix, 161, 232, 234–38, 245, 250–51, 272–74, 281, 356, 393
Healy, Ian 365
Heaslip, Tanya 89
Henderson, Sara 343
Henri, Lucien 185
heritage listing 230, 255, 257, 333, *ill.* 42
Heysen, Hans 113, 309
Hicks, David 240
Hicks, Sir Frederick Stanton 236
Hills hoist 9, 242, 280
Hirst, John 158, 160
Hitchcock, Maria 193
Hobart 188, 202, 259, 288, 353
Hobsbawm, Eric 292, 359
Hockey, Joe 307
Hogan, Paul 16, 18, 342
Holden viii, 3, 9, 12, 16, 17, 242, 280, 296–307, *ill.* 53, 54
Holidays 1, 44, 122, 123, 214, 304, 327, 376, 377, 381 *see also* tourists and tourism
Holt, Harold 117
Honours 34, 59, 64
Hopkins, Livingstone ('Hop') 160
Horne, Donald 329
Hornung, EW 81
horse-racing 331, 333, *ill.* 58
Hotham, Governor Charles 31
Howard, John 13–14, 16, 31, 98, 99, 179, 181, 194, 217, 244, 333, 335, 344–45, 368, 385
Hughes, Davis 327–28
Hughes, William Morris ('Billy') 12, 339
Humphries, Barry 99, 117, 240, 293 *see also* Everage, Dame Edna
Hunt, Arthur Atlee 226
Hunter, Governor John 79
Hurley, Frank 249, 253

I
Iemma, Maurice 267
Immigrants *see* migrants
India, Indian symbols and Indian–Australians 21, 45, 66, 116, 158, 260, 369
Indigenous Australians *see* First Peoples
industrialisation 9, 89, 255, 261, 286, 297–98, 303, 326, *ill.* 46
Iraq War 179, 218, 333

Ireland, Irish symbols and Irish–Australians 23, 24, 66, 69, 157, 173–74, 185, 199–200, 241, 376, 378
Irwin, Steve 18, 89–90, 100
Isaacs, Clarrie 351
Italy, Italian symbols and Italian–Australians 26–27, 30, 117–18, 244, 329

J

James, Maude Wordsworth 23, 86–8, *ill.* 14
Japan and Japanese symbols 11, 48, 51, 101, 131, 162, 164, 193, 215, 216, 220, 239, 247, 289, 305–06, 355
Jardine, Douglas 363
jewels and jewellery 23, 54, 66–67, 69, 87, 125, 185, 252, 354, *ill.* 1, 14
Johns, Amelia 180
Johnston, George 114
Jones, Alan 333
Jones, Philip 136
Joyce, Alan 48, 294
Joyce, Barnaby 16, 376
Jungarai, Gwoja *see* Tjungurrayi, Gwoya

K

Kamilaroi people 357
kangaroo 1, 3, 6, 8, 15, 16, 17, 18, 21, 22, 24, 38–52, 84, 87, 93, 116–17, 131, 135, 142, 152, 154, 158, 164, 196–98, 201, 203, 306, 323, 349, 363, *ill.* 2, 7, 56
    Boxing Kangaroo 37, 44–47, *ill.* 8, 9
    kangatarianism 51
    Skippy 45–47
Kata Tjuṯa 2, 311, 315, 318
Keating, Paul 13, 178, 217, 345
Keir, Stephen 336, 337, 340
Kelaher, Tip 340
Kellermann, Annette 84
Kelly, Ned 20, 220, 234
Kelly, Vivienne 89
Kernaghan, Lee 16, 343–44
King, Philip Parker 130
Kingsford Smith, Sir Charles 34–35, 37
Kingston, Peter 265
Kipling, Rudyard 159
'kitsch' 3, 136, 141, 240
Knight, Michael 319
knights and dames 14, 34, 59

koala 8, 18, 21, 115, 131, *ill.* 2
Kociumbas, Jan 133
koel 78
Kokoda 13, 24, 215, 342
kookaburra 2, 8, 77, 135–36, 348
Korea 175, 216, 294, 307
Kraft 19, 234, 236, 241, 242, 244, 384, 409
Kukatja people 350
Kunwinjku people 348

L

la Meslée, Edmond Marin 71, 74–75
La Perouse 23, 131
Laalaa, Mecca *ill.* 49
Lake Tyers 131, 132
Lambert, George 226
lamington 9, 240, 283, 288
Lang, Jack 262, 265
Langer, Justin 365, 366–67, 370
Langford Ginibi, Ruby 316
Lardil people 350
larrikinism 3, 46, 47, 83, 208, 213, 215, 217, 218, 220
Lauder, Elizabeth 22, 200
Laugesen, Amanda 375
Lawrence, Charles 360, 366
Lawrence, DH 81
Lawson, Henry 30, 82, 147, 148, 149–50
Leach, Vice Admiral David 64
Leach, Helen 284
Leak, Bill 265
Lebanese Australians 180
Ledger, Heath 240
legal issues 8, 56–57, 140, 215, 252, 272, 368, 378 *see also* copyright, national symbols and ownership, trademarks
Leggett, Mark and Susan 237–38
Leong, Hou 16
Leunig, Michael 265, 268
lifesaver 1, 12, 21, 237, 270–81, *ill.* 48, 49, 50
Lindsay, Darryl 204
literature 23, 27, 34, 44, 81–83, 85, 107, 114–15, 147, 149, 159–60, 189, 243, 252, 264, 306, 312, 316–17, 322, 332, 338, 340
'Little Boy at Manly' 160, 164
logos 5, 6, 11, 18, 21, 48–49, 83, 177, 293, 356, 377
Lonely Planet 322

Longstaff, Sir John 110–11, 226
Lucas, Beryl Llywelyn 111
Luhrmann, Baz 9, 342
Luritja people 178
Lyons, Joseph 60
lyrebird 8, 198

M
MacCannell, Dean 140
McCubbin, Frederick 148, 150
McDonald's 5, 17
MacIntosh, William 203
Mackay, Kenneth 83
Mackellar, Dorothea 67, 111
Mackennal, Bertram 226, 227, 228
McGuire, Walter 357
McIntyre, Scott 24, 218
McLachlan, Noel 124
McMahon, Elizabeth 66
Maiden, Joseph 187, 192
Malouf, David 381
Mannix, Archbishop Daniel 173
map 3, 8, 21, 23, 65–76, 87, 93, 106, *ill.* 2, 12, 13, 24
marriage equality 100, *ill.* 16
Martin, Toby 133
mates and mateship 21, 36, 85, 142, 146–51, 189, 276, 305, 335, 338–40, 345, 358
Matthiessen, Peter 123
Mayo, Eileen 204–05
meat pies 17, 306, 372
Melba, Dame Nellie 84, 324
Melbourne 9–10, 21, 26, 44, 84, 93, 96, 97, 99, 114, 121, 163–64, 173, 187, 189, 197, 244, 245, 259, 260, 262, 265, 298, 301, 324, 360–61
Melbourne Cricket Club 360–62, 364
Melbourne Cricket Ground 10
Melbourne Cup 278
Melbourne Exhibition Building 171, 259
men and masculinity 22–3, 37, 97, 100, 110–11, 116–17, 125, 148–51, 159–67, 198, 209, 213–14, 270–71, 274–80, 293, 303, 318, 336–39, 371, 374–75 *see also* baggy green, bushmen, digger, lifesaver
Men at Work 243
Menzies, Sir Robert Gordon 12, 60–62, 94, 170, 174–77, 301, 302, 304

Merivale, Herman 59
Michelet, Jules 71–74
Migrants and multiculturalism viii, 8, 20–22, 36, 62, 68, 77, 105, 117, 133, 160, 175, 179–80, 185, 218, 222–23, 224, 241, 243–44, 262, 265–66, 275, 325, 336, 354, 374, 410 *see also* race and ethnicity
middle eastern Australians 37, 168, 180, 218, 278, *ill.* 49
military symbolism 3, 11–12, 63, 100, 136, 156–59, 165, 172–75, 189, 215, 275–77, 295, 297, 339–40, 355 *see also* digger
Miller, Keith 359
Minang/Menang people 130
Minogue, Kylie 4, 21
Minties 17
Miss Australia 94, 156–67, *ill.* 5, 27, 28, 29
Miss Universe *ill.* 50
Mitchell, Austin 293
modernity and modernism 12, 33, 83, 89, 97, 132, 162, 165, 203–05, 225, 228–30, 234, 251, 261–63, 275, 286–88, 292–94, 300–03, 324–26, 329–34 *see also* postmodernity and postmodernism
Mojo 16
Moll, Eugene 203
Monarchy, monarchs and royal hangers on 7, 12, 14, 21, 40, 41–42, 53–64, 77, 84, 92–93, 98, 135, 145–46, 157, 176, 190–92, 199, 200–01, 203, 277, 331, 335, 344, 362, *ill.* 10, 11, 48 *see also* Queen Elizabeth II, Queen Victoria, royal visits
Monkman, Noel 253–54
Moore, David 265
Morgan, Maxine 166
Morton, Tex 139
Mountford, Charles 312
multiculturalism *see* migrants and multiculturalism
Munyarryun, Djakapurra 133
Murdoch, Iris 332
Murdoch, Billy 360
Murrumurru, Dick Nguleingulei 349
music 1, 22, 24, 82–83, 84, 85, 87, 89, 128, 151–53, 313, 322–34, 338, 342, 345, 354, *ill.* 15, 28 *see also* Sydney Opera House

N

Nabegeyo *ill.* 64
Namatjira, Albert 113–14, 309
Nathan, Isaac 82
national anthem 4, 13, 37, 151, 176, 177–78, 181
national colours 13, 14, 21, 105, 108–11, 115, 183, 293, 360–62
national dress 9, 335, 339, 341, 346, *ill.* 50 *see also* Akubra
national flower 4, 12, 104, 183–89, 192–93 *see also* wattle
National Gallery of Australia 42–43
National Museum of Australia ix, 7, 10, 319, 349
national parks 46, 51, 154, 246, 254–57, 314–15, 318
national symbols
    aesthetics of 30–31, 105, 108–10, 113–14, 185–86, 203–04, 226, 242, 251, 310, 353–55, 359–60 *see also* art, decorative arts, design
    ambiguity of 4, 31–32, 36, 55–56, 107, 167, 180, 205, 218–19, 347–51, 357
    and appropriation of indigenous symbols 6–7, 77–85, 104, 130–32, 135–37, 140, 317, 356–57 *see also* First Peoples, boomerang, cooee, rainbow serpent, Uluṟu
    and diversity 20–21, 24, 133, 167, 240, 243, 271, 278–80, 325
    and emotion 3, 15, 21, 23, 25, 32, 49, 51–52, 60, 83, 111, 119, 149, 175, 206–07, 209, 266, 315–16, 340, 364, 383
    and patriotism 15, 19, 34, 37, 51, 60–62, 85–88, 92, 98, 101, 104, 110, 157, 172–74, 180, 184–88, 197, 210, 242, 294, 340, 343
    and protest 7, 14–15, 36, 100, 114–15, 169, 178, 182, 199–200, 328, 333, 351, *ill.* 29, 40, 57, 58
    and self-consciousness 8, 13, 50, 77–78, 81–82, 154, 273, 344, 346
    and the future 11, 109, 115, 150, 156, 182, 227, 257, 319, 334
    and the past 11–12, 16, 23, 64, 85, 113, 141, 154–55, 156, 235, 241, 244, 275, 278, 280, 282, 292–93, 302, 306–07, 334, 336, 338, 347, 350, 356, 367
    commercial aspects of 8–9, 14–16, 18–19, 24, 50–51, 98, 135, 137–38, 140–41, 149, 152–54, 178, 193, 197, 214, 217, 242, 254–55, 268–69, 293, 306, 313–14, 364–65, 368 *see also* advertising, Akubra, Holden, Vegemite
    disagreement about 2–3, 12–15, 31–36, 50–51, 63–64, 85, 109, 132, 199–202, 204–05, 185–87, 189–93, 218, 221–26, 238–40, 262–63, 271, 277–80, 282, 298–99, 326–30
    disrespect for 23, 24, 46, 51, 108–11, 314–18, 351 *see also* national symbols, laughing at
    dissemination of 3–4, 6, 8–9, 14, 19, 22–23, 27, 36–37, 43, 81, 85–86, 88, 113, 128–31, 135, 179, 185, 211–13, 216, 251–53, 263–65, 342, 368, 374–75 *see also* advertising, postage stamps, schools
    distinctiveness of 3, 8–9, 29, 40–41, 82, 102–04, 147, 171–72, 183, 206, 209–11, 228–29, 260, 272–73, 292, 308, 339
    exclusionary role of 3, 19, 30, 37, 41–42, 65, 110, 159, 276, 278–80, *ill.* 13
    falling out of fashion vii–viii, 10–12, 15, 32, 88–89, 136, 230, 305, 307, 324
    in international context viii, 4, 10, 16–18, 22, 39, 41–43, 45–50, 75–76, 81, 84, 116–17, 136–37, 162–65, 167, 188, 192–93, 239–40, 265, 269, 271, 273, 275–76, 280–81, 319, 321, 322–23, 330–33, *ill.* 2, 9, 56, 57 *see also* Australia House, baggy green, postage stamps, tourists and tourism
    laughing at 20, 23–24, 32, 44–46, 89, 212, 245, 362, 371, 374–75, *ill.* 42
    meanings attributed to vii, 2–5, 9, 12, 20–24, 33–34, 36–37, 43–49, 52, 61, 82–83, 85–86, 97, 120, 129, 132–33, 136, 140, 142, 146–47, 157–59, 167, 168, 189, 195–97, 205, 206–07, 220, 223, 239–41, 244, 248, 265, 283, 289, 318, 323–25, 332–36, 339–40, 343, 346, 347–53, 356–57

'natural' vii–ix, 8–9, 11, 85, 106–07, 109–10, 115, 135, 141, 185, 196, 248, 251, 272–73 *see also* gum tree, kangaroo, wattle
of other nations viii–ix, 8–9, 11, 17, 23, 29, 56, 66, 67, 77, 92–94, 97, 99–101, 107, 116, 128–29, 132, 141, 156–59, 162–64, 174–77, 182, 185, 191–92, 195, 199–201, 224–25, 260, 282–86, 322, 355 *see also* flag, Union Jack
official 6, 13, 45, 48, 63, 91, 98, 136, 157, 158, 171, 178, 183, 188, 192, 193, 197, 199, 206, 212–13, 223, 335, 362–63 *see also* coats of arms, currency, crown, flag, postage stamps, wattle
origin myths about 6, 85, 143–46, 151–52, 169–70, 194, 201, 207, 212–14, 270, 282–94, 311, 336, 338, 347–50, 358–60
ownership of 18–19, 135–41, 241–42, 278–79, 282–83, 362–70 *see also* legal issues
popular acceptance of 6–8, 23, 26–29, 30, 34–37, 40–43, 62, 78, 81, 85, 88, 113, 128–31, 143, 152–53, 172–73, 177–79, 185–89, 197–205, 207–08, 211–12, 232, 235, 244, 252, 263–65, 274–75, 290, 302–04, 333, 375–76
recognisability of 2, 3–5, 8, 18, 25, 40, 43, 50, 67, 77–78, 102, 135, 157, 215, 259–60, 265–67, 269, 271, 276, 292, 308, 310, 322, 332, 344, 364
reproducibility of 3–5, 62, 77, 86, 202–03
unifying role of 3, 19, 20, 37, 55, 59–61, 64, 67, 71, 88, 108, 124, 133, 170, 172, 177, 180, 194, 196, 199, 209, 223, 280, 294, 319, 348–49, 356
visual images of 3, 5, 10, 36–37, 39, 41, 77–78, 102–15, 148–51, 156–57, 160–61, 205, 242, 308, 309–10, 323 *see also* design
nationalism 7, 12, 15–17, 82–85, 89, 104–05, 109–14, 135–36, 150, 202, 206, 217, 238, 240–41, 283, 293, 338, 341–42, 346
Nelson, Brendan 179
New Age 317, 354
New South Wales 11, 32, 58, 68–69, 92, 157, 162, 188, 197, 201, 228, 262, 270, 273, 326, 371 *see also* Sydney
New Zealand and New Zealand symbols 29, 32, 56, 73–74, 77, 79, 87, 101, 107, 132, 144, 158, 164–65, 182, 191, 207, 209, 210, 232, 234–35, 282–95, 378
Newson, Marc 48
Nganjmirra, Titus *ill.* 11
Nicholson, Captain John 29
Noble, Jenny 349
Nolan, Sidney 310, 353
Noongar people 130, 351–52, 357
Noonuccal, Oodgeroo 114
Norman, Greg 16, 117, 343
Northfield, James 336, *ill.* 44
nostalgia *see* national symbols and the past
Nurse, Sir Paul 237

O

Oakes, Charles 273
Ocker 16
O'Donoghue, Lowitja 319
O'Grady, John 117–18, 252
Olsson, Kristina 322
Olympic Games 45, 99, 264, 341
    Melbourne (1956) 96
    Sydney (2000) 18, 19, 99, 105, 133, 178, 265, 269, 280, 307, 319, 322, 333, 335, 355
Our Lady of the Southern Cross 33, *ill.* 5

P

Packer, Kerry 333
Palm Island 131, 133, 135
Palmer, Nettie and Vance 252
Parish, Steve 106
Parker, Harold 228
Parliament House
    New 7, 105
    Old 14, 94, 174, 176, 177, 194, 203, 221, 224
Paterson, AB 'Banjo' 82, 147, 151–53, 208–09
Patterson, George 17
pavlova 2, 3, 4, 9, 29, 144, 282–95, 413, *ill.* 52
Pavlova, Anna 284, 289, 292, *ill.* 51
Pedley, Ethel 46
Pell, Cardinal George 33

Pelsaert, Francisco 38
Peris, Nova 319
Perth 187, 239, 248, 259, 284, 293, 351, 357
Philippines 164
Phillip, Governor Arthur 58, 67
Photography 14, 16, 21, 97, 100, 105, 106, 113, 114, 125, 137, 248, 251, 253, 261, 264–66, 308, 310, 312, 314, 318, 322–23, 345, 354, 371, 375, 376
Pigafetta, Antonio 27
Pitjantjatjara people 311, 319, 416
platypus 8, 198
Portugal 28, 104
Portus, John 361
possum 15
postage stamps 3, 8, 91–101, 183, *ill.* 16
postal services 63, 91, 92–100, 105, 201–02, 378, 379–80 *see also* postage stamps
postcards 8, 21, 71, 106, 112, 251, 263, 266, 322–23, 332, *ill.* 18
posters 8, 88, 244, 251, 261–62, 275, 308, 373, *ill.* 44, 46, 60
postmodernity and postmodernism 10, 13, 140, 293, 319
Praed, Rosa 82
protest *see* national symbols and protest
Ptolemy, Claudius 26
Purgatorio 26

Q
Qantas 16, 47, 48, 99, 135, 294
Queen Elizabeth II 6, 14, 21, 53–55, 57, 59, 60–61, 93, 94, 135, 170, 176, 192, 203, 277, 325, 331, *ill.* 10, 11 *see also* monarchy, monarchs and royal hangers on
Queen Victoria 62, 63, 157, 159, 199, 228
Queensland 32, 75, 92, 133, 151, 182, 233, 234, 246, 251, 254–55, 270, 346, 380, 381 *see also* Brisbane, Gold Coast, Toowoomba

R
rabbits 173–74
race and racism 36–37, 61, 136, 163, 167, 168, 180, 182, 191, 220, 252, 265–66, 273–74, 306, 320–21 *see also* migrants and multiculturalism, national symbols, exclusionary role of
Radcliffe-Brown, AR 352

radio 21, 34, 77, 235, 267, 278, 340
Rainbow Serpent viii, 7, 19, 347–57, *ill.* 62, 63, 64
Ramson, Bill 145
Rawson, Mina 286–87
reconciliation 7, 13, 14, 178, 181–82, 267, 319–20, 355–56
Reed-Gilbert, Kerry 136
refugees 21, 22, 25, 31, 76, 181
Reid, Sir George 221, 225
religion 29, 33, 69, 94–97, 218, 315, 349, 352, 377 *see also* Aboriginal culture and symbols, Christianity
Relph, Arthur 274
republicanism 12, 31, 33, 35–36, 57, 64, 82, 150, 157, 174, 178, 181
Returned and Services League of Australia (RSL) 63–64, 169, 174, 178–79, 207, 214, 216, 218
Richards, Duncan 120
Riddle, Tohby 53–54
rising sun 10–12, 156, 161, 215, 218, 227, 355, *ill.* 24
Roberts, Tom 208
Robeson, Paul 324–25
Robinson, John 357
Robinson, Ray 364
Rogers, Denis 368
Rosebank School 349
Rosella tomato sauce 16, 83, 135, 241
Ross, 'Captain' Henry 30
Roughsey, Dick *ill.* 62
Royal Society for Prevention of Cruelty to Animals 49
royal visits 6, 40, 41–42, 53–55, 59, 60–61, 62, 135, 170, 176, 277, 331, *ill.* 48
Royer, Augustin 27
Rudd, Kevin 14, 244
Rudd, Steele 43, 82, 338
Russell, HC 74–75
Russia 162, 284
Ryan, Norman 326–27

S
Sachse, Herbert 284, 293
Samoan symbols 29
Santa Claus 94, 96
Sarah, Michael 244, 410

Sargood, Sir Frederick 170, 175
Satour, Catherine 182
Saunders, Will 333
Savage, Georgia 243
Saville-Kent, William 253, *ill.* 43
Sawer, Geoffrey 380
Schmitt, Hugh 293
schools 20, 62, 67, 70–71, 84, 88, 171, 172, 173, 174, 175, 177, 179, 189, 193, 235, 243, 327, 333, 337, 349, 353, 363, 372–73, 375, 376 *see also* children
science 32–33, 108, 235, 237–38, 256
Scooby-Doo and the Legend of the Vampire 1–2
Scott, Mark 232
Scott, Montagu 157
Scotland and Scottish symbols 185, 199, 201
scouting 84
Scruby, Harold 169
shark 1, 45, 116–27, *ill.* 21, 22
Sharp, Martin 265
Sheep and wool industry 9, 40, 41, 51, 116, 150–52, 228, 310
Shields, Bevan 382
Shorten Bill 375, *ill.* 68
Shorter, Lucy 185–86
Simpsons, The 44
Siwes, Darren 57–58
Skippy the Bush Kangaroo 45–46
Slater, Michael 365
slouch hat 1, 11, 12, 215, 218, 278, 339–40, 358, 367 *see also* Akubra
Smith, Steve 370
Smout, Arthur 177
snakes 87, 116, 198, 320 *see also* Rainbow Serpent
Snowy Mountains Hydro-Electric Scheme 21, 325
social class 12, 34, 36, 53, 150, 154, 185, 300, 303–04, 305, 325, 338, 363, 372 *see also* egalitarianism
social media 2, 9, 22, 24, 218, 371, 375–76, 382
Sorenson, Edward S 142–43, 151
South Africa and South African symbols 17, 79, 120, 159, 189–92, 365, 370
South African War 152, 159, 175, 219, 297, 339
South Australia 6, 11, 62, 68–69, 70–71, 120, 189, 228, 270, 372, 377, 378 *see also* Adelaide
Southern Cross 2, 8, 26–37, 86, 156, 168, 171, 197, 200, 201, 360, *ill.* 4 *see also* flags
souvenirs 3, 6, 18, 23, 62, 85, 87, 99, 128–29, 131–32, 134, 137–41, 263, 318, 346, 354
Sowden, William J 189
Spain 28, 344
Speedo 242
Spielvogel, Nathan 107
sport 16, 24, 40, 42, 45, 83, 97, 99, 100, 136–37, 183, 214, 248, 342–43, 367, 369, 370 *see also* bushwalkers, cricket, golf, football, lifesaver, Olympic Games, tennis, wrestling
stamp collectors 91–92, 100 *see also* postage stamps
Stephen, Sir Ninian 315
Streeton, Sir Arthur 226, *ill.* 5
Strehlow, TGH 313
Stuart, John McDouall 309, 315, 416
Stubbs, George 39, 42–43, 47, *ill.* 7
Sturma, Michael 117
Sturt, Charles 309, 416
suntan 117, 271, 274–75, 278
surfing 117, 277, 343, *ill.* 21 *see also* lifesaver
Sutherland, Dame Joan 99, 324
swagmen 20, 147–48, 151–54, 209, 214, 230 *see also* bushmen
Switzerland and Swiss symbols 77, 92, 194
Sydney 6, 9–10, 18–19, 33, 34, 41, 53, 58, 62, 68, 84, 88, 93, 105, 106, 124–26, 129, 157, 163–64, 178, 180, 185–87, 190, 197, 270–04, 280, 307, 336–37, 355, *ill.* 22 *see also* Sydney Harbour Bridge, Sydney Opera House
Sydney Harbour Bridge 1, 5, 9–10, 14, 21, 23, 55, 106, 131, 223, 259–69, 275, 322, 355–56, *ill.* 24, 46, 47
Sydney Opera House 1, 3, 5, 9–10, 14, 18, 21, 55, 106, 223, 259, 260, 265–66, 322–34, 335, *ill.* 57, 58, 59
symbols and symbolism *see* national symbols
Symonds, Andrew 370

T

Tasmania 32, 65–66, 68, 87, 103, 108, 124, 184, 270 *see also* Hobart

Tasmanian tiger 127
tattoos 26, 36–37, 86, 126, 130, *ill.* 6
Taussig, Mick 302
tea 41, 42, 53, 143–48, 151–55, 186, 242, 244 *see also* Billy Tea
television 9, 11, 22, 45–46, 99, 105, 213, 217, 235, 269, 280, 294, 306, 342, 365
Tench, Watkin 129
Tennant Creek 131
tennis 99, 245
terrorism 267, 269
Thailand 67
Thomas, Edward and Helen 90
Thomas, Harold 7, 178
Thomas, Rover 350
Thompson, J Walter 234
Thomson, Joanne 90
Thornhill, Michael 305
Thornton, Don 287
Timor-Leste 69, 218
Tjungurrayi, Gwoya 96–97
Tjukurpa 311, 315
Tomkins, Henry 154
Toowoomba 33
Torres Strait Islanders *see* First Peoples, flags, Torres Strait Islander
tourists and tourism 1–2, 10, 66–67, 87, 106, 113, 115, 118, 128–37, 140–41, 216, 239, 248, 260, 263–64, 267–69, 308–19, 322–23, 335, 346, 354, *ill.* 19, 20, 23, 24, 55
　government involvement in 18, 21–22, 48, 97, 135, 140, 223, 275, 314–15, 342
　tourism industry 7, 18, 85, 87, 120, 122, 130–35, 137, 140–41, 155, 187, 248, 251, 253, 257, 263, 268–69, 312, 314, 318–19, 338, *ill.* 44
trade unions 34–36, 97, 255
trademarks 3, 6, 8, 15, 19, 83, 87, 135, 232, 336, 340, 368 *see also* advertising, copyright, national symbols, commercial
Trompf, Percy 261, *ill.* 46
Trumper, Victor 361–62, 365, *ill.* 66
Turnbull, Malcolm 24, 321, 345, 375
Turner, Grant 374
Turner, GW 290
Turner, Victor 4, 383
turtles 247–49, 410
Twomey, Anne 56

U

Uluru vii, viii, 2, 5, 7, 14, 18, 21, 137, 308–21, 335, *ill.* 55, 56
United States and United States symbols ix, 36, 48–50, 94, 101, 117, 128–29, 132, 162–65, 175, 234, 239–40, 286, 296–99, 342–43, 376, 378, 382
Utzon, Jørn 324–34

V

van Raalte, Henri 113
Vaughan, John 169, 178
Vegemite 1, 5, 9, 14, 16–17, 19, 55, 81, 232–45, 292, 298, 335, *ill.* 41, 42
Veron, John 'Charlie' 265
Vespucci, Amerigo 27
Vicks VapoRub 242
Victa lawnmower 9, 16, 241, 280
Victoria 45, 92, 96, 108, 115, 144, 162, 167, 171, 173–74, 233, 270, 339, 354, 378 *see also* Melbourne
Vietnamese Australians 21
Vietnam War 100, 216, 293, 328
Virgin Blue 37

W

Wadawurrung people 354
Walker, Fred 233–34
Wallace, George 340
'Waltzing Matilda' 98, 151–53, 399
Wangkatjungka people 350
war memorials 182, 213, 215, 219, 264 *see also* Australian War Memorial
waratah 12, 46, 104, 111, 131, 185–88, 192
Ward, Russel 145–46, 343
Wardill, Major Ben 361, 362
Warlpiri people 97
Warne, Shane 21, 370
Warner, David 370
Watson, Chris 172
wattle 3, 183–94, *ill.* 5, 10, 28, 32, 33
Waugal (or Wagyl) people 351, 357
Waugh, Mark 367
Waugh, Steve 358–59, 365–70, *ill.* 65
weather 74–75, 256–57, 272, 308 *see also* climate change, environmental issues

Weaver, Rachael 39
Webster, Nikki 133
Weet-Bix 16
Western Australia 40, 65, 68, 92, 119, 123, 124, 130, 187–88, 193, 242, 270, 275, 351, 378 *see also* Perth
Wheatland, Bill 329
whiteness 6, 85, 88, 93, 109, 112–15, 158–59, 163, 180, 191, 222, 244, 278, *ill.* 13 *see also* immigrants, race and racism
White, Patrick 99
White, Richard 294
Whitlam, Edward Gough 12, 36, 89, 98, 330
Wilkinson, Roy 343
Williams, Buddy 89
Williams, Marjorie 138
Williams, RM 16, 342, 346
Winton, Tim 123
Wiradjuri people 136, 145
Wollaston, Tullie 199, 204
Women and femininity 19, 22–23, 86, 149, 156–67, 188–89, 213–14, 216–17, 271, 278, 285, 288, 293, 295, 305, 318, 336, 343, 345–46, 368, 372

wool *see* sheep and wool industry
World War I 9, 88, 90, 136, 165, 173, 187, 189, 201, 207, 209–15, 217, 227, 275, 297, 339 *see also* Anzac
World War II 11, 47–48, 174–75, 215–16, 230, 234, 237, 276, 288, 298–99, 399–40, 355, 372 *see also* Kokoda
World Youth Day 33, 333, *ill.* 5
wrestling 125
Wright, Donald viii
Wright, Judith 254–55
Wulguru people 130
Wyatt, Ken 182

Y

Yawuru people 346
Yeomans, John 329
Yolngu people 133, 417
Young, Peter 369–70
youth and 'young Australia' 33, 36, 37, 41, 82, 109, 155, 156–66, 180–81, 185, 194, 216, 220, 237, 273–74, 277–78, 305 *see also* children, schools